The Chess Artist

The Chess Artist

Genius, Obsession, and the World's Oldest Game

J. C. Hallman

Thomas Dunne Books ⚇ New York
St. Martin's Press

THOMAS DUNNE BOOKS.
An imprint of St. Martin's Press.

www.stmartins.com

Design by Ralph Fowler

Library of Congress Cataloging-in-Publication Data

Hallman, J. C.
        The chess artist / J. C. Hallman.—1st ed.
            p.   cm.
        Includes bibliographical references (p. 333).
        ISBN 0-312-27293-6
            1. Chess—Anecdotes.   2. Chess—History.   3. Hallman, J. C.—Journeys—
    Russia (Federation)—Kalmykia.   I. Title.

    GV1449.H35   2003
    794.1'092—dc21
    [B]

                                                                    2003046872

First Edition: September 2003

10 9 8 7 6 5 4 3 2 1

CONTENTS

ACKNOWLEDGMENTS

A LOT OF PEOPLE HELPED THIS PROJECT COME TOGETHER. As a writer, I've been lucky enough to be able to call upon the wisdom of the likes of Scott Anderson, Frank Conroy, Charlie D'Ambrosio, Tom Grimes, Bill Lashner, Mary Marbourg, and Jean McGarry.

Others offered support or specific skills. These include Mary Jean Babic, Connie Brothers, Mike Delaney, John Donaldson, Rosemary Evans, Ivan Ginov, Tim Gosman, Amy Hallman, Peter Hallman, Brigita Krasauskaite, Kristi Meardon, Kathy Merkey, Julie McDowell, Barry Neville, Boris Pakhomov, Macon Shibut, Deb West, and Judy Zimmer.

Then there are those who brought the book to fruition. These include my agent, Giles Anderson, and those who published the book: Tom Dunne, Carolyn Chu, and all the good folks behind the scenes at Thomas Dunne Books and St. Martin's Press.

Finally, I owe a debt to my parents.

Thanks to all for your friendship and generosity.

Kalmykia
AND
Surrounding
Region

Moscow

RUSSIA

Volga

UKRAINE

KAZAKHSTAN

Volga

KALMYKIA
(Baghdad
1,000 Miles)

Ketchenery
Elista

Chernozemelsky

CASPIAN DEPRESSION

Lagan

Black
Sea

Caspian
Sea

CHECHNYA

GEORGIA

TURKEY

AZERBAIJAN

N

IRAQ

| 0 | | 250 Miles |
| 0 | | 250 Kilometers |

Map by James Sinclair

The Chess Artist

Prologue

If I lose badly I will feel like committing suicide.

—GM Nigel Short

IT WAS THE FLY THAT WOKE ME, A KALMYK HOUSEFLY AS big as a grape. Bigger in the blur of myopia. I mistook it at first for something much larger near my feet, then it landed on the blanket in front of my nose and ascended again when I jolted. My eyes focused as best they were able, and the lazy swim of a fat fly offered diagnosis of the churning flush of my brain. I was drunk in Russia.

There was a knock at the door, and I recognized the trope: the beginning of the day, the gap in action filling in at once with plot. I stood up. I was in the strange weakened state of alcohol recovery when the down of it has worn off but the headache has yet to arrive. Shame and chemistry. It would blossom soon, like a flower opening to sunlight and torture, but for now it was a kind of limbo: I would not be acting like myself for some time, but the future would become a past uninterrupted by further failure of memory.

It was Glenn at the door. Glenn was a chess player, a self-described chess artist. He was thirty-nine years old, a boyish African-American man with dimples and a tender smile. Glenn's skin was the color of the dark squares on a fine chessboard, a perfect mahogany. His hairline had begun a ragged retreat, but he had a giggle so girlish he sometimes seemed like a teenager. His vocabulary was urban, but his accent was neutral. He neither drank nor cursed. He was a parent once, possibly twice. A few years back he had spent a number of days in jail for reasons I was still unclear about. He had played chess while on the inside. Shortly after I met him, I asked Glenn which was more important to his identity, the game or his race. He considered the question seriously a moment. It was odd for him because he tended to pride himself on supplying quick answers to everything, as though logic made every question simple.

"I'm a chess player first," he said, finally. "Then I'm black."

It was the combination of the two that made him a rarity—in the entire history of chess, more than fourteen hundred years, only a few dozen black chess players have achieved the rank of master or higher. This is because chess, generally a cold climate game, failed to penetrate Africa at the beginning of the second millennium. Glenn was one of the few.

Teetotaler that he was, the shame he wore for me now suggested I would spend the better part of the morning distributing apologies.

"I know I wasn't on my best behavior last night," I said. "But it was only here, right? It wasn't with Galzanov."

"No," he said. "It was all over. You tried to hug our maid when she didn't want to be hugged and stuff." Glenn had never been drunk in his life, and he was proud of it. He had the advantage on me, and his manner was efficient in generating guilt even though I knew of his habit of trying to induce sobriety in everyone he met.

"What time is it?" I said.

"It's 9:15. We have a meeting with Galzanov at 9:45. Downstairs. Suit and tie."

He left me standing at the door, content to allow me to collapse and shrivel up if that's what would happen. I locked the ancient lock, and the room was back to the deep hum of the Kalmyk fly as it clicked against the window trying to get out into Russia. I followed. Our rooms were on the fifth floor of the Elista Hotel, one of only two hotels in downtown Elista, Kalmykia. Kalmykia was a desperately poor Maine-sized republic on the northwest coast of the Caspian Sea. Here, a chess movement was underway. The republic's president, Kirsan Ilyumzhinov, a former chess prodigy, was using the game, I believed, the way tyrants used religions to unite people. Many thought he was mad and, possibly, a murderer. I wasn't sure what I thought, and that's why Glenn and I were here: to interview Ilyumzhinov and visit his pet project, a mysterious place called Chess City.

I looked across Elista at tree height, over roofs and a sporadic canopy of leaves. Just behind the hotel an alley served as parking lot and maintenance yard—men worked on cars, and a dirty brown dog wandered. On a neighboring street, aboveground sewage pipes shaped a squared-off threshold that marked entrance into nothing. Many wires hung between the city's buildings, sad droops of potential as numerous as ornaments. The buildings were all of the same block brick, an architectural surrender to the elements that would have made sense if it had been a moon colony. Smokestacks for some kind of power generator stood near the edge of the city, and past them the squatty supports for power lines ran off into the sand of the North Caspian steppe, yellow-brown in the distance.

I removed my clothes and took solace in the fact that, drunk as I had been, I had managed to change into the sweats I slept in. The room was cold. Heat in Kalmykia, in all of Russia, would not be turned on until October 15th. It was state controlled. Furthermore, hot water and electricity were regulated to help Kalmykia pay off debts to neighboring regions. In the bathroom a square of elevated tile amounted to my shower. I turned the red-painted knob in vain. The icy feel of the water sent a shudder up my shoulders, but dehydrated as I was it struck me as potentially delicious anyway. But I was as drunk with propaganda as I was with vodka. Do not drink the water in Russia.

I climbed up onto the shower and looked down at its grid of tiles, like a chessboard. The elevated pedestal was somewhat like a square itself, to which I had moved or been moved. I used a pipe snake showerhead to spray myself, the whole thing awful and self-inflicted. The water did not cure me, but it did grant an illusion of sobriety. When I was dry, even the room's 13 degrees felt passable. I put on one of my suits.

Bad drunks tease the ego: flaws inflate, finer characteristics recede if you're willing to admit they ever existed at all. Assurances that you did not behave badly amount to nothing; assurances that you did make you want to jump out a window. I sat and waited for Glenn. My friendship with Glenn over the last year and a half had become an inadvertent tour of chess, and if the chess movement in Kalmykia was an experimental use of the game, then my time with Glenn was an experiment of a different sort. I was an accidental chess historian. I studied the game. Glenn was my guide. I didn't know it when I met him, but during our friendship Glenn would force me to play blindfold chess with him in public; together we would explore the dusty crevices of New York's chess underworld; we would one day crash a Princeton Math Department game party; we would attend one of the largest chess tournaments in the world; we would visit a prison in Michigan and a murderer in Virginia; we would host a Mongolian Women's International Master from the opposite side of the planet; and finally we would fly to Russia, to a newly born chess state, where we would be received by Galzanov, a young suspicious press secretary armed with a bottle of vodka that was specially flavored with medicinal "grasses" and emblazoned with a portrait of Kirsan Ilyumzhinov.

I recalled a chess writer who had noted that chess was the only game in which players were forced to resign, to admit defeat. In most games time simply ran out while you were losing. Chess players were KO'd every time they lost, and they remained conscious throughout the ordeal. The agony was significant, the writer said, and now, waiting for Glenn, not really aware that I was still under the influence of Kirsan's magic vodka—only now did I truly understand what it meant to lose an important game of chess. The drink had been ritual, but the "grasses" could have been anything, and our first evening in Kalmykia had been an effort to find out what we wanted with the president. My imagination burbled with lost history—I remembered arguing with Glenn, I remembered someone saying, "Massage, or just sex?" My stomach wrung itself dry as I tried to find logic in the decision-making protocol I had employed for the last twenty-four hours. I felt an intense need to dream.

There was another knock at the door. I opened it expecting Glenn, but it was one of the maids, perhaps the one Glenn said I had tried to hug. It's possible—I wanted to hug her now actually. She held a scrap of my clothing, a Nike shirt with a tear under the arm. I wasn't sure how she had obtained it. She began speaking, and I caught the idea, the dear woman, that she blamed herself for the tear, that she must have done it while scrubbing it. She mimed sewing to suggest that she fix it. It was too great a task to explain to her that the tear had been there for several years, that I was actually fond of the shirt because it was torn, so I gave her a hundred-ruble note to fix it—I had a thick pocket of such notes. She nodded and said, "*Spasibo,*" and when she was gone I was left again with the sick and absurd sense that I had lost a kind of game.

CHAPTER I

Developing Your Pieces: ♟

The Pawns are poor men. Their move is straight, except when they take anything: so also the poor man does well so long as he keeps from ambition.

—Innocent Morality, John of Waleys, thirteenth century

My chief intention is to recommend myself to the Public, by a Novelty no one has thought of, or perhaps ever understood well; I mean how to play the Pawns: They are the very Life of this Game; They alone form the Attack and the Defense; on their good or bad situation depends the Gain or Loss of the Party.

François-André Danican Philidor, 1749

THE OFFICIAL RULES OF CHESS ARE NOT CALLED RULES. They're called laws. Article 5.6 of *The Official Laws of Chess* (Collier Books, MacMillan Publishing Company, New York, 1986) describes the moves of the pawn. (a) is simple: "The pawn may only move forward." (b) is slightly more difficult:

> *Except when making a capture, it advances from its original square either one or two vacant squares along the file on which it is placed, and on subsequent moves, it advances one vacant square along the file. When capturing, it advances one square along either of the diagonals on which it stands.*

So begins the difficulty of the game.

The history of chess can be loosely understood through the history of pawns. In the beginning, almost everything moved like a pawn. The most common chess-origin myths claim the game was invented as a tool for instruction in war, an effigy of battle. The actual origin is lost, but the war-game myth and metaphor is apt enough to have influenced its evolution: Early piece movements were limited just as the movement of men and animals in early combat was limited, and as war technology advanced so did chess pieces. The pawn captures on the diagonal, it has been suggested, because foot soldiers kill by thrusting their swords sideways.

When chess arrived in Christiandom around the year 1000 it struck Europeans as intriguing but slow. The game had hopped the information divide between Europe and Arabia, but not much instructional literature came with it. Still, Arabian chess—*shatranj*—flourished on the new continent.

Arabia had played the game differently, however. Arabian players rushed their first few moves to what was called a battle array—*ta'biya*. Each player would make a dozen or more moves without considering their opponent's moves too closely. In modern chess, this would be unthinkable. The Arabians blitzed to their pet arrays, and the game of slow, alternating moves didn't properly begin until a capture was made. Europe didn't know of this, and they played the slower game from the outset. The difference of opening style was apparent even as late as 1865, when Vincenz Grimm, a Hungarian chess player, visited Syria:

> For the first time that I played with an Arab and invited him to commence the game, he made with incredible rapidity 10 or 12 moves one after the other without in the least troubling himself about my play. When I asked in astonishment, "When does my turn come?" he rejoined in just as much astonishment, "Why are you not moving?"

Arabian chess produced and analyzed a broad range of *ta'biyat* and gave them colorful names—The Torrent, The Strongly Built, The Slave's Banner—a contrast to the modern practice of naming openings after players. But even the great Muslim masters, beginning with as-Suli, expressed doubt over playing so quickly through the opening. As-Suli had tapped into the subtle art of deep strategic play. But the Muslim game was steeped in tradition, and his suggestion that it was careless to rush to *ta'biyat* went unheeded. The reluctance to evolve would contribute to the death of *shatranj*. Now, it's chess's lost civilization.

In Europe, they did not know of *ta'biyat*. But without even playing cards to compete with, chess was popular even though it was slow. Still, it was not long before the adventurous Christians began to experiment with the pieces. The pawns, perhaps as early as the thirteenth-century, acquired the option of moving two squares on their initial move instead of one. The game was accelerated. The double move created the incongruous situation that a pawn, moving two squares instead of one, might skip past a square that was controlled or attacked by an opposing pawn. Quite wrong. Thus was born a new law, *en passant*, in passing, the right to capture a pawn that moves two squares on the square that it skips. The law reads nearly as gibberish. Initiated in the fifteenth century and not universally accepted until as late as 1880, the *en passant* law demonstrates the unruliness of chess, its heinous incomprehensible baggage, and its habit of defying simple translation into language.

The Arabic word for pawn had been *baidaq*—foot soldier. This was directly translated into a number of European languages, and continued to evolve from there: Latin, *pedinus;* Italian, *pedona;* Spanish, *peon;* English, *pawn.* The names of the pieces and their movements weren't the only changes the Europeans made to the game. The writers of the moralities were quick to recognize the allegorical potential of chess, not simply as metaphor for battlefield melee, but for abstract conflicts as well. Depicting chess accurately in literature took a backseat to using it to score philosophical points. In *Les Eschez amoureux,* a fourteenth-century morality in which a woman plays a game of chess with the devil, the conflict is moral and religious with a theme of temptation. Here, the pawns represent not foot soldiers but opposing character traits: The lady's pawns are charity, humility, loyalty, love of God, etc., and the devil plays with inconstancy, slander, perjury, blasphemy, and fiction. The moralities helped to change the understanding of chess's main metaphor—the allusion grew to a vision of the chess array as representative of the nation-state. *The Game and Playe of Chesse* of Jacobus de Cessolis, copied so frequently that it rivaled the Bible, explained the pieces and pawns as representing society's economic stratum, the board a miniature Babylon. Each pawn now stood for a different element of human infrastructure: labourers of the erthe, physicyens and cirugiens, tauerners and hostelers, drapers and makers of cloth, etc. Chess would eventually bow to this more symbolic vision of the game, a number of countries changing the name of the pawn from foot soldier to the corresponding word for "peasant"; Danish, *bonde;* Hungarian, *paraszt;* Czechoslovakian, *sedlák.* Hermann Hesse would take this a step further in naming the main character of his 1946 Nobel Prize–winning novel, *The Glass Bead Game,* Joseph Knecht. *The Glass Bead Game* first seems based on the Asian game go, which is played with small stones, but then chess references start popping up and one realizes that "knecht" is a North German word for peasant and pawn. Joseph Knecht rises from nothing to be a master of the glass bead game. He is a promoted pawn.

Pawn promotion was the final frontier for pawn laws. A pawn may "promote" to a higher value piece if it manages to inch all the way across the board. On arrival at the final rank, it is transformed, like a battlefield promotion. Pawn promotion altered the game dramatically after more European tinkering accelerated the moves of the queen *(firzan)* and bishop *(aufin)*. Around 1500, both became what are now called "line pieces," able to traverse the entire length of the board in a single move. This indirectly empowered pawns. When the queen became the most powerful piece on the board, chess realists—those who held that chess should be a microcosm of melee—were pitted against those who preferred the speedy, aesthetically pleasing improvements to the game. The questions raged. Eight pawns representing eight queens-in-waiting initiated early sex-change debates. The lawyers in Italy's Lombard universities sat down to nagging questions—if a player contracted to mate his opponent with his d-pawn, could he then promote that pawn, give mate, and claim victory? The decision was well known enough to be later invoked in a legal case that involved an actual bishop promoted to archbishop.

The realists lost: Multiple queens was permissible by the seventeenth century. The character of the chess endgame was forever changed. Now, after all the pieces had been exchanged, the game degenerated from an attempt to give exciting mate to a race for a decisive pawn promotion. An early pawn advantage meant a replacement queen thirty or forty moves later. Still, Europeans, charmed and hypnotized by their new powerful pieces, tended to undervalue pawns. Recorded games between 1500 and 1700 reveal overzealousness with pieces, a fetish with the "tactical" exchanges that gave one side or the other an immediate advantage. If Arabians had been in love with their battle arrays, then five hundred years later the Christians were in love with their pieces. And just as as-Suli, the Arab champ, offered advice to the *shatranj* community on a subtlety he sensed in the game, so did François Philidor, a French chess player and composer, offer the chess world the advice on pawns given at the front of this chapter, a quotation that is usually given incomplete and translated differently as, "Pawns are the soul of chess."

Philidor's remark on pawns and his general understanding of chess would go unappreciated in his lifetime. Others would pick up the mantle of his work much later and trace his inspiration back to sources even closer to 1500, the convenient date for the birth of modern European chess. An advanced understanding of pawns laid the groundwork for William Steinitz, the first recognized world champion, whose teachings would eventually evolve into "positional" play, where deep strategy aimed to exploit small weaknesses twenty or more moves further along in a game. Steinitz, like many before him, stressed occupation of the center with pawns, but also emphasized attention to pawn structure, with separate teachings for connected pawns, isolated pawns, doubled pawns, and pawn majorities. Steinitz looked for tiny advantages that could translate into favorable endgames, where the promotion of a pawn was the goal.

Pawn chains and pawn storms have come since; the modern Dragon Variation of the Sicilian Defense is named for a generous assessment of black's pawn skeleton, like reading heroes into the stars. Pawn moves were among the first in chess to evolve, among the last to gain universal acceptance. And of all the suggestions to change the game since—new files, new pieces that move in alien ways—none involve the pawns.

CHAPTER 2

Mutant Message from Forever

The love of the game has, on occasion, bordered on fanatical mysticism.

—Dr. Anton M. Somalai, 1980

There may be an analogy in totalitarian states, or states which are autocratically led even if they are democracies, but in a real democracy there should be no particular resemblance to chess.

—Lord Callaghan

IN 1857, AN ENGLISH JOURNALIST NAMED FREDERICK edge found himself in New York around the time of the first American Chess Congress. Edge was not a chess player, but nevertheless he was appointed one of four secretaries to the event. In its course he found himself fascinated by the characters of the chess world and by the United States's twenty-year-old chess sensation, Paul Morphy. Edge had previously written a book about slavery and would go on to write a book about a famous U.S. naval battle, but from 1857–59 he became obsessed with chess and Morphy both.

The first concrete chess reference in the New World went back only as far as 1734, though chesslike games among Native Americans have been cited as proof of the migration across the Bearing Strait. Thomas Jefferson and Ben Franklin were both avid chess players, and a chess book written by the latter became the first chess book printed in Russia, in 1791. Paul Morphy was a Creole born in Lousiana in 1837. He was a competitive chess player at the age of eight, and among the nation's best by thirteen. He was the first to realize simultaneously the complete potential of pieces in the form of tactical play and the subtle strategy of positional play. He grew to be a small, frail man who could pass for a woman. He wanted to be a lawyer—rumor claimed he could recite most of the Civil Code of Louisiana—but he could not practice until he turned twenty-one. He called his passion for chess a "chess fever." In 1857, he traveled to New York for the Chess Congress.

"Who that was present on that evening," Edge would later write, exaltingly, "does not remember Paul Morphy's first appearance at the New York Chess Club?"

In 1858, Morphy decided to travel to Europe, where the best chess players resided. He announced that he would go to England. Already returned to London, Edge recognized the opportunity—he would handle Morphy. Even before the young American arrived, Edge latched onto him, making himself a known quantity in English chess circles by claiming he was Morphy's public relations manager.

Morphy arrived in London just as he turned twenty-one. He dominated everyone he played. The British press claimed he looked like Abraham Lincoln. Edge represented Morphy in match negotiations and served as a consultant for the events Morphy would participate in. The two men pursued Howard Staunton for an informal world championship match, but talks disintegrated with Edge engaging in the kind of nasty politics—unreasonable demands and public slander—that has since become common in the game. Morphy and Edge traveled together to Paris for matches and a now famous eight-board blindfold display, the celebration of which caused a riot. Morphy was notoriously lazy, and Edge returned letters for him and recorded scores of his games that otherwise would have been lost. When Morphy became ill and wanted to go home, Edge wrote to the clubs of Europe pleading with them to request that Morphy stay on. Edge sent a certificate of health to Morphy's family in Louisiana. But they were not convinced. Morphy's brother-in-law came to Paris, and Morphy and Edge were separated after six months together.

Morphy returned home to a hero's welcome. The United States suffered from a sense of national inferiority to Europe, and Morphy was the first American to have achieved world supremacy in anything. James Russell Lowell, one of the Fireside Poets, called Morphy's chess exploits a "new clause to the Declaration of American Independence." Two months after Morphy's return, Edge wrote him a plaintive letter: "I have been a lover, a brother, a mother to you; I have made you an idol, a god..." Edge completed a book about their travels in 1859.

But Morphy gave up chess. He returned to New Orleans and began a descent into madness. He never practiced law and was tormented by feelings of persecution. In 1863, Morphy wrote of the game, "It is, to be sure, a most exhilarating sport, but it is only a sport; and it is not to be wondered at that such as have been passionately addicted to the charming pastime, should one day ask themselves whether sober reason does not advise its utter dereliction." He traveled once more to Paris, but played chess only privately. He became a recluse, wandering the streets of New Orleans. He was cared for by his mother and sister until he died of a stroke at age forty-seven.

"Without [Edge's] nagging," the *Oxford Companion to Chess* later suggested of the two men's relationship, "many Morphy games would have been forgotten. On the other hand, Morphy himself was not grateful to someone who was an irritation and yet indispensable. Perhaps the interplay between them had a bearing on Morphy's later mental problems."

GLENN AND I WERE STUDYING TWO-MOVERS WHEN THE PILOT announced that we were nine thousand meters over Newfoundland, approaching cruising altitude. The plane was yet tilted slightly up, a Lufthansa flying crib crammed with technology and communications equipment: pop-down monitors, flight data and trajectory graphics transmitted through the cabin, phones capable of retrieving E-mail. We sailed through the sky as perverse testimony to modernity. We intended to fly faster than history.

To say that Glenn and I both studied two-movers isn't quite correct. Glenn held his problem book up before him—a compilation of more than five thousand practical chess positions—chose one that caught his eye for reasons I would never understand, stared at it, and then passed the heavy tome to me and waited in the plane's engine pulse silence until I solved it. This could take a minute or two. Usually, I was distracted by the question of whether Glenn had already solved the problem or was solving it now, without looking, racing me to the finish. Sometimes I would actually divine the composition's answer—the initial move, its gush of logic, the subsequent artful checkmate—but more often I would hazard a guess, pronouncing the name of the piece and the algebraic notation of the square I intended it to occupy.

"Rg4?"

If I was correct and sounded confident, Glenn reached for the book to find another; he did not believe in praise. If I was hesitant, he would question me.

"What if he plays queen check?"

"Uh . . ." and I would return to the problem to work it through.

If I was wrong, his disdain was palpable and he would explain it as though scolding me, consulting only the hazy afterimage of the position deep in his mind's eye.

"How you gonna play Rg4? He's got a bishop on b7. He just checks you."

Glenn and I were not studying two-movers; *I* was studying.

We flew on the autumnal equinox, leaving Boston in summer to arrive in Frankfurt, and ultimately St. Petersburg, in the fall, hopping seasons just as we would cultures. When the plane veered east and headed out over the Atlantic, we turned into an accelerated night and history sped up ten kilometers below us. The plane leveled off, and Glenn put the problem book away to rest. I looked about the cabin, hoping to find someone he could play with. A man two seats away was absorbed in a paperback whose title chimed: *Mutant Message from Forever*. I had been reading chess history for about a year by then, and suddenly all I had learned about the game led me to conclude that the non sequitur of the title was intimately connected to chess. The game was one of those things that because its source could not be traced was probably of extraterrestrial origin, a message from forever.

There were no likely chess players about. Glenn was quiet beside me now, either dreaming or studying variations, it was a fine line between the two. Because we were traveling to a region of Russia whose technology could not match even Lufthansa's, our trip was really only half planned. Officials of Kalmykia had proven difficult to reach by phone, and E-mail had vanished into electronic ether. We were unsure how we would be received, or *if* we would be received. We would not arrive in Kalmykia for several days—we had two nights each in St. Petersburg and Moscow—and I worried about Glenn as a traveling companion. We had known each other for eighteen months, but our chess adventures to that point had not taken us far from home. Historically, chess players are complainers, paranoiacs, creatures of habit ready to go to the mat over the slightest details of accommodation. Glenn was only a master, but he could complain like a world champion. It would be best to keep him playing the game.

He stirred beside me. "Yo, Hallman," he said, "if we get into a fight over there, don't kill the person."

"Okay. Why?"

"It's less paperwork. You can half kill 'em, but if you kill 'em there's all kinds of paperwork." He paused and whistled a few notes. He was an accomplished whistler capable of the hypnotic vibrato that separated simple tweeters from musicians. "If we get into a fight, I'm going to seriously injure my individual."

He gave a vigorous, boyish nod, a common gesture that he usually produced after saying something borderline outrageous.

I reached into my bag for an envelope of notes.

"You ready to get to work?" I said.

"Man. Messin' with my vacation already."

Long after I had immersed myself in chess history, I had been comforted by the advice of Edward Winter, a noted chess historian. "If historians have the knowledge and documentation and players have the expertise in chess praxis," he wrote, "why don't the two work together?" It was the formula I had devised with Glenn, but while he was a solid master it was unclear whether I could rightly be called a chess historian. The envelope was filled with chess quotations I had been collecting over the last few months. Literary chess references are an important tool to the chess historian, and they are the primary source for pinning the birth of chess at approximately the year 600. To arrive at this date, historians calculated the number of years it took for chess to enter literature in societies where the date of the game's introduction was known, then simply subtracted from the earliest references. Though chess references in literature are a bounty for the chess historian, chess players tend to have mixed feelings over how the game is used by writers. The quotes I had for Glenn were recent, and as an experiment I gave them to him without the authors' names attached.

I asked him to respond only to the chess in each passage, what he thought of the various understandings of the game. William Hickling Prescott (*The History of the Conquest of Mexico*) and Thomas Bullfinch (*The Legends of King Arthur*) were both "pretty weak," according to Glenn. Robert Louis Stevenson (*New Arabian Nights*) was "pretty silly," while Lewis Carroll (*Through the Looking Glass*) was "pretty good." John Locke ("An Essay Concerning Human Understanding") used chess, he said, to deliver "a layman's version of the Theory of Relativity." Charles Lamb (*The Essays of Elia*) used it "just to seem kinda esoteric," and Francis Bacon (*The Essays*) used chess to "make his preceding and future passages sound more interesting." Jack London's (*The Son of the Wolf*) use was good, but his notation was bad; Melville got an equally split decision—in *Benito Cereno,* he was "very good," while in *Billy Budd,* he was "trying to get the reader to not like chess too much." Cervantes (*Don Quixote*) "read okay," and Bram Stoker (*Dracula*) was "kinda funny." When Poe ("Murders in the Rue Morgue") suggested that in chess, "what is only complex is mistaken . . . for what is profound," Glenn responded, "That's a ridiculous statement. It's a fallacy with a lot of writers who believe that humans are unable to understand a lot about chess." The writers began to fall into categories for Glenn—those who tried to make themselves look good by employing chess, and those who tried to fit it into some kind of theory or approach. More recent writers fared better, but with conditions. Mailer (*The Fight*) "was obviously a chess player," but his argument comparing Muhammad Ali's rope-a-dope to a chess flank attack showed he had fallen "into the same trap that a lot of people who don't play chess fall into." Nabokov (*The Defense*) was nice, "but it could have been worded better." When Tolstoy (*War and Peace*) suggested that chess was like war and that players looked for their mistakes only in the opening of games, Glenn said "he should have interviewed some good players before he started talking about how a good player feels." He was nearly lecturing now, and his response to Montaigne (*Essays*), who suggested that chess was a "ridiculous diversion," was a description of the game's odd predicament in the world, and a boiled-down version of the question our journey was meant to answer: "The problem is, where does chess fall? You really can't put chess in a science room or a laboratory. Surely, you can't put chess in the Olympics. And the question is, if you can't put it anywhere, what use is it?"

He gave a tired, exaggerated shrug—another common gesture that indicated arrival at a disappointing terminus. I had been giving Glenn exercises like this for months; he alternately found them exhilarating and depressing. For the last two hours, he had been speaking into my tape recorder's small microphone, and a sweet old woman across the aisle had watched all along. Now she waved.

"I think she thinks you're interviewing me," Glenn said.

"I am," I said.

We landed at 5:55 A.M., German time, having traveled eight thousand kilometers, six hours into the future, and from an American summer to a European autumn.

GLENN HAD CHOSEN TO PUT FAITH IN THE ANTI-SOVIET PROPaganda that had been circulating in the United States for three-quarters of a century. He believed Russia was cold twelve months a year. In our six bags, he'd packed seven liters of water and what he believed would be enough food for the month: five large cans of assorted nuts, several packages of granola bars, and more than twenty tins of sardines that he listed on his customs declaration form as "Wildlife Products." He counted himself prepared.

At the Frankfurt airport, it took us awhile to give up on looking for directions in English and rely on international symbols. We humped our bags, heavy with Glenn's food, through the terminal.

A British traveler watched us play a game of chess at a restaurant during the layover. When our game was finished, he interrupted to chat and ask where we were headed.

"Russia," Glenn said.

"The thing about that part of the world," the man said, nodding, "and I've been there a few times, is the toilets. You can't use them. You haven't seen anything like them in the States. It's ghastly. Take your own lav paper everywhere."

Glenn was pleased—on top of all the food, he'd sneaked half a dozen rolls of toilet paper into our bags.

On the flight from Frankfurt to St. Petersburg, I produced another envelope, this one filled with news clippings of Kirsan Ilyumzhinov's volatile career as a chess politician and a real politician. Glenn thought it was silly that I wanted him to read the clippings—to his mind, Ilyumzhinov was my job and his job was to play chess. But he agreed with some prodding, and we passed the photocopied pages back and forth on the plane. The Western press had not been kind to Kirsan. And it was clear from even a few articles that Kalmykia, while absurd enough to make good copy, was simply too small to merit the serious attention of international journalists. Their knowledge of Kalmyk history was limited, and absurd factoids of Kalmyk life were plagiarized and exaggerated from one news source to the next. This was complicated by the fact that much of what had been happening in Kalmykia *was* pretty absurd, and that Kirsan, unschooled in the art of the sound bite, was prone to statements that made him look crazed. I'd been reading about Kalmykia for a while by then and knew most of the articles by heart, but I read through them again with Glenn.

Kirsan Ilyumzhinov had been born April 5, 1962, in Elista. He'd been a rough-and-tumble child, but a straight-A student and the republic's chess champion at age fourteen. He went to school in Moscow, graduating from the prestigious Institute of International Relations in 1986. The Kalmyk people were of Mongol descent, having migrated across Asia early in the seventeenth century, and Kirsan's ethnicity came in handy when he graduated and found himself at the right place with the right skills. In 1989, a Japanese-Soviet joint venture, Liko-Raduga, was looking for someone to open and manage a Moscow branch office. Liko-Raduga sold cars and cattle skins, ran restaurants and commercial art exhibitions, had interests in gambling. Kirsan passed tests and interviews, got the job, and caught the capitalist tsunami in Russia when it was gaining speed and running deep. He made a fortune, and in 1990, at age twenty-eight, he felt the call to public service. He was elected a member of the Russian Parliament and shortly thereafter became president of the Russian Chamber of Entrepreneurs. He sat perched atop fifty corporations with an annual turnover of $500 million. He first won the presidency of Kalmykia in 1993, at age thirty-one. Historically, Kalmyk rulers had been called khans (some chess sources list "khan" as the Kalmyk name for the chess king), and for journalists, it was shooting fish in a barrel when Kirsan said, "Kalmykia needs a khan, but one who'll come by democratic means." "The New Khan of the Steppe," as he was soon known, seemed to have a creative interpretation of democracy, however—reports had him offering one hundred dollars for every vote and "a cellphone for every shepherd." Kirsan promised to turn his little nation into another Kuwait based on modest oil deposits discovered in the republic. He modeled himself loosely on Western leaders, but when he once started a speech, "I have a dream . . . ," he wasn't talking about the Promised Land, he was talking about making Kalmykia a tax haven like Lichtenstein. He ran on a platform of get-rich-quick and future shock, and was promptly elected. His first official action was to disband the Supreme Soviet of Kalmykia, which consisted of 130 members. He replaced them with a 25-member Parliament. Over the next several years, he would declare independence for Kalmykia several times, only to take it back. In the 1993 Russian coup attempt, according to news sources, Kirsan first lent his support to parliamentary forces and only got back in line behind Boris Yeltsin when it became clear that the coup would fail. Although it was inauspicious at the time, another early action of Kirsan's presidency was the country's chess movement—the presidential chess decree, handed down in 1993. This was more fodder for journalists, who would latch onto the lunacy of making chess mandatory in schools across the country. The problem was compounded when Kirsan stacked his plate even higher; in 1995, in addition to being reelected president of Kalmykia, he became president of the *Federation Internationale des Echecs,* FIDE, the international chess organization.

While there are 350,000 people in Kalmykia, there are an estimated half-billion chess players worldwide. Chess events in Kalmykia appeared where economic promises went unfulfilled. In 1996, the Karpov-Kamsky World Championship match was held in Elista, though FIDE was a struggling organization at the time, battling for legitimacy as the world's then-highest-rated player, Garry Kasparov, was not considered a member. The idea of the world championship had split some time before. As an organization, FIDE was a political entity whose queerness could be extrapolated from the basic psychological profile of any individual attracted to chess. Intelligent, introverted, science-minded, meticulous, prone to depression and insanity. FIDE operated like a pseudogovernment, a mock United Nations. Its leadership was the result of worldwide politicking, complete with backstabbing, international elections, and Third World voting blocs. FIDE had taken control of the world championship in 1946. As the game flourished through the late '40s and '50s, so did FIDE continue to grow. Soon it was possible to become a chess professional without even being a player. The chess politician traveled the world, lobbying for votes and coalitions, a piece in a larger game of policy and political intrigue. By the '60s, results of FIDE matches began to have political impact outside of chess. Actual governments exerted influence over chess government. The goals of grandmasters and chess politicians diverged—who knew best how to control the laws of the game? A series of world champions proved problematic: Bobby Fischer absconded in '75, Anatoly Karpov's reign was marred by illegitimacy, Garry Kasparov never stopped fighting with FIDE officials. Eventually a group of players tried to revolt, in 1993, forming their own organization outside the auspices of FIDE; but the effort fizzled out in politics of its own. When Kirsan Ilyumzhinov, the first real politician to become a chess politician, inherited FIDE, there were arguably three world champions: Karpov, who got it back when Kasparov gave it up; Kasparov, who took it with him when he left; and Bobby Fischer, who claimed to have never given it up in the first place. Kirsan promised to bring order to the chess world.

For the most part, the Kalmyk people went with the program. Poor as they were—Kalmyk incomes were half the average of a depressed Russia—they didn't seem to mind that Kirsan drove around town in a Rolls Royce and was reportedly a billionaire. He was the prosperity that had come of their sacrifice, a kind of living cathedral to demonstrate their collective worth. They needed a cathedral substitute, as the unstable land of the North Caspian steppe prevented any structure in Kalmykia from standing more than nine stories high. To his credit, Kirsan had taken steps to restore Kalmyk culture after seventy years of Soviet repression: Along with chess, the Kalmyk language was being taught in schools, and artisans and musicians had been sent to Tibet to learn traditional arts. Kirsan was confident of his relationship with the people. "Irrespective of what I tell people," he told reporters, "I give them instructions on a subconscious level, a code. . . . I am creating around the republic a kind of extrasensory field, and it helps us a lot in our projects." More practically, he pitched himself as a kind of Robin Hood—he once seized $216 million from a Russian bank on the grounds that Kalmykia had overpaid its taxes. Moscow promptly cut all financial ties. Power began to take its totalitarian toll on Kirsan: Reports appeared that he wanted to chop the hands off of thieves, put drunks in cages in public, and legalize polygamy. "In my country," he said, "there is only one man who plays politics, and that is me. The other men have to work, the women have to bear children and the children have to play chess."

Internal dissent began to form in Kalmykia, perhaps born of the resentment of a man trying to be two presidents at once. Rumors began to float: Money from the sale of forty thousand tons of Kalmyk oil wound up in Kirsan's personal bank account, $12 million meant for flood victims went missing with Kirsan as the primary suspect, and another $10 million in wool subsidies similarly disappeared. Reports came in of State Duma deputies breaking off investigations without cause, and of tax ministers authorizing refunds on shady deals. Witnesses to irregularities died conveniently, and a carful of Kalmyk documents crashed and burned in transit to Moscow. When a team of investigators came to Elista, they found the truly bizarre: Ilyumzhinov had declared "Youth Self-Government Week." Kirsan and forty of the republic's officials had temporarily abdicated, each leaving behind a youthful "double" to run the government in their absence.

Most prominent among Ilyumzhinov's critics was Larisa Yudina, editor of *Sovietskaya Kalmykia Segodnya* (*Soviet Kalmykia Today*), the republic's only opposition newspaper. By 1998, *Soviet Kalmykia Today* had been banned—it was being printed in a neighboring region—and Yudina, investigating Kirsan's various dealings, was routinely threatened and harassed. Ilyumzhinov dismissed Yudina as a Communist because her paper was called *Soviet Kalmykia Today*. In fact, Yudina was regional cochairman of the pro-Western political party, Yabloko. "[Kirsan] claims he is a modern ruler," Yudina told another journalist. "But democratic freedoms and rights are violated here more than anywhere in Russia."

Kirsan had long since adopted a policy of taking on more and more projects when things became difficult. The upcoming 33rd Chess Olympiad offered the opportunity to rally Kalmyk resources and distract the populace. He quickly committed Elista to host the event, despite being told that it was unlikely the city—with a total of two small hotels for fifteen hundred chess players—could be ready in time. Kirsan simply made more promises, first suggesting absurdity: He would create a small chess nation within Kalmykia, an autonomous chess republic inside another autonomous chess republic, and this chess nation would have its own president, its own parliament, and would thrive within Kalmykia the way the Vatican thrived within Italy. Surprisingly, the plan was too ambitious for Moscow, and Kirsan was soon scrounging for money to fund even a scaled-back version of the dream—Chess City. Kalmyk architects were sent abroad for inspiration—it was to be a futuristic city, a way for Ilyumzhinov to fulfill promises. At the same time, he realized he had to play ball with Moscow. Where once he had wanted to do without Russian help altogether, he was now asking for funding for Chess City and the Olympiad. To almost everyone's surprise, construction on Chess City began. Elista itself was beautified, Olympiad posters hung up everywhere beside photos of Kirsan with the pope, the Dalai Lama, the head of the Russian Orthodox Church. Chess City rose from the steppe, its main building, Chess Palace, a five-story pavilion with a huge glass front wall, emerging like a beacon of modernity from land that was slowly reverting to desert. Dozens of cottages grew around it. Up to the end, no one was sure whether Chess City would be ready in time for the Olympiad.

Yudina had been busy as well investigating one of Kirsan's successes. Kalmykia was now a large tax shelter. Nobody was sure it was legal, but corporations could register in Kalmykia to avoid paying local taxes. Ilyumzhinov had failed to turn Kalmykia into another Kuwait, but he had succeeded in turning it into another Delaware. Yudina smelled rat. Half the fees for the service went to Kalmykia, the other half went to a company called ARIS (Agency for Development and Cooperations) controlled by Kirsan. Some believed this money was being used to fund Chess City. Early in June 1998, Yudina got an anonymous call that promised incriminating information about ARIS. She got into a car in the middle of the night, and her body was found a few days later, brutally beaten and repeatedly stabbed, in a pond near Chess City.

It was no help to Kirsan that the two men arrested for the crime were former presidential aides. Still, he denied all knowledge of the murder. The *Christian Science Monitor* quoted Yudina's husband as saying that the two aides were "merely pawns" but made no mention of the irony. That Ilyumzhinov had ordered the killing became a quick given. Boris Yeltsin called it a political assassination. "We must find the murderers," he said. Despite all the talk, there was no direct action against Ilyumzhinov, and the two aides were scheduled for trial in another region. Kirsan took it in stride: When asked about the murder on television, he said it was sad, called for justice, and then announced that he would be running for the Russian presidency in 2000. He soon reneged.

The scruples of the chess world were tested with the murder's proximity to the upcoming Olympiad. Chess players and officials who weighed in on the matter tended to blunder at either end of the spectrum. Those in bed with FIDE claimed the murder didn't have anything to do with chess or said they had known Kirsan was a repressive dictator, so what else was new? At the other end, a small percentage of chess players tried to form a boycott of the Olympiad, but they tended to believe every accusation against Kirsan that surfaced. "Mass theft, drug-running, white-slavery, murder," wrote Larry Parr, a former editor of the United States's *Chess Life*, "oh, heck, nothing's too good for chess." Sarah Hurst, a British chess writer, was more methodical, but similarly emotional: "At this moment I am ashamed to be a chess player."

The boycott failed, and the 33rd Chess Olympiad in Elista came off with only minor delays. A computer system installed at the last minute made it the most technologically advanced Olympiad to date. Quashed was the notion that Kalmykia could not get things done, and for the most part it seemed the Kalmyk people benefited from the attention the Olympiad brought the republic. Kalmyk hospitality was praised the world over. The success of the Olympiad—considered successful less for its grandeur, perhaps, than for its having happened at all—killed the interest of the international journalists: The scheme of Chess City wasn't so interesting if it worked. In Kalmykia itself, the Yudina murder took its toll, and a few more threatening phone calls took care of what opposition was left.

International news from Kalmykia abruptly stopped at that point. My Internet searches came up dry after the Olympiad. Kirsan himself continued to make headlines for changing, with the swipe of a pen, the entire structure of the FIDE World Championship. It went from its boxing-style title-holder tradition to an NCAA-style knockout tournament to be held biannually. This was called the trivialization of the world championship.

When Glenn completed the articles in my file, he gave another dismissive shrug and cuddled up against the window to sleep. He had probably skimmed most of it. I tried to remind myself why I had thought bringing him to Kalmykia was a good idea. Both Glenn and Kalmykia had used chess as a fundamental building block of their identities. This was odd because Glenn was not a grandmaster—indeed, he did not even make his living from chess—and Kalmykia, even while situated in Russia, had not produced a grandmaster from within its ranks. What seemed to unite them was a simple interest in the game not based on simple excellence in chess. This suggested a dimension to the game that hadn't been considered.

Late in the sixteenth century, the Oirat tribes in Mongolia—who would eventually produce the Kalmyks—adopted Tibetan Buddhism as their religion. The Kalmyks have been Buddhist ever since, making them the only Buddhist nation in Europe. But the reason the Oirats adopted Buddhism in the first place wasn't faith, it was politics. Buddhism brought cohesion to the Oirat tribes, who then became a force in post-Genghis Khan Inner Asia. Kirsan Ilyumzhinov was a Buddhist and had taken steps to revitalize religion in Kalmykia—all religions were welcome, in fact. But his interest in chess and his use of it, I thought, was similar to the Oirats' use of Buddhism 450 years before. He had used chess the way a dictator used faith. Kirsan had been known to quote Stalin—"Trust is good, control is better"—and chess was the tool he was using to unify and mollify his people.

The international journalists would have agreed, I thought. Interest people in chess, control chess, control people. For me, there were just two problems: I kind of liked Ilyumzhinov, and I liked the idea of chess as a religion. Between the lines of the news reports something clicked, and it bothered me that the journalists' work was sloppy. A chess nation sounded strange to a Western ear, but Glenn and I were coming from a culture where many children and not a few adults spent countless hours and dollars playing mindless games on their television sets. Chess was arguably beneficial. So who was absurd? Everything that came out of Kalmykia suggested Kirsan was an evil madman, but I clung to the hope that he was inventive and quite sane. The Yudina murder was a hitch, but my true sympathies lay with the Kalmyk people. The Russians, and then the Soviets, had written their history in the past; and now that the Soviets were gone, the Western press was trying to assume the job. By plagiarizing one another's stories, they sacked their own credibility. I realized that as a chess historian who believed chess was being used as a religion in a strange corner of the world, I lacked a little credibility myself; but that was why I had brought Glenn, now asleep beside me, for whom chess was a religion as much as it was for anyone. Glenn was a chess monk. If I took him to Russia, I thought, the usefulness of the game would be laid bare.

We had been over Russia for a while by then, I realized. Glenn and I had discussed the Edge-Morphy journey to Europe before we left, and we had laughed at how history seemed to be repeating itself in our friendship. But really I was worried. Glenn wasn't worried because he was an American, and he knew that just this fact would see him through. I thought alternately of chess and of the pond where Yudina had been found. The idea of our journey struck me as at one moment whimsical, with Chess City looming like a real-life Oz in the distance, and at another moment frightening, with Kirsan as the mad Kurtzlike tyrant waiting at our river's headwater.

CHAPTER 3

Writing Sonnets in Public

*Communicating with the outside world is a tricky business. . . . Nonplayers
unnerve us.*

—Andy Soltis, Karl Marx Plays Chess, *1991*

*Also, the milieu of chess players is far more sympathetic than that of artists.
These people are completely cloudy, completely blinkered . . . madmen of a
certain quality, the way an artist is supposed to be and isn't, in general.*

—Marcel Duchamp, *1968*

MY FAMILY HAD A POOL TABLE IN THE BASEMENT WHEN
I was a boy. I spent a lot of time down there. I didn't really play pool
so much as use the table as a kind of fortune-telling device. If I broke
and ran off nine balls in a row, I thought, good things would happen.
Much later, in my chess research, I learned that the chance mechanisms of many games—dice, lotteries—had their origin in religious
rites. As a boy attempting to participate in my own oracle, I acted
out an age-old transition from pagan augury to ancient ritual.

In college I played pool for money, which approximated another
transition of chance mechanisms—from organized religion to gambling. Gambling inaugurated for me a fascination with games that
was half indulgence half anthropological investigation. I became
competent in poker, gin, bridge, and pool.

It was my interest in games that eventually led me to seek work
as a casino dealer—another subculture to investigate, another seamy
facet of my personality to indulge. I went to dealer's school, received
"degrees" in several gambling games, and started work in Atlantic
City. It was fallacy. Whatever hypothesis I had thought to test mu-

tated so badly that it needn't have existed at all. Play was fiction, I came to learn. Play was alternate space. Puppies and children know intuitively that play matters, and to mature is to simply confuse play with nonplay, to assign seriousness to that which is still whimsical. Casino dealers understood this, I learned. They appeared to be playing but were not. They occupied the same space as players, but were wholly outside the universe of the game.

Early in my dealing career, I saw irony in the fact that dealers sometimes played chess in their break lounges. Play a game to work; play a game to rest. Dealers' lounges varied from casino to casino, but a few central features were consistent: It was always a windowless room deep in the bowels of a huge hotel, there was always mismatched furniture and soda fountains and coffee machines and banks of pay telephones. Dealers inhabited these removed caves that could double as bomb shelters, the space all littered with plastic cups, unfolded newspapers, snipped coupons piled like confetti, and it might have resembled the commons room of an insane asylum, scattered pockets of people sometimes whispering, sometimes screaming, sometimes sleeping amid the madness. It was here that I played my first games of decidedly unserious chess as a dealer. Initially, chess did not strike me as a proper game because it had no chance mechanism. I found it intense and frustrating and I didn't really like it, but occasionally I succumbed to a mysterious desire to play. I was drawn by the cleansing effect it seemed to have on my mind, wiping away the occasional humiliation of the casino.

Splicing together a stint in graduate school with my dealing career, I had, before I knew it, become a journeyman dealer, hopping from house to house. One summer I jumped from one casino to another for two bucks more per hour. I didn't see the new dealers' lounge until my first day on the job. I started at 4:00 A.M., worked an hour, and walked to the lounge for my break. I was surprised to find, near the row of vending machines, an entire table devoted to chess. Two paper boards submerged beneath a plastic sheet, and two sets of pieces scattered over the squares like a battlefield's corpses. No one was playing. I sat down to watch reruns of the day's talk shows, and looked back at the chess table again only when a man appeared and sat down before the boards. He was in a suit, a pit boss. He arranged the pieces in their opposing arrays, then planted his chin on his palm to wait. I walked over.

"Can I?"

"Come on," he said.

To play chess with someone before you know anything at all about them is to accelerate the normal course of learning their personality. Even though I did not play chess very well, I could discern things about the pit boss from how he played. He was aggressive and stubborn. He appreciated creativity, but preferred the thrill of winning. The scolding he gave himself when he erred suggested self-esteem problems, and the casualness with which he eventually resigned suggested he was also resigned to his life caught in the vortex of the casino, this industrial dungeon that was more his home than his home.

"You got me," he said, after we had played awhile.

I began playing a lot then, almost every break. Thick crowds of players and observers gathered around the dual chess table to the annoyance of those forced to navigate the oblong bulk of us. The players were a sampling of men from all over the world, muttering to themselves in the languages of five continents, from Peru to Nigeria to Micronesia to Vietnam, but trading barbs with the foul vocabulary of our common English. I would later note a parallel between the chess community at the casino and the chess community of early Arabia—chess in the lounge existed as chess did one thousand years before and five thousand miles away, when play was ragged and banter from opponents and observers was commonplace. As with most chess communities, the characters of the lounge were colorful. One man, a Jamaican named Chaplin, chanted slowly while he played: "Hey, all you sinners," slowly rocking to and fro, "turn the lights on!" Another, Bing from the Philippines, whistled annoyingly past his sharp mustache. Michael—a young black man who studied the Moors—punctuated his moves with a repeated tidbit that drew the metaphor between the game and physical assault: "*Ow!* I'm *hurting* you!" And James, a statuesque ex-boxer and ex-marine, put all that he'd learned about homophobia as a jarhead to use in hushed lectures that he delivered when in command of a position: "Can you feel me inside you, baby? Do you like it, you little bitch? Oh, *yeah!* I'm ramming you. You like that meat, don't you, little girl? You like my big thick meat. *Yeah!*"

I first heard that there was one very good player among us from a man named Bob who did not play at all. This player, I was told, had been written up in local newspapers and company in-house news-letters for exhibitions he'd given, and his reputation as a man ob-sessed was common knowledge even to those who avoided the chess table altogether. "People say he's like a grandmaster or something," Bob told me. "I don't know, but get this. A couple years back, he gets married, right? Goes on his honeymoon. And then I see him in the lounge, playing chess! Dude's supposed to be on his honeymoon, and here he is in the dealers' lounge."

It was Glenn, of course, and from then on I kept my eyes open and asked around about him. But he was a ghost, a lingering mini-legend who would materialize, it seemed, only when the effect would be greatest. After a few weeks, I gave it up. Then one day a woman sat across the chessboard from me and asked me to teach her how to play. It was flirtation, and I was flirting myself as I ran through the moves, hurrying through to the moment when we could begin a game that might lead to more than flirting. But Glenn was watching. And just as we began our game he descended, handsome, friendly, and boyish. I noticed the ironed seams of his shirtsleeves, sharp enough to slice bread.

"You shouldn't conduct a game until you know all the rules," he said.

"*Conduct* a game?" I said.

He nodded vigorously and walked away.

"I guess you've got to be a member of the chess club," I joked. My friend smiled, but our moment was ruined. We gave up the game, sat in silence, and fondled the icons before us.

I DIDN'T SPEAK TO HIM UNTIL THE FOLLOWING WEEKEND WHEN I finally saw him play for the first time. Glenn attracted a lot of attention in the lounge because he played with a clock. He handled the pieces differently as well, with a kind of graceful deftness, and it was easy to recognize in him the telltale aura of expertise. Everyone knew that he almost never lost. Glenn was responsible for the fact that the chess table in the lounge existed at all—it was his baby, his personal fiefdom—and he was used to people approaching him with half-hearted interest in the game. He handed out advice that went ignored, books that weren't returned. When he finished his game, I introduced myself. He gave me his card, which had nothing on it except a tiny pencil drawing of his profile, his proper U.S. Chess Federation (USCF) title, master, and his P.O. box number. There was no phone number.

"You have a computer?" he asked.

"Yes."

He took the card again and wrote on the back, chessclub.com. Then he shook my hand and said, "Develop your pieces." I had no idea what it meant. He turned away and just like that he seemed to forget about me.

That night I went to the Web site and downloaded a program for access to the most popular site for chess play on the Internet. The site came up quickly and efficiently. Its main feature was its matches-sought graph, a quadrant of axes overlaid with a scattering of flickering dots, each representing a chess player somewhere in the world waiting to play a game. It worked like this: interface with someone's dot and a board would appear, a digital timer ticking at one side of the screen. The dots on the graph appeared and disappeared as regularly as raindrops pattering against a window. Dozens of games started every few seconds. I was transfixed. Had there ever been a science fiction writer who didn't predict that it would be a game to make us a small world after all? And here it was, chess players of the global electronic community gathered together to the small world of a single graph, which somehow made a perfect kind of cyborg, millennium-terror sense. I was future shocked.

I would come to learn that chess tended to trail only the military and pornography in the exploitation of new technology. It's no accident that the proper date of the birth of modern chess corresponds neatly with the invention of moveable type. Although many chess players would argue that the game has evolved to a perfect state, a more likely hypothesis is that chess arrived at a viable state and then dominated by riding the coattails of printing and technology. Just as the world's religions had evolved toward monotheism, so had chess lurched toward a single set of laws through technological advancement. Inaugural uses of the telegraph and the telephone included chess games played across great distances. An early space flight featured a game played from orbit. It was in computer research that chess found its neatest niche, from there helping to drive the future of technology. A chess-playing computer had been suggested as early as 1864, and the first machine able to carry out a "program" was invented in Spain in 1914 and called Ajedrecista for the Spanish word for chess, *ajedrez*. A 1944 German program used chess to help create a symbolic computer language based on logic rather than mathematics, and subsequent computer researchers used the game as a model for decision-making processes. When chess-playing programs began to come into their own in the '60s and '70s, almost no chess player missed the opportunity to publicly underestimate the potential of machines. Garry Kasparov suffered the greatest humiliation. In 1989, as world champion, he said, "Ridiculous! A machine will always remain a machine. . . . Never shall I be beaten by a machine!" Eight years later, he lost a match to Deep Blue, at the time the most powerful computer ever made, and became the computer age's John Henry. What even nonchess players understood was that something sacred and human had been eclipsed.

But the Internet Chess Club (ICC) was a wholly different matter. If Deep Blue was the theory, then the ICC was the human application. Watching the heavenly twinkle of its matches-sought graph, I might have been looking through a window into a vague and still-growing frontier. Apart from the dozens of brands of chess software, those blips appearing and disappearing were people, mechanized and electrified, boldly inhabiting a future that awaited the rest of us.

The next time I saw Glenn, I told him that I had signed up for membership with the ICC. His eyes lit slightly.

"Yo, listen," he said, "I loaned my computer to a girl, a very beautiful girl. I don't have access to it. Do you think I could come over and—" He let his eyes complete the request.

He came by that night, and the next several, and played chess on my computer for hours. He always stayed until I asked him to leave. I learned that the ICC was much more than just a playing site—it was a giant electronic chess room frequented by many of the world's leading grandmasters, who gave on-line lessons and simultaneous exhibitions for chekels, the currency of chess. Any member of the ICC could watch any game currently underway on the site, calling it up and observing the moves instantaneously as they were played from anywhere on the planet. These contests might be one of a handful of wild chess variants or normal European chess in one of three categories of time control: bullet, blitz, and standard. On the main chat channel, players bantered, argued, and flashed one another in most languages I could recognize. The handles they used were based on philosophers, cartoon characters, composers, scientists, historical figures, and biblical figures. A robot, MrSpock, gave hourly automated lectures with titles like "The Knight Sacrifice on g7, Part 1," and there was frequent coverage of major tournaments from everywhere, live over-the-board games from Linares or Dehli or Las Vegas fed into the Web and arriving on-screen with the commentary of anyone who chose to comment. The ICC was more than chess TV; it was global voyeurism, which was basically what I was doing as I sat by Glenn's shoulder and watched him scan the matches-sought graph for a likely opponent.

"Dude don't know the Grünfeld!" Glenn might suddenly bellow as he ran through a common opening. "Playin' the Grünfeld against *me!* Look at 'im push. No, no, no. That move would be winning except for my next move." He moved with my mouse, which he invariably found to be too sticky for serious Internet play. "That oughta make him want to give up chess! Look at that; I love it when they screw up. Weak joker. Resign!"

Glenn and I quickly became friends, and the floodgates of his chess hospitality opened wide. One afternoon, without asking, he loaded into my computer a chess program and a database of almost 1 million recorded games dating from as far back as the sixteenth century. Four of them were his own. Glenn also loaded into my computer twenty erotic pictures of his favorite model and a program that caused them to shuffle full screen, automatically. "No hands, Hallman," he said, smiling. He began giving me chess lessons, introductions to openings, the Ruy Lopez or the Evans Gambit. "You want a lesson?" he would say, always proceeding before I rightly agreed. He gave me books and told me I could be 2000 strength in four years. He always told me to develop my pieces when we parted, and eventually he explained that it meant the timely deployment of one's chessmen.

I came to realize that Glenn was kind of a lonely man, a serious player cast adrift in a world of nonplayers; and in Atlantic City, to be honest, I kind of felt the same way about reading. Glenn and I were drawn to one another simply because we were both passionate about something that no one else around us seemed to care about. Glenn had been in the casinos longer than I had, and he had no particular home to speak of. He rented rooms in other peoples' houses and carried most of his important belongings in a discount backpack that he kept with him at all times. These included his chess clock, a set of chessmen, several chess books, a toothbrush, some clothes, and printouts of computer analyses of his games that he handed out to people who didn't even know how to read chess notation.

GLENN'S RATING ON THE ICC HAD REACHED AS HIGH AS 2561, which, if it were an over-the-board rating, would be world-class. But his rating tended to fluctuate, and Internet ratings tended to be inflated. He was a strong player, but not world-class.

When I had known Glenn for just a short time, I went to New York City for a meeting. I arrived early and did some walking, and stumbled across the Manhattan Chess Club, then on Forty-sixth Street. The main shop was below street level. I went down and in. Glenn had told me the name of the man who worked there, Mitchell, and here he was, just as described, shelved like the ornate pieces and chess furniture on sale in the cramped front room. I was the only customer. I tried browsing, but one does not browse in a chess shop. I walked to the nearest revolving carol of self-printed chess pamphlets and examined one. Before I had scanned even a couple of the indecipherable pages, Mitchell popped out from behind the register and plucked the pamphlet from between my fingers.

"How strong are you?" he said.

He meant my rating. Glenn had taught me about ratings. In the United States and on the ICC, an average player started at about 1200, then gained or lost points relative to the rating of players he either beat or was beaten by. Each step of 100 points was like an informal grade. At 2000, one became known as an expert. The first title threshold, master, was 2200. Titles above that, international master and international grandmaster, were awarded based on performance in tournaments with ratings of their own. The rating system of chess scared me a little because it seemed like something out of the Knights of Columbus. I feared chess oaths.

"1500 tops," I exaggerated to Mitchell.

Like most men who work in chess shops, Mitchell was slightly chubby, somewhat disheveled, a little awkward socially, but with an intelligent glimmer in his eyes. He wagged the pamphlet before my face. "This is not for you. Over here we have something that might be better for—"

I interrupted him to replace one ruse with another. I told him that I was a writer, and that I was thinking of writing something about chess, and would he mind if I looked around in the back a little, where people played and tournaments were conducted? Mitchell looked at me out of the corner of his eye, and I knew it was time to raise the ante of my lie—I told him I was working with a master. Mitchell knew Glenn's name at once and, nodding, assured me that Glenn was not a master, he was a *strong* master. He said I could look around, but told me to be quiet if I went upstairs because a grandmaster was giving a lesson.

I wanted to see a grandmaster. I walked back behind the shop into a room that reminded me at once of the dealers' lounge, fluorescent, windowless, cluttered, with newspaper clippings and tournament results posted all over the walls. Except for the eight or nine chessboards gathered tight in the center of the room, it looked like a garage that needed fumigation. Upstairs, it was cleaner without being decidedly clean, comfortable only relative to the floor below. Chess tables pressed in against either wall, but only one was occupied, a man on each side speaking softly and clicking pieces. But they weren't playing. Rather, they were talking about playing. They were talking about playing as though it was the most important discussion that would be held in the throng of the city that day. I used an examination of portraits of the world champions as a pretense to edge closer, but I could not determine which man was the grandmaster and which was the student.

Glenn was pleased that I had visited the club and dropped his name, and he asked repeatedly what Mitchell had said about his rating. For chess players a rating is as important as a face. When Glenn's sank, his mood became sour and difficult. When it rose, he was happy again. Apparently, the step of visiting the club entitled me to his history, and he delivered it one evening after our lesson.

For most American chess players, the ascent of Bobby Fischer to world champion in 1972 marks the beginning of their interest in the game. Fischer has a habit of spouting insane invective, but his reign as champion is still the point from which most American players measure time. But this didn't apply to Glenn. Rather, like Fischer himself, Glenn's interest in chess seemed to spawn from nothing. He had first seen the game played at an air force base where his parents worked. As he watched a game for the very first time, Glenn began to understand. "I saw that f7 was weak without even knowing what f7 was," he told me. He was infected at once, motivated in part by a desire to beat his brothers, and at fifteen he quit romping with other children after school to study chess at home. In a chess book he received from a teacher, he read that there was a player somewhere in the world who could play four games at once without sight of the board. Glenn figured he could do at least one.

His first blindfold exhibition, at age sixteen at a mall in Virginia, came before his first tournament game. His opponent was a reporter from a local paper. The exhibition was written up and marked the beginning of his tepid celebrity.

His path into chess from there was of a standard formula—he bounced into the subculture, began playing in tournaments, received the advice and support of high school teachers and other players. He made expert at twenty and master at twenty-five, which put him into that highly select group of black chess players, a subculture all its own. When I met him, he still hoped to become the world's first black grandmaster. Like almost every chess player before him, Glenn had gone to college to study mathematics only to drop out. He took a job driving a truck. After a year he lost a promotion to a white man and quit on principle, which put him in a difficult spot. "I messed up," he said. "I had never worked on anything. I had never built anything. All I knew was chess." He moved north to enter the casino business. He was energetic in the job, far more friendly than most, and he sometimes impressed players by playing blindfold chess with them as he dealt. In 1995, he said, he married a woman for her breasts. The comment was meant as a joke to cover up the error it had been. His single victory over a grandmaster came in the three-day interval between the wedding ceremony and his honeymoon. That was why Bob from the dealers' lounge had seen Glenn playing chess when he should have been in Jamaica. The union lasted only ten weeks but produced his daughter, Emerald, and it was the aftermath of divorce that somehow landed him in jail. "She lied in court," he said about it. No problem, though: Looking at five long days in the slammer, Glenn simply tore up the prison rules, made chess pieces from the scraps, and taught his cell mate how to play. "Let me tell you something, Hallman," he said, his tone level and solemn, "I saw guys in there who would never make 2400."

As a dealer Glenn made more than forty thousand dollars a year, but he had never owned a car and only rarely saw his daughter. He claimed he was broke most of the time. I realized what was happening the first time he asked me for a loan—four hundred dollars. "The tables were not kind to me," he said, with the dimpled smile he used to get himself past awkward moments. He was a gambler. It wasn't unusual for dealers to be gamblers. Or chess players. I gave Glenn the money, and he paid me back on exactly the date he said he would. Three days later he was back for another loan. The cycle continued, and Glenn seemed to operate on the assumption that our chess lessons were appropriate compensation for interest-free loan sharking. I once asked him if I could watch him gamble, but he shook his head and changed the subject.

One day he arrived at my door wearing a face more grave than I had ever seen on him. It was an expression that spoke of news both good and bad, a beautiful death or fouled-up birth. He handed me a Sunday newspaper magazine insert. Chess was on the cover. A man named Maurice Ashley had just become the world's first black grandmaster.

Glenn had played more than four hundred tournament games, which I would come to understand was something like saying he had written four hundred sonnets, in public, while opponents who didn't particularly like him tried to write better sonnets using the same words. Glenn believed tournament chess was a weak spot in my chess education. I was a strange student, starting with the game's most recent incarnation, the Internet, and working backward. Glenn always treated gaps in my chess understanding as serious character flaws.

"Say you're in a tournament," he told me, trying to give me the feel of it. "You make a move. You get up from the board. You go *outside* the building. You get something to eat. You *eat* it. You go back in the building. You go back to the board. And it's the same position. The guy hasn't moved yet. *Then* you're playing chess."

One night after work he suggested we drive to Philadelphia, where the World Open was currently underway. The World Open drew over one thousand players for sections ranging from grandmasters to people who played more poorly than I did. We wouldn't be arriving until late, well after play had concluded for the day, but it didn't matter—the chess players would still be up and about in the Skittles Room. "Skittles" was another word for speed chess. Every tournament has a Skittles Room for casual interaction among players.

As we entered the hotel, Glenn shook my hand and said, "Hallman's first chess tournament."

The hotel was of the type that catered to conventions, which meant that it was clean and big, but decorated by an accountant. Its hallways had the feel of broad tunnels far beneath the earth, a chinked-out network of caverns where a replica of society would play out until it was safe to return to the surface. Operating like businesses, chess organizers in the United States had been using hotels for decades, so that chess tournaments now had more in common with plant and dog shows than with sports or art. I had expected something gala, but "open" was the operative word and gala had been the first thing cut from the budget.

Traffic was light in the cave as Glenn and I entered. He knew exactly what hallway led to the Skittles Room, a shrouded conference chamber where thirty or so players were still playing quick games on tables covered with industrial tablecloths. In a corner a man was lecturing about a chess position to impress a pair of girls, and near the middle of the room a gang of haughty chess-talented teenagers gripped beer cans, cool for maybe the first time in their lives. Glenn found a man named Gist, another of the players of the black chess subculture, and I watched them play for some time, two or three dollars a game. Glenn won for the most part, and the room's mood was lively. But I found the Skittles Room depressing. It was like the dealers' lounge again. In the United States chess has failed to become much more than a game, a diversion. I found that I wanted organized chess to be a thing that elevated culture, and when I eventually heard of Kirsan Ilyumzhinov's chess movement I wondered if crafty Russians had beaten us to it. Here in the Skittles Room, chess was still just a toy.

As a player myself, I tended to favor one-minute chess. One minute, in which each player has sixty seconds to complete all their moves, isn't even chess to most serious enthusiasts. Tournament games can last more than six hours. One minute, or bullet, can last no more than two minutes total. The dimension of time, I thought, added something to the game. The base thrill of one minute made my organs cinch and shrivel. A nice mate produced in sixty seconds could keep me happy for days. In Glenn, the seduction of one minute was apparent, as it was for many grandmasters who played on the ICC. They could go on for hours, jacked into the quick drama. Many players spoke of having caught the chess bug, or of being hooked on speed chess, but the language was always euphemistically light.

"*Drats!*" I heard Glenn mutter once, employing the only vague curse I ever heard him use after four consecutive losses on my computer. "I'm playing like a jerk! I've *got* to beat this guy."

He wasn't talking to me. But he meant it—he *had* to, or else. I left him there for a while. I walked my dog, went to eat, saw a movie, and when I came back he was still there, his face inches from my screen. He had never stopped.

I never played more than eight or ten games in a row—even this I found exhausting—but it was not long before a quick check of my ICC history revealed that I had played thousands of games of chess. I wasn't sure if I was already an addict, but looking around the Skittles Room, panning across its watered-down machismo and bent personalities, I realized something. I didn't want to be a serious chess player.

On the drive home, I spoiled Glenn's victorious mood with the news. I was still interested in the game, I told him, but I realized that I was not talented and didn't particularly want to be. I told him I wasn't sure what chess's strange rhetoric was all about, what it meant, but that I still wanted to find out. This did not necessarily have anything to do with playing, I said. Glenn was disappointed that I would never study chess to the point where I could offer him companionship, but he was happy that I was still interested in the thing that held him fixed. Still, I'd put him in a reflective mood, and as we reentered New Jersey he asked me what people at the dealers' lounge, the people who had watched him age ten years and knew him well, thought of him.

"To be honest," I told him, "they think you're kind of weird."

He stared out the windshield, gathering righteousness. "Pff. I think *they're* weird for not developing their pieces."

THAT NIGHT I LOGGED ONTO AN ON-LINE BOOKSTORE AND typed in "History of Chess," expecting to sift through twenty thousand or so matches of limited relevance. I had no idea there would be an exact match, but up popped H. J. R. Murray's *A History of Chess,* dated 1913. It was exactly what I was looking for: an account of the game from its origins up to the modern era. Originals cost as much as a decent used car, and even the reprint was out of print. It took four months to arrive.

A History of Chess, simply "Murray" among chess historians, is the game's latest definitive work. The book was the result of more than a decade's research by Murray, who traveled widely to discover unpublished texts that referred to chess. Printed at more than nine hundred pages, the work included entire documents in Spanish, French, Arabic, and Hebrew, so that it was unreadable by anyone, probably, except Murray. Between 1900 and 1913, Murray published thirty-five articles in *British Chess Magazine,* disseminating his findings in serial. Finally, he was ready to publish in book form. But before the thousands of quotations and footnotes, before the hundreds of diagrams and charts, before the endless chess analysis for the scores of chess variants he had discovered or learned, before the complex codes he had constructed to refer to the ancient texts—before it all, Murray listed his errata. There were nine proofreading mistakes in the book. All of them had been caught.

Life began to change after I got the Murray. As I worked my way through it, I took dozens of pages of notes. I drew geographically based time-line charts of the movement of the game and scribbled down rare bits of chess writing that I found pleasing. I posted it on my walls. I read other texts, as well: Glenn brought over his twenty years' worth of *Chess Life,* the thin slicks coming to sit on my shelves and on the back of my toilet. I downloaded a chess screen saver for my computer. I kept a chess set ready in my house at all times. I tried to buy a pair of chessboard-patterned nylons for a woman I was dating, but she said she would never wear them. I told her I would. By then I had come to realize that my meeting with Mitchell at the

Manhattan Chess Club had been prescient, that I wanted to write something about the game. But I still didn't know what it was.

My relationship with Glenn began to change. Now that I was a layman historian, our bond became a version of the classic conflict between player of the game and student of the game. I was now equipped to debate points with him—he was forced to admit that the knight had not always been called a knight—and before long I came to an understanding of what my role in our relationship would be. What was more interesting than Glenn's skill, I thought, was his devotion to chess. I admired the sacrifices he had made for the game—his maturity, his family—even as those sacrifices sometimes seemed ill-advised. In a way I wanted to save him from himself. We were an even odder couple now. He was black and I was white, and we were like chessmen opposed on a board that was the game itself.

IN 1834, I READ, A CORRESPONDENCE MATCH WAS PLAYED between chess clubs in London and Paris, teams of more than a dozen men on each side contributing to a contest that would last two years. It was one of the earliest examples of organized international play, an event that helped create the climate of national competition that resulted in chess organizations and FIDE. By then I was not surprised to learn that I already owned the games of this match, each of them stored on the database Glenn had installed on my computer.

My first exercise for Glenn was to invite him to my apartment to show him one of the games. Glenn was surprised by the new additions of chess history on my walls, but wasn't really sure how to understand my interest when I still didn't understand chess.

We sat down before my board. I told him nothing of the game before I began to recite the moves to him—only that his job was to guess who was playing, and what year it had been played. Interested in the puzzle of it, he agreed. White was London, and black was Paris.

"That white failed to get in c4 at some point means it's probably before 1950," Glenn said. "There's an early queen check—people don't really do that now, so before 1920. If the players were famous, I'd say it was pre-1900. As well, black is a pawn gobbler. You don't see too many gobblers after 1900."

The experiment tested a hypothesis—that expertise in chess, knowledge of the opening theory that had come about in the last couple of hundred years, amounted to a kind of historical study. It wasn't good enough for a player to simply memorize the moves—one had to know where they'd come from, the exact etymology. Glenn could look at a game and just from the moves tell me when it had been played. What was it if not a study of history?

Frequently, he made the moves of the game before I spoke them aloud, anticipating the maneuvers that a handful of men had debated for days in a fraction of a second and being correct perhaps four out of five times. When he was wrong, he would say, "I prefer g6," or "Ng4 is silly. Who's this guy with this stupid knight move?" After we played white's tenth move of the game, Glenn stopped, covered his eyes, reported the location of each piece on the board without looking, and then suggested a tenth move for black: "Bxc5 is the most logical."

He was right.

"By today's standards," Glenn said of the game, near its conclusion, "this wouldn't even be published. Everyone knows that a knight on f3 is worth a couple pawns. It's that white has so many tempos. After white's thirtieth move, black should play Kd8 and resign."

Black had done just that 165 years before.

MAYBE A WEEK LATER, I CAME ACROSS AN EDITORIAL IN THE *Washington Post* titled, "The Tyranny of Chess." "In some Godforsaken corner of the Russian empire," the columnist wrote, "the impossible has happened. A chess fanatic has seized power." He called Chess City a surreal Potemkin village. "God help us."

I called Glenn and told him my thoughts. I began following Kalmykia on the Internet, searching for its history. Our trip was still many months away, and we'd have other chess adventures before we left; but the next time I saw him at work, I overheard him speaking to another dealer, a pretty girl.

"We're going to die in Russia!" he told her.

CHAPTER 4

The Theory of Commodes

The Pioneer palaces were a bit amateurish—there was a network of schools, sports schools, and chess was one of the items on the curriculum. . . . Chess had a very special reputation in the country, it was seen as the very important ideological weapon. That's why the regime needed the crown, needed top players to defend its intellectual pride.

—Garry Kasparov, 1993

The reader can see that I am beginning to show distinct signs of paranoia myself. That's what you get when you think too much about Russia.

—GM Hans Ree, The Human Comedy of Chess, 1997

"BEFORE THE SEVENTH CENTURY OF OUR ERA, THE EX-istence of chess is not demonstrable," wrote Prof. D. W. Fiske, in a tone of solemn import common to chess historians. "Down to that date it is all impenetrable darkness." By demonstrable he meant chess references in literature. The earliest chess reference actually came from a sixth A.D. 590 Sanskrit prose romance called *The Vasavadatta,* a passage describing the rainy season: "The time of the rains played its games with frogs for chessmen, which, yellow and green in color, as if mottled with lac, leapt up on the black field squares." The debate over the truth birthplace of chess centers on China and India, but the matter will never be resolved. The game had penetrated Persia even by the time of the earliest chess references. Chess's rapid spread would become a characteristic feature of its history. It caught like fire, moved like a virus. Persia gave the game the words "check" and "mate." The Persian word for king, *shah,* mutated first into Latin's *scac,* and eventually into "check." The Persian word *mat* meant "at a loss" or "helpless." *Shah mat* meant "checkmate."

Arabia promptly sacked Persia in 638 and took the game, but the timing was problematic because it was not clear whether chess was looked upon favorably by Islam. Muhammad had died just six years before, and nothing in the Koran really seemed to address chess, except of course its prohibition on idolatry, which is why chess pieces are shaped the way they are today. Despite the uncertainty, early caliphs played chess widely, and after a good deal of dispute—a mad Egyptian ruler once tried to outlaw the game, and at least two other leaders expressed hatred for it—chess fell into a category of behaviors undesirable but not forbidden. The game was popular throughout the Islamic Empire, from Pakistan to Spain, by 750. It would be more closely associated with art in Arabia than at any other time in history. A ninth-century text was titled *Elegance in Chess,* and one caliph was said to explode at his courtiers when they interrupted a game to point out the beauty of a garden. "Stop," said the caliph. "As-Suli's skill at chess charms me more than these flowers." Arabia would suffer no shortage of myths as to the game's invention. One tale claimed the creation was meant to appease a king who had run out of enemies to defeat, another credited the invention to an Egyptian sage the Greeks called Hermes, and still another said it was intended as a tool of military instruction for an incompetent warrior prince.

Chess entered Western Christiandom before the Crusades, around the year 1000. It had been on the continent of Europe for a while. If you were to plot an invasion of Europe from the south, you might accidentally re-create chess's triple-pronged sweep across the Christian-Islam information divide. Chess entered Byzantium by hopping the Bosporus Strait in what is now Turkey. Here it became *zatrikion,* and just as the Eastern Empire was cut off, so was the Byzantine game isolated and eventually absorbed, after more conquests, into Arabia. Muslims in Spain, specifically the Moors, allowed the game passage into Western Europe, and the chess language of Spain and Portugal shows Arabic influence even today. The Central European invasion came through Italy, the game either riding merchant trade in Venice or war when the Saracens conquered Sicily, and the first reference to chess in Christiandom proper is a bequest of chessmen in the castrensian will of Count Ermengaud I, dated 1008. As in Arabia, chess received a mixed critical greeting in Europe even as it flourished. Early in the twelfth century it was included in a list of "knightly accomplishments," but late in the same century there was an attempt to ban it as an "unprofitable addiction." Christiandom offered its own set of origin myths. One morality attributed it to an Eastern philosopher, Xerses, for the purpose of correcting the manners of an evil king, and a medieval problem book claimed it was invented at the siege of Troy by a Trojan knight and his lady.

In Asia, the game spread out in an initial wave from its birthplace, moving north and eventually giving birth to *xiangqi* (Chinese chess), *tjyang keui* (Korean chess), and *shogi* (Japanese chess), all of which are played with pieces placed on the intersections of lines rather than inside squares. Arabic chess passed through Asia in a second wave after Arabia sacked India in the eighth century. From there, chess swept through Southeast Asia piggybacked on Buddhism. Religion, Genghis Khan, and Western colonization assisted the spread, but in the meantime chess had descended onto the country where it was to find its most profound expression—Russia.

Russia is not the birthplace of chess, but it is the heart, a transplanted critical organ. Three theories attempt to explain how chess came to Russia, but each is insufficient on different grounds. The first is that Genghis Khan's Mongols brought the game when they overran Russia around 1200, but there are references to chess in Russian ecclesiastical literature prior to the invasion. The second theory suggests chess arrived from Byzantium through the Serbs and Bulgarians, but this is suspect because the Russian name for chess is the Arab-influenced *shakmaty,* rather than *zatrikion.* The last theory is the most likely, though the evidence for it is only circumstantial: A trade route running from Baghdad to the mouth of the Volga River allowed Russian merchants access to the Muslim world, and chess stowed away on boats that rode the Caspian Sea home. Regardless of which theory was correct, the game quickly achieved popularity in Russia, and after the Mongols came and went and the Eastern expansion began, the country became a cauldron of Asian and Muslim varieties of the game. Chess was played by the Czars. Ivan the Terrible, one apocryphal tale goes, was about to sit down to a contest when he was afflicted with the disease that killed him. A "cult of chess" flourished in the Russian court through the seventeenth century. Chess sets of amber and ivory are among the royal treasures, and a special troupe of craftsmen, *shakhmatniks,* were employed to make and repair these sets and boards of other games as well. Chess references popped up in ballad literature and heroic epics.

European chess didn't arrive in Russia until Peter the Great opened the empire to foreign influence. Peter I was a player, and the floppy leather board he used during military campaigns eventually wound up at the State Hermitage Museum. Even before the introduction of European chess, Russia had an international reputation of strong chess traditions—a Russian embassy of more than fifty men who went to France in 1685 led one Frenchman to conclude that the best French players were schoolboys by comparison. Similarly, in 1673, a papal envoy inside Russia wrote: "At this game nowadays both old men and children spend all their time on all the streets and squares of Moscow." European chess was among the many Western fashions Peter I facilitated when he took the throne in 1689. This completed the Russian trifecta: They had now received chess influence from each of three possible directions, east, south, and west. Even if India or China was the home of chess, Russia, by the early eighteenth century, was a kind of focal center, a boiling stew of chess ingredients from all over the world. Russian diversity made reconciliation of the variants difficult, and as late as 1854 the most widely practiced form of Russian chess included rules clearly influenced by Mongol sources. Even in modern Russian chess, the bishop is known as *slon,* making it the only country in Europe to refer to the piece by the word for "elephant," the original Asian designation.

Mikhail Chigorin, in the last quarter of the nineteenth century, was the first Russian player to devote his life completely to the game. Others had paved the way for him, but he was the first to work toward a unified chess identity in Russia and the first to achieve significant results in international tournaments. He played for the world championship twice. He promoted the formation of a national chess association in Russia, but the first such organization wasn't founded until six years after he died. The Bolshevik Revolution came along quickly thereafter, and, as had happened with the United States, a feeling of national inferiority to Europe led the new Soviet government to search internally for a sense of hegemony. There was chess. The third All-Union Congress in late 1924 announced that it regarded chess "as a political weapon that must be used in order (a) to give to the working masses, tired after their daily labor, a rational leisure activity, and (b) to exploit the significance of chess . . . to give a new impetus to the growth of intellectual culture and the training of the mind among the laboring masses." Proponents claimed it was useful in the struggle against superstition—"a living piece of propaganda against religious delusion"—and the new chess movement was put under the jurisdiction of the Supreme Council for Physical Culture. The council's chairman, Nikolai Krylenko, had been Commissar for War in the revolution and was later Commissar for Justice. Krylenko was one of the most feared men in Europe and has been said to have done more to popularize chess than anyone in history. Under his leadership, the national chess movement began with Chigorin as the posthumous poster boy. Chigorin had been bold and crafty, emblematic of all that was to be Soviet. In Leningrad alone the number of registered chess players jumped from 1,000 in 1923 to 140,000 in 1928. The first Russian to become world champion, Alexander Alekhine in 1927, proved problematic, however: He was labeled a White Csarist, and he publicly attacked the Soviet regime.

When Alekhine died in 1946, the time was ripe both for FIDE and for the Soviet School of Chess, which by then had gestated for a generation. While the older schools of chess—the Modenese movement, the hypermodern movement—were revolutions in which a leap in chess understanding had been made, the Soviet chess machine was more a political ploy than a sporting movement. By then chess theory had arrived anyway. After the '20s there would be no more major revelations in the game, and refinements in theory were limited to ultrafine tuning and depth of analysis.

The Soviet government hoped chess excellence would boost production among the workforce, but it turned out that all chess players really wanted to do was play chess. After Alekhine died, Mikhail Botvinnik became the new world champion and poster boy. Chigorin and Botvinnik were opposite prototypes. Chigorin had had a long beard and drank. Botvinnik looked like a nuclear scientist and was one of the first chess players to advocate physical training. His success was hailed in *Pravda*: "We value this wise game, standing on the frontier between art and science . . . Our great teachers Marx and Lenin devoted themselves enthusiastically to chess. . . . The U.S.S.R. is becoming the classical land of chess." Chess continued to develop in Russia within a constraint: Winning was now more important than creativity. International domination was an imperative. Players who lost had support revoked or reduced. Authorities exerted pressure on creative players who succeeded anyway, as they were risky, and the government's financial support cast shadows of doubt over the nationalistic dogma delivered by Botvinnik and others. The KGB would become the Keystone Kops of the chess world: Rumors spread that the organization was involved in fixing tournaments to favor Soviet players, that they employed Soviet psychics to sit in audiences and direct damaging mental beams at opponents, that they harassed and threatened the families of chess dissidents.

Soviet chess dominated the two decades after WWII. They seemed to be winning the Cold War as well, the arc of Sputnik describing the success of the Soviet system. But if Soviet leadership found losing the race to the moon dispiriting, they must have found Bobby Fischer even more so. Fischer had been on the rise for some time. Most of the stories about Fischer's early life are already shrouded in exaggeration and myth. "All I want to do, ever, is play chess," he is supposed to have said as a young man, capturing in one line the bizarre hold the game sometimes exerts on the young. After his first experience with a woman, a prostitute, Fischer is supposed to have emerged with the comment, "Chess is better." Some stories don't even involve him: In the late '50s, a group of his supporters, in a discussion of the boy's obvious mental illness, considered seeking help for him until someone wondered aloud whether he would continue playing if he "got better." The meeting promptly broke up. Fischer's mother was Jewish, and he was brought up in a Jewish household. His father had been absent his whole life, and he was self-sufficient by seventeen. For a time he seemed perfectly functional—he wrote a column for *Boys' Life,* did a television commercial for Xerox, and won money to play in his first interzonal tournament by appearing on a game show. But he was uncouth and probably disturbed. Were it not for his arrogance, Fischer would have echoed Morphy perfectly—an American sprung from nothing, destined to change the chess world completely. Soviet authorities must have been baffled by this kid from Brooklyn who marched toward them inexplicably, like the force of capitalism itself. Worse, he became popular in Russia, his madness understood as an expression of freedom. The love was not returned—Fischer studied Russian chess books, but otherwise spoke poorly of Russians.

Fischer might have played for the world championship in the '60s if it weren't for his own eccentricity and Soviet collusion against him. His run through the turn of the decade is probably the best performance chess has ever known, repeatedly dominating and sometimes blanking world-class opponents. His '72 World Championship match in Reykjavik, Iceland, received more press than any chess match in history, mainly because its struggle seemed to describe the Cold War. Chess metaphors had been used for the Cold War for some time, and a sentiment that was supposed to have run through the echelons of U.S. international relations said, "We play poker, they play chess." With Fischer, the United States played chess, too. The symbolic meaning of the '72 match would have been far more significant in the Soviet Union than in the United States, and chess interest in the United States leapt dramatically—Fischer was on the cover of *Life*, chess was suddenly on television, and eventually a Broadway musical was based on the contest. The first of many books of the match sold two hundred thousand copies. Negotiations almost prevented it from happening at all, and Henry Kissinger is said to have intervened when Fischer threatened not to play. Fischer won convincingly, even though the match was marred by paranoia from both sides: One of the players' chairs was x-rayed for insidious devices, and a careful examination of suspicious lighting fixtures turned up two dead flies. Since 1927, virtually all the world champions have come from within Russia, but for three years in the early '70s the title was held by a man so demanding and bizarre that he frequently drove away those closest to him. The Soviet Union was forced to explain why the combined resources powering their subsidized pastime could not prevent one crazy American from unseating them all.

But Fischer was as easy to hate as he was to like. He was paranoid, and people really were out to get him. After he won the world championship, it was Fischer himself who was driven away. Fischer tried to use the pulpit of the title to return the world championship to pre-FIDE traditions. Most agreed that his changes would be good for the game, but when not all of his demands were met by FIDE, he refused to defend. The title went to Karpov by default, and the hitch step sent chess into a tailspin. Fischer, the man who had single-handedly added an all-important straw to the already-strained back of the Soviet Union, vanished from the chess scene. He became active in a California cult. When he was mistakenly arrested for bank robbery, he wrote a rambling account of the incident titled "I Was Tortured in a Pasadena Jailhouse!" Bizarre anti-Semitic commentary became a prominent feature of his personality, and another popular story spread that he had all his fillings removed to prevent radio signals from penetrating his brain. By then Fischer had as much in common with Lee Harvey Oswald as any American: He had been to Russia, he had ties to Cuba (he had given Castro a copy of his book), and he claimed he had been victimized.

Arguably better chess players have come along since Fischer, but no one, not even Russian players, underestimated his contribution to the game. Former world champion Mikhail Tal called him "the greatest genius to have descended from the chessic sky." GM Raymond Keene said he was "a kind of angry chess god incarnate." Long before I ever thought of Glenn as a chess monk, the term had been applied to Fischer, living in seclusion, playing only private matches.

In 1998, Fischer gave a series of rare live interviews to a radio station in the Philippines. The interviewers tried to keep him talking about chess, but Fischer's delusions had taken over. He told infantile Jewish jokes and rambled conspiracy theories of a "Jewish world government" that was attempting a "mega-robbery" of his assets. The transcripts went on for pages:

> The Jews control the courts. It's just a charade they go through. It's Façade City, you know—Façade City. . . . This is just a conspiracy against me by the Jews . . . those filthy filthy bastards. You know they're trying to take over the world. . . . You know they invented the Holocaust story. . . . The United States, they're gonna grab me, put me in jail, and who the hell knows? Maybe I'll quote unquote commit suicide. . . . The fucking Jews want to destroy everything I've worked for all my life. There was no Holocaust. The Jews are liars. It's time we took off the kid gloves with these parasites. . . .

Since 1972, chess has been in a kind of stasis, waiting for the Cold War to end and the dust to settle. Soviet players appeared to replace Fischer, but the certainty of a single world champion was lost to the public consciousness and all the matches that have been played since have had the shadow of Fischer looming over them. When the Soviet Union fell, stipends to chess players in Russia ended. The Pioneer Palaces that had once taught chess to promising young players now converted to an "economic game" designed to simulate Western capitalism.

When Glenn and I arrived in Russia, chess had been on the decline for a decade. I wasn't sure what we'd find. But I knew what I thought: If chess was a tool of national identity, then Russia had dropped the ball and Kirsan Ilyumzhinov had snatched it up and run with it to Kalmykia.

ST. PETERSBURG WAS LIKE A CITY CHOPPED OFF AT THE KNEES. Down low it was like any other city, but everything stopped at a uniform five stories above the ground as if the entire downtown had been reduced by a huge blade passing overhead. Really, it predated elevators. The cars of the city were so old that I could count the firings of their pistons, and the wooden planks holding the trolley tracks in place bounced into the air as the heavy trains rumbled over them. Taxis parked wherever they could stop on wide, seamless streets, and islands of vehicles shaped impromptu lanes. Looking down alleyways in St. Petersburg was like looking through a time door into a world of a different century, into Dostoyevsky's underground.

Chepukaitis spotted us almost at once at the small chess club we found on our second day in St. Petersberg. It wasn't quite right to say that Chepukaitis was a hustler, because he was actually good. But he had a hustler's instincts, and when he saw Americans at his club it spelled opportunity. The day before, Boris, a translator I'd hired on the Internet, looked at Glenn and me strangely when we eschewed his offer of sightseeing in favor of a chess park. There, we'd learned that chess in Russia was subject to rules of hospitality. Initial games were playful and polite, then the sparks flew. We also learned of Chepukaitis's chess club and an upcoming tournament. Chepukaitis arrived after the tournament began. Glenn was playing; Boris was outside smoking. Chepukaitis approached at once, recognizing in me the telltale signs of a chess mark, whatever they are. We stumbled through a greeting without a common language, and even without knowing what he was saying I could take a guess at his body language. When Chepukaitis's young, pretty wife arrived and Boris returned we had enough access to each other's words so that I knew I was right.

The chess clubs in Russia were like brothels—they weren't marked with signs or addresses, people just knew where they were. The chess room was a large converted porch—its wooden brick floor was smooth as though once exposed to the elements. It was a basic classroom setup—a desk for the director at the front of the room, and twenty-five chess tables lined up in rows. The color motif was asylum green, and small metal vessels on the floor showed where the roof leaked when it rained. As we waited for the tournament to begin, our presence attracted some attention. But not because we were foreign. It was our chess clock. Russians were no longer impressed with blue jeans and ballpoint pens, but their chess clocks were ancient devices in the style of '50s radio units. We had a Chronos—the sleek, hot new clock of the United States. As a rule, the business of chess clocks suffered from R&D lag, and the Chronos was really just a simple digital mechanism housed in a metal casing. Two toggles for the clocks, a single options button, and an LED readout that would have looked antiquated in anything but a chess clock. When we first produced it, a few men sneaked glances at it, and one finally mustered the courage to ask for a look. He touched its button as though he had never touched a button before in his life and laughed when it beeped and its readout materialized. Others wandered over, and the man held it up as though it was a marvel, as though it deserved a higher station in life than he himself. He spoke for a moment, and Boris translated as the others continued to play with it.

"He says he would gladly pay five hundred dollars for such a device," Boris said.

Glenn's first-round opponent in the tournament was a young, quiet, dark man who first objected to our digital clock, then agreed reluctantly. They played on Board 1. I didn't see the game because, when Boris disappeared to smoke, I was approached by an older man in a dirty suit coat. He was short, and his hair grew wild. He spoke no English but showed off his bad teeth and caps of precious metals. Thick tufts of hair strained from his ears, and his eyes expelled great quantities of mucous. It was Chepukaitis. He was a legend, we were told.

Glenn dropped out of the tournament to play with him. Chepukaitis offered to play three-minute blitz for ten rubles a game, but Glenn insisted on a stake six times higher, two dollars. Chepukaitis shrugged and agreed. Their first game was a draw, and the small crowd that had gathered to watch seemed surprised and pleased. But the Russian honeymoon was over. Chepukaitis shrugged for the last time. The old hustler's lips formed a pout as he played, but it wasn't wise to trust his expressions. He often folded his hands in front of him as he thought, clutching them like restraints against impulsive moves. He won nine of the next ten games. He asked for a break to smoke, and I offered to buy him lunch.

"I must be tired," Glenn said, as we walked to the restaurant. He was sad at the losses.

"Give yourself a break," I said. "He's a legend."

We took a small back room at a neighborhood restaurant. As we ate, Chepukaitis and his wife told stories through Boris that gave an incomplete but revealing portrait of Chepukaitis and made it apparent that his status as a legend was his own doing. Chepukaitis had always lived in St. Petersburg. He had survived the siege of Leningrad from 1941–44, but when he finally escaped he could not afford college. He believed chess came originally from the sunken island of Atlantis; and another myth, this one about himself, said that as a young man he had once gone to the Balkans with only a chess clock and returned with a bagful of money. He was a five-time blitz champion of St. Petersburg, but had never achieved a title because he lacked the money to travel to the necessary tournaments. He had been a blitz specialist even in the years when blitz chess was out of favor because Botvinnik had declared it not serious. Tal, Korchnoi, Petrosian—they all had come to play with him when blitz was forbidden. When Bobby Fischer came to Russia at age fifteen, he lost ten games in a row to Chepukaitis. Like Glenn, Chepukaitis made a habit of carrying the evidence of his accomplishments around with him, and he showed us his books and an article that had been written about him in a Polish journal. As Chepukaitis spoke, little bubbles of saliva formed on his lip, and flecks of it projected out from his mouth to snowflake down to his chin and lapels. He was cynical about the current status of chess in Russia. "It is nothing," he said, swatting at the idea. "Ten or twenty years ago, chess was necessary. In the '80s, there were one hundred chess clubs in St. Petersburg. Now there are two." Chess as a tool of ideology, it seemed, had failed Chepukaitis, but Russia's transition to capitalism had made for a delightful endgame to his life. He had met his wife at a tournament—she was beautiful, thirty years his junior, and rated over 2000—and the Internet had afforded him his first formal job: He worked for a chess Web site.

After lunch, we returned to the chess club, and Glenn and Chepukaitis sat down to play some more. I chatted with Chepukaitis's wife and mentioned the Yudina murder in Kalmykia. In a country where journalists disappeared with regularity, she recalled it at once. She didn't commit as to how she felt about it, and I didn't press because I knew of at least one journalist who had been asked to leave Kalmykia after asking about Yudina. I discovered that Boris had a bad habit: Sometimes he was so interested in the conversation I was having that he simply quit translating and began a conversation of his own. I interrupted him once to find that he had been forming a revolutionary opinion.

"It is impossible to say anything against Ilyumzhinov and stay alive in Kalmykia," he said.

Boris had a master's degree and had written his thesis on optical information systems, but now he made his living running a Web translation service. Mostly he wrote letters for American men looking for Russian brides. He didn't like the work, but there was enough of it. Boris had a dim view of Kalmykia, having been there on a long trip he'd taken through Russia a number of years back. The water there was as trustworthy as the politicians, he remembered.

"To tell the truth," he said, "I was once shot at in Kalmykia. I was drunk. It was a pellet gun, at our car. I said to my friend, 'I wish we have a gun to shoot!' Later, I look back and I am glad. It was why I stopped my travels."

By then the chess room was as crowded as a tavern. The tournament was still going on, but other matches were happening as well. I stepped over to watch Glenn. It wasn't going well. Chepukaitis glanced up at me, and, in that instant, the old hustler did not look as though we had just been making chess jokes at lunch. Instead, he looked at me as though I was an enemy. The whole room, in fact, seemed to have adopted the same bad vibe, and just a moment later two arguments over tournament games broke out at once. The Russian contest at this level was apparently decided by the volume of one's protest. The men went straight to screaming at one another, and others screamed as well, for silence. The director appeared from behind his desk to settle things, but before long he was screaming too, making chopping motions with one hand to emphasize his words. I didn't know Russian history too well, but it seemed to me at that moment that the chess room was a puppet show depicting the post-Soviet disorder—a vague core of authority blindly attempting to establish control over many groups at odds with one another.

In the end Glenn won four games against Chepukaitis and drew three. He lost thirty-nine. The seventy dollars was a third of what he'd brought for the entire month of our trip.

"Hey," I said, knowing he would take it hard, "you won more than Fischer did."

"Fischer only played ten games," he said.

THAT NIGHT, BORIS ACCOMPANIED US ON THE RED ARROW train to Moscow. Glenn slept across from me, his jacket pulled up over his lip and nose like a Bedouin. The cabin beds were short, and his knees crimped toward his chest, but he slept soundly. The train was all lullaby, the gyroscopic jostle of the tracks, the steady click of the wheels like the eighth notes of some slower melody, the stars stationary out the small window, all of it a lull of travel nostalgia, a cradle or warm womb, Glenn and I like twins incubating in that cramped space. It was too early to sleep. I watched out the window, looking for features of the Russian night, but after the boring industry outside St. Petersburg, I saw only darkness. A light appeared from the right, and another train vaulted by us on a parallel track, a twenty-second blur of vaguely understood metal. When it was gone, it seemed odd that the stars were still in place. I brushed my teeth for a moment with my forefinger until they felt clean to my tongue. We had been gone only two nights, but already I felt the anxiety of rootlessness, the emotional film of hygiene practiced on the fly.

Earlier, Glenn had beaten me three times at blitz in the restaurant car. The prices of food on the train were so wildly inflated they had little business. The service was slow, and we had plenty of time. The only other man in the restaurant did not even look at us. Boris was getting used to the idea that Glenn played chess for money, and when we finished, he asked what our stake had been.

"Pride," I said.

Back in the cabin, Glenn crimped into his little bed. I left him to use the train's bathroom. On the airplane from Boston, the toilet basins had been lined with teflon and the flushing mechanisms seemed to employ a sophisticated firearm technology. On the train, the toilet was a steel hulk that flushed like a blunderbuss. When I returned to the cabin and told Glenn about it, he frowned and opted for biofeedback. It wasn't necessarily a wise decision as the rest of our journey would be a trip backward through the evolution of commodes.

Rumbling toward Moscow in the middle of the night, this didn't seem such an absurd thought, and I wondered if anyone had considered a theory of commodes. I scribbled in my notebook, "Toilets as Historicity," but didn't know what to do with the thought. I asked Glenn how he was feeling about the trip. I was worried because Chepukaitis had had his way with him. But Glenn seemed fine and said that he'd like to take a trip like this every other month. We fell silent at this, and before long he pulled his jacket over his face and his breathing grew loud across from me.

I wrote for a while in my notebook, then turned out the light and looked through the window, waiting for sleep. The Russian night was absolute. Another train passed us, a ghostly reflection of our own midnight whoosh, a drumming of wind and a sputtered clanking, and then it was gone, its passengers asleep like Glenn, breathing metric volumes and dreaming of the morning when they would wake to sore limbs, slobber on their cheeks, and the miracle of new life granted overnight while they slept.

MOSCOW'S MEDIA TOWER—A 530-METER BABEL TOPPED WITH A bouquet of antenna visible from most places in the city—had caught fire and burned shortly before Glenn and I went to Russia. The Russian submarine *Kursk* had sunk about the same time, an explosion making a coffin of it at the bottom of the Barents Sea. In the weeks to come, Russia's war with Chechnya would flare again, and bombs would explode in the underground passageways of Moscow, acts of terror inflicted so frequently they lost that which was terrible about them.

We were never searched so thoroughly as when we went to the U.S. Embassy in Moscow to register our presence in the country. We were shuttled past a line of Russians, then asked to empty our bags for the marines waiting on the inside. Upstairs, five parties waited at some kind of cultural affairs division—Glenn and I, and four men doing paperwork for Russian brides, the women sitting quietly nearby, still and beautiful, trying hard in leather, lipstick, and high heels to resemble the photos that had landed them their ticket out.

When our paperwork was complete, we took a walk through Red Square. Glenn wanted to talk about the Russian brides, about Russian women in general. The sheer number of beautiful Russian women we'd seen challenged all the assumptions Glenn had made about Russia, and they offered him a slate on which to calculate wacky theories. Moscow was a city of pin-up girls. A beautiful woman in leather pants and spiked heels might just as easily strut through the doors of a modeling agency as from an alley that led to a slum of world-class blight. Russian women were building capitalism from the top down, and they had quickly mastered some of its most basic principles. When they stood still at a street corner, it was easy to mistake them for a poster stretched along the brick wall behind them.

"Russian women have a nice shape," Glenn told Boris, as we passed first Lenin's Tomb and then a stone platform where beheadings had occurred not so long ago, really. "In America, about half are too big. Not healthy. Not true here." He looked up at the Kremlin looming before us, and at Red Square's cathedral plopped down like a bit of the Emerald City tornadoed to Kansas by mistake. "Russia! I appreciate the architecture. I appreciate the women."

I needed to get him back in front of a chessboard. I demanded for the second time that Boris take us to play chess. In St. Petersberg, Boris had been surprised at this, but now he was beginning to understand. He hailed a taxi.

At Moscow's Central Chess Club, Glenn played back and forth with a man who was a "candidate master," Russia's equivalent to Glenn's master ranking. The Russian men who gathered around to watch were hulks sheathed in long, wool coats. They were either literally old or prematurely old thanks to the conditions of the country, with burn marks on their knuckles from cigarettes, fingernails the color of pus. I noticed one man among them simply because he was blond and young, and asked Boris to introduce us. His name was Aleksandr. He told us what he knew about the club, then offered to take us to another chess club where another blitz tournament was scheduled to start shortly. A famous grandmaster was supposed to attend. I interrupted Glenn with the news.

"Arbakov will be there," I said, pretending I knew the name well.

"Arbakov?" He looked up and smiled at his opponent. "For Arbakov, I will go."

The four of us squeezed into a small taxi. Aleksandr was from

Chechnya. His house had survived two wars only to be destroyed eight months before, and now he was unemployed in Moscow, staying with friends.

"I'm sorry about your home," Glenn said.

Aleksandr nodded, and I asked him about chess in Chechnya. The wars had destroyed much in the country but not the game. Even Shamil Basayev, Chechnya's ex-prime minister and sometime warlord, had an interest in the game, Aleksandr said. Between wars, when Basayev lost the Chechen elections, he stole a tactic from Kirsan Ilyumzhinov and became president of the Chechen Chess Federation. He put on a tournament in 1997 with a prize fund of five thousand dollars. Aleksandr took third place in the event but seemed to have no love for the rebel leader.

"Number-one terrorist," he said.

I let a moment go by and then suggested, "Chess always survives."

Aleksandr stared wryly out the windshield. "Thanks God."

The new chess club was down one of Russia's ancient alleyways, and we walked under the stone arch of its mouth into a courtyard that had not done much but age since the nineteenth century. That quick we had traveled back to a decade when speed chess had been outlawed in Russia and relegated to operations like speakeasies. Aleksandr approached a huge locked metal door. The door was not in good shape, sitting slightly ajar, and Aleksandr put his lips to the open crease and shouted *"Shakhmatist!"* After a moment, another of Russia's inexplicable beauties let us in as she let herself out. We watched her transport into the future of the Moscow we'd left behind.

The chess room was below street level, a dark and cramped stretch of chambers lit by bare fluorescent bulbs and decorated with surreal pop art—the Virgin Mary levitating over a house, a crucifix over a red drape. The creatures who played chess in this room were troglodytes who posed as men during daylight. Aleksandr inquired for us—Arbakov was a no-show, and we were too late for the tournament. There was good news, however. A grandmaster was on hand to give lessons, and he would play with Glenn.

Glenn scanned for a familiar face. "Who's a grandmaster?"

The grandmaster was a short, pudgy, recent inductee named Dragomaretski. We saw him over in a corner explaining something to a student, and his credentials made it across the room before he did: a three-time blitz champion of Moscow. We weaved through the room's buckling pillars to the table where they would play. Glenn had learned his lesson from Chepukaitis and agreed to the ten-ruble stake this time. He tried to equalize with the suggestion that they play one-minute chess. There was some chuckling from the crowd, and Dragomaretski agreed. He was a small, nervous man, but somehow he was comfortable with the nervousness he inspired in others. When the game began, it was a spastic dash of play, and even the five-minute blitz games around them seemed methodical and dull by comparison. Dragomaretski was faster than Glenn, and it was soon apparent that there was nothing Glenn could have done to equalize. He lost six games before registering his first victory. I tried to encourage him—any victory over a grandmaster is worth remembering—but he was hard on himself and complained that the Russians were talking during the games. Dragomaretski himself kept up an introspective dialogue during play, like a pitcher talking to his baseball. Glenn won only two of the next twenty-one games, and they were done in forty minutes. After they shook hands, Dragomaretski came running to me for the greedy payoff, 220 rubles, about eight dollars. He shuffled back to his private table.

Glenn was sad but sat down to play some with Aleksandr. Boris and I found the chess room's manager to ask for an interview.

"He says he is too busy," Boris said, shrugging. He didn't believe it, as the room was already beginning to clear out.

We watched Glenn for a while, and then I set off to find the bathroom. I wandered down a dank hallway like a dungeon corridor and passed an open doorway. It was the chess room office. Inside, the manager was seated at his desk, his head lowered before him. He slowly banged his forehead against the surface of the desk, as though being tortured or sucked by something between his knees. Another man stood on the other side of the desk. He waved me farther down the hallway the instant he saw me. I continued on and soon arrived at the conclusion of the theory of commodes. There was no toilet in the bathroom, and it was a bathroom only in the sense that it was where the chess players shat. A hole in the floor was covered by two planks, the wood near the rim rotting, splintered, and stained from the splash of men with illness or poor aim. I left my water there, but came away thinking of Russia as a nation of mighty sphincters.

Back in the main room, Boris approached me with news. "I was told," he said, "there is a man here. A chess player. He is Kalmyk."

He pointed to one of the tournament tables, to a young man with Asian features and long, black hair. In Russian fashion, he wore a sport coat over a sweater. Boris introduced us when he finished his game, and it turned out that the first Kalmyk we met in Russia was the only titled Kalmyk chess player there had ever been. His name was Baatr Shovunov. He was an international master. He was friendly and warm and readily agreed when I suggested he play a game with Glenn. There was a line for Glenn by then, Russians who wanted to play with an American, but I squeezed Baatr through to the front. Their five-minute game turned complicated and interesting, and they both ran low on time in a complex and furious endgame. Everyone was pleased when it ended in a draw.

It was getting late. Dragomaretski left without saying good-bye. I chatted with Baatr a little more, as Glenn continued playing.

"You know," Baatr said, "there is a story, a Kalmyk fable about the creation of chess. Do you want to hear it?"

"Tell me," I said.

He paused a moment, putting the story together in his mind. "There was a boy, a shepherd boy watching his herd. Suddenly, he noticed that two of his goats were playing a strange game with stones. The boy sat down to watch them play. And when the game was finished, the boy was an old man. This was the birth of chess."

CHAPTER 5

Developing Your Pieces: ♞

The foot of the Horse is very light in the battle;
He goes by a crooked path,
His ways are crooked and not straight,
Three Houses are his boundaries.

—*Abraham b. Ezra, 1283*

Those well-cut similitudes of Castles, and Knights, the imagery of the board,
she would argue (and I think in this case justly), were entirely misplaced
and senseless. Those hard head-contests can in no instance ally with the
fancy.

—*Charles Lamb*, The Essays of Elia

THE KNIGHT'S BASIC UNIT OF MOVEMENT IS THE MOST bizarre of the pieces, the most nonsensical. That it jumps over other chessmen is believed to represent the leap of a horse, but that it jumps crookedly is taken as a given. Among amateurs, the movement is usually described as an L-shape, two squares up and one over, or two squares over and one up. But this description leaves out a good deal, and definitions that aspire to exhaustion become exhausted themselves. I once mentioned the difficulty to Glenn.

"It's not difficult," he said. "The knight can move to the nearest squares of opposite color that are not adjacent to the original square."

What the knight's move lacks in simplicity it makes up for with consistency. The knight's move has not changed throughout the history of chess and is a litmus for determining whether chess variations from odd corners of the world truly belong to the chess family. If a game has a piece that moves like a knight, then it's chess.

Most agree that the original chessboard was derived from a board used in an earlier Indian game called *ashtapada*. *Ashtapada* was played on an 8 × 8 board of squares that was also called *ashtapada*. Games played on the *ashtapada* were usually race games in which pieces completed a tour of the board so as to arrive at something frequently called "home." The knight's move may antedate chess itself in the form of a puzzle inspired by those early race games. This puzzle is called the Knight's Tour. The basic challenge of the Knight's Tour is to make as many knight's moves as possible on a board without repeating a square. Early attempts to master the puzzle aspired to only half the board. When this was mastered, the entire board was soon solved. Reentrant Tours came along next, in which the knight completes its tour with a leap to the square on which it began (eight million solutions), and then tours that would turn the chessboard into a vast magic square when each of the knight's leaps was correspondingly numbered (2,032 solutions). The Knight's Tour is an odd medium of expression: Arabia used tours as a delivery vehicle for poetry, printing words of a poem on each square so that the poem would read as the tour was completed; and later, mathematicians devised formulas to discover tours of distinctive patterns. The many solutions of the Knight's Tour recall the many theories of the origin and spread of chess itself, a larger puzzle with a similar pantheon of potentially perfect solutions.

The knight was originally a horse. The name was left alone in most cultures and languages, the relevance of the horse valid even if it didn't represent cavalry. The horse was demoted to a single horseman on entering Europe and eventually became a medieval knight. The writers of moralities understood the knight as a Christian interpreting his faith in a militant spirit. The piece itself became a steed and continued to be represented by a horse's head. The knights of many early chess sets were carved as simple inverted L-shapes, and while this described the movement of the piece fairly well, it's generally believed that the shape was a crude approximation of a horse's head.

The modern knight is basically equal to the bishop, though the value of the piece is subject to context, style, or preference. Knights are considered slightly weaker because they lack range. Knights are volatile—on the edge of the board they may be poorly positioned, attacking as few as two squares, but in the center, protected from behind by a pawn, a knight is an elegant bastion, threatening eight squares at once. Viewed from above, a knight's sphere of influence, of attack, is circular, and more imaginative chess writers have described a well-outposted knight as a potent octopus. When knights protect one another, they shape a figure-eight, a double ring of attack, but at the same time they are vulnerable: When one is threatened, the other becomes weak as well. When a knight attacks two pieces at once, it is said to "fork" them, a subtle way of describing its influence as pronged. In the Arabian game, forks were well known, and a special name was reserved for a knight's fork of the opponent's king and rook, forcing an advantage—*Shah Rukh*. The maneuver was so highly valued that a series of Mongol princes were given the name.

To give mate with a pawn is almost an insult. Historically, the value of such a mate has reflected cultural mores: In the West, a pawn mate might force the loser to pay double in a game played for a stake. In Japanese chess, pawn mates have been considered bad form, dishonorable. To give mate with a knight is delicious. In the otherwise two-dimensional universe of the chessboard, the knight's move is counterintuitive, and to mate with a knight is to arrive at the essence of chess's spirit, an understanding of the force of the men beyond the gross threats of line pieces. A smothered mate is even better: Trap your opponent's king inside his own men, use his pieces as though they are your own, then attack him with a knight when there is nowhere left to run. "A perfect 'mate' irradiates the mind with the calm of indisputable things," wrote A. G. Gardiner. "There are 'mates' that linger in the mind like a sonnet of Keats."

The first time I gave mate with a knight, I called Glenn immediately. He came over, and I showed him the game. He ridiculed my opening play, pointed out missed tactics in the middle game. But he became silent as the finish approached, and I knew he was calculating the moves just as I had during the game, and when the knight mate came, a corner of his mouth turned up, and his lips parted slightly. He huffed a tiny laugh and shook my hand.

CHAPTER 6

Epideixis

The blindfold game contains everything. . . . If one could see what goes on in a chess player's head, one would find a stirring world of sensations, images, movements, passions, and an ever changing panorama of states of consciousness.

—*Alfred Binet,* Mnemonic Virtuosity: A Study of Chess Players, *1893*

. . . this exertion seems absolutely miraculous, and certainly deserves to be recorded as a proof, at once interesting and astonishing, of the power of human intelligence.

—London Morning Post, *May 28, 1782*

THE FIRST BLINDFOLD CHESS PLAYER WAS A BLACK MAN. Sa'id bin Jubair was born in the same century as chess itself and died early in the eighth century. He was the first player to actually turn his back to the board. His fame for blindfold chess rivaled his fame for politics. One legend suggests that he took up chess to disqualify himself for a judgeship. And when he was executed for his part in a revolt, his executioner was said to believe that God would punish him once for each of his murders, but seventy times for the death of Sa'id bin Jubair.

Arabia trail blazed the field of blindfold chess only to be forgotten. A date for the first blindfold chess players to enter Europe is given as 1265, and in 1331, there was a report of a Muslim who could play two blindfold games simultaneously. A sixteenth-century text tells of another Muslim who could play four games at the same time, and in the following century the ante would be upped to ten by a man who could correct his opponents' mistakes even as he played.

Early Europeans valued blindfold chess—in particular players from the Lombardy region of Italy, who were among the first to make a scientific inquiry into the game. But the Muslim blindfold tradition had been forgotten when European chess appeared and wiped out the older game. Late in the eighteenth century, the blindfold displays of Philidor, playing two or three games at once, attracted the attention of news sources. Even Philidor's uneven results in these displays mystified journalists, who strained their vocabularies to find language appropriate to their awe. Philidor's public displays would set the tone for the next 150 years, and blindfold chess exhibitions would help to promote the game and offer players a source of income. The number of simultaneous games would rise quickly. Paul Morphy would play eight games at once in 1858, Harry Pillsbury played twenty-one near the turn of the century, and Richard Réti broke the record a generation later with twenty-nine, only to be eclipsed by Alekhine at thirty-two and Koltanowski at thirty-four.

Blindfold chess is the game's sideshow event. It's not considered pure chess, and there's a tendency to think it's a trick, cheap magic. There is little consistency in reports from blindfold players on how it *feels* exactly. Some describe a great strain on the mind and being haunted by positions, others claim it is effortless. All find it difficult to articulate the process. Hype tends to win out. Paul Morphy's friends warned him that playing more than eight games at once might lead to brain fever—he dismissed the suggestion, but eventually went insane—and Soviet authorities, as with blitz, banned blindfold chess altogether in 1930.

FOR CHESS PLAYERS IT COMES DOWN TO A CHOICE: ONE CAN become a tournament player, a nomad following the informal event circuit; a chess hustler, living on the cheap, sometimes cheating friends and counting on the ignorance of opponents; or a chess performer, a traveling act doing simuls and blindfolds. Glenn had remained poised between all three. He truly excelled in nothing. But his speed game was better than his tournament rating would suggest, and the four games he could play while wearing a blindfold was more than most titled players.

The first time I played Glenn while he was blindfolded, I wasn't supposed to play him at all. It was still early in our friendship. He had invited me to attend an exhibition he was giving at a women's fund-raising event, an evening put together by local housewives. The event was held at a small museum constructed on a sinking hillside so that its architecture incorporated short flights of stairs all over, a labyrinth turned gallery. There were many different levels and rooms, all filled with table exhibits set up for the night. These included buffets from local restaurants and bakeries, amateur crafts, a silent auction, and Glenn's blindfold exhibition. A variety of folk musicians had been sprinkled through the rooms so that their music just barely overlapped as I moved through the crowd, like picking up adjacent radio signals on a mountain road. The scene was a mesh of common-denominator culture and casual indulgence. It felt like a political event.

"Yo, Hallman," Glenn had said that afternoon, "are you coming? I'll be wearing a green suit."

"A green suit?"

"It's green! You gonna make it?"

I recognized now that this had been Glenn's way of telling me that it would be a somewhat dressy affair. As with his attempts to teach me chess, Glenn frequently wound up communicating something entirely different from what he intended to communicate, the result perhaps of his having lived for so long inside a subculture whose language was completely unique. But by that time in our friendship, I had given up trying to understand him completely, about chess or anything else, and our talks often ended with vague, non sequitur draws.

1851 marks the date of the first international chess tournament, held in London, an event commonly associated with the Great Exhibition put on in London that same year. A massive glass-and-metal building, the Crystal Palace, was constructed specifically for the London fair, just as Chess Palace, with its massive glass facade, would be constructed to host Kirsan's Chess Olympiad 147 years later. Reading chess historians on London 1851 and the Great Exhibition, I got the impression that the two went hand in hand, and that chess had taken its place alongside the great engineering marvels and advances of the day. But accounts strictly of the Great Exhibition alone don't mention chess at all; and its exhibits—items from the countries of the British Empire meant to represent their industrial, military, and economic superiority—were dismissed as tasteless junk by contemporary designers. An envelope machine, a big diamond in a birdcage, kitchen appliances, a two-ton orchid, stuffed frogs arranged in human poses, a Swiss army-style knife with eighty blades, a steel man of seven thousand parts. Immediately after the Great Exhibition closed, the Crystal Palace was moved and went on to be used for hobby exhibitions—cats, dogs, flowers, honey, pigeons, motor cars. Also there were sporting events: polo, cycling, archery, rugby, croquet. But no chess.

But let's say it was a little bit true: the chess tournament in London in 1851 was held in the Crystal Palace, but perhaps as a still-obscure sport or art, or whatever it was, chess was relegated to some obscure corner of the structure, back behind the vase made of mutton fat and the stuffed elephant, and only chess players would remember that they had been there. If so, then its exhibition was not so different from its faint echo more than a dozen decades later: Glenn's blindfold chess display at a quirky museum in New Jersey.

Lost in the wined-up crowd, I tapped a woman's shoulder and asked after the chess player. "Back and down," she said, waving, "back and down." I shouldered through the noise, looking over the museum's permanent exhibits, the dug-up trash of Native Americans, the passable paintings of locals artists. At last I spotted Glenn in the green suit. I had feared a leprechaun's gleaming tuxedo, but Glenn's green suit was a very dark green, and he looked good—dapper, charismatic. His display included a table set up with two chessboards, and alongside them stood propped-up posters with lists of his various accomplishments and photos: Glenn leaning over finished games he had just won, shaking hands with people and smiling. He was well-practiced at such poses.

I was late to the affair and had missed the main exhibition he had given some time ago. But another was scheduled soon. Glenn and I shook hands. Shaking hands was important to Glenn, something about the formality of the greeting canceling the awkwardness of routine social interaction. Glenn would shake my hand even if it was only ten minutes since I last saw him, his large putty palm replacing words he found less intimate than touch. His grip was never firm; it was not angry as some men's are. It was a shake without a subtext.

"Thanks for coming," he said. "I'm glad you're here. The guy I'm supposed to play . . . he's not here. We need you to be my victim."

He smiled and flashed his dimples. I balked at first. Despite all my time on the Internet, I was not a good chess player. The week before I had thrilled at beating an international master in a one-minute game, but by then I was well read enough to know that it didn't really mean anything. Also, I have always hated performances—I cheered Henry James when he decried photography for its annihilation of surprise—and while Glenn had played in public often, I had, apart from the dealers' lounge, only played chess in my apartment, where losing was private if not painless.

Glenn set about constructing a list of arguments as to why I should consent to the match: They really needed me to play; I was supposed to lose so it was okay; I was not as underdressed as I felt I was; and if I played, it would really be as though I was part of the exhibit. I finally agreed, and at once a nut of nervousness fashioned in my stomach. My mouth began to water, and the room suddenly seemed much more crowded.

Glenn wandered off to greet admirers, and during that time I met Judy Zimmer, the mother of one Glenn's students. She was one of the event's organizers and had arranged for Glenn to participate. I had spoken to Judy through chats on the ICC, where we had once had a long conversation about Glenn and his well-being. We were both just getting to know him at the time, each of us assuming the other knew him better, and we had both recognized something in him worthy of appreciation and study: a kind of boyish helplessness coupled with unlikely genius. The brand of friendship was hardly a new phenomenon—a ninth-century Muslim writer had once told of wealthy people who kept chess players in their households: "A parasite may be pardoned his intrusion upon other people's society . . . only on the condition that he is endowed with certain talents, as a knowledge of chess. . . ." Glenn was intriguing because he was good at something; but in addition to chess, Glenn was good at marketing his secrets. In guiding Judy and me into friendship, Glenn had used separate sets of facts, and in our chat we realized that if we shared our respective information, each of us would know more than either alone. On-line, typing and pausing, we hedged over respecting Glenn's trust, then dropped all pretense and told each other what we knew of a lost child, a very angry ex-wife, and Glenn's five days in jail. Even in consultation, his story was enough of an adumbration to keep us fixed.

More than anything else, we were simply charmed at the idea of a hapless chess player, and watching Glenn play was a vicarious pleasure for both of us. Judy and I spoke a bit, exchanging a smirk that assured our mutual betrayal would never surface.

The time came to play, and Judy made an announcement to the milling crowd that chess master Glenn Umstead would now make a demonstration of blindfold chess. Glenn, with the help of an assistant, made a fuss of putting on an elaborate blindfold, all of it reminiscent of the showy preparations of a knife thrower. I was only vaguely aware that I was the target. Before I sat down to play, I briefly doubted Glenn's ability to beat me blindfolded, and I asked Judy if I should dump the game if it looked like I would win.

She smiled. "Nah, crush him," she said.

Glenn allowed himself to be settled into a chair by his assistant and called out his first move, d4, his queen's pawn. Queen's pawn openings tend to be slightly more complicated than king's pawn openings, and I knew at once that this would not be another of our instructive games. He would not risk a public loss to teach me something. I wasn't even sure which moves black could make against d4. I decided to play a conservative game (not necessarily a good idea), so as not to become overextended (the result is that you get a "cramped" position), and to keep my pieces close to home so that I would not fall for a quick mate in six or seven moves. I also thought that if I managed to avoid a predictable opening, something Glenn was familiar with, I would have a better chance of crossing him up. We played back and forth, Glenn's moves called out over his shoulder quickly and played on the board before me by the assistant. Another assistant moved stenciled cutouts of pieces across a large demonstration board for the crowd. I avoided early exchanges of pieces on the theory that more chessmen would be harder to keep track of. But soon enough there came a move that jolted my nervous system. "Queen takes rook on a8," Glenn said, as calmly as asking for the salt. I looked at the board. I had opened a diagonal, or he had opened a diagonal, I wasn't sure which, but a diagonal had opened up, running from corner to corner, and Glenn had slid down there in his mind to snatch a rook that I had yet to even move. I let a moment go by, and then joked, "Okay, so I didn't see that," and the crowd behind me, thirty people sipping local wine and nibbling local pastries, laughed predictably.

But I was angry. I didn't want to lose easily in front of a roomful of people. I took a moment and composed myself. Glenn's queenside rook was stuck on its original square, and it was not going anywhere anytime soon, so I reasoned that the loss of a rook at this early stage wasn't so serious and that I had positional compensation for it. We played on, and I tried to complicate as much as I could. Before long I got the sense that the people behind me were becoming interested, and perhaps they were even pulling for me. I heard murmurs and suggestions, but ignored them and threw myself into concentration. Glenn seemed to have threats everywhere. It happens that way when you play a much stronger player. It's a little like magic, but it's not a trick: Those things he saw he saw because he had trained himself to see them. It was neither ESP nor simply science. Chess was one of the sticks by which the world had decided to measure itself, to gauge our civilized progress, and blindfold exhibitions were less matters of freak shows and savants than public experiments, a look-what-we-can-do-now demonstration of logic, artistry, and brainpower. In this way blindfold chess players were something like the sophists of the fifth century, whose displays of tricky oration were called *epideixis*—exhibitions. Like chess players, sophists were nomads prone to vagrancy and parasitism, and their deeds made them seem like miraculous beings, heroes of athletics. And like a blindfold chess specialist, the sophist's business was to exhibit knowledge and defeat a rival in a public contest. Blindfold chess belonged to the lineage predating and including sophists—medicine man, seer, thaumaturge, poet. There was no sleight of hand in blindfold chess, but viewers came away feeling they had witnessed something mystic and divine.

Though not perfect. Sometime in my middlegame with Glenn, I spied an unprotected bishop in line with my queen. I had neither seen it coming nor recognized it as soon as it was my turn. I hesitated. One of the first things Glenn had taught me was to never quickly accept material from a stronger player—it was always granted with a greater plan in mind. Already a rook up, Glenn could easily sacrifice his bishop for a devastating positional advantage. I looked over the board, but saw no reason why I could not grab the bishop and end a few of his threats. I made the move, and Glenn twitched visibly in his chair. He hadn't seen it. His offside rook was still uselessly undeveloped; his queen wasn't doing much in the corner. My position was not bad, it seemed. There was some audible murmuring in the crowd behind me, and I wondered whether I should dump the game after all. Then I thought no, a win here would make up for the times at my house when Glenn mated me quickly, mercilessly, without saying a word, simply reaching for the clock to reset it. This game would be my vengeance for every perceived sleight. I made a move or two without much thought, trades of pawns and bishops that surely could not hurt me, until suddenly Glenn's pieces, without his ever having witnessed the board, somehow seemed to congeal around my gathered knights and king. How it felt like cheating! When a good player uses his pieces together, it feels as though they are not bound by the laws of movement that make up the game. Harmony in the army allows pawns to advance like spiders sliding down their own silken tethers, and pieces to leap wherever they wish. The figures themselves decide which squares are safe and find a way to cinch an unworkable knot. Soon, I was surrounded. And then came the familiar painful sequence, that sequence in which you have only one move to make, and this invariably leads to another move you must make, and you realize that your opponent has anticipated all this even if you haven't, and that he knows where you're going even if you don't.

"Rook takes h7 mate," Glenn said, and he turned around and peeled off his blindfold dramatically without waiting for confirmation, without looking at the board for even a moment. The applause of the crowd began, and Glenn approached me and said, "You played well." He offered his hand, a thumbs-up shake. I took it, and he held me a little more firmly this time, a little more threateningly, but not, I realized, so that he could add injury to my insult, but so that we would be held there for a photographer—it was Judy—who had planned for this shot from the start; and I forced a smile through my angst, the pain of being beaten and photographed at once, and in the flash that made me a trophy I hated photography, not because it annihilated surprise, but because it preserved mine.

CHAPTER 7

Nothing Can Be Lost in Elista

*In the days of the Chosroes, as it was reported, the old town of Naysabur
had been originally laid out on the plan of a chessboard with 8 squares to
each side.*

—*Mustawfi, 1340*

It's Iceland . . . or the Philippines . . . or Hastings . . . or . . . or this place!

—*"One Night in Bangkok,"* Chess, The Musical, *1985*

EARLY WRITERS ON CHESS FOUND THE NEAT MATCH BE-
tween the grid of a city and the grid of a chessboard irresistible: They
suggested that cities with patterns of 8 × 8 streets were modeled
after the *ashtapada.* The problem was that chess hadn't been around
when the cities they described were built. One thousand years later,
in Cessolis's morality, the chessboard was said to represent Babylon,
its sixty-four squares a neat mathematical segue from the city's four
sixteen-mile walls.

Kirsan Ilyumzhinov's Chess City wasn't the first chess city to get
off the ground. The first may have been mythical: The series of Mongol princes who had been named *Shah Rukh* shared their name with
a town that their father, Timur, built on the banks of the Jaxartes.
When news of the birth of a boy and the completion of his new city
reached Timur while playing chess, it was said, he chose to call each
by the name of the maneuver he had just perpetrated on his opponent. The town became Shahrukhiya and flourished until the thirteenth century. More concrete accounts of chess towns include a
report from Iceland of an island sixty miles off the northern coast
whose inhabitants were addicted to chess. More recently, the conditions of the 1993 candidates' match between Nigel Short and GM Jan

Timman at San Lorenzo, Spain, led one chess journalist to claim that "what the cross is to Christiandom, the gridiron is to the town of San Lorenzo." But the best-documented chess city is Ströbeck, Germany, in the Harz mountains. Chess playing in Ströbeck was recorded just about as soon as the game entered Europe. By 1616, Ströbeck had a strong reputation as a chess-playing village. Though inhabitants were said to be very good players, foreigners lured by legends reported that the natives were of only average ability. Still, chess was central to the identity of the town, and in 1823, an endowment was set in place to ensure the life of chess in the city. During WWII, the Nazis made a propaganda film of Ströbeck's famous living chess displays. Interest in the game dropped in the first half of the twentieth century; but in 1952, a chess revival began and the game became compulsory in Ströbeck schools. Modern Ströbeck has a chess museum alongside its chess tower and holds an annual chess festival.

THE MORNING WE WERE TO FLY TO KALMYKIA, I ATE BREAKFAST with Boris while Glenn showered. So far Glenn had managed not to drink any Russian water and had eaten little Russian food, but the effects of malnourishment and dehydration in him were still indistinguishable from laziness. I was glad to be free of him for a time.

After bread and caviar, Boris and I tried for one last contact with Galzanov in the hotel lobby. The president's press secretary had been our first contact in Kalmykia. In the months leading up to our trip, Galzanov had seemed alternately elated and annoyed at the prospect of our visit. From the United States I'd spent dozens of frustrating hours in the middle of the night attempting to secure a phone connection with him, and when I got through the message was always an abrupt assurance that everything was just fine. Now Galzanov told Boris that everything was ready. Boris didn't know what to make of it.

"He sounded not happy," he said.

At the airport Boris found the counter where we would check in. He cautioned us about the airport itself—the terminal we were in now was safe, but we shouldn't wander. The warning made me keenly aware that in a few moments Glenn and I would be alone in Russia, obvious Americans, with no one to translate for us. Glenn shook Boris's hand and told him to develop his pieces.

We headed to the gate. While we waited to board, Glenn discovered that one of his shoes had split open. We were both in suits on the off chance that we would be meeting Kirsan immediately, and Glenn had bragged that this particular pair of dress shoes had been an excellent bargain—they were of very high quality, he said, but he had purchased them used at a tuxedo shop for almost nothing. He was genuinely surprised when the seam along the instep split open. I was happy to see him suffer for a bit. Glenn was proving a difficult traveling companion, and my arms hurt from the weight of all the food and water we were carrying to make him comfortable. The money we had for the trip was already strained because he had brought to Russia very little cash. Before we'd left, Glenn had given $750 to two women he was dating at the time. Between what he'd already spent and what he'd lost to Chepukaitis, he had less than half his money left. And already he was complaining. When he was unhappy with the planning or the accommodations I had arranged for us, he whined like a retiree who was certain that his money was worth better than this. When his shoe split, I enjoyed it fiendishly. But it proved only a minor problem for his keen chess mind. He walked off to buy a package of chewing gum and chewed a stick until it was of gluelike consistency. He pulled the gum into workable lengths and pressed the strips into the damaged leather. He stood on the shoe until only a white line remained that he colored in with ink. When he was done, he had fixed more than his shoe—he had repaired the error of having bought it in the first place, and he had replaced his inability to spot quality with perky resourcefulness. He nodded enthusiastically.

Our jet was a little, fat rear-loader, and we fired into the bright sky like an ICBM. There wasn't room for us to sit together, and up the aisle Glenn's head lolled to one side before we leveled off. I fell asleep as well and woke ten minutes from the Elista airport. The plane banked to give us our first glimpse of Kalmykia. From the sky, the North Caspian steppe was flat and featureless, the vast cracks of its many shelves looking like old wounds, scars long since gone to pliable flesh. They snaked along the land down paths of least resistance, young, slow canyons. Then they were gone, replaced by the small outlying structures of airports the world over. We landed hard, stopped fast, and the jet U-turned and drove back to a small terminal.

I exited first, crapped out onto a cracked and weedy runway. A greeting party stood on the chilly concrete: a chorus line of half a dozen made-up Kalmyk girls in bright traditional costumes, red gowns with gold-and-black stitching all over, and dark braids of hair under ornate headdresses. Each held bowls of either Kalmyk tea or balls of ceremonial dough. There was a TV crew there as well. For something less than a second I entertained the notion that the reception was meant for Glenn and me, something from Galzanov. But the girls did not come rushing forward, and the man with the TV camera kept it pointed off at an angle. I stepped to one side to wait for Glenn, moving underneath the jet's wing and settling in beside a tall Kalmyk man dressed in what looked like a safari vest. He stared at me.

"Are you Hallman?" he said.

"*Da.*"

"I am Bair. I am with the press office. We have a van to take you to Elista."

"Excellent," I said.

Excellent. I had been in Kalmykia for roughly twenty-five seconds before breaking the one rule I had made for myself—I wouldn't slip into the role of self-righteous American who expected catering. In half a minute the scene had found synchronization with the screenplay of every bad spy movie ever made. Bair would be our trusty scout. He was a head taller than me and appeared intelligent, and somehow his vest made me think of him as quite capable of leading us around Kalmykia. The reception was for the Russian minister of health, Bair said, who was arriving in Kalmykia to attend a Congress on Traditional Medicine at Chess City. Like the Crystal Palace of London 1851, Chess City doubled as an expo center when it wasn't hosting chess tournaments. We watched the reception when the relevant man appeared, the girls finally pressing ahead to deliver their tea and doughballs, and it was all very ceremonial, though ceremonial in a way that seemed staged. The cameraman was sure to catch it all. Much in Kalmykia was like this, I would come to believe—there was not only an effort underway to return to the Kalmyk traditions that had been repressed by the Soviets, there was an attempt to record those ways. In Kalmykia the introduction of chess, the attempts to reintroduce Kalmyk culture, even this greeting out on the windy tarmac was as much the creation of tradition as adherence to it. This was what had made Kalmykia such an easy target for the international journalists. Ilyumzhinov was attempting the impossible: He was trying to leap from the Third World to the First, and at the same time reintroduce old ways. Through chess, he wanted Kalmykia to move backward and forward at the same time.

"BECAUSE OF ME, BUDDHISM CAME TO KALMYKIA," TELO RIN-poche lectured over the phone from Colorado. "Because of me, the construction of the monastery started. That's what they craved for; that's what I gave them. Why did I leave? Because all the money in the country was spent on Chess City."

Long before Glenn and I arrived in Kalmykia to confirm every sneaking suspicion of Soviet propaganda about Americans, there had been another who had paved the way for us. Long before us, there had been Telo Rinpoche.

In 1942, during the Great Patriotic War, Kalmykia was occupied for several months by the Germans. When the Red army pushed the Germans out, the republic was left in ruins and the Kalmyks found themselves with a choice: Soviets or Germans. Soviet repression was distinct in Kalmyk memory: land, language, and religion had been stripped away from them just a few years before. During the occupation, the Germans forced the Kalmyks into labor, but, playing on frail Kalmyk loyalty, they also permitted Buddhist services. When the Germans left, some five thousand Kalmyks went with them. When the war ended, the refugees were put into displaced persons camps by the United Nations. Ineligible for immigration to the United States on the basis of race, the Kalmyks languished for seven years before the Tolstoy Foundation pulled a fast one on the acting attorney general. They argued that the Kalmyks were "Caucasian" because they had been living in the Caucasus for 250 years. The Kalmyks were reclassified, and Kalmyk-American settlements eventually emerged in New Jersey and Philadelphia.

Telo Rinpoche had been a Philly kid. He was first-generation Kalmyk, the ninth of nine children in a family that was broken and dysfunctional before he even came into it. His birth name was Erdne Ombadykow. "When I joined the monastery in India, I was given the name Tenzin," he explained on the phone. He was an amiable speaker with a cute chuckle. I had found him long after he had left Kalmykia behind. "Later, I was given the name Telo. Now some people say Rinpoche."

At five years of age, Rinpoche had begun to show an interest in monkhood. At a very young age, his mother told a BBC documentary about Rinpoche's life, he would thrill at pictures of Thai temples. While his siblings dreamed of being firemen and policemen, Rinpoche always wanted to be a monk. As it happened, the Dalai Lama was just about to make his first visit to America, and a private audience was arranged. "I remember it was in New York City," Rinpoche said. "We met at his hotel. I think we spent a good half an hour with him."

Before the Dalai Lama recognized in Rinpoche the reincarnation of a dead lama, he must have recognized opportunity. It was 1979, the fall of the Soviet Union was visible on the horizon, and the history of lamas in Kalmykia was far from a model of Buddhist purity. His Holiness spied a shrewd tactic. With the Soviet Union beginning to teeter, Kalmykia would need a lama, and Rinpoche was like a pawn with the potential to promote, a kid throwing the shadow of a god. I asked Rinpoche whether His Holiness had meant for him to go to Kalmykia all those years ago.

"I don't know," Rinpoche said. "I can't speak on his behalf. I can't say. That hasn't even crossed my mind."

In New York His Holiness suggested to Rinpoche's mother that if the boy was interested, and she was interested, then the best thing would be for him to receive training in India. Much later Rinpoche's mother would admit that the Ombadykow family troubles contributed to her decision, and when she left Rinpoche with the monks it was at best a chance for a prodigy to strive for immortality, at worst an elaborate form of day care.

"It was a very warm feeling you received when you came here," Rinpoche said, referring to the yards in the monastery teeming with monks his own age. He was giving an interview for the documentary. "After I got here, six or seven months later, I got the feeling that I was not an ordinary person. We used to play a lot, play house. But instead of house, we used to play lamas. The kids would put me on a mattress and carry me. Later, they said I was recognized by His Holiness as the reincarnation of a lama."

When Rinpoche was given his name and title, it meant that he was just about as close to godhood as a mortal could get. Tibetan replaced English as his best language, but did nothing for his Philly accent. He returned to the United States in 1987 for almost a year, an interval of temptation. A visit from a teacher contributed to his decision to return to the monastery, but by then Rinpoche's odd mix of acculturation had a firm grip: He returned to India with a passion for rock music and a subscription to *Newsweek*.

In 1989, the Soviet Union fell ahead of schedule. The Dalai Lama made his first trip to Kalmykia in 1991, and the nineteen-year-old Rinpoche tagged along. Buddhism in Kalmykia was in a poor state. Communism had offered many temptations, and those Buddhists who had been highly educated had long since passed away. Rinpoche was surprised by the topographical fact of Kalmykia—he'd expected it to be mountainous like Tibet, but instead it was flat, arid steppe. Still, it was exciting to make an impression. "It was an eye-opening thing for the Kalmyk people. I mean, when we first got there, they were offering the Dalai Lama alcohol. To the Communist world, to offer vodka is something special, and if you don't accept it, they get offended. So to them it was like, What's wrong with this guy? When we came to Kalmykia, people saw the pureness of a monk."

A year later Rinpoche was back at his studies in India when he received a telegram from Kalmykia, an invitation to attend an "Extraordinary Conference" the following week. Since the visit with the Dalai Lama, he'd had no contact with anyone in Kalmykia. "I took off the very next day. I had to travel up north into India, three days by train, catch a flight. When I flew into town, they were having problems organizing their Buddhist revival . . . they needed leadership." The conference was two days of plans, testimonials, and laments. At the end of it, they were ready to take action. "Somebody stood up and said, 'I definitely suggest Telo Rinpoche to be our head, to guide us in reviving Buddhism. How many of you vote for him?' And everyone stuck their cards up in the air!"

Before formally accepting the post, Rinpoche returned to request an audience with His Holiness. The Dalai Lama was hesitant as Rinpoche had yet to finish his studies. The plan had come together too soon, but it was a chance to lend assistance to Kalmykia.

Rinpoche was twenty-one when he went to Kalmykia with his idols and heavy metal music, thinking he could simply be a lama who spread the dharma, but once he arrived he realized that a monk on a spiritual frontier did not have the luxury of being a simple preacher. To get anything done, he would need to become political. "All of a sudden," Rinpoche said, "out of the blues, I got into a certain position and had no experience." Still, he went about his job enthusiastically. He went on Kalmyk television and allowed awkward questions in order to attract young people—"You're not interested in girls? Doesn't a good female impress you?" Kirsan Ilyumzhinov came into power shortly after Rinpoche arrived, and Rinpoche saw the energetic young leader as an opportunity. He suggested to Kirsan that Kalmykia create a Department of Religious Affairs, with Rinpoche as cochairman.

The Department of Religious Affairs scored him an office in the House of Government. The department would be the bridge he would use to raise funds to build his vision for Kalmykia—a temple complex on the scale that would eventually be used for Chess City. But while five years later Chess City would go from conception to hosting the Olympiad in a matter of months, Rinpoche's temple complex would fall prey to politicking and the crunch of Russia's struggling post-Soviet economy. Seated in his office next to a small model temple, he told the BBC documentary crew of the first one-and-a-half years of fruitless effort and profound inflation. The film crew continued to follow Rinpoche through his first crisis of faith. The Kalmyk people wanted to be led; Rinpoche wanted to teach them to lead themselves. If the spiritual revitalization of Kalmykia had seemed difficult but doable on his first trip, economic and political realities made it seem impossible now. "This is crap! This is totally crap!" he mused for the microphone. "Why don't I just escape from it? Why should I deal with other people's problems?"

He headed to India for another audience with the Dalai Lama. "Since the election of the new president," Rinpoche told His Holiness, "things have become better. He's made religion a part of the state." His Holiness grunted approval in brief spasms of monk chant. He perhaps sensed the subtle fib in this and maybe realized that trouble was brewing and that the mistake was his own from long ago. He advised Rinpoche to return to India to continue his studies.

Rinpoche was too invested in Kalmykia to leave it by then and returned to Russia to continue the transition from monk to bureaucrat. But the seeds of his discontent had been planted, and his faith was beginning to shake. "I don't think I really know what I want," he said. "On one side, I've been getting pressure. Just because of Kalmykia, my teacher, my family, I remain a monk." On the other side, it was political: his boss at the Department of Religious Affairs was little more than a baby-sitter, he decided. "The Kalmyk government looks at me as a young kid they want to control." Rinpoche had begun to tap into a conundrum far more absurd than the fact that he was a monk who liked listening to the Smashing Pumpkins. He was a god-puppet. Kirsan and the Dalai Lama had each tried to play him like a chess piece of their own array. Eventually, he told people he was giving in to His Holiness's request that he continue his studies in India. He recorded a terse good-bye on Kalmyk television, and left Kalmykia in 1994. But instead of heading to India, he went to Philadelphia for Thanksgiving, having already decided that he would not return. After the holiday, Rinpoche headed West rather than East. He went to Boulder, Colorado, where there was a growing community of Tibetans. It was in this interval that he disrobed. Years later, when I got him on the phone, still the poorly spoken but undeniably sincere man who had once almost been a god, I asked him if there was a procedure to disrobing.

"There're two ways of doing it," he said. "The first is asking permission to leave your teacher or your guru. The second is breaking your vows."

"What did you do?"

He laughed softly at the memory of whatever had made him mortal again. "I pretty much broke my vows. Yeah."

FROM THE AIRPORT IT WAS A TEN-MINUTE DRIVE INTO ELISTA, a city of about one hundred thousand people. Founded in 1865, the town had grown quickly, though in 1918 citizens on the outskirts of Elista still built *kibitkas,* the round, mobile tent structures the Kalmyks had lived in for centuries as nomads. The telegraph came to Elista in 1912, motorcars soon followed. The Kalmyks had started out in tents, had moved to thatch-style houses, and had finally settled on the concrete microdistrict apartments that Glenn, Bair, and I began to pass as our van rolled into the city.

Journalists who attended the 33rd Chess Olympiad in Elista were quick to remark that the buildings between the airport and the town had been made over, but only on the sides that faced the road.

The evidence of this was still there—huge gleaming posters depicting stories-high chess pieces and scenes of Kalmyk happiness affixed to the sides of buildings like flags of victory. Glenn marveled out the window at the idea of chess displayed prominently. Bair smiled at him. But just as the bright, traditional outfits of the greeting party at the airport starkly contrasted with the bland runway and the blank steppe beyond, so did the colorful banners inadvertently call attention to the crumbling, industrial structures to which they were attached.

The city itself was a similar contradiction. It was like a newly planted garden already gone to pot, but at a single glance it was difficult to tell if things were actually getting worse or getting better. All over were the signs of Kirsan's attempts to invigorate the town—new plants here and there, skeletal arch structures meant as support for ivy that had never caught on, new stone statues standing before buildings cracked and repaired with alternate shades of cement. Elista had trees, but weeds were more plentiful in the city, and if the steppe was any measure, the weeds here always won, collapsing on everything like a storm of linked pawns. It was impossible to determine whether Elista was suffering from neglect or a particularly cruel face of nature. There was almost no advertising in Elista—none, that is, apart from the chess posters and billboards at the side of the road, more limelight for FIDE and the Olympiad, and blown-up photos of Kirsan consorting with the heads of religious traditions. Ilyumzhinov had apparently recognized the competitive nature of the relationship between advertising and propaganda, and chose to control both. I asked Bair whether Kirsan was in the country, but Bair remained quiet on the matter, politely deferring all serious inquiries to Galzanov, his boss, whom we would meet in an hour or so. To keep us occupied, Bair did a little tour guiding, naming the street we were on—Lenin Street—and pointing out the statue of Lenin in Lenin Square. The Kalmyks did not have the same relationship with Lenin that other Russians did. He had been one-quarter Kalmyk; and when the Soviet Union fell, Bair said, rather than take down Lenin's statue, the Kalmyks had simply turned it so that it faced out into the steppe.

Bair brought us to one of the city hotels—Hotel Elista—and informed us that we would be staying here for several days until the Congress on Traditional Medicine was over. Then we would move to Chess City. The hotel was old and functional, set squarely in the center of town. Glenn and I were given separate accommodations. The rooms felt far away from things American, far from leisure. Briefly, I looked out my window at the breadth of the city, across the same view over which, the next morning, I would drunkenly formulate a theory on the relationship between chess and shame. As I watched, a gang of crows swooped into town and took up a squawking residence in a large tree.

Downstairs, Bair said he would take us to Chess City for a quick tour, and then we would head back to the House of Government to meet Galzanov.

"Excellent," I said.

Chess City sat out on the outskirts of town, a small suburb now two years old. In all my searching on the Web for it, I had found only a picture of the inside of Chess Palace; it was an oddly angled Echeresque photo of some phenomenon of design that gave me nausea but not a good sense of what the place looked like. I was excited as we approached Chess City, passing a cement wall on which children had painted colorful profiles of chess pieces. Then came the city, surfacing out of the wreck of Elista, a slip of grandeur and color spoiling the blight surrounding it. It was a gated community—a guardhouse stood at the entrance and the entire compound was surrounded by chain link—and we passed first through a parking lot that came equipped with six wrought-iron rooks, three meters high, positioned as though for some odd chess problem that could be solved on the surface of the lot. Chess City extended gently downhill from there: fifty or sixty of what were called cottages but which struck me more as prefab condos, each of their blueprints unique, but all of the same difficult-to-describe blend of architectural influence. Some of the homes were iced over with stucco; others were brick. The plastic roof tiles probably looked clay in photographs. The arched or pointed roofs seemed sometimes Gothic, other times Victorian, occasionally French. We idled into one of the streets past a row of the chess statues that sat all about Chess City, winners of a contest that had been held when the neighborhood was going up. The most famous of these was a simple waist-high pawn that had Mickey Mouse ears attached to its head.

"People just call it Mickey Mouse," Bair said, laughing.

Like everything else in Kalmykia, Chess City was under assault from the steppe weeds, whose aggressiveness made the streets look untended, the tall brown stalks taking up residence in the squares of dirt meant for sapling pines. Despite the appearance, the streets were busy when we pulled in, the Congress on Traditional Medicine in full swing. We came up along the rear of Chess Palace; it was like an overturned cone five stories high. The front was entirely glass. Squared-off office-style space embraced the cone from behind. Bair led us up three short flights of steps and through the building's airlock of glass doors. Inside, the Congress on Traditional Medicine hovered in greeting mode, a cocktail party. The palace was filled with chess tables, hundreds of them used for conference furniture at times like these. Two Kalmyk girls seated before chessboards beckoned Glenn and me toward them, mistaking us for attendees. Glenn waved, but we followed Bair. He showed us first around the ground level—there was a huge chessboard set into the floor, black-and-white squares of alternating impressive stone, the walls here covered with photos of the plans of Chess City and the miracle of its emergence from the desert. There were many photos of Kirsan in a construction helmet; and even Chuck Norris, that American movie icon of squinty grit and plucky adaptability had come by for a visit during construction. He had met Ilyumzhinov in Moscow while opening a theme restaurant. There were many photos of Norris's visit, walking with Ilyumzhinov, the two men flanking a beautiful Kalmyk woman who was their translator. They had strutted meaningfully about the muddy construction site. In one shot, Norris chewed the ear support of his sunglasses, trying to look like a thoughtful businessman as he surveyed a model of the finished vision of Phase I. Two years later, the model would be on display in Chess Palace, and was now situated just behind us, a prophecy fulfilled. But the look on Norris's face, even as he tried to take the project seriously and knew he was being photographed, said, "What the hell is happening here?" Norris was still famous in Kalmykia as being the most prominent celebrity to have ever visited the republic.

Bair led us eventually to the base of a spiraling open staircase that spun up through the heart of Chess Palace's cone like a twirled streamer. We ascended slowly. On the second floor was a coffee shop, a large mural along one wall depicting the chess world champions, men and women both luxuriating under shade trees in a verdant pasture. Kibitkas and livestock filled the green background. On the third floor was open space for more chess tables; and on the fourth floor, a smaller pinnacle, I looked back down at the space spread out below us and recognized the cropped and dizzying section of the photograph I'd seen. Looking out the broad windows from here, it was possible to see into the land beyond Chess City, the beginnings of wilderness that I would eventually explore while looking for the pond in which Larisa Yudina's body had been dumped. The land of Kalmykia, brown, sere hills across which even now a tiny shepherd was steering tiny cows, could only by generous fantasy have inspired the vision depicted on the mural two floors below.

We rode the elevator back down, a glass-walled machine that gave us a princess's entrance onto the ground floor. We left Chess City in a rush, hurrying back for the meeting with Galzanov. Kalmykia's House of Government stood on Lenin Square, an eight-story rectangle of minimalism topped with three flags: Russia, Kalmykia, and FIDE. Inside, the House of Government was like a film noir hotel, the elevators tight, the hallways shady, fluorescent lights occasionally burned out so that while it was often possible to see well down the corridor, the next step might be black as ink. The outgoing regime had looted the House of Government when Kirsan first won the presidency in 1993. On his first day, he and his people had had to send out for paper for their first decrees. Now, Bair strode ahead of us confidently, like a miner down a passage he'd dug himself. It was late for the working day. A single slice of light came from a door standing ajar, and we followed Bair's silhouette directly to it. We entered the office of Galzanov's secretary as though happening on a campfire in the middle of the steppe.

Galzanov's secretary sat erect at her desk, looking so unoccupied that it was quite natural to guess that up to the moment when she'd heard our footsteps she was quite busy with something she would rather we not know about. She was thirty and pretty, but she had the sad, spent look of whores and addicts; the mascara under her eyes was tattoo, and the bags below that were age and weariness. Galzanov was busy, she told Bair, looking at the door that led from her office to his. We waited fifteen minutes. I examined a row of chess books on a shelf. Bair showed me the published books of the Olympiad, and a copy of Kirsan's autobiography, *The President's Crown of Thorns*. He said Galzanov would present a translation and other books to me as gifts.

Galzanov finally appeared, boisterous and friendly, throwing aside the door to his office. He was quite tall for a Kalmyk man, a decimeter shy of two meters, and his features seemed more traditionally Asian to me than most Kalmyks. He had high, sharp cheek bones, a thick lick of hair flopped about his head like the fleshy plume of a quail, and a tooth was missing from the left side of his smile. To our eyes, he could have passed for forty, but he was twenty-seven. We would later learn that he had been one of the youths who had taken over a government post during Kirsan's Youth Self-Government Week—he had acted as press secretary, then simply stayed on in the position.

Galzanov's office had a television and a chess table set up in a corner. Bair had told us that Galzanov was a fine player, and that he prided himself on his blindfold ability—we anticipated a blindfold match between him and Glenn. Galzanov's conference table was strewn with issues of the republic's many newspapers, and the four phones in the office rang almost continually, the electronic bleats like four species of Kalmyk animal. Sometimes Galzanov answered these phones with a spoken word or two before hanging up, and sometimes he ignored them completely so that I understood why I'd spent hours in the middle of the night listening to beeps from 7,500 kilometers away. Now, before we sat down, he answered a phone, responded *nyet* to one question, *da* to another, and then hung up and turned to face us, beginning to speak as he searched his desk for clean spots to settle his elbows.

He formally welcomed us to Kalmykia and went through a few details of our accommodations. Bair, now Galzanov's mouthpiece wholesale, said for Galzanov that his assistant, Bair, would be our guide and translator. He would be with us at all times at a rate of five dollars an hour. Bair looked at me almost desperately as he quoted the figure, and my nod of agreement was not good enough.

"Is that okay?" he said.

"Yes."

He seemed relieved. We would have the use of a car, Galzanov went on, but we would be required to pay for petrol. Then they asked for a business card. I'd been warned about business cards in Russia. To Russians, they were as good as the badge on a sheriff, and to not have one was sufficient grounds to bring your very identity into question. Why would one not have a business card? Galzanov wasn't looking for the information it would contain, as I'd delivered everything about us in several letters. Russians apparently loved some abstract notion of business, the formal conduct of it an affirmation of worth. Having a business card was like having a chess rating. It meant you were in the game. I didn't have one. I didn't have one because as a writer with a contract I was independent. I produced the contract instead, which I had because I'd also been told that Russians loved impressive-looking paperwork. Though he couldn't read it, the contract seemed to please Galzanov immensely.

Glenn had said all along that he would go to Russia simply to play chess, that he fully intended to remain on the sidelines of all nonchess situations, but I could sense he was becoming antsy now that such a moment had actually arrived. His remedy was to worm into the proceedings by producing the huge problem book that we had passed back and forth on the plane. To Glenn, the problem book was a miraculous phenomenon, a sacred text, and he introduced it with flare, repeating three times that there were 5,334 problems inside, that it was the finest problem book to ever appear in the English language. He failed to calculate that this was precisely the kind of moment in which one would deliver a diplomatic gift carried across some great distance.

"Is this for me?" Galzanov said. He happily turned the pages of the heavy book.

"Uh," Glenn said, "okay."

"*Spasibo.*" And like that the book was gone. Galzanov turned a few more pages and nestled it atop some paperwork. Then he turned to me. "What kind of a scientist are you?"

"Excuse me?" I said.

"Your . . . theory. In your letters."

This was the beginning of a miscommunication the extent of which wouldn't become clear until sometime later. He referred to something I'd come across in reading Kalmyk history and the Murray at the same time. There was a parallel. In tracing the movement of chess through the world, Murray had been confused by similarities between Russian and Mongol chess around the year 1600. A likeness in the rules of the two worlds, he felt, could not be explained by independent developments in the game. As well, he had cited the notes of adventurers who had traveled to Tibet late in the eighteenth century. These adventurers claimed that chess in Tibet was identical to chess in Europe. Furthermore, the adventurers described "Cal-mucks" among the Tibetans who were particularly skillful at the game. To Murray, these were separate mysteries, but though he'd studied migrations he seemed ignorant of the Kalmyks' movement through Asia from 1600 to 1800. This was precisely what I had learned of them. Very early in the seventeenth century, an alliance between two Kalmyk tribes in Djangharia, now a northwest province of China, allowed both groups to shuttle westward to escape Chinese pressure. The first Kalmyk contact with the Russians came in 1606. The rela-tionship with the Russians would always be testy, but the Kalmyk migration from Djangharia continued for many years. As Buddhists, the Kalmyks maintained constant relations with Tibet. They consid-ered returning to Djangharia as early as 1644, but the exodus wouldn't actually happen until 1771, when more than 150,000 Kal-myks departed Russia in what was the world's last great migration of nomadic people. Most died on the trip, and those who made it back were absorbed into the growing China. The Kalmyks who had been left behind—caught on the wrong side of an unfrozen Volga River in an unseasonably warm January—were the ancestors of today's Kalmyks.

I hadn't had any illusions about discoveries in chess history, but the dates and mysteries matched nicely. The Kalmyks had had plenty of time to learn the European brand of chess that had just arrived in Russia and return to Tibet with it in time to impress adventurers in 1775. The implication was that the history of the Kalmyks was twined together with the history of chess—their people and their story played an important role in the spread of the game. I liked the idea that the Kalmyks were significant in chess history—it gave meat to Kirsan's decision to employ it as a tool of tradition and unity. I had included what I'd found in my letters of introduction. There, I'd spelled out a boiled-down version of it, thinking that Kirsan had probably soured on Western journalists, but might be won over by the research. But I'd received no response to the letters, and when Galzanov asked me what kind of a scientist I was, it was the first acknowledgment that he'd even received them.

I apologized and told him that I wasn't a scientist—I was a his-torian, sort of. I said that I hoped the idea could be the foundation for introductions to Kalmyk scholars who would surely be able to point out its errors. Galzanov asked me to spell out the theory, and I repeated it to him just as I had in my letters—there wasn't much more to it. Still, he seemed to enjoy hearing it.

"I don't know this theory," he said, "but it sounds very good, and I hope that it is true. I am sure we will be able to arrange for you to meet some of our Kalmyk scientists. Now, if you like, we can end our meeting and have dinner."

"Excellent."

"Do you have any questions?"

"Yes. Is President Ilyumzhinov in the country?"

Galzanov folded his arms on the table in front of him, scanned the papers scattered before him as he spoke, and then looked directly into my eyes as Bair translated his words. "Mr. President is still in Australia, attending the Olympics, where chess this year, I'm sure you're aware, is a demonstration sport. From there, he will go to the Philippines for several days to meet Mr. Bobby Fischer. We hope he will return to the republic by the weekend. We will be able to arrange an interview for you at that time."

I nodded, and it's from there that my memory crosses the event horizon into the evening's black hole of drunkenness. The very night began to accelerate, and soon we were seated at an almost empty restaurant with a bottle of vodka on the table with Kirsan's picture on the front. Kirsan Ilyumzhinov was a small, thin man, and in the bottle's photo he was dressed in traditional winter garb, a white coat and a thick, white fur hat, and the smile on his face seemed to contain the knowledge of what his flavored vodka would do to me. We all made the obligatory toast, Glenn making sure that everyone at the table knew that this was only the sixth or possibly seventh time alcohol had ever touched his lips. I remember Galzanov challenging Glenn to a game of blindfold chess with dinner as the stake, and the pleasant mood that had come over us once business was concluded was almost lost to the names of openings. What for Glenn was the Caro-Kann was, according to Galzanov, the Najdorf, and the two of them went back and forth across the table over the matter, needing no translation, the names of moves like a scientific language fixed and used universally, Glenn's repetition of "Kann, Kann, Kann," sounding like a deprecating mispronunciation of the Kalmyks' ancestral leaders. I interrupted to point out that there was a vast misunderstanding of Kalmykia in the West. In fact, on maps I had seen in the United States, the Volga River passed directly through Kalmykia, and Elista was on the Caspian Sea! Perhaps, I suggested, the discrepancy of opening names was a similar miscommunication between our nations. This seemed to please everyone. "No problems, no problems!" Galzanov said, and he kept refilling my glass with vodka that was as tasty as it was devious. This was my last bit of straight chronological memory. "We are normal civilian people!" I recall Bair saying to me in a random toast. It was suspicious, but I supposed he meant to distinguish us from Glenn and Galzanov, the blindfold combatants. Then he leaned forward for a man-to-man whisper: "If you need anything official, tell Galzanov now. If you need anything later, tell *me*." Lost to the thrummy medicinal buzz of Kirsan's vodka, I don't know if I even responded. The next day I discovered the only evidence of the rest of my activity for the night: a message in my notebook, scrawled in a barely readable font of drunkenness, its inspiration and meaning long since sacrificed to chemistry and good times. "Nothing can be lost in Elista!" I had written, and while it may have referred to my passport, which did go missing for a time, it certainly did not refer to either my good sense or my innocence.

"I'VE HAD SO MANY TRAVELS, SO MANY ADVENTURES," TELO Rinpoche told me on the phone when he became confused for a moment about his own chronology. "I have everything out of order!"

Rinpoche's efforts in Kalmykia did not end when he left the country and disrobed. Not long after he moved to Colorado he became involved in the Tibetan Freedom Concert project. The organizers asked Rinpoche to guide them in India and assist with an audience with the Dalai Lama. Rinpoche agreed, but might have regretted it when His Holiness spotted him in a crowd with his hair grown out. Their first meeting was awkward, but eventually the Dalai Lama forgave him, laughed, and with a swipe like the one that had granted the young Ombadykow godhood, His Holiness simply took it away and told Rinpoche that he could continue as a lama without being a monk.

After the audience, Rinpoche decided to stay in India for a while. The extra time allowed him to visit an old confidant, a woman named Ngawang he had met at a festival years before. They had spent one day together, but it was all they'd needed. Now that Rinpoche was disrobed—he went to see her, and three weeks later he proposed.

Ngawang relocated to Colorado with Rinpoche, and Rinpoche began a jet-setting lifestyle between the United States and Kalmykia, to which he returned in 1995. This time around he avoided the Kalmyk government, gave up his limousine and his apartment, and took a room at his aunt's. The split was made easier by the fact that the Russian Federation had declared the Department of Religious Affairs unconstitutional. Rinpoche's return was awkward as the people who had once seen him as a god were now forced to contend with the knowledge that he wasn't even a monk. "Before, I was a cup," he explained to Kalmyk television. "Now I am a broken cup, but still a cup."

The price of politics in Kalmykia had gone up in his absence, and Rinpoche soon found himself accused of financial mischief, just as Kirsan would be accused. "I was called into the president's brother's office one day," he said. "And when I was accused, I said okay, that's it. After that I went back to my office and said, you know what, I made the wrong decision. I'm going home. And once I went out the door, my assistants got on the phone like crazy."

Two hours later, there were one hundred angry demonstrators outside the House of Government, yelling and shouting, threatening to skin the president's brother alive.

"Why? Because I was leaving. Now I knew the trick. I knew they were going to try to butter me up. So I told my driver, hey, take me to my friend's place. And guess what? The president's brother came to my aunt's house and waited. And he waited for me. And he waited. The next day I went home and there they were. They hadn't slept all night. That's when I told them off. And ever since then, the whole attitude changed. That was the real turning point."

Rinpoche had finally figured out how to conduct business in Russia, but it came at the price of his faith and the illusion that he could make a difference spreading dharma. Ironically, progress on the temple project materialized—Rinpoche established a monastery school for Kalmyk boys, and construction on the main temple began. But by then Rinpoche was spending less and less time in Kalmykia. In 1997, the temple was completed and opened, but even this did not bring him satisfaction as Kirsan wound up with the credit. Credit is what the president would take, too, for the creation of Chess City, which would go up on a grander scale than Rinpoche's temple and in a fraction of the time. Rinpoche had been skeptical of Chess City from the beginning; and when it was complete and the Olympiad was over, he scoffed. "Chess City doesn't impress me. It never has. I don't think the money was used wisely," he told me. "Unless there is some kind of vision down the road that we are not aware of. What is Chess City being used as now? Of course, they have to say they're making money. Otherwise, they become a total joke." While Chess City was still under construction, Rinpoche was hard at work on another project: the Dalai Lama was planning on visiting Kalmykia again. But summer 1998 gave Rinpoche three more reasons to question his devotion to the republic: Chess City was completed, Larisa Yudina was murdered, and the Dalai Lama's visit was canceled because of a potential coup in Moscow. "I was basically out of energy," Rinpoche said. "I was ready for some kind of a change. I just kind of took off and never looked back." When I talked to him on the phone, he hadn't been to Kalmykia in two and a half years. He now had a job as an import/export manager and a three year-old son, Jungkar.

I steered our conversation back to Yudina and asked him whether he thought the fact that Yudina's body had been found near Chess City was significant, and whether it was possible that Kirsan actually wasn't responsible for the crime.

"You know," he said, "the very first impression I got was that it was a setup. Because if he was involved, it would have been done a whole lot more professionally."

"Meaning what exactly?" I said.

"Huh?"

"How would it be more professional?"

"You know, you hear about political leaders who disappear and nobody knows what happened. You hear about some deputy going on an official trip to one of the regions and then all of a sudden disappearing."

"But that never happened, did it?" I said. "It never happened that anybody in Kalmykia disappeared without a trace, did it?"

Rinpoche hesitated. "In Kalmykia?"

"Right."

He chuckled for a moment. "Uh, I can't tell you who, but yeah, it has happened. Some of my friends . . . they've been lost, and when they appeared again they didn't want to talk about it. People disappear for six, seven months, and all of a sudden they show up, and it's like, is it a ghost? Is it really you?"

When Rinpoche next spoke to the Dalai Lama in 1999, he was surprised to learn that His Holiness was familiar with the Yudina matter. "He asked me, 'Do you think the president did it?' I said, 'I have no comment; I don't have enough information to make a decision.' He said, 'Okay, I understand,' and that was the end of that conversation."

By the time Glenn and I arrived in Kalmykia, Telo Rinpoche was well on his way to becoming an unperson. Of the photos in the streets of Kirsan meeting religious leaders, none were of Rinpoche. Nor was he listed in the books about Elista we were given. The entire time we were there, no one mentioned Telo Rinpoche. And when I asked Bair, walking in the halls of the House of Government, where the Department of Religious Affairs was, he looked thoughtful for a moment and said he didn't recall such a department having ever existed at all.

"YO, HALLMAN," GLENN SAID, THE FOLLOWING MORNING, after my interlude of remorse, on our way down to meet Bair and Galzanov, "something's wrong with the hot water in my room."

"They probably don't have any," I told him.

"Nah, they gotta have hot water."

"Why?"

"They got a restaurant, don't they? How would they have hot water in the restaurant?"

"Stoves, probably."

"Nah, man. Ask Bair or somebody."

In Glenn's mind, we had arrived at the cusp of civilization, and it was my job to yank him back from the edge. Bobby Fischer had lost as many friends as he'd made with unreasonable demands, and losing at chess in St. Petersberg and Moscow, doing without hot water, and denying himself almost all forms of nourishment but nuts and sardines had sent Glenn into a spiral that was amplifying his own mild version of Fischer's psychosis.

"Last night," I said, as we waited for the elevator, "did I say anything about Yudina?"

"No, you just poured Kirsan's vodka into your coffee. Stuff like that. You weren't acting like yourself. Just be yourself." He looked at the floor as he spoke, his mind working on other things. "We gotta get some hot water."

Bair had been coming up to meet us and was on the elevator when it arrived on our floor. He was just as hungover as I was. "We had fun," he said, with a shrug. We drove to the House of Government to meet Galzanov, but he was not in his office. He was busy with the Congress on Traditional Medicine and would meet us for lunch, we were told. We would sightsee until then, visit Kalmykia's Buddhist temple. On the way there, Bair spoke of the history of Buddhism in Kalmykia, how the Kalmyk people had kept their spirituality alive by hiding ancient Buddhist icons throughout the era of Soviet repression. The revival of Buddhism in Kalmykia had included the sculpting of a huge Buddha sheathed in Mongolian gold that was in the temple we would now visit.

"Now," Bair said, "Kalmykia is a part-corporate, part-republican state. All religions are welcome."

I was listening carefully. I realized that we were heading to Telo Rinpoche's temple. But just as Kirsan's vodka had caused backup, gridlock, and even negative flow along my intestinal tract, so did my thinking seem prone to sticking and derailing. I changed the subject completely. Back in the United States, I had read that ancient Kalmyk warriors were skillful with whips and could kill a man on horseback with a single strike. I asked if there was any lingering tradition of whips in Kalmykia. But Bair had never heard of such a tradition.

"Who would we whip?" he said, and laughed as though it was a punchline.

"Bair," Glenn said, after a moment, "there's something wrong at our hotel. There's no hot water."

"I don't think the hotel has hot water."

"The knob in my shower! It's red! They've got to have hot water."

Bair looked at me, and I shrugged. "I don't think so," he said.

Like Chess City, the temple sat out on the outskirts of town. A small yellow-roofed structure nearby commemorated the Dalai Lama's first visit, and a monks' house stood a couple of hundred meters away. Though the temple was the only building of Telo Rinpoche's expansive plan to be completed, it was still the largest Buddhist temple in Europe, standing boxlike on the edge of the steppe, compact and solid. The construction was modern—two paved roads led up to the entrance, an island of dirt between them long since conquered by weeds. To the left and right stood small shelters for the rows of upright drums ceremonially spun by visitors. One was for entering; the other for exiting. As we got out of the van, a maroon monk shuffled up and hurried by the spools, like a kid dragging a stick down a picket fence.

The work of decorating a Buddhist temple is a particular art, and when the Buddhist revival began a few young Kalmyk artists were sent abroad to study the technique. Their work was now on display on the front of the temple, intricate, bright murals of contorting Buddhist gods. We climbed the first short flight of stairs toward them and walked down the row of holy spools. Glenn made each cylinder a rite. When one of them stuck, he stepped back and gave it a crank. Inside, a service was in session, metal gongs clanging as we removed our shoes and stepped into the temple's court of worship and observance.

It was Rinpoche. The gilded statue of Buddha, three meters high in the lotus position, with a golden Buddhist robe thrown over one shoulder and a hand the size of a palm frond on one knee. Mongolian gold and all, the suggestion was decidedly Rinpoche, Erdne Ombadykow, the kid from Philly who'd gone from spiritual rags to spiritual riches and back again. The similarity was remarkable, preadolescent mustache and all. "Quite a few people have said that to me," Rinpoche said later, when I told him there was a resemblance. "I don't know if they were just trying to make me happy or not." The statue sat on a dais at the back of the church, eyes gazing out over the heads of those gathered before it, slightly crossed, staring into something like a hypnotic spiral of enlightenment, though with Rinpoche's vaguely confused expression as well, his knowledge that he'd been given an impossible task in an impossible place. Now the Kalmyks were stuck with a god who'd absconded. They were victimized again, teased by another superpower. I was beginning to understand why Galzanov and Bair behaved with a manner that triggered my paranoia gland. They knew that as a writer I would be gunning for them. And wouldn't I? One of the international journalists had described Kalmykia as a "Swiftian caricature of a nation gone mad," but while the Kalmyks had no idea who Swift was, they knew that I was probably there to tap into a history that read like raw satire.

Glenn asked Bair what in the temple was made of plastic. The extent of Glenn's knowledge of Asiatic culture was pretty much limited to the dangling trinkets in Chinese restaurants in the United States. "I don't think anything is plastic," Bair said. Glenn seemed to doubt this as he surveyed the tables brimming with icons, the frills hanging from the ceilings, the back wall filled with shelves of statues and boxed scrolls. I decided to move away before Glenn started asking how much things cost. Up by the Rinpoche statue, there were photos of the Dalai Lama. I looked over the old icons that proved the perseverance of the Kalmyk people, dozens of fist-sized Buddhas of aging brass better traveled than most Kalmyks, in some cases having come from Djangharia four hundred years before.

One side of the chamber was partitioned off for the Kalmyk artists who were still at work on painting the inside of the temple. I peeked behind their stretched sheets. The artists had scaffolding up, through which they were weaved like men navigating barbed wire, and the walls behind them were covered with pencil drawings of images they would fill in with color and detail. The men were contorted, the twisted figures on the walls accidental self-portraits, and only one of them was so positioned that he could turn and look at me. I nodded at him when he did, and he paused before smiling, as though to ask himself whether he could smile. I was an American, which meant that I was like Rinpoche, which meant that I was a kind of threat, a probable disappointment. He decided to risk it, and when he smiled I cherished it as the first expression of genuine affection I had received since entering the republic.

CHAPTER 8

Developing Your Pieces: ♝

The alphins are the various prelates of the church, Pope, Archbishop, and their subordinate bishops . . . [They] move and take obliquely three points, for almost every prelate's mind is perverted by love, hatred, or bribery . . .

—Innocent Morality, *mid-thirteenth century*

Some three days since, the King long studying how to play a bishop, the Marquis of Winchester blurted out, "See, Sir, how troublesome these Bishops are in jest and earnestly." The King replied nothing, but looked very grim.

—Letter from York of Lewis Boyle, *c. 1640*

FOR A TIME ELEPHANTS WERE BIG IN THE HISTORY OF chess. Both because the bishop was originally an elephant, and because elephants—real elephants—became evidence in debates over the game's birthplace. A dominant theory that chess was invented as a war game in India came under attack by historians who favored China. But India-proponents argued that since there were no elephants in China as of the year 600, China could not possibly be the homeland of chess. The China-proponents shot back: there *were* elephants in China, or had been. The commentator Tso claimed that elephants were employed in a battle between the states of Wu and Ts'u in 512 B.C. The elephants decided nothing, and the debate continued.

The original elephant—*gaja,* in Sanskrit—leapt two squares along the diagonals, capturing on the second square. It was a weak piece, able to occupy a total of only eight squares on the board. An elephant could neither attack another elephant nor protect its partner, the way knights could. In keeping with chess players' tendency to treat beauty in chess as a function of likelihood, mates given with the elephant, as with pawns, were valued highly and could earn a multiple of the game's original stake.

As with the queen, chess realists absorbed by the game's war metaphor were scandalized at the elephant: Clearly, an elephant in war was far more powerful than an elephant in chess. Two attempts were made to correct the error. The first allowed the elephant to leap along the ranks and files rather than along the diagonals. This doubled the number of squares the piece could occupy, but still allowed for the problematic image of an elephant jumping at all. The second revision—associated with Buddhist centers in southern India—made the piece more potent and logical. The elephant could now move to any of five squares—three directly in front, and two diagonally to the rear. This represented the elephant's five limbs, counting the trunk, and made it lumbering and powerful. But the move disappeared when Muslim conquerors brought their own game and their own elephant back to India.

Along with Persia, the Muslims translated the elephant into their own language, *pil* and *al fil*, respectively. *Al fil* came to dominate just as Islam did. The elephant went over well in Asian versions of chess, but when the game crossed into Europe, it brought with it only the adopted word and a reputation of being a somewhat sneaky piece. Chess moves that are not strictly "straight" are considered stealthy, underhanded. Europe's *aufin* was quickly labeled a thief or a spy, and eventually the nonsense of its name sent the Europeans searching for replacements that captured its unlikely efficacy. Alternates included Italy's *alfiere,* meaning "flag bearer," France's *fol,* meaning "fool" as in court jester, Latin's *alphicus,* meaning "leper."

Even before the leap to Europe, the elephant had been represented by a small figurine with two pointed knobs protruding from the top. In decorative sets, the piece would be carved as a complete elephant, but in more rough-hewn sets the two small protrusions suggested tusks. Once the game came to Europe and the elephant was lost, the two knobs began a centuries-long approach of one another in the changing interpretations of wood carvers, moving mysteriously like continents or glaciers, closing until they appeared to form a cleft. The piece was otherwise bald, and was already called a sage or an old man in some countries. Because of the cleft, the small knobs taken for a mitre, the *aufin* began to be called "bishop" in

England. It fit with Europe's habit of thinking of the chessmen as a lineup of medieval power brokers, but it wasn't a flattering representation because the piece was still thought of as devious. But even this satisfied the realist. The visit of the papal legate Otho to Oxford in 1238 is believed by some to have inspired an indictment of "alphins" given by the author of the Innocent Morality. Otho had a reputation of being greedy and unscrupulous, and his visit caused a riot. It was only a short time later that the name bishop began to spread. That a sneaky piece should be named for a priest caught on quickly, and artisans came to carve the piece as a bishop even in countries where the name remained *aufin*.

It's also possible that the piece came to be known as bishop simply because so many priests played. Religions all over the world felt threatened by chess for the power it exerted over their clergy. John Zonares extended the Western church's condemnation of dice play to include chess: "Because there are some of the Bishops and clergy who depart from virtue and play chess . . . the Rule commands that such shall cease to do so . . . if a Bishop or elder . . . do[es] not cease to do so, he shall be cast out." Some time later, in 1550, the Protohierach Sylvester tried a similar tack in Russia: "But the man who does not live according to God and the Christian life . . . who practices all kinds of diabolical gratifications . . . plays *zerniyu, shakh-mate* [chess] and *tableu* . . . verily they shall all dwell in hell together." These bans were invariably imposed after chess had already etched itself deep into the minds of priests, and they had little effect.

The exact origin of the modern bishop move is lost. But a chess variation from Ströbeck Germany, called "Courier," provides convincing evidence for a piece of the puzzle. Courier was played on a board twelve squares wide by eight squares deep. There were twelve pawns, and extra pieces with exotic moves. The game was named for one of these, the courier, which moved like the modern bishop, as many squares as it wished along any diagonal, unable to leap, but capturing as it moved. The range of the piece fulfilled the promise of motion in its name. The courier proved aesthetically pleasing, but the Courier game never caught on outside of Ströbeck. Around 1500, the piece made the leap to the 8 × 8 board. Another substitute name appeared, "archer," for the distance of its influence, but it wasn't until warfare itself evolved that an even better nickname surfaced: In analysis, modern players often call a bishop on a long diagonal a "sniper," a description that captures both its range and its shiftiness.

Like the knight, the modern bishop has strengths and weaknesses. It's a line piece, but it's limited like the *al fil*—each bishop can only move to thirty-two squares of the board. Bishops are distinguished from one another by the color of the squares upon which they move—each player has a light-squared bishop and a dark-squared bishop. In addition to advancing the theory of pawn play, Steinitz helped define the potential of bishops. Bishops can be "good" or "bad," meaning powerful or ineffective. The strategic theory of chess that began to form in the late nineteenth century often centered on the assessment of good and bad bishops.

Bishops and knights are the flip sides of a coin: They have almost the same average value at the start of a game, and together they comprise the array's minor pieces. A knight forks the opponent's men; a bishop skewers them: a stabbing metaphor for each. But while the surprise of a knight is that at any moment it may prove surprisingly strong, a bishop, as a line-piece whose strength is known, tends to surprise only by being suddenly neutralized, proved weaker than one has reckoned. A bishop is a glass weapon, a fragile hypothesis.

CHAPTER 9

The Chess District

Fair play is nothing less than good faith expressed in play terms. Hence the cheat or the spoil-sport shatters civilization itself.

—Johann Huizinga, Homo Ludens, 1950

The student that needeth chess or cards to please his mind, I doubt hath a carnal empty mind; if God, and all his books, and all his friends, &c. cannot suffice for this; there is some disease in it that should rather be cured than pleased. . . .

—Anonymous letter, 1680

GLENN WAS THIRTY-NINE YEARS OLD BUT HAD NEVER owned a car. In Russia the fact would have been entirely unremarkable, but in the United States, at Glenn's income level, it was a quirk. As a result, he was a proficient patron of commuter services. On our first trip to New York together, via a near-empty Greyhound, he demonstrated his practiced manner of sleeping on the jostling carnival ride of buses: He fixed his body proper in the aisle seat and leaned across toward the window using his backpack as a spinal support ledge. The position made him something of a human shock absorber; and the violent jarrings of the bus—each divot in the pavement amplified through its rolling slinky—while these for me were ruptures that prevented sleep, they were for Glenn a gentle rocking that made the trip restful and perhaps therapeutic. It was a chess trick: He had turned the disadvantage of the bus to his advantage.

Before he fell asleep, Glenn and I had spoken of what it meant when chess players said they "had" a move. The peculiarity of chess language had come to interest me. Even inside the chess world, there was disagreement over the precise definitions of words like "sacrifice" and "gambit"; and even "opening," "middlegame," and "endgame" were imprecise descriptions, closer to adjectives than nouns. The way chess players used language contributed to their otherness. Chess players everywhere were a little bit strange, but it was only in Russia, first by a militant state, then by a wacky but possibly benevolent dictator, that that otherness had been employed, and perhaps confused, with something more mystical. I didn't tell Glenn, but sometimes I worried that Poe had been right: chess was complex, but not profound. Still, I tried to understand it, and every time I heard Glenn say he "had" a move, I piqued. "He has that move," or "I didn't see he had that move." A simple verb had been conscripted for something complex. I considered the contexts in which I'd heard it, scribbled out a definition, and read it to him as we rolled out from Atlantic City.

He blinked and said, "What are you talking about?"

I read it again more slowly.

This time, he frowned. "No, man, a guy has a move when . . . he has a move!"

I took issue with him, and we went back and forth as a man a row in front of us worked unabashedly to create and expel a ball of phlegm from his throat. Glenn was just as unabashed while talking chess in public, and when he next spoke, after an interval of staring out the opposite window, it was lecture loud and meant as a gem for whoever would listen to it.

"All right, man," he said, "to have a move means you have a resource available to you. It can be offensive or defensive. It means you can improve a winning position or prolong a losing position."

He shrugged and performed a gesture that was new to me, opening his palms suddenly and at the same time contorting his face to an expression of exaggerated surprise. He saw that I did not understand, and repeated it again, as though I simply hadn't heard him. And then again, until I finally understood that it was satiric. It wasn't his own surprise; it was mine. It was criticism.

"What about an equal position?" I said, pressing on. "Wouldn't an unlikely move that preserves an equal position also be a move that a player 'had'?"

"What are you talking about, 'had'? When would he say that?"

"I don't mean it literally. I just—"

"Tournament players never talk during games, man."

The man in front of us sneezed. Whatever disease he was combating was not beaten by his phlegmball, and now his body was initiating its own attack. Glenn cringed. One of his chess player quirks was an irrational fear of germs. He always wiped his palm before handshakes, telephone handsets before dialing. He leaned to one side as though a quick glimpse of the man would hint at the extent of his contagion. Then he nodded to me and got up to move one row farther back, edging out of range of both the man's cloud of infection and my weird theory of the game. It was clear that Glenn did not like talking about chess in this way—as with many chess players, that which was not the game itself was uninteresting to him. I had to concede: While we might have gotten closer to a definition of "to have" in chess, we would never get it exactly right. To have a move could mean nothing more nor anything different from having a move. That was chess.

The bus took the exit to the Garden State Parkway, the whole shaky thing leaning impossibly to one side. The anonymous bangs of the road's imperfections came like accurate flak on the underside of a B-17. Glenn was the veteran flyer in all this. He ignored the doom, arranged his backpack, and assumed the pose that allowed him to sleep, that made him one with the bus's brand of logic.

IN NEW YORK, AT THE MANHATTAN CHESS CLUB, MITCHELL recognized me immediately, and he smiled at Glenn and me as though he had caught us in a conspiracy. This time there was another man in the shop, actually shopping. The man was looking to buy a piece of chess furniture. He was clean-cut and buttoned-down, and you knew he couldn't play chess if for no other reason than that he smelled good. He was leaned over, peering across the surface of a low wooden chess desk. A scuff mark showed on one of the white squares.

"Who's messing with the board?" Glenn said. "It's all dinged up."

"It's this man's," Mitchell said. "I just saw him do that."

The man was miffed. "It's my board, so I'll do what I want," he said.

We had interrupted Mitchell and the customer in a conversation about chess clocks. In addition to his board, the man was trying to decide between analog and digital time pieces. Glenn inserted himself in the discussion. The customer was looking for a simple answer to a simple question—which was better—but both Mitchell and Glenn knew it wasn't a simple question to begin with.

"It kind of depends," Glenn said.

"The analog would be good," Mitchell said, "if you were going to be playing FIDE tournaments in the next year or so. But you're not."

The insult of this went over the man's head as he fingered the buttons of the sleek digital device.

"Do you play speed?" Glenn said.

"Not really," the man said.

"Because if you're playing someone who's really fast—I mean *really* fast—then the analog is no good because it doesn't register moves under a second."

The man gave a dumbfounded smile. "There are people who can really move that fast?"

Glenn and Mitchell nodded slyly.

"You mean they can"—he mimed the motion of an entire move—"they can pick up the piece, put it down again, and hit the clock in less than a second?"

"Well," Mitchell said, watching the man's hand, "not like that. Smoother."

The man shook his head. He couldn't see it. In his mind each move was a singular event, but chess moves are not really independent of one another. The fastest moves in speed chess are those that are part of a plan, a sequence of captures, maneuverings. There is the other player to consider as well—just as his pieces may become backward weapons of your own, so may you plot as his clock ticks. Speed chess is a dance. It's more complicated than simply making a move in a second.

"Now this clock," Glenn said, gesturing to the digital, "this clock can register less than a second. Less than a tenth of a second."

"Maybe more," Mitchell said.

"So it's better?" the man said.

"No," Glenn said. "If you're playing a tournament game with a time control of two hours, or even half an hour, then this one is better." He moved back to the analog, demonstrating the bright stems of the buttons: they could be seen from a distance.

"So if you wanted to stretch your legs or whatever, you could still see it was your move from across the room," the man said.

"Right."

"Of course," Mitchell said, wagging the digital, "this has the lights on it." But even the man could see the disadvantage of bulbs that could burn out.

Now the question was even more confusing. The customer decided two salesmen was one too many, and he and Mitchell began to discuss the matter in quieter voices.

I wanted to get moving, but but Glenn spotted a book deep in the shop and made for it. It was useless to try to stop him. In a moment he was poring over pages of diagrams, the book held close to his face like a bowl of fried rice. I wandered back into the rear of the shop, the dirty garage, to see if my chess education had changed my perception of it. It was the same grimy pieces scattered across the same paper boards, but this time around I thought I knew why chess tended to favor disrepair. Chess players did not make money. The impoverished state of their pieces and equipment was a badge of honor. In chess, it was ideas that gleamed: If you cared too much about how white the pieces were, or what the board was made of, or even if you thought too much about the very fact of pieces and boards, it only meant that you weren't thinking enough about the game.

"Glenn," I said, "let's go."

He was on to another book by then, peeling pages slowly. "One second, one second."

He arranged to buy several copies of his huge problem book, one copy for Emerald, he told me, then aged three.

"By the way," Glenn said, "I read that you were moving."

"Yeah," Mitchell said. "Hopefully in time for the Open. The club will be at the New Yorker Hotel. The shop will be closed. Kaput."

Glenn let it sink in. The Manhattan Chess Club had been at its current location for years; but with a permanent membership of under two hundred they had been evicted.

"Man," Glenn said, "What's a chess club without a chess shop?"

Mitchell shrugged. "A chess club." And he went back to his difficult sale of a digital clock.

WE TOOK THE SUBWAY DOWNTOWN TO THE CLOSEST THING that New York had to a chess district: two chess shops, Village Chess Shop and Chess Forum, opposed to one another like bishops fianchettoed on the diagonal of Thompson Street. Thompson Street was just south of Washington Square Park, which was the heart of Manhattan Chess, a broad circle of cement chess tables in the park's southwest corner. The Marshall Chess Club was a few blocks to the north, and Fred Wilson's Chess Shop, specializing in books, was a few blocks east. We went to Fred Wilson's first.

I knew of Fred Wilson through Glenn. Glenn routinely purchased copies of a small instructional chapbook that Wilson had written and passed them out to people who showed an interest in the game. Wilson was a player of roughly Glenn's caliber, but he had also written chess history and so constituted a bridge between us. Once Glenn had gotten used to the idea that I preferred history to the game, he had suggested we visit Wilson's shop.

The shop was in the kind of old and cramped office building where you expected to find collection agencies, dentists near retirement, struggling divorce attorneys, and private dicks. We got off the elevator and turned left three times before coming upon Wilson's store, a tiny, crammed-with-books room. The rooms across the hall from Wilson's were being used for the conduct of some kind of psychological treatment requiring absolute silence: A small noise machine masking background sound sat on the floor before each door. When Glenn and I arrived, someone cracked one of the doors just wide enough to shush us with a sound identical to the little machines at our feet.

The shelves that lined the walls of Fred Wilson's Chess Shop cut its square footage by 25 percent. The books were organized with a system that probably only Fred Wilson knew completely. He was a slim man, gone to salt and pepper in both his hair and mustache, and his eyes had a tendency to dart.

He was glad to see us. "Business is slow," he said.

In addition to the chess shop, Wilson gave weekly chess lectures and ran a number of chess programs in private New York City schools. He'd been at it for twenty-five years. He had written five books and edited two others. Like many chess personalities, Wilson was an unassuming man for whom prolonged eye contact was a significant effort. I liked him even as he seemed wary of us. A woman, his wife, I thought, sat in a corner of the room and seemed more normal, flipping through a newspaper. But she was content to let him run the show.

Glenn asked after books by Smyslov and Polgar, I asked for anything about history. Wilson was never stumped, and pulled books from the shelves, leaning slightly to pull a title off the left wall, then taking a single step and leaning again to pull a title off the right. He handed them over without comment. As with Mitchell, chess and power salesmanship did not go hand in hand. Wilson became animated when I asked him about a chess writer, a man who, like me, had visited the chess world from the outside to write a book about Bobby Fischer.

"He's a fucking asshole," Wilson said.

Wilson's wife did not react—she'd heard the rant before. Wilson was worked up enough now to show us a game of his that had been printed in *Chess Life*. The game's pivotal moment was Wilson's offer of a queen sacrifice. The position forced resignation, and Wilson described the game as "cute and quick."

"Two diagrams!" Glenn said. The magazine had published two small chessboards alongside the list of moves, visuals that depicted the game at important junctures. Glenn was impressed. "Most 2200 people are lucky to get one."

"Yeah," Wilson said. He went on about the difficulty of actually getting the game printed, politicking for it, and sending in notes.

I bought several books of history. Wilson seemed pleased by the sales and gave me change from his pocket.

"Two diagrams!" Glenn said as we made our good-byes. "Two!"

"Yeah," Wilson said.

"Yeah, two," his wife said, speaking for the first time from the corner of the room's confusion. "We're on our way."

THE CHESS CORNER OF WASHINGTON SQUARE PARK WAS A bubble of lawlessness, a sphere where the addictive quality of chess aligned with the addictive quality of all the pharmaceuticals for sale in the same arena. The police occasionally made arrests, but the chess corner was like a pet shop fish tank filled with guppies—every once in a while the net came down and snatched someone away, but after the slight turmoil everyone went about their business. In winter, chess players could be found in the park dressed in huge down jackets, the only problem presented by the cold being the difficulty of moving pieces while so encumbered. In summer, many went shirtless and angled for the few tables that got shade. The boards were inlays in heavy cement. Some time back, I heard, chess players all over the city had been rounded up in an antigambling sweep. But the joke was on the authorities: A judge eventually ruled that chess for money did not constitute gambling. Modern courts have somewhat loosely identified three categories of game: wholly luck (blackjack, craps), combinations of luck and skill (backgammon, pocket billiards), and wholly skill (chess, checkers). Rulings varied, but courts tended to agree that statutes against gambling applied only to games of chance.

Glenn, who played in Washington Square Park even though he didn't particularly approve of the players there, suspected the day was too windy for chess. The temperature wouldn't scare the players, but a heavy wind was a miniature tornado that could carry off a complicated position and a hustler's lunch. It was late March. There were several games underway, but to Glenn it wasn't much of a crowd. We approached a game where two black men sat playing, one younger and leaned forward so that he looked directly down onto the pieces, the other older and leaned back, his hands in his pockets and his grizzled face frozen: a hustler's concentration. Several kibitzers stood about the board, men relaxed and watching silently, only slightly more expressive than the players.

"Sweet Pea!" Glenn said, interrupting the game boisterously and addressing the older man. "Yo! Sweet Pea!"

Glenn had told me about Sweet Pea, though only a fragment. I leaned to one side to verify it: Sweet Pea was a very short man who sat on top of stacks of newspapers to make himself the same height as his opponent.

Sweet Pea looked up from his game as though to examine a cloud whose peculiar formation had drawn his attention for some reason, but gave no indication of recognizing Glenn at all. The form swirled away, and he went back to his game.

Glenn raised his eyebrows, and we moved over to where the other park inhabitants were gathered. Two men had boards and pieces ready to play, and two other games were stuck in their openings. Glenn circled around behind a dour white man in a down coat. Cigarette smoke tumbled from his lips like the last breath of a dying man.

"Russian Paul!"

Russian Paul looked up at Glenn, but did not even hesitate in an attempt to place him. He went back to his game at once, played a move, and hit his clock. He fished into one of his down pockets for another cigarette.

The park had me on edge. I flinched when something touched my elbow. One of the men waiting had recognized me as a chump and came on to me with his beggar's manner. He wore jeans and a denim vest, and the white stubble on his face stood out like the trees of a tiny forest scorched to ash.

"Excuse me, would you like to play a few games?"

I put up my hands. "No, thanks. I'm not a player."

The man shrugged. "Something cheap. Dollar a game."

This tactic I knew from poolrooms: When your mark seems intimidated, lowball them just to get them playing, then worry about the bet later. The gambling of chess was different from the gambling of pool, though. For chess players—as with Chepukaitis—hospitality was part of the con.

"No, thanks," I repeated, and the man frowned and forgot me.

By then Glenn had begun his own negotiations with another man. But they broke down at once and he made his way over to me.

"Man!" he said. "You see these guys? They don't even say hello to you! I haven't seen Sweet Pea in four years, possibly five. He didn't even acknowledge me."

"Maybe he forgot."

"He didn't forget me. You never forget someone you lose money to. Ridiculous." Indulging a vision of chess as ritual combat, Glenn had borrowed for the game the backward morality of a gunslinger. But in his mind the battle was contained to its quick interlude. Beyond that, what was most important to him was that chess foster a community. Chess players shared their otherness and should watch one another's backs. The players in the park, however, were content to niggle and hustle, to act out cheap confrontations. The park wasn't a chess community; it was chess anarchy.

Glenn shook his head at the scene, defeated. "Let's go to Thompson Street."

We entered the Village Chess Shop first. The two chess stores and playing rooms of Thompson Street were sepia photocopies of one another form fitted to unique architectural arrangements. The wood of the chess shops was invariably dark, weathered by a stratus of nicotene smoke and a precipitation of ancient sputum. As with Wilson's shop, the walls were crammed with books and display cases. The books were volumes sometimes self-published, chess going on in the year 2000 not so differently from how it had gone on in the year 1000, and the many sets of chess pieces for sale were a queer form of history marking the millennium in between. Theme sets fell into three categories: wars, cultures, novelty. War included the English and American civil wars, WWII, Napoleon, the Alamo, and the Crusades. Cultures ranged from Brazilian to German to Chinese to African to Russian Village. Novelty featured characters from *The Simpsons, Star Wars, Star Trek*, Marvel Comics, *Lord of the Rings, The Muppet Show,* and the Book of Revelations. The pieces were sometimes designed by artists long dead, and regardless of origin all the little men wore the same tiny shawl of dust. The actual players who lingered here were like a convention of actors who had each portrayed Rip Van Winkle in some stage production. And they were all still in costume, clothes thin from repeated unwashing, hair long and spikey and clumped into locks, cigarette smiles, dried skin, twitchy fingers, and a steady smart gaze framed by eyelids soft as clothy paper. These men manned the counters and shuffled pieces and talked trash while seated at rows of wooden card tables.

Glenn moved into the Village Chess Shop as though it were another home of his. He looked over the crowd of men using clamshells as ashtrays, then smiled to me and said, "Players!" As a master, Glenn was minor royalty in the chess shop equation: He wasn't at the game's pinnacle, but he was better than 98 percent of all tournament players, and it was enough to impress the casual regulars of most chess shops once they heard the word uttered. There were half a dozen games going on at 2:00 in the afternoon on a Wednesday. One man at a center board was the alpha among them, and his European-accented stream of hostile play-by-play filled the room.

"Quack, quack!" he said to his opponent. "Quack, quack! What are you going to do with this absolutely horr-ee-bull position? Quack!"

Glenn crab walked around behind the players, squirming past them as though moving to a theater seat. "Quack, quack!" he announced to all of them.

The alpha looked over his shoulder at Glenn's easy smile, but didn't respond. He turned back to his game. "Quack, quack! Give it back!" he said, and snapped off a bishop. Then, during his opponent's moment of hesitation, he said, "I can't wait for de blunder! I can't *wait* for de blunder!"

"No blunder," his opponent told him, mumbling.

A slow stream of classical music burbled out from speakers hidden somewhere in the room. A nearby wall was covered with newspaper clippings—most were stories of the last few decades' chess dramas, but one was an article about the chess shop itself, how walking through its door was like traveling back in time, but the clipping itself was quite old, yellowed and beginning to rot at the corners.

There was a seat open at the fifth board, but a position was in place and a cigarette burned near the empty chair. Opposite, a young man sat erect.

"You play speed?" Glenn asked him.

The young man gestured at the pieces. "I'm waiting to finish this one."

"All right," Glenn said, and he shook the man's hand. He quacked one more time, said good-bye to everyone, and nodded us out the door.

The Chess Forum was half a block away, identical arrangements of chess pieces, bookcases, broken coffeemakers, and piped-in sonatas conforming to an L-shaped blueprint as cramped as a soup kitchen. Though the Village Chess Shop had been quite busy, the Chess Forum, for no reason I could understand, was empty except for one man sitting at a board with the pieces waiting, his legs draped over a chair. A chicken lunch sat on the next board over.

"Hey, there," he said to Glenn at once, with a salesman's smile. "Do you play chess?"

"Occasionally," Glenn said.

"Occasionally," the man repeated. "That's good."

"Now and then," Glenn added.

The man giggled a little, an odd play with fluid stuck in the back of his throat. He was balding, olive-skinned. "Would you like to play some chess now?"

"Possibly, possibly. What's your name?"

"Oh," the man said, embarrassed, "you can just call me Mustache." The mustache above his lip was sparse and unremarkable.

Glenn grinned at me. "Mr. Mustache! You can call me Mr. Beard."

"Okay," Mustache said.

Glenn took off his coat, and laid it carefully across a chair. "What do you play?"

"Five minute."

"Want to play two minute?"

Mustache grinned and his eyes widened, but he did not look away from the board. "Five is fine."

Glenn settled into his seat. "What's the—?" He did not need to speak whatever word for bet he might have chosen.

"Two," Mustache said. He fumbled with a tape recorder that he planned to turn on while they played.

"Touch move or clock move?" Glenn said. Gambling had helped cement the finer rules of chess, including the question of what actually constituted a move. Originally, any touch of a piece was an obligation to move that piece, but after chess clocks were introduced, there was a choice. The question gave players something to haggle over.

"Clock move," Mustache said.

"Touch move!" Glenn said. "I can't have you touching all the pieces!"

Mustache giggled again, gargling spit. "I play clock move."

"Nobody plays clock move."

"Nobody?"

"You're gonna be touching all the pieces! You're gonna have fingers all over the pieces!" He pointed at Mustache's lunch. "Greasy fingers with chicken grease."

"Clock move," Mustache said, and with the set of headphones over his ears he was ready to begin.

"All right," Glenn said. "Clock move."

Mustache turned on first his music, then Glenn's clock.

They played quickly through a Sicilian Defense, slowing somewhat as they arrived at the middlegame. Another chess player appeared in the shop—another suddenly middle-aged Van Winkle, groggy and disorganized—and as brazenly as Glenn had entered the Village Chess Shop the man attempted to solicit games from two kibitzers. They didn't take the bait.

"Jesus, it's a chess room!" the man announced. "You'd think someone would want to play chess!"

Just then Glenn launched the first combination of moves that tipped his hand as a player: He slid a bishop to a square where it could be captured at once, but taking would create positional havoc for Mustache.

Mustache gleaned the import of the move, and his reaction was both to the board and to what he now knew of his opponent. "Oh," he said.

"What's wrong?" the new chess player said.

Mustache hesitated, did not look up, and only spoke when he reached to make his move. "Guy's a professional."

Glenn's response was immediate, his hand firing smoothly through the move and shooting to the clock. He touched his plunger gently. Mustache had chosen a path that gave Glenn a pawn and a tempi, and they moved quickly through another stage of the game, slowing once more when Mustache found counterplay. Glenn eyed the board with his head slightly cocked, his expression so vicious and dead he might have been watching film footage of some atrocity, a pan across a field of skulls. Such pauses in speed chess are pregnant with drama—the hoarded seconds tick away, and the loss is haunted by the knowledge that the game may not be decided by checkmate or resignation, but instead by one of those precious twinkles of conserved thought.

Glenn made his move, slow in a psyche: it was strong enough to execute with patience. Mustache squinted at the board, then pushed his a-pawn.

What happened then surprised all of us who were watching. "Illegal move," Glenn said, and he immediately began gathering up the pieces, destroying the position and realigning them for the next game. In speed chess, any illegal move—a failure to avoid check, a pawn that advances too far—counts as a loss.

"Hold it," Mustache said, stripping away his headset. "What are you saying?"

"Look," Glenn said, "you had the threat to check with your queen, right? So how can you push to a5 if your queen can go to a4?"

"Are you saying I pushed the pawn two squares?"

Glenn wagged his head. He felt the move had been deliberate, and he was as discouraged as he had been in the park. He would not answer the question when he knew well that Mustache knew the answer. Instead, he went through it again, explaining that the pawn had double skipped past a square that Mustache's queen had been threatening to occupy. If the move had been legal, then there would have been no such threat. As with the uniqueness of chess language, this was incontrovertible evidence to a player, and Glenn's arguments won over the pair of kibitzers.

"Okay, so you're saying I moved it two squares. I thought they were doubled is all."

Glenn set the clock again. "That's two," he said, meaning money, not squares.

"I'll play you one more," Mustache said, and the battle started over again.

If tournament chess was in any way a scholarly pursuit—and I was beginning to think it was—then the last 150 years of tournament play was like a dialogue conducted among a loose community of players and thinkers. Theories were tested, and theory expanded. By contrast, speed chess was like simple talking, the rash hashing out of contrary opinion. And from the Internet to chess shops to Skittles Rooms at tournaments, it was the far more common phenomenon. Speed chess, it seemed to me, was life as it was lived, rather than life as it might be. It was the difference between symphonic orchestration and jazz improvisation, a composer's craft entirely different from the intuition of jazz performers trading fours. Which was how I came to think of Glenn and Mustache as they began their next game for the same token two dollars, though the stakes seemed to have gone up now with how the last game ended. The middlegame this time was a tight web fraught with tension and complexity, and Glenn played a combination that involved the temporary loss of his queen. It was a tricky maneuver, and Mustache could have lost more than his own queen in return if he had not played it right.

"You don't miss anything," Glenn told him.

Mustache was too engrossed to respond, thinking, listening to his music, eyes flicking hungrily over the pieces as though over meat sautéing in a pan. He seemed unaware of it when he began to tootle along with the song playing in his ears, half words half whispered.

"Night Train...te de da...on the Night Train...ooh...ta da...." Mustache began moving his pawn mass forward, wholly enraptured by the game and his song. "...Ooo-ee-ooh...Night Train... aah-da-da..."

The kibitzers laughed, but Glenn and Mustache ignored them, rushing toward a rook vs. knights endgame. The bulk of theory—the work of several centuries' worth of chess scholars—has determined that rook vs. knights is a won position for the rook, but the rules of speed chess destroyed theory. Both men's clocks ticked below ten seconds, the digital displays now counting off tenths, and the players' moves suddenly accelerated like sprinters after the final turn. Not in any sport or game I have watched or played have I felt anything to quite match the visceral shock of a live chess game that descends into the hostile ballet of two players in time trouble. No extra inning, no hurry-up offense, no photo finish, no river card showdown quite imitates the intoxication of watching two players in an exchange that measures the extent of their wits and the intelligence of their fingers. Mustache fell silent from his singing. Together, his hand and Glenn's, churning gyroscopically, drew a quick invisible figure eight over the board, on its side like the symbol of infinity, moving from the pieces to the clock and back again. The moves themselves were crisp, the pieces occasionally wobbling on their squares, spiraling on their base like a top and sometimes being snatched up again before coming to rest. When Glenn's clock read 3.0 seconds, I realized I hadn't breathed since it read 30.0.

Glenn dropped his rook to a knight fork, but the knight wound up in a corner where it controlled almost nothing, and by then Mustache had almost no time remaining. Glenn made a few king moves, three or four in the space of a second, and then he stopped suddenly and pointed at Mustache's readout. Glenn's own read 0.9.

"You're down."

"Damn," Mustache said. "I had that one, too." He produced four dollar bills and spilled them onto the table. "I enjoyed it," he told Glenn, though it was an effort.

"What's your real name, Mr. Mustache?" The fight was over now, and Glenn genuinely wanted to become friends.

Mustache grinned, still stung by the loss, and tilted his head. "Oh, no."

Glenn shrugged and put on his coat. He shook hands with Mustache and tried again for friendship. But it was no good, and I wondered if Mustache's bitterness wasn't proof that chess could never amount to anything like a religion for the simple reason that chess players' otherness drove them apart as often as it pulled them together. Just as we were leaving the shop, we passed another chess player coming in, another Van Winkle soiled and soggy. He looked up as we moved by him, and his eyes ignited at the sight of Glenn.

"Glenn!"

"Willis!"

The two had known each other for many years, and Glenn, who refused to take the seat next to mine in movies for what it might suggest to the people behind us, threw his arms around Willis in a strong embrace. Willis had a one-tooth grin, a single canine pointing crookedly toward the interior of his mouth like the maw of a kicked-in jack-o'-lantern. He was about 2000 strength, Glenn said later. I was jealous of their intimacy. They talked quietly for a moment, some short reminiscence and a chance for Glenn to remind him to develop his pieces, and then Glenn and I were in the street, hailing a cab.

"I don't understand it," I said. "You're afraid of sneezes. You're scared of a sick guy on a bus. And then you give this guy a big hug."

"Willis and I go way back! We'll die in the trenches together."

"Yeah," I told him, "of malaria."

?!

CHAPTER 10

In those areas the climate was cold and severe, quite different from the baking hot climate of the Caspian region. And the Kalmyks died in droves.

—*Aleksandr M. Nekrich*, The Punished Peoples, *1978*

In the course of time such displays of virtuosity fell more and more under a strict ban, and contemplation became a highly important component of the Game. Ultimately, for the audiences at each Game it became the main thing. This was the necessary turning toward the religious spirit.

Hermann Hesse, The Glass Bead Game, *1943*

IN 1943, ALL THE ETHNIC POPULATIONS OF SOUTHERN Russia, including 170,000 Kalmyks, were deported to Siberia. In 1958, the exile ended, and the 73,000 Kalmyks who survived limped home to a remapped Kalmyk nation. In 1996, Kirsan Ilyumzhinov commissioned a large bronze monument to the event. In 2000, after visiting Kalmykia's Buddhist temple, Bair continued a sightseeing tour, hampered by our hangovers, by taking us to the monument on a small hill not far from Chess City.

The monument was at the end of a street that ran alongside a herd of dilapidated apartment buildings. A short stretch of railroad tracks ran up to the base of the hill, symbolic of the trains that had been stuffed with the peoples of the Caucasus. From the end of the tracks, a cement path led up to the monument, spiraling around the hill three times. We started up.

Even centuries before Stalin, Russia had played an odd game along its ethnically populated southern frontier. Pitting races and nations against one another, Russia maintained the peoples of the Caucasus in group form as a buffer against invasion. Like chess pieces, they could simply be used to gather tempi or harvest material. The government itself was largely ignorant of the lifestyles of many of the one hundred nationalities that lived inside its borders. Ignorance led to paranoia, and as the Soviet Union began to feel threatened by its neighbors, they were forced to acknowledge that some of those neighbors weren't neighbors at all, but citizens. More than a million ethnic Soviets turned and fought on the German side during the Great Patriotic War, which prompted Stalin, who assumed that if one ethnic Soviet was against him they all were, to deport the lot of them as soon as the tide of the war turned.

Kalmyk families were given twenty minutes to pack their belongings, and on the month-long journey in livestock cars between one-quarter and one-half of them died. The history of the Kalmyks in Russia to that point had been a slow-motion ethnic acculturation. As early as 1730, Russian money had become as viable a currency as livestock for the nomads. Throughout the eighteenth century, Russia attempted but failed to convert the Kalmyks to Christianity, but a slow policy of dependency on Russian products forced the Kalmyks into a sedentary lifestyle. Russian laws slowly replaced the informal justice of nomads. Where once the Kalmyks had been fierce warriors, they were now described as phlegmatic, deadened. But it wasn't until Stalin died and the Kalmyks returned from their deportation that Russian became the first language of communication among Kalmyk families.

The monument stood cold and still, a vast slab of melted-together images: a giant horse, a fetus inside a womb, a hugely muscular man's back, a crowd of Kalmyk faces. I walked around the statue several times, contemplative, yes, but at the same time hoping that my revolutions would counter the spin of my stomach like the tail propeller of a helicopter. My eyes were off Glenn for too long: When I came back around from another revolution, he was asking Bair how much the monument was worth.

"You mean like how much could you sell it for?" Bair asked.

"Well," Glenn said, "yeah."

"Who would buy it?"

Glenn chuckled and shrugged and gave up. Bair smoked and I felt my stomach again attempt to dislodge itself from its warm socket. I looked out at the land beyond Elista. It was ghostly and unnatural, a mild, messy spread of hills, bald and dead. It looked like a land that had once been rich, with features and fauna now wiped from its dry surface, and scanning across it was like looking across a corn field where the crop has just been taken down. Eventually, I asked which was correct: "steppe" or "steppes." No one seemed to know the proper plural form. As well, steppe was supposed to be a verdant ocean of treeless pastureland. But Kalmykia was slowly reverting to desert as a result of various ecological plagues, and the very definition of steppe seemed to have been yanked out from beneath it.

A small Kalmyk bird sailed by overhead, repeating an electronic bleep. It occurred to me, sick and inebriated still, that my current state was a pretty good lesson in what had happened to the Kalmyks when they were forced into Russian ways and collectivization. I was pretty damn phlegmatic. As well, the tight grip that Russia had kept over the Kalmyks was present in the form of Bair, who, it turned out, was an agent of the FSB, the Federal Security Service. The FSB was the reincarnation of the KGB, the fall of the Soviet Union just a hitch step and an acronym shift for the country's intelligence network.

"Oh, yeah, yeah, yeah," Rinpoche told me, when I mentioned Bair later. "He used to work for me. After I let him go, he called me up and said I want to join the service. I said go for it."

Bair took us to a restaurant called Ice to await lunch with Galzanov. Glenn and I would be encouraged to patronize just three restaurants in Elista, modern places that, like Chess City, represented Kalmykia's aspirations to the industrialized world. The restaurants were always either completely empty or completely full for a banquet. Kalmyk meat was as tough as the tough Russians, and a helping of peas was about nine peas.

I ordered sturgeon, but my confused stomach refused it, and I munched instead on my twelve kernels of corn. Glenn picked at a chicken. Bair, who had continued to make me suspicious by repeating the phrase "just between you and me" something like half a dozen times in the first twenty-four hours we knew him, disappeared twice to call Galzanov, and both times Glenn and I were silent while he was gone. Glenn had not played chess in almost two full days. But it was just the prologue of his problems, and as far as he was concerned I was the author of all of them. When Bair returned from his second call, he didn't explain why Galzanov was missing. He suggested that we rest for the remainder of the day and meet again tomorrow.

THE NEXT MORNING I KNOCKED ON GLENN'S DOOR. HE WAS still in bed, but he hadn't climbed under his covers. Rather, he had slept in his long coat with its hood deployed, one arm thrown across his eyes in a facsimile of his bus-riding posture.

"What's wrong with the heat?" he said. "Hotels in Elista are like going camping."

I explained that heat in Kalmykia was state-controlled and wouldn't be turned on for another two weeks. He stared as though my face would betray the joke of this, then shook his head. The night before I had walked down the hall to Glenn's room to find him watching Russian television, staring at the screen forlornly. I asked him if he wanted to take a walk around Elista at night.

"Galzanov said we don't go anywhere without Bair," he said.

"Doesn't that seem strange to you?" I said. "It's just a walk."

"We don't even know if it's safe, man. I don't want to walk around Elista. I don't need to walk around Elista."

He hadn't removed his eyes from the screen, and I left him there for the rest of the evening.

Now I waited for him to dress, and we walked to the House of Government for a morning meeting with Galzanov. We would meet with Galzanov regularly in the mornings to discuss plans for the day. It was a gesture to organization, which was lacking, as the plans were rarely followed, and each day in Kalmykia seemed to proceed along trajectories of laziness and whim. That morning Galzanov got a break from his telephones long enough to play a few games with Glenn over his small wooden set. Galzanov held a cigarette in the same hand he used as a prop for his forehead as he played. Smoke sifted through his hair and drifted away to help compose the room's heady Russian atmosphere. In Galzanov's office, the Russification of the Kalmyks took the form of vague political dread and the odor of Russian tobacco.

The plan for the day included an afternoon meeting with members of the faculty of the newly formed Institute for Humanities Research, a school that had been created to help with the redistribution of Kalmyk tradition. The members of the institute had been made aware of our arrival and my theory of Kalmyk chess and would speak with us that afternoon. Galzanov had also taken the liberty of inviting to his office the republic's leading chess teacher, Sergei Badminov, who arrived presently.

Badminov was a small, dark-haired man of indeterminate age. He was dressed in a patterned shirt and an entirely different pattern of tie. He moved with a penguin totter. He arrived during one of Glenn's games with Galzanov, and introductions were delayed until Galzanov lost a piece and resigned.

"After the disintegration of the Soviet Union, the Soviet chess school split," Badminov said. "Some grandmasters made their own private schools, but the problem with those schools is that they cost money. If you have no money, then no sessions. We took the system of the Soviet school. Our players do not pay for sessions. It is open. The president helps with financial support. Talented children should all have the same conditions for studying chess."

I asked about chess in Kalmyk schools, and Badminov felt a need to defend the decree to a Western sensibility. He assured me that chess was not obligatory in Kalmyk schools despite what the international journalists had trumpeted across the globe.

Across his desk Galzanov was taking a phone call, shouting gutturally into the handset, "*Oom*-stead! *Oom*-stead!" he said, repeating Glenn's surname for whoever was on the other end.

We told Badminov that we had met Baatr Shovunov in Moscow. Shovunov was the only titled Kalmyk, Badminov admitted, but even he was no longer the best chess player in the republic. A fourteen year old named Sasha had won the most recent Kalmyk championship. But the real gleam on the Kalmyk horizon was a seven year old named Sanan. Sanan had arrived in Elista the year before to play in a children's tournament, and Badminov had discovered him. Kirsan had become the boy's benefactor, providing money for grandmaster training, and Sanan's family had relocated to Elista so he could study. The boy had met the president and played chess with him, but Kirsan won both their games. Badminov joked of a rematch.

Galzanov asked if we would like to meet Sanan before heading to the institute. The idea was so remarkably spontaneous it seemed orchestrated. The meeting was arranged with a single call along Kalmykia's troubled lines.

. . .

THE CENTRAL ASIAN STEPPE WILDERNESS HAS BEEN COMPARED to the Arctic in terms of desolation and scant wildlife. There's more, as the forever-changing ice face of the Arctic, thunderously cracking and shifting, resembles the slow swells that form the steppe landscape. The North Caspian steppe is an ocean of earth—once it was seafloor—whose waves crest on a millenial scale. The land moves. Elista was an isle of trees in the steppe sea, but the land cared little for the civilization that barnacled it, and the fact that it moved, that it breathed and heaved, was evident in the city's roads, marked with craters and giant swollen pimples like tortoises sleeping under the asphalt. Elista was a small town, but taxis were everywhere because cars were an outrageous expense. The drivers knew the ever-changing roads the way riverboat pilots knew their stretch of the river. They knew how to jam the gears just right to hop a crack in the street like a bloodless wound, how to gun over a mound without becoming ridiculously balanced atop its summit. The taxi drivers, and the driver of our van as we made our way to Sanan's, executed the roads expertly, surfers catching a sluggish tide.

Sanan's house was not yet complete, but his family had already moved in. The home was in a community going up on a descending tract of muddy land, a wave swelling down, and our van had to steer through an obstacle course of dirt bulbs to get close. The rule of Russian homes, we would discover, was that the outside of a building told you very little of what the inside would look like. Sanan's outer yard was yet strewn with weeds and building materials, but the inside of the house was quite comfortable, their living room equipped with a helping of leather furniture, several plants, and a picture of the Dalai Lama. Sanan's father, Slava Sugirov, was a businessman. His mother, Zanda, was a pretty housewife caught by surprise in her apron. Sanan himself was a short, shy, chubby-faced boy every bit as cute as he was talented. His smile was a wide-toothed impression of a chipmunk. At seven he had already been featured in Russia's *64 Chess Review*, but he had not yet attended school. He had his own bedroom, no small accomplishment for a Kalmyk child, but really you could argue that the whole house was his as it had all been paid for by Ilyumzhinov. Sanan's bookcases were crammed with play paraphernalia and chess books. He had a signed football, a Robot Commander, and plastic army men arranged in careful rows. In the middle of the room stood his chess table, neat but large for him, and it was to here that we, Bair, Badminov, Glenn, Sanan, and myself, retired as Slava and Zanda prepared a welcome meal of caviar and Kalmyk tea.

Sanan seemed confused by the company at first, happy but uncertain. He started the clock in his first game of blitz against Glenn and quickly became all business. The chess pieces filled his palms like gourds. His captures were slow because of it, awkward transfers. But his mind knew exactly where the clock was, and he reached without looking to smack it, his eyes never shifting from the position developing before him. Glenn did not go lightly on children—once, after a blindfold exhibition at a school, I watched him dispatch a line of children one after the other like a grim Santa—but he did slow his moves some to compensate for a child's inability to manipulate the pieces. For the first time since I had known Glenn, I wanted him to lose. Losing to a child would only make things worse for Glenn in Russia, but I didn't care. When Sanan looked up at me from the game, his cute face had become a puss as sour as that old hustler, Chepukaitis. Or better, it was like a photo of the Dalai Lama I had seen, aged seven or eight and perched atop a mountain of holy pillows at the outbreak of the Great Patriotic War. It was this thought that made me realize what Sanan was exactly. If Telo Rinpoche's plans for a temple complex in Kalmykia had been replaced with Chess City, then Sanan was the replacement for Rinpoche himself. The boy was a chess chosen one.

Sanan dropped a bishop to Glenn, and it appeared to everyone that the game was over. But in another move or two Glenn's queen was trapped. "Oh," Glenn said, and he licked his lips as he did when he realized an opponent was stronger than he had reckoned. He lost the queen, but was able to salvage material for it and only when Sanan was down a bishop again did he reach to stop the clock, smile, and offer his little hand for congratulations.

We gathered in the living room, where our meal was ready, bowls of Kalmyk tea and cuts of bread onto which we smeared the tiny slimy beads of caviar. Kalmyk tea was one-part Russian tea, one-part cream, and a dosage of salt. It was a special recipe to alleviate thirst and hunger.

"My boy was very curious one day," Slava said, when I asked how Sanan had become interested in chess. "I played one day, and he just wanted to look. Later I showed him some moves, and it became interesting to him. It's his nature."

I turned to Sanan. "How do you feel when you win, Sanan?"

The boy's eyes shot to Bair for the translation, and he answered quickly. "Okay."

"And when you lose?"

"The same," he said, and everyone smiled.

"His age is seven and a half," his father went on. "He wants to be a GM. He is doing much in it. Sergei Badminov is part of our family. He is teaching him. We live in Elista now, but if in the future he is a master or a GM he will visit many towns and countries and it will be useful for him."

Back in Sanan's room, Glenn paused before their next game to show Sanan where we lived on his world map. Sanan scrambled up onto his couch to get as close to Glenn's finger as possible. On the map the United States was small and stuffed away in a corner. Sanan stared as though peering hard enough would allow him to make out the streets and buildings of America.

Everyone was pleased when Sanan won the next speed game from Glenn. We cheered when Glenn resigned, and Sanan looked up, not at all certain what we were happy about. Only I knew Glenn well enough to recognize the disappointment in him. He asked Badminov what he had thought of the games, and Badminov shrugged and said Sanan should have won the first game as well. Glenn smiled, but it accelerated his disintegration. He had come to Russia hoping to beat grandmasters, and now he had lost to a seven year old.

I caught Bair glancing at his watch as Glenn sat down with Sanan to show him a chess puzzle involving four knights moving inside a nine-square block. We all discovered how difficult it was to explain the parameters of an odd puzzle to a seven year old through a translator.

"He's just a kid," Bair said, trying to convince Glenn to skip the exercise, as by then we were late for the institute.

"Just a second," Glenn said. "It's just these *nine* squares. He can move whatever knight he wants." He started in on a visual metaphor, making puppets of his hands to indicate plots of land. "Let's say you've got two islands. One here, and one here. You want to build a bridge between them. There're many ways to build the bridge, but the important thing is the *idea* of the bridge."

He went on for a time, and Sanan solved the puzzle as soon as he understood it. We hurried through a series of happy snapshots outside the house, posing by the van, then waved to the family and sped off to the institute.

Murray wrote:

> *Certain peculiarities of play that began soon after 1600 to appear in chess as played in different regions of the Central Plain of Europe are identical with some of the special features that exist in Russian chess. . . .*

Of the three rules Murray referred to, at least one was clearly of European origin. The other two were Indian. The first of these attempted to compensate for the slowness of pawns by initiating the game with a set number of moves from each side. The second rule seems nonsensical at first: A player who is stalemated, who has no legal move available to him, wins the game.

Both rules had moved east from their origin in India. To the west, the Muslims began their games simply by racing to set positions, and stalemates were a draw as in modern chess. As the game moved east, however, multiple moves at the beginning of the game became common, and stalemate was either not permitted or, as in India, Java, and China, counted as a victory for the side that received it.

When both rules appeared in Russia and then Europe around 1600, according to Murray, it was odd as they had leapfrogged over many of the intermediary stages commonly associated with the movement of chess rules. The stalemate rule jumped from Russia to England, where it thrived for two centuries, but this could be explained by contact between England and Russia in the years in question. How the rules had arrived in Russia to begin with was a mystery. Murray knew that the odds of Asia and Europe developing the same rules independently were long and believed that "the existence of common rules must presuppose a relationship." But he could not find any better explanation than the one that was already in place: the Mongol control of Russia, beginning around 1225 and lasting until 1380. But

375 years lay between the initial Mongol influence and the rules' appearance.

In the end Murray left the matter undecided, a prominent but characteristic absence in the history of the game.

Murray was well aware of the Kalmyk chess tradition. He cited references stating that "the Kalmucs likewise play at chess . . . as we do," and "the Calmuck Tartars play at chess and backgammon," but better descriptions came from Westerners who had traveled to Tibet. Late in the eighteenth century, an adventurer described the tough "Calmacks" he had encountered in Teshoo Loombo:

> Among the Tartars, who have come some three, and some four months' journey on pilgrimage to the Lama, I have met with some masterly chess-players. . . . Some of the Tibetans are also acquainted with chess, which they have learned from the Calmacks, but they are, I think, far inferior to their masters. . . .

Another example came from the nineteenth-century travelogue of a pair of Jesuits:

> The Tartars and Thibetians are likewise acquainted with chess; and, singularly enough, their chessboard is absolutely the same as our own. . . . What is still more surprising, these people cry "chik" when they check a piece, and "mate" when the game is at an end. These expressions, which are neither Thibetian nor Mongol, are, nevertheless, used by every one, yet no one can explain their origin. . . .

Murray appeared to have never wondered how or why it was that European chess should have popped up so suddenly in Tibet. The Tibetan name for the game was *chandaraki*, which proved that the Tibetan game derived from India's *chaturanga*. For Murray, however, the fact that Tibet did not lie on the main caravan route that had brought much of Indian culture to China was sufficient explanation for the discrepancy between Chinese and Tibetan chess. The lay theory I had sent to Galzanov explained it all a little better, but of course couldn't be proved.

The Kalmyk scientists were staring at us. They numbered a roomful, thirty or so cultural scholars, a group made up of very old crinkly men who could at least remember rumors of the time before the Bolsheviks, and very young men and women among the new learned elite of Kalmykia. Our van had arrived at the institute in a rush.

Sanan had made us an hour late. We shuttled into the building, cutting down its cold, tall hallways to a room that was reserved for us. Until the final minute I believed the meeting would be a private conversation with two or three scholars who would prove warm and insightful, gentle with my theory's gaping holes. Also, I hoped to use the theory to find someone willing to discuss the Yudina murder, a member of the hibernating Kalmyk opposition.

The scholars filtered in—in their wait, they had drifted into the hallways or back to their offices. Glenn and Bair and I were led to seats behind the long end of a conference table, with most of the Kalmyk scientists filing into chairs against the far wall. I gradually realized I was to be the speaker. The Kalmyk scientists eyed Glenn and me suspiciously—we looked much younger to their eyes, we were on the arm of a Kalmyk who was widely known to work for the FSB, and they had been told that a pair of Americans had arrived to explain their history to them. The Kalmyk scientists were proud of what they had come to know of themselves. What they didn't know was who we were or what we were doing there. Glenn began to squirm beside me in an effort to make himself physically smaller and perhaps even invisible. I held out the hope that the setup of the room was yet another misunderstanding, but in a moment a woman at a desk called the room to order and introduced us, pronouncing Glenn's name just as Galzanov had done on the phone earlier that morning.

Then they waited.

Bair gave me a moment, and leaned over. "Tell them your theory," he whispered.

I didn't look into the audience as I spoke. I talked to the table. It wasn't the first time I'd gone through the theory since arriving in Kalmykia, and my tendency was to abbreviate it. But I gave it to them, arguing that two of the mysteries in the history of chess—a similarity in rule between Mongol and Russian chess around the year 1600, and the appearance of European chess in Tibet in 1775—could well be explained by the history of the Kalmyks, who made contact with Russia in 1606 and returned to China in 1771. I presented the information as empirically interesting, at the end wedging in the caveat that Glenn and I were not scientists and that we were unsure what they had been told about our project. I said that we had come to Kalmykia to learn rather than teach. Then I opened the floor for insight that might either support the theory or refute it outright.

My entire presentation lasted perhaps four minutes.

It took the scientists a moment to register that it was over, and when they did I needed no translator to interpret the telepathic group message ricocheting through the room: *The Americans are weak!* After a moment, a man in a thick mustache and with his legs crossed in the effete way of academics chose to speak for the whole of them.

"I wonder," he said, "do you have a business card?"

I exhaled and explained that I did not have business cards. I told them Galzanov still had my contract.

"What is your specialty?" said the man with the mustache.

I ran down my eductation, but it wasn't until I mentioned, entirely in passing, a second undergraduate major in psychology that any of the Kalmyk scientists reacted. *"Ah, psikhologhiya!"* they muttered.

The woman who had brought the meeting to order stepped in then to repair the disorder I'd made of it. She announced politely that an error had been made, and she suggested that we end the meeting in its current form, dismiss the majority of those present whose disciplines were unrelated to chess, and reconvene with just those scientists who might have something to offer my theory.

The Kalmyk scientists jumped up like a roomful of students at the dawn of summer recess. Five or six remained for the workshop session that would go on for nearly two hours, but even those who had left would occasionally return to check on the progress of the meeting, poking their heads in the door, or actually reentering and sitting for a bit, as if to observe the progress of a large snake consuming some animal. Before we began again, however, there was a moment to assess those scientists who'd stayed behind, each of them moving forward so that they sat across and around the conference table, some of them cracking open the bottles of water that had been stationed there. To the far right was a quite heavy man who spoke in a halting English he was proud of—already he had sparred with Bair over the definition of particular words, and later Bair would confess to a troubled history with the man, though he refused to elaborate. Next to him was Kalmykia's lone chess problemist, a man whose name I would eventually learn was Basaev; he was dark, with sunken cheeks and large eyes that made him look like a smudged figure from a Munch painting, baffled by pain. Next in the row was Vaskin, a kindly, chubby old man with an ornate cane and a beret, whose smile said more about his hearing loss than about what he thought of my theory. The man with the mustache came next, followed by one or two others; and finally, to our far left, a woman, Deliash Muzraeva, a Tibetologist, who during the meeting managed to sustain a smirk for so long that it became natural to wonder whether an appearance of intellectual contempt wasn't simply the natural state of her face. For some reason, I got the idea that Muzraeva would be the most likely scientist to open up about the Yudina murder.

The woman who was chairing the meeting formalized it once again with a question. Was my theory a theory that was generally accepted in the West, or was it more one man's suggestion, a hypothesis or idea? I admitted that the latter was the case, then argued that in English there wasn't really a significant difference between theory and hypothesis, especially as applied to more imprecise sciences. The scientists were first offended by the use of theory to describe something less than accepted dogma and second by my explanation of English vocabulary. The difference between theory and hypothesis sparked a heated debate among everyone present. Glenn touched my elbow.

"Hallman! There *is* a difference between theory and hypothesis."

"Okay."

"A *big* difference!"

"All right," I said. I wanted to tell him that I had never used the word "theory" to begin with—Galzanov had. But I was already coming to the realization that I had made the same mistake Stalin had in regard to the Kalmyks. I had expected that a link between Kalmyk history and chess history would be attractive to the Kalmyks because of the chess movement. I had assumed uniformity among them even after reading their history of endless internal dispute. Glenn and I must have looked to the scientists like agents of the Ilyumzhinov regime attempting to spread chess propaganda. And probably we were being used for just that. It was the first indication we had seen of hostility to the presidential chess decree. If anyone was to object to it, I thought now, it would be the intellectuals, and the Kalmyk scientists had the role of intellectual down: They wore the shaggy formal clothes of professors, the sweaters and tweed that allowed them to pass for having it together.

They proceeded to attack my idea. "Have you read Linder?" asked

Basaev, glaring across the table so that he looked ever more frightened and Munchian. I had not. I hadn't even heard the name. Basaev explained that Isaak Linder, Russia's version of Murray, had written extensively on Mongol chess. I later found Linder's books and discovered that, like so many chess writers, Linder had relied almost exclusively on Murray for early research. There was nothing in Linder to refute the suggestion, but for Basaev the fact that Linder had not made it himself was its damnation.

"Quite right," said the fat man to Basaev's left, in hesitant English. "Because the Russian history of Mongolia was too close, too close. In the thirteenth century, the Mongols invaded Russia and conquered it. They ruled Russia for two hundred years. Do you know the history of the Golden Horde?"

"Yes," I said, and I went on to explain that the problem of the Mongol occupation of Russia as an explanation lay in the fact that several hundred years had elapsed in the interim.

"There were many succession states after the Golden Horde," the fat man said. "Russia had many contacts with them. Maybe the influence of these Oriental countries and Muslim countries can explain these facts you describe."

I was beginning to get annoyed because there didn't seem to be any clear reason why they had dismissed the suggestion; it simply wasn't in keeping with what they believed history to be. I had formulated the theory only to guarantee our passage to Russia, but now I found myself defending it, arguing with the very people whose trust I had hoped to enlist, digging in like any misunderstood chess historian rebuffed by mainstream academia.

"Doesn't that strike you as being just as possible as a Kalmyk explanation?" I asked the fat man.

"I think it's very dubious," he said.

I cringed. "Dubious" was a word chess had adopted and assigned its own specific punctuation sequence to indicate a bad move. Because chess was played in many cultures, common comments delivered in the analysis of games were abbreviated to a vocabulary of symbols. !?, for example, meant "interesting." ?! meant "dubious," a move that looked good but was unsound.

"You are quite right that the Kalmyks were well-acquainted with chess playing. But they came to Eastern Europe only in the seventeenth century."

"Which is precisely when Murray noticed the rule similarity."

The fat man grimaced. "But if you are right, it would need great exploration of the history. It would need correction and—" he trailed off into Russian and began to debate something with Bair.

There was to be no real structure to the meeting, and a man far off to the left took the opportunity of the moment's chaos to change the subject completely: He named a few of the important American chess players of the past—Reshevsky, Fine, Fischer—and asked if there were any young players in the United States who might soon emerge as a potential challenger to the world championship.

I gave the question to Glenn. He sat up in his seat and leaned forward over the table as if to speak into a microphone.

"Right now," he said, "no."

And he leaned back again. The answer seemed to surprise the scientists not at all.

The man with the mustache had had a revelation: Either he was completely won over by the lucidity of my theory, or he had come to realize that his career would be better served by throwing support behind whatever Ilyumzhinov was trying to cram down their throats. "Your suggestion," he said, "is very interesting. It might be productive. If you look into Kalmyk folklore, you can find stories about India, Tibet—even about chess. So your theory is possible. How to prove it is another question. You mentioned chess rules. I would like now to introduce Mr. Vaskin, who knows a great deal about the Kalmyk version of chess."

We all turned to Vaskin. Vaskin was the institute's ancient emeritus, a folklorist and craftsman, but appeared to embody too much of the Soviet era for the younger Kalmyk scientists. Their respect for their elders was tested by Vaskin's forgetfulness and poor hearing.

"In 1238," Vaskin said, starting up as though power had been restored to an automaton, "chess came to Europe with the help of merchants. This game came from India. Chess appeared in Europe as a result of the Great Silk Road, and our people. Kalmyk chess is quite different from other games. Our elders kept the history of Kalmyk chess."

I interrupted to point out that it was well-known that chess had arrived in Europe certainly by the year 1000, via Arabia. But Vaskin hardly cared for any theory but his own.

"The Kalmyks brought Asian chess to Europe!" he said. "Not

Arabia! I started to play Kalmyk chess when I was five years old. All my family played with the Kalmyk rules. We didn't even hear of European chess until I was eleven. My mother lived until she was ninety-two. She played only the Kalmyk way. She knew sixty-four special prayers, and one was about chess. Before we would play, we would say this prayer. Chess is also mentioned in the Kalmyk epic poem, *Djanghar*."

Vaskin paused for a moment, and when no one interrupted he took it as a signal to launch into another lecture, a description of the twenty-two differences between Kalmyk chess and European chess. He spoke at length, repeating himself often. I realized as he went on that our presence at the institute wasn't so much a failure of communication as it was a clash of faulty remembrance, dueling dubious histories. Sweet as he was, Vaskin's history was more bizarre than my own. Still, I felt a small measure of victory when he came to the Kalmyk rule for stalemate and said that if white gave stalemate to black, then black won.

Muzraeva, the smirking woman, spoke for the first time when Vaskin had exhausted himself. She asked why I had come to Kalmykia if I was interested in chess—weren't there more interesting chess countries I could have visited, such as India or The Netherlands? I defended the choice as Kalmykia had truly become something of a chess hub, the Olympiad, a world championship match, and a number of tournaments having been held here, but really she was tapping into my search for absurdity in the republic.

"You mentioned Kalmyks in Tibet in 1775," Muzraeva said. "What part of Tibet did they visit?"

I admitted that Murray had not been specific, and that academic historians had a much higher threshold for the completeness of information than did chess historians.

Muzraeva frowned. I pleaded to her with my eyes in the hope of making a connection, but she only looked back with bemusement. She dismissively suggested that information about chess could possibly be found in stories of pilgrimages to Tibet.

The man with the mustache leaned forward, still my champion. "Your theory is an explanation for how chess spread through the world. You can find some proofs in Kalmyk folklore. In the end I'd like personally to say that your suggestion is very productive, and I quite agree with you."

His colleagues were not convinced. But it seemed that our meeting was over, at least in the sense that everyone present had decided how to feel about what had been said. The woman who had begun the meeting brought it to conclusion by enumerating the points against my theory: The year 1600 was not the only wave of Kalmyk migration, and the history of the Mongols in Inner Asia was more complex than those migrations would suggest.

She leaned forward and peered across her desk. "Your theory sounds very nice," she said, "but are you now ready to accept that it has been proven untrue?"

ELISTA WAS GETTING BETTER, I DECIDED. IT WAS A PLEASANT town in the morning. Lenin Square and the House of Government stood at the head of a large, flat central park latticed with pathways, some of them wide swaths lined with wooden benches, others just frazzled stripes of cracked cement that led off into the wilderness. The paths were all being converted from Soviet asphalt to brick, teams of construction men at work here and there, and the sections of Elista that were already complete hinted at the quaint atmosphere the city would achieve if the money held out. There were new statues all about, abstract figures of Kalmyk themes and huge monuments to Pushkin, to the heroes of the Great Patriotic War, to the original singer of the *Djanghar*. As well, there were scraps of modern ethnic architecture popping up: the Sun Gate, a wide and tall pagoda-influenced shelter standing on stilts near Lenin Square; and closer to Hotel Elista, a small gazebo of the same style housing a cement chess table in its center.

Kiosks stood all over Elista; they had been popping up just in the last four or five years, the first embodiment of a free-market economy being shops like booths in a market. Of course. The kiosks were the size of horse trailers, small semipermanent structures with the FIDE symbol emblazoned on the front, and they sold everything from bags of tea to alcohol to postcards and stamps. A more formal market, something like a Value Mart in rows of plastic tents, had cropped up first behind Hotel Elista, but had long since begun to creep out into the city itself. Here for sale were socks, shoes, school supplies, kitchen utensils, makeup, medicine, nylons, pots and pans, clocks and watches, bootleg movies and tapes, the many symbols of

Western capitalism seeping in just as the market itself was seeping in, the Tweetie Birds and Reeboks and Brad Pitts. Legal money-changing stores were all about, their rates printed on sandwich boards, but men who would change dollars illegally were more plentiful and hugely more convenient. I bought four small packets of shampoo and a deck of cards.

The night before, after the institute, Galzanov had lost dinner again in a blindfold game with Glenn. My hangover had long since transformed itself into dehydration and exhaustion, and I ordered a pitcher of ice water at the restaurant. I drained my glass three times. Also I ordered fruit, browning slices of apple and banana that I gobbled for their vitamins. Glenn frowned at me like an aristocrat who would rather starve than eat the food of the rabble. He wasn't really wrong. There was something sour in the water, and the fruit was far from fresh, but still my body screamed for the stuff, and as it all began to metabolize inside me I felt not the cessation of hunger, but the faint biological understanding of nourishment.

Galzanov and I talked books over dinner. He had studied philology at Kalmyk State University, and he was well read: Pushkin, Dostoyevsky, Dickens, and Shakespeare under his belt. At one point, he and Bair consulted quietly with each other and then emerged to ask about a word in English. Bair imitated Glenn's hand puppets of earlier in the day to help illustrate a story that was even more chess-like.

"If you've got one army," Bair said, "or one group of guys here, and another group of guys over here, and maybe there's going to be a fight, and a couple of guys from one army go forward to find out about the other group, what is this called, please?"

"Reconnaissance," Glenn said.

"Intelligence," I said.

"Intelligence, *da*," Galzanov said, and I caught the quiet accusation of it. The scientists at the institute had been suspicious of us, and so was Galzanov. Who *were* we exactly? We were the couple of guys. Kirsan's vodka had done its damage, but apparently it had failed to betray us. I looked at Glenn to see if he had come to this same conclusion, but he had other things on his mind.

"Do you want to see something amazing?" he announced.

"Sure," Bair said.

"Okay. But not here. Wait until we're outside."

He nodded, and Galzanov and Bair looked at one another like men in for a treat. They didn't know it, but Glenn was going to whistle for them. Whistling was something that Glenn did at a certain stage in his relationships with people. To whistle for someone meant something to him, somehow sealed friendships. We walked through Lenin Square a short while later, Bair, the FSB agent, and Galzanov, the press secretary who'd sold his soul to a tyrant, leading the way.

Glenn stopped and said, "Okay, this is good. Are you ready?"

They nodded.

He spread his feet slightly. Then he sucked in his ammunition and shaped his lips to a pucker as if for a kiss, just a tiny hole in the center of his embouchure like the pupil of a fat, fleshy eye, and when the first note sounded from between his lips, it was effortless and took just right to the architecture of the buildings around the square so that it seemed perfectly supplied by an electronic amplifier at some distance from us. It was "Over the Rainbow," which was not usually his first choice, though I'd heard him do it before. On the octave shifts he swelled up and down like the slide of a trombone lusting each of the notes in between, and on the longish tones he held steady for a moment before the slow pulsation into vibrato. Galzanov continued to smoke, but Bair froze at the first note, squinting and looking off toward Lenin's metal shoulders, cocking his head to one side to adjust his ears to the music. The tune was not perfect, nor did it transcend ridiculousness, but it did for a moment lower the stakes of all the mystery between our parties. Later Galzanov would threaten us with karaoke, which seemed his preferred instrument of torture, a kind of all-natural sodium pentathol to get people loosened up and talking. But Glenn had no such agenda. His song was a calculated effort to remind the rest of us of things simple and peaceful. He continued the performance through to when the bluebirds flew and then trailed off, and the three of us applauded him in the windy evening.

The night ended with a request that we do a television interview the following afternoon and a promise from Galzanov that the four of us would go hunting in the steppe that evening.

The morning brought the first day of fine weather in Kalmykia, but for Glenn it was no reason to step outside the hotel or even leave his bed. I went alone. After the market, I walked back to Elista's central park, this time into an overgrown area of it. The weeds here were unchecked, man-sized, with tentacles like groping, rubbery arms. Fall being the time of marriage in Elista, a wedding party passed me, on their way to the Sun Gate for its photo-op. I walked on and came to the cement bust of one of Kalmykia's old leaders deep in an unkempt corner of the park, back where it was possible to find a cow tied to a tree for the day. The old leader had not put his face on enough calendars to be remembered properly. Moss had begun to grow on his cheek, lesions like an angry parasite intent on making a monster of him.

I returned to the hotel an hour before we were to meet Bair. I found Glenn awake, still in his jacket and bleary-eyed before a Kalmyk newscast. He didn't appear to have slept at all. I left him and returned a short while later, but he had done nothing more to prepare himself for the day.

"We're supposed to be there in twenty minutes," I said. I was frustrated and annoyed with him. "You're not ready. What's going on?"

"Plenty of time, plenty of time," he mumbled. "Go back to your room, I'll meet you there in a little bit."

Two minutes before 11:00, he appeared, rushed and sweating. We hurried to the House of Government where Bair was on time, but Galzanov was late. As we waited, Glenn produced the noose of a pretied tie from his pocket and strung himself up using a glass door for a mirror. He put on his cheap pair of sunglasses, and Bair laughed and whispered to me, "He really does look like FBI man. Don't tell him I said so!"

When Galzanov finally arrived, he was wearing the same suit from the night before. His complexion was mottled, and he was moody and irascible. He would not accompany us until that evening. The plan would be for us to visit a school in Elista to see the presidential chess decree in action, then the television interview, and then to a lake in the countryside for hunting, and perhaps karaoke after that. It was slowly becoming apparent to me why the Kalmyks took Chuck Norris seriously as a model of masculinity. And Kalmyk hospitality seemed little more than a fulcrum of control to keep us in sight and in check.

The principal at the school had a photo of a pretty Hollywood actress on his desk where his wife's picture should have been. A pink lump grew on one of his eyeballs. The principal bragged that his school was home to Kalmykia's chess champion, the fourteen year old Badminov had spoken of. The children in the chess classroom stood on our arrival, a polite group of well-behaved kids in rows. As with the institute, they expected us to speak, but here it was easier to deflect the request and I asked them to simply go about their lesson. Glenn was invited to play with one of their stronger players, another seven year old, and he lost the first game. It didn't matter to the children, Glenn was a star anyway, but I could see the damage the loss did to him.

The chess teacher had a large mole in one of his eyebrows, and one long hair squirmed out a decimeter from his neck. He corrected Badminov in saying that chess was in fact obligatory in Kalmyk schools, though only for very young children. There were extra lessons for those with talent, and it became optional later. The classroom's chess pieces were rudimentary figures, wood sets like a child's toy blocks.

"Of course it helps to develop the mind," said a cute girl in a black turtleneck and ponytail when I asked her about the game. "It is very useful in other subjects. For example, mathematics."

The boy next to her was willing to weigh in on Ilyumzhinov. "He's famous. He plays chess. As far as I know, he's a candidate master."

I moved the pieces for Glenn in a display of blindfold speed chess, putting my finger to my lips for silence when his young opponent's time ran out. When Glenn won the game, the teacher scolded the boy for not resigning the position earlier.

"Why didn't you see checkmate coming?"

"I didn't see it," the boy said.

"You should treat your opponent more respectfully!"

Glenn continued playing offhand games with the kids, and as soon as we had a free moment, they surrounded us for autographs, thrusting forward books and slips of paper. When we simply signed our names, they pushed the signatures back and asked for wishes.

"I hope you become a grandmaster!" I wrote. "I wish you happy chess!"

The Chess Champion of Kalmykia arrived. The boy's name was Alexander Utnasunov—Sasha. He was a plump kid with long hair, tinted eyeglasses, and a pair of pointed-forward lips that made him look like a rabbit toughened by life on the steppe. Earlier in the summer, Sasha had scored a victory over Alexander Grischuk, a young grandmaster phenom, and later that fall Sasha would be Ilyumzhinov's choice to represent Kalmykia at the FIDE World Championship tournament in Delhi, one of only one hundred players in the world invited to the event. Sasha was a quiet boy, his eyes far older than his years, and he had become Champion of Kalmykia at the same age Kirsan had been when accomplishing the same feat. Later, we would come to know Sasha much better, but by the time he arrived at the classroom, we were late for our interview on Kalmyk television. Sasha and Glenn played only a single game. And though Glenn won, neither it nor the swarm of children who followed us out of the school, shaking Glenn's hand, asking him for more signatures and wishes, and shouting their bits of treasured English, compensated him for having lost another game to a seven year old.

"I hate losing to kids, man," he said, once we were safely in the van. "In the States, I lost one speed game to a seven year old in my life. In Kalmykia, I've lost two games in two days."

The driver set off into Elista. Glenn opened the button of his collar but left his tie cinched. He refused to look at anything but the rows of cement houses skidding by us, and for the time being his mood seemed to prove the theory that blindfold chess was a terrible drain on the mind.

"You look sad," Bair told him.

"I just hate losing to kids."

The interviewers were waiting for us in a small garden adjacent to the television building. Glenn and I sat side-by-side on a bench, neither of us wanting to be particularly near the other, while the cameraman dodged and darted around us, collecting the angles from which the story would be culled. The interview was half interrogation: Both the interviewers were women in a tough mold. What kind of a scientist was I? they wanted to know. Misinformation seemed to travel the republic on the efficient frequency of gossip. I corrected the error again and prepared to explain why I did not have a business card. Why had I chosen to come to Kalmykia? they asked. I took another tack with this question this time, saying that chess was a cultural artifact of anthropological import and an untapped tool of history, and that the story of the Kalmyk people, apart from being rich with chess heritage, was a tale so full of abuses by powers both

East and West that the Kalmyks, it had been suggested, had suffered more than the French fleeing from Moscow, more than the children of Israel wandering in the desert, more than the English or the Greeks during their times of plague. No response. Would my book be a work of fiction? they asked, and I explained that it would be a story that was true. They looked at me as though I had spoken of warm snow, and then one of the women repeated an earlier question as though the interval of just a few seconds would result in a more incriminating answer. The heart of the dilemma, I guessed, was in trying to explain journalism as it was practiced in the West to people in a country that had never had a free press. I tried to feed Glenn one of their questions, but they were intent on making me stumble. I risked looking at Glenn as Bair translated my responses: he was rigid as a corpse beside me, and when I averted my eyes I accidentally looked directly into the lens of the camera. I turned away at once.

"So," the first interviewer said, "do you know President Ilyumzhinov?"

The question was the center of the interview's vortex, the cachet of sharing air with Kirsan that strong, and on its answer hinged the question of whether they would continue wasting time with us. We had not yet met the president, I said, but we had been promised an interview. This was the response that the interviewers wanted in that it allowed them to conclude that we were not as newsworthy as they had been led to believe. They thanked us curtly and stripped away their photogenic scarves.

"Why didn't they ask me any questions?" Glenn asked, back in the van. Bair shrugged. Glenn had always wanted to be famous, and in Kalmykia he was, at least to a greater degree than at home, but he was finding it wholly uncomfortable that his fame was not adoring. When we began moving again, Glenn slouched down in his seat, mournful and spent. I was tired, too. It was odd. The night before we had had significant time to rest, and we had been awake today for only four or five hours. I told Bair that I intended to skip hunting that evening.

"Why?" he said. "Just go!"

"I'm tired. I need to sleep."

He assured us that we would both be given guns. But the formula of firearms and a nearby lake struck me as too close to the formula of the pond where Yudina had been found.

"It's the countryside!" Bair said. "It's good. Go!"

We bounced along for a moment, and then Bair asked if it was possible that he be paid for his first four days of translation.

"How much?"

He shrugged. "Two hundred?"

Back at the House of Government, Glenn and Galzanov played a few more games, both men tired and moving slowly with the pieces. Galzanov had already told us that one of his problems with chess was that he did not know how to quit once he began playing. It was similar to his life, I thought, an addiction to the power of his position, that whirlwind high of fast living and political intrigue. When Galzanov announced last game before the hunting expedition, I told him I did not intend to go along. It was the first moment when either Glenn or I had refused a Kalmyk suggestion. Galzanov appeared upset at first, but it faded.

"No problems," he said.

Glenn decided to go on the hunting trip, returning to the hotel first so he could change clothes. I went to speak with him before he left. It wasn't clear why he was going hunting. He was inebriated with the effects of not eating, not drinking, the breakneck pace of the week, the dark side of fame, and the shock of losing games of chess to clever Kalmyk children. Inexplicably, he chided me for getting drunk on our first night, repeating his scolding again and again like the drunk he abhorred. He so faithfully believed in his illogic that eventually I became angry and left him as he had left me. I was asleep in my room before he passed my door on his way to a dark lake somewhere in the steppe, having never been told what animal it was he would hunt.

I WOKE AFTER ONLY A FEW HOURS TO THE DARK HOTEL ROOM and the black city out my broad windows. I drank some water, therapeutically, and turned on the television in time for the Kalmyk news. There were two stories about events in Elista, and then a forty-five-second spot about Glenn and me, most of it head shots of me with my lips moving while commentary neither my own nor Bair's came in voice-over. I heard my name and then Glenn's among the quick Russian. They had kept the shot of Glenn's dour profile as I glanced from him into the camera, and for an instant, as the spot rolled, I looked out from the television and into my own eyes again, where I registered as suspicious even to myself.

I left the hotel to walk through Elista at night, retracing my steps of the morning. The city was sinister in the dark, and it was strange to be in its streets and yet feel the firmament so close; stars like candles hung on tangled strings just a few meters overhead. I walked once more the paths of the park, serenaded by an odd species of cricket and drawing stares from couples pressed on benches. The smaller paths now led into vertical walls of black. In these darkest areas of the park, Kalmyk teenagers gathered to drink, their cigarettes like orange fireflies that flared on drags taken for their warmth. I saw a young man and a young woman stumble out from between some shrubs, where they had sneaked to kiss or piss.

I sat down on a bench to take some notes, but it was only a moment or two before a woman appeared at my side. She was short, wore a knit wool hat, and had a growth the size of a marble on her lip. She was drunk. She nestled in beside me, spooning our thighs, and for a time she tried to communicate with me, repeating phrases that I couldn't have made out even if I had understood Russian. She smiled and shook her head. Finally, she gave up on sentences and forced just one word through her lips.

"Ha . . . Haa . . . Hallman!"

She knew me. Probably from the same newscast I had just watched. She pronounced the "H" of my name like a throaty Russia "Kh." She saw from my eyes that she had identified me correctly, and the instant of communication gave her license to begin her pitch again, pressing closer now, a proposition or just begging. The scene caught the attention of a Kalmyk man a few meters off, another Elista street person who smiled and wandered over. He seemed to want to help me escape, and to do so he sneaked up behind the woman and slid a hand into the pocket of her jacket. She panicked and as the two began to struggle, I got up and moved away.

I walked under the Sun Gate and headed into Lenin Square, where the three flags over the House of Government whipped loudly and Kalmyk women crossed the expanse arm in arm, laughing in the last bit of passable weather before the steppe's windy winter. I examined a row of students' art posted to the wall of a government building, the children having been asked to make paintings detailing what they'd been taught of the sufferings of their ancestors. It was the revision of history at work, or the revision of the revision. Kalmykia had been cut out of the twentieth century and asked to juggle varieties of history. Now the Kalmyks were on the move again, wandering emotionally if they could not wander literally. But the direction was still unclear. Was Kirsan's Steppe Code closer to the American Constitution or to Stalin's Constitution of 1936? With the chess decree, had the Kalmyks been given promises or been made fools of? The dilemma always returned to the impossible assignment of moving backward and forward at once. Ilyumzhinov had tried to use the game—both the intellectual discipline he believed it afforded and its international political infrastructure—as a new steppe across which the Kalmyks could roam. They needed new pastures. But it still wasn't clear whether chess could be such a thing. The experiment was ongoing, and my two walks of the day, one in light and one in dark, represented its polarity of potential: hope and fear.

GLENN WAS IN HIS ROOM WHEN I RETURNED TO THE HOTEL, but he was tired and promised to relate the story of the hunting trip the following day. By morning, however, another event had eclipsed it: He believed that he had witnessed an attack of some kind during the night, a girl accosted by several men in the alley parking lot below our windows. He pointed down to where it had occurred. The woman, he said, had screamed for a time and was pushed to the ground. The sight had affected him deeply. I asked how he felt.

"I feel bad because I didn't help the girl," he said.

Glenn looked worse today than the previous morning, the battering of an entire Russian life compressed down to a week for him. My room was closer to the attack he described, and though he claimed it had been loud enough to rouse him from sleep, I had heard nothing. I suspected he had dreamed it.

"I mean your health," I said.

"I'm tired. I shouldn't be losing to little kids. And I shouldn't miss e4 when Galzanov attacks my knight." He continued looking out the window. "Look at that. They've got a gate down there. What's that for?"

It was a standard wooden beam to block vehicles that did not belong to hotel guests. "It's a parking lot," I said.

"They don't need that, man."

Somehow it was evidence. He walked to the television and turned it on. I asked him again if he wanted to go for a walk. It was another beautiful day in Elista.

"What I want is a hot shower," he said.

"Glenn, do you think you're healthy?"

He stared at the television screen. I tried again.

"Are you convinced you're healthy?"

"Hallman," he said, "I'm all right."

"Why don't you get some sleep?"

"Hallman, the room is only so big for all these suggestions."

"I don't know what that means."

He didn't respond, and I left the room. A short while later, Bair failed to meet us in front of the House of Government, and the guards on the ground floor told us that Galzanov wasn't in either. Glenn spent the rest of the day moping about the hotel, and I took another walk through Elista. A phone call finally came that we were to meet Bair in front of the House of Government at 6:00. We would move to Chess City that night. By 6:20, Glenn was as agitated and upset as I had ever seen him. The smiles of the guards inside the House of Government suggested we were the victim of a joke. I'd long since decided that paranoia in Russia was the easiest of emotions, easier than love. Glenn became more and more somber, both his will and the skin of his face drooping sadly. I tried to prompt a conversation about what was happening, to generate in him some of the same suspicions I had been having of Bair. But Glenn's mind would allow him to consider only the truth of a situation, the facts of which he could be as certain as a mate-in-three. Conjecture was out of the question. Theory was only that which was essentially fact. He stood like the statue of Lenin just a few meters before us, frozen but withering awfully as the fading light approximated his mood.

"What do you think is happening here?" I asked him.

"I think Bair is late."

"But what do you think that indicates?"

"I think it indicates he's late."

"But why?"

"Because he's not here yet."

There was a pause, and we shuffled across the sidewalk, killing time. An old Kalmyk woman spotted us from across the square and approached, begging rubles, and when I gave her the coins in my pocket she went through a series of complex gesticulations and *spa-sibos,* wishing me good health and a good death. When she left, my eyes moved to the concrete, falling precisely to a small crevice in the cement that a steppe grasshopper had assumed for its tomb. It filled the spot neatly, looking mummified somehow, and might have been there for a thousand insect generations.

Finally, Glenn began to respond to my question. "You know, man, I was out hunting yesterday. We drove forever. We were supposed to hunt geese, but it was too dark when we got there. Everybody had guns. They all seemed friendly, but you never know. The middle of the steppe. And then that girl last night. I should have helped her. If that can happen to her—" He looked at me with only the vaguest suggestion of speculation, his imagination taking the form of fear, and it was the first time I could remember him guessing at anything. "I'm tired of being nervous all the time. I've seen enough of Kalmykia."

CHAPTER II

The Queen of Mongolia

She was out to win now. She would hammer at his weakness. She loved it. She loved attack.

—Walter Tevis, The Queen's Gambit, *1983*

As to whether a professional chess player would be a more suitable husband, it depends on whether I am still a strong chess player. If not, then a chess player is no use to me.

—WGM Xie Jun, *1990*

I LIKE YOUR IDEA ABOUT WRITING CHESS HISTORY IN KAL-
mykia, Baagi typed. *But I want to say this place is different than you are thinking. Kirsan Ilyumzhinov is the heart of this little republic and chess there. They do have nice tradition of chess, but they never have been center of chess until Kirsan. This republic of Russia is fallen down by economics and politics. People are fighting for their life every morning and living for their dinner.*

I was an American chess historian, Baagi was a Mongolian Women's International Master, and from my apartment in New Jersey I was watching her play, from her apartment in Utah, in the Internet's first international chess tournament, which wasn't really anywhere except in the minds of its participants. The event was held on the ICC. Baagi and I had met only electronically. She played the first round with a grandmaster from Argentina, then against a Bosnian international master living in Dallas. I was enthralled watching her games, the tangled idea webs of chess passing fast as light from her to me. We talked via the ICC's chat feature between rounds. Baagi was an experienced international player. She had played in the 33rd Chess Olympiad in Kalmykia, she spoke Russian, and she had met

Kirsan. That's how, before round three, she came to address our trip to Kalmykia.

Baagi's full name was Battsetseg Tsagaan. I had met her through Glenn, who had met her on the ICC while playing. A few games and some typed trash talking had spawned a friendly rivalry. I was intimidated by titled players on the ICC, but to Glenn titles didn't mean much compared to good chess and one day he told Baagi to say hello to me. She was as friendly as he was. When I apologized to her for not being a good chess player, she criticized my insecurity. *I don't like your comment about yourself,* she typed. *I never care what rating you have. As long as you love chess!*

A three-way friendship began to form, and often I watched the two of them play very late at night. The teasing became triangular, and I read both their jibes.

Yo, Baagi is mine, Glenn typed.

You see how he loses? Baagi typed. *You see?*

Baagi's handle on the ICC was "Bercmgl." I didn't know what it meant. Her full name included her title, so whenever she appeared on my screen the handle and the letters "WIM" came after it. The ICC's metaphor of a chess room was sustained by an automated notification program that sent out an announcement whenever a grandmaster logged on: *A hush fills the room as GM—— walks in!* On the day of the Internet tournament, my screen filled with hushes. The event was sponsored by some company or other and had as a first prize fifteen-hundred dollars and a paid trip to Iceland to play in a live tournament with several of the world's best players. This was enough to attract some pretty strong players in and of itself: 63 grandmasters (of a total of roughly 750 worldwide), and 94 other FIDE-titled players, including Baagi, which made the first cyberevent competitive with the largest live events.

Now, round three was about to begin.

Glenn was at work at our casino. Chess players in the United States have long noted that even menial labor tends to pay more than a life in the game, and if players couldn't afford to attend events that would allow them to progress, then Internet chess was the promise to change all that. The ICC monitored as many games in four days as the USCF rated in an entire year. It was the consensus that this was just the beginning. And the very first Internet event was already one of the most well-attended tournaments in chess history.

Baagi, playing from her living room while her two sons watched movies just next to her, had done nothing more than roll out of bed to play her first game in South America, a second in North America, and when round three began she crossed the Atlantic to her third continent of the day, to play a guy named Dmitri from Copenhagen.

Do you want to know what my handle means? Baagi typed to me, after she'd beaten Dmitri with a neat tactic. When she told me I realized I should have guessed it. The *c* was pronounced as an *s*, and Mongolians tended to substitute *b* for *f*, *Berc* was "fers"—*firzan*, queen—and *mgl* was Mongolia. *Bercmgl* meant "Queen of Mongolia."

LIKE THE HISTORY OF HISTORY, THE HISTORY OF CHESS IS A history of acceleration: Nearly every significant change to the game has seen it become faster in one way or another. With speed as the litmus, one would tend to favor China over India as the true birthplace of chess, as the older Chinese games—those predating even *xiangqi*—were even slower than India's *chaturanga*. Even the earliest incarnations of recognizable chess had rules meant to keep the game moving. Though the European changes to the game made the pieces abstractly faster, games of chess could still take a concrete eternity to complete. Games on the chess island off the coast of Iceland were said to last for weeks, and peoples of Northern Siberia at the turn of the twentieth century were reported to think nothing of allowing a contest to run through to a second day. Games at London 1851 had lasted sometimes twelve, sometimes twenty hours. Up until the modern era, chess was an upperhemisphere amusement for royal courts—a conspicuous waste of time for long winters. As the game speeded up, it trickled down both the economic ladder and the globe itself to become an amusement favored by cultures on the economic fringe. For Indian filmmaker Satyajit Ray, in his movie *The Chess Players*, the acceleration of the game served as a metaphor for British imperialism and intrusive Western technology.

The invention of chess clocks was the collision of literal speed with that of the abstract speed of quick pieces. Fluctuations in the balance between opposing concepts of time shaped the evolution of the game after its laws were established. Once chess became abstractly faster, it became more practical and more interesting to see the new "fastness" executed quickly. Early time controls required each player to make twenty moves per hour. Running out of time was a loss by forfeit. When pendulums replaced hourglasses, the time control changed first to thirty moves in two hours, then to forty moves in two and a half hours. These time controls would be followed by secondary controls—something like twenty moves per hour for everything after move forty. The standard time control for most of the modern era became 40/2½, 20/1.

Five-minute chess first became popular in the early twentieth century and went by a number of names: rapid chess, skittles, blitz. Chess with a flat time control of just a few minutes did not lend itself to deep theoretical games. This helped inspire lightning chess, a different kind of control in which each move was allotted ten or twenty seconds. This made it more difficult to run completely out of time. But lightning chess by itself was incomplete. The idea eventually merged with flat blitz, creating more complicated chess rules: a player would start with x minutes, and then be awarded y seconds for each move played. When Baagi played in the first major Internet tournament, each player started with five minutes, and a five-second "increment" was added after each move. If in the Middle Ages chess players had been forced to debate chess laws, then in the modern era the debates focused on how long the game would last.

What no one would deny was that time controls—and time trouble—made chess more exciting. Chess has often been compared to a drug, and Hans Ree attributed its high to time: "Time trouble is an addiction, perhaps even a physical addiction to the opium-like substances secreted by a chess player's brain during the time trouble phase." As a game, chess accelerated of its own accord, and tournament directors' experiments with clocks and time schemes were attempts to keep pace with its evolution. Time trouble was generally reserved for the last stages of a much longer contest, but the emergence of one-minute chess saw games *begin* in time trouble. The intense and sudden struggle was the goal rather than a tournament rarity. The Internet was perfectly suited to one-minute chess.

This was the state of the game when I came to it. After I'd met Baagi, I was able to watch her and Glenn play ten or fifteen bullet games consecutively, an entire match compressed down to half an hour. Capablanca had shocked his contemporaries by giving 5-1 time odds to the world's elite in 1914, but ninety years later playing a game in a minute still wasn't considered valid chess. Neither "one-minute chess" nor "bullet" was listed in my *Oxford Companion to Chess,* but bullet was easily the most popular time control on the ICC. Most ICC players, including many grandmasters, played far more bullet games than three minute, five minute, or any other time control. And in the same way that the dealers' lounge at the casino recalled thousand-year-old chess communities, so did one-minute chess throw the game back to Islamic styles and practices. I invented my own *ta'biya.* I put together an opening system of eight moves that were the same regardless of what my opponent did. Glenn hated my *ta'biya* because it didn't occupy the center, but I liked it because I usually came out of the opening with a time edge. My bullet rating rose. It continued to climb until it was higher than my ratings for slow chess. Before long I began to encounter many others on the ICC who played as I did, and when we played each other, each of us racing to pet positions, it was communion with history.

"That's not chess," Glenn said, a curmudgeon who didn't want to see the game evolve beyond his own learning, "that's just moving fast." Which was true—and that was the point. Even in tournament play, it was sometimes possible to exploit time to one's advantage. Mikhail Tal, considered one of the most exciting players the game has seen, said of his 1960 World Championship victory, "I know I made what appeared to be bad moves at times, but they served the purpose of making my opponent use up time." In every game of bullet, there came a moment when the entire metaphor of chess broke down, when the little battle of opposing armies ceased to apply, and players—grandmasters often among them—raced their pieces about the board, simply moving until their opponent ran out of time. Chess had emerged from early race games, and looked to be returning to them. In bullet, the skill, perhaps no less artful, seemed to be the ability to recognize the moment when it was wise to abandon chess completely, to allow it to evolve within its tiny instant.

GLENN AND BAAGI PLAYED ABOUT EQUALLY WELL. SOMETIMES Glenn would dominate, and sometimes Baagi would beat him effortlessly. When Baagi won, she would ask me to teach her idioms that she could use to tease him. I'll beat you silly, I taught her. I'll beat you like a red-headed stepchild. The next time they played, Baagi announced: *I am gonna beat you silly until you are like red stepchild!*

Glenn doubted that Baagi could beat him in a live game. "She's strong, man," he said. "But there isn't a woman in the world that can beat me one minute over-the-board."

If you stand before a globe and point fingers directly into Atlantic City, New Jersey, and Darkhan, Mongolia, the two fingers will aim almost directly toward one another: the cities are on opposite sides of the world. Glenn learned to play chess at age thirteen, Baagi at four. Which meant that sometime around 1976, the two of them were learning to play chess at just about the same time, as far apart from one another as humanly possible; and neither had any idea that they would one day meet, first electronically, and then in person with the help of a zealous chess historian who hoped to show that chess and the Internet could help destroy barriers of culture, race, gender, and geography, and that there was at least one woman in the world who could beat Glenn in over-the-board bullet.

But that didn't come until much later, long after Baagi played round four in the Web tournament, in which she went back to Argentina to play a FIDE master. The game was a slow, positional dance, and once she was in time trouble Baagi displayed her endgame knowledge to scrape out a sixty-one-move draw. *Gosh!* she wrote of the game, when it was complete. Just as Glenn used "Drats!" as his choice exclamation, Baagi said "Gosh!" in response to anything that was suddenly disappointing, or disappointingly sudden.

We had been friends for a few months by then. The relationship had first been limited to the Internet, then she called me one afternoon. I realized our mistake at once: Glenn and I had been pronouncing her name as though she was made of plastic. "Baaaahgi," she said. "Like sheep." She had a deep, gravelly voice, a sudden infectious laugh, and even when her English wasn't perfect it expressed a truth proper grammar missed. It wasn't long before she told me her history; and if Glenn's story as a chess player had made me think he needed to be saved, then Baagi's chess upbringing and the sweet story of her husband made me think she could save *us*.

BAAGI OWED ALL THE SUCCESS OF HER CHESS CAREER TO HER father. As a young dad, he had liked to relax with chess when he came home from work, and when Baagi was four years old she started to go along with him to the small park where people of their complex gathered to play. Baagi sat in his lap, and he allowed her to move the pieces as he instructed. This was how she learned, and one day, her father said, she showed him how he could win a game with a clever bishop move.

She remembered her years in the little park as the most enjoyable chess of her life. A table would always clear for her when she arrived, and small crowds would gather to cheer the thousands of offhand games she played before ever having a teacher. "Hey, don't get picture of me milking cow," she told me, of her parents' farm. "I don't know all that stuff because I was a princess all the time for only chess." As with Glenn, an encounter with a journalist had helped motivate her— a newspaper story about the young girl genius appeared after she won her first trophy. By the time she was in the seventh grade, her father could no longer beat her. He became more serious then, and brought in an expert named Sukhbaatar. Sukhbaatar taught Baagi opening knowledge, and every night after study time they played a few games, recording the moves and signing the scoresheets when they finished. She didn't play well in tournaments at first because she was used to the more raucous setting of the park, but when she became accustomed to formal tournament conditions success came quickly. In 1984, she became Women's Champion of Darkhan.

In 1987, Baagi's father had a stroke and was unable to watch her play in her second Women's Championship of Mongolia. She had placed fifth the year before, but this time around she won both the championship and became the youngest Mongolian ever to achieve the title of master. Her father recovered with the help of a bonesetter, but he could no longer travel with his daughter. Baagi went on to win the Women's Championship six more times, and became famous across Mongolia. Stories of the young, small-town girl—renamed Battsetseg of Darkhan—appeared on radio and television. She traveled on her own, winning tournaments—Tonshuul-International 1989, Gdansk 1989. In 1990, she was ranked ninth on FIDE's world-wide list for women under twenty. In the same year, Baagi became the first Mongolian to win a zonal championship, and it was from this tournament that she achieved the title of international master.

In the meantime she had come to know Enkhbat (EK) Tegshuren, a young up-and-coming Mongolian player. They saw one another often, playing in competitions between cities. EK was a university student—he would achieve a degree in hydroengineering—and though their relationship was close, it was simply friendly at first. Once, when Baagi was in the tenth grade, she and EK played in a tournament in the Mongolian countryside near Irkutsk. Baagi thought of EK as a big brother, but when she won the tournament and EK signed her award "To My Loving Sister," Baagi swooned. It was her first instant of romantic inclination.

Several years passed before Baagi and EK would come to know each other any better. Because Baagi was already famous by then, EK wondered whether he was good enough for her. 1990 found them both representing Mongolia at the Chess Olympiad in Novi Sad. The Mongolian men's and women's teams were housed in the same building. One day Baagi was studying alone in her room when she heard someone in the hallway whistling a Mongolian tune. She opened the door and it was EK.

Novi Sad was Baagi's career highlight. She scored 9.5 out of 13 on first board against grandmaster opponents, and the Mongolian team won first place in the second division of the Women's Olympiad. 9.5 out of 13 was an excellent result, but perhaps not as good as the result of her decision to open the door to her future husband. Together, they would use the game to make a life for themselves, and have the two boys who sat nearby in Utah as Baagi played chess and chatted with me.

Now, I am kind of crazy mom, she wrote. *Studying full time, working part time as tutor at math lab, and staying on ICC. I am too much attracted on it!*

IN ROUND FIVE BAAGI WAS PAIRED AGAINST A PLAYER WHOSE handle was "WhitneyHouston."

Whitney Houston! Baagi typed. *My favorite singer!*

The game was intense, and the handle WhitneyHouston was sinister for its brazen anonymity. WhitneyHouston played well, but made a slight mistake in the endgame that empowered Baagi's remaining knight, and she gobbled up a pair of pawns and won in seventy moves.

Gosh! Baagi wrote. *Really gosh!*

Several weeks before I had found Baagi's old games in my computer database. She had played in Azov, Nuremburg, Moscow, Manila. She had sat across from a women's world champion, and she had beaten a contender. I printed her scores from the Novi Sad Olympiad and called Glenn to tell him I had an exercise for him, more anonymous games.

He came by that night after work. He walked about my apartment for a while, reading some of the chess quotations I had collected. He was in a sour mood: He had lost his master ranking the week before. He was trying to see it as a value—he would be eligible for the expert section of that year's World Open—but really it drained him. Baagi's style confused him. Sometimes he thought the games were distinctly American, other times tacitly European. He cited a broad range of strengths and dates. "This was definitely after 1982," he said of one game. Another was obviously 1990–present. Sometimes, though, he couldn't make up his mind. Games were either modern contests between weak masters, or they were grandmasters from the '30s. "This looks like it could be Réti or somebody," he said once. Another game put Baagi in the company of Gulko or Shabalov. It was all high praise.

"That's Baagi?" he said, when I revealed it. He looked at her final winning position. "*Man. Baagi is strong.*"

It was rare for Glenn to grant women praise. Chess players often found happiness in marriage to other chess players, but Glenn had not been so fortunate; and the general disconnect he experienced in his marriage and romance had ignited a smoldering misogyny in him. "She doesn't like it that I play chess so much," I had heard him say of more than one of his fleeting relationships. Once, Glenn told me, he had spent all day on the phone trying to track down a woman whose picture he had seen in a chess magazine, a young Nigerian player. Her name was S. Chidi. Glenn did not speak the language, but he managed to get through to a relative of Chidi's who redirected him to a chess tournament where she was playing. He called the tournament and was told she was married.

BAAGI'S SUCCESS IN INTERNATIONAL CHESS INSPIRED THE Mongolian government to devote resources to the game. Opportunities for Mongolian chess players increased dramatically. Baagi's greatest successes corresponded perfectly with the country's transition to democracy. But corruption pushed Baagi and EK to the decision to leave Mongolia in the mid-'90s. They thought of Germany first, but Baagi's coach happened to meet a representative of a Utah state college. A meeting was arranged. Baagi came to the United States first as a student, and completed the paperwork for EK and their sons. They had kept their heads above water since then by teaching chess, tutoring math, and working after-hour cleaning jobs for sometimes twelve hours at a stretch. They played blitz games with one another with chores as a wager and saved money to travel and compete in tournaments. In the few years they had been here, they had managed to play all across the country—EK was a 2400 player, and Baagi, by rating, was ranked fifth among women in the nation. Not long after we started speaking on the phone, she asked me to help her with applications to the University of Texas and the University of Maryland, where there were chess scholarships available.

During the Internet tournament, I decided to sponsor Baagi and EK to come to the World Open that year. It was still six months off, but Glenn was already studying for it. I was just as interested in the tournament as I was in organizing a bullet match between Baagi and Glenn in our dealers' lounge. I thought of the setting and the opponents as the most unlikely chess match ever held, proof that the game could truly unite people.

I spent all day watching Baagi play. When the Internet tournament was over, I felt like I'd read a novel in one sitting. Baagi and I typed back and forth awhile longer even though her boys and my dog were growing restless. I offered to pay her plane fare to the tournament. She was excited, and we made a deal—I would spring for the tickets, and she would play the match with Glenn.

Before then, though, Baagi and EK would play another live tournament in Las Vegas. She asked me to root for her. *I will play with top GM in first round. If I beat him, that would be big surprise for him, yeah? Well, I will try my best. Check broadcast in Las Vegas. If it is shiny sunny, that means I am doing alright!*

CHAPTER 12

Developing Your Pieces: ♖

Thow shalt mate hym with a Pon at v draughtis yf thou play wel affter thy Roke, and if thou knowe itt not thou shalnot mate hym at ix draughtis ffor he woll tel his draughtis for cause of thi Roke.

—The Ashmole Manuscript, *1470*

. . . but when the rukh gets behind them and attacks them from the rear, he destroys them just as horsemen in war destroy the foot soldiers.

—as-Suli, *c. tenth century*

WORDS LIKE PAWN, ENDGAME, AND STALEMATE HAVE transcended chess, entering the common vocabulary with definitions inspired by the game, though the meanings have slipped. Although the movement of the rook is like the knight in its constancy through chess history, the name of the piece is a point of debate among historians and illustrates the way in which chess interacts with language, first reacting to it, then helping to determine it, then being forgotten by it.

The rook's movement and its strength relative to the other pieces has generally suggested the mechanical, vehicles or articles of war. Most often, the rook is infrastructure. As a line piece that can access all the squares of the board—moving in a straight line on either ranks or files and capturing along its path—the rook combines the abstract potentials of the knight and the bishop. Before the piece came to be represented by the figure of a crenelated castle tower, a depiction that appeared between 1524 and 1550, the rook was often portrayed as a two-headed shape. Early carvings of both bishops and knights were upright figures with some kind of aslant protuberance; early rooks had two such projections. In ornate sets it was a knight with two horse heads instead of one. Early chess players knew well the relative values of chess pieces, and the shape of the rook, regardless of what vehicle, structure, or creature it seemed to resemble, suggested a value roughly double that of the knight. This still holds true: The modern rook's value is generally considered to be almost twice that of either the bishop or the knight.

The rook began as either a chariot or a ship, and as with the debate over bishops and elephants, chess historians argued over what role ships would have played in the military affairs of nations central to the dawn of chess. Murray was certain that the term *rukh* meant "chariot." But cultures adopted foreign chess terms as often as they translated them. This created problems. Arabia understood that *rukh* meant "chariot," but at the same time *roka* was Sanskrit for "ship." As the game traveled into jungly Southeast Asia, a ship on the chessboard made a lot more sense than a chariot, and *roka* was familiar to Hindus there, while *rukh* was foreign. The pull of chess realism was such that ship displaced chariot independently in a number of nations. As the game moved through Asia, piggybacked on Buddhism, the transformation of the rook paralleled the evolution of war, in some countries inspiring an additional piece, the cannon, which like the rook could capture at any distance, but which was required, like a projectile, to leap over an intervening piece. Among other Asian peoples, the rook was transformed into the carts or wagons familiar to nomads.

Europe experimented with a number of images for rooks: Germany tried *marchio,* lord of the marches, England tried *duke,* and a fifteenth-century morality listed rooks as *judges* for three reasons: a rook cannot play until a way is opened for it; a rook is in danger when on the same color as the king; and a rook loses power when it is "in the King's palace" (i.e., not yet castled). In the end the Christians adopted the word "rook," but without a proper definition they looked locally for what it might mean. *Rocca* was Italian for fortress. When the chessboard came to be viewed as a miniature nation-state, fortress won over and now castle and tower are as common a name for the piece as rook. That the fortresses move, and move quickly, was a stretch, but by the Middle Ages the metaphor of the game had already begun a transformation. The movement of rooks might well suggest an expansion of territory rather than a flanking maneuver on a particular battlefield. One chess historian suggested that the new carving of the rook as a castle was meant to suggest the rolling wooden towers used in sieges. Though a compelling image, the writer cited no reference for the supposition, and it seems just as likely that the towers were inspired by the rook as the other way around.

Rooks are major pieces along with the queen. They are stronger when they are "connected" or "doubled," occupying most often the same file but occasionally the same rank. Adjacent to one another or with no friendly piece in between, connected rooks exert an influence stronger than that of a solitary queen. To force a win with major pieces is common, but it's a mistake to think of rooks as inelegant because they are brutish. How a rook works in conjunction with another rook is sublime on a less easily accessed level. Even alone, rook moves can seem unusual. The exact opposite of the knight, rooks are more desirably placed at the edges of the board than near the center. Strong rook moves toward the center of the board thus offer the aesthetic beauty of breaking the "rules" that dictate solid play. What's now called the "mysterious rook move" originally meant the movement of a rook to a closed file as a preemptive measure, but the term is coming to mean any rook move that occupies or traverses the center of the board. The tactical fireworks available to a rook generally come in the form of sacrifice, trading itself for a knight or a bishop in a maneuver called "sacking the exchange." The rook's glory is vicarious.

Although the word "rook" itself has been dropped from many languages in favor of tower or castle, its influence lingers in heraldry—images of the two-headed piece appear in the coats of arms of families with rooklike names: Rookwood, Rocold, Rochlitz, Rochow, Rochette, Rochemore, and others. But whatever impression the word "rook" originally may have made, it's now phasing out. Even the earliest chess historians couldn't say what the word truly meant, and the non sequitur of it confused or displeased those who would make chess a microcosm. Rook was heinous from the beginning.

Nonchess players use pawn as similar to puppet, a lamentable small and expendable figure. Lost is the image of a phalanx of pawns preparing to promote one of their own. We use endgame and stalemate mostly in the context of sporting events and politics, stages in campaigns that are the most boring for the titillated fan. Both uses are incorrect, of course. The very fact that an endgame in chess is appreciably finite gives it a kind of excitement that perhaps only a scientist can appreciate, and the art of engineering a stalemate from a lost position is a precious phenomenon in chess. The same brand of journalists who tittered in print at the idea of Chess City employ chess terms regularly, occasionally unaware that they have done so. Chess itself is approaching the linguistic obsolescence that the rook already knows, both of them lingering anachronisms of unknown origin.

CHAPTER 13

Illuminating Ilyumzhinov

. . . by means of this game emperors consult with demons concerning victory: it is a temptation of Satan.

—c. sixteenth century

Now you know as well as I that the Glass Bead Game also has its hidden diabolus, that it can lead to empty virtuosity, to artistic vanity, to self-advancement, to the seeking of power over others and then to the abuse of that power.

—Hermann Hesse, The Glass Bead Game, 1943

IN 1616, THE FIRST TRIBES OF KALMYKS HEADING WEST toward the Caspian Sea cast enough of a shadow to bring Russia to cut off relations with China. The Kalmyks' first 150 years in Russia were largely defined by the question of whether they would remain an independent nation or become subjects of the czar. They enjoyed several decades of near autonomy under the leadership of Ayuki Khan, who ruled the Kalmyks three hundred years before Kirsan Ilyumzhinov.

Ayuki had been born in Djangharia in 1640, the same year of the great meeting of Oirat and Mongol leaders that established Tibetan Buddhism as the glue binding Inner Asian peoples. Ayuki spent his first twelve years in Djangharia, then traveled to the North Caspian steppe with his grandfather, Daichin, who ruled the Kalmyks until 1661. Ayuki's father became khan, but died just eight years later.

Resistance to Ayuki's ascension appeared immediately from Kalmyk leaders in the east, south, and west. Ruthlessness was the solution: Ayuki formed a temporary alliance with an uncle, Dugar, and asked Russia for help. Once the alliance was no longer necessary, Ayuki slandered his uncle and led a campaign against him.

History forgives betrayal: Evil becomes shrewd in a few generations, murders downgraded from crimes to maneuverings like chess moves. Ayuki had become familiar with strategy and tactics. Wealth and power brought him prestige among neighboring peoples, and the broken alliance with Dugar presaged his handling of a series of oaths Moscow asked him to sign. Russia wanted loyalty from Ayuki, but he was defiant, courting relationships with foreign powers. Throughout the late seventeenth century, the Kalmyks would be a prized ally and a feared enemy for their warriors' horsemanship, which allowed them to move efficiently across the steppe. They were known to rush behind an army's lines and sack unprotected towns. The Kalmyks were like a rook that could sneak past pawns and wreak havoc on an opponent's seventh rank. A common maxim of chess states that a threat is more powerful than its execution, and fear of the Kalmyks was enough to dissuade enemies from marching against them at all.

In 1688, Ayuki granted himself the title of khan, and two years later the official title arrived from the Dalai Lama. In an early exercise in propaganda, Ayuki made the preposterous claim to being a descendant of Genghis Khan, and soon thereafter he signed the first document with Russia that acknowledged the two as equal powers.

Opportunity came in 1697: Ayuki brokered the first firearms deal with Moscow, and back in Djangharia the Oirat khan died, offering a lure of power. Literal lust compounded the lust for influence. Another Oirat leader discovered that Ayuki was planning to assassinate him and promptly absorbed sixty thousand Kalmyks. And in 1701, Ayuki was caught in an affair with one of his daughters-in-law. In the wake of the sex scandal, his sons postured for power as though Ayuki was already dead. The weak khan was forced to flee to Russia, and with its help the king run worked. By the end of the decade, Ayuki's power had been restored.

Ayuki used every tactic he knew to maintain a precarious balance in the second decade of the eighteenth century. Kalmyk prosperity continued for a time. In 1722, Peter the Great visited Ayuki to request horsemen for a campaign. The two men met again a few months later so that Ayuki could secure his choice of heir. But both men would be dead within three years, and the agreement would have little influence in the ensuing power struggle.

When the real succession crisis began, Kalmyk society was rent by internal war. They would never again enjoy prosperity in Russia. Ayuki had been a bridge. He was born in the same year the Oirats adopted Buddhism, and he died the year the Bible was first translated into Kalmyk.

IN FRONT OF THE HOUSE OF GOVERNMENT, GLENN ASKED THAT we wait awhile longer for Bair, just the promise of a hot shower worth the suffering of whatever we would endure. He gave up by 7:00, and we stumbled back to Hotel Elista.

By then I'd had a chance to begin Kirsan's autobiography, *The President's Crown of Thorns,* which Galzanov had handed over in exchange for Glenn's problem book. In Ilyumzhinov's description of the '93 coup attempt, he proved that Russians were just as susceptible to Russian paranoia as non-Russians were. He believed that the Russian White House had been irradiated during the days of unrest, with the goal of mollifying those inside, and he cited an expert in "psychotropic warfare and zombifying tactics" who suggested that guards outside the building had been given drinks spiked with "mind-bending ingredients."

I'd had the crazy thought that Glenn and I had been drugged, and not just with funny vodka. It seemed possible in Russia, where paranoia itself could have been the effect of something slipped into your mutton. But I was feeling much better after my policy of forcing down water. Glenn was still drinking very little, eating and sleeping less. His best hope for recovery, I thought, was chess, and when we got upstairs I suggested that we play in his room for the rest of the evening. I was surprised when he agreed. I stowed my satchel in a closet, and when I went down the hall I found Glenn on the telephone. It was a woman from FIDE's Elista office, he said. Just an hour before, they had been informed of our arrival in Kalmykia. They would call again later. Glenn and I reacted to the news with identical skepticism. We set up our board and pieces.

I wanted to play, but Glenn insisted I needed a lesson. He gave me instruction on safe opening play for black. A good rule, he said, was to establish one of four central pawns to the fourth rank early on. "You're never gonna have a good game with black unless you understand this principle," he said. "No matter what you do, you're forced to put one of those pawns on the fourth rank. The position tells you which one. Failure to do so will automatically give you a bad position."

"Let's play one," I said.

He went on as though I had not spoken at all, moving forward a little in his chair to begin shifting the pieces. "Suppose something like this happens. You can still play a move like this. And if he takes again, then knight takes pawn, with complications." His fingers clicked the pieces against one another, the sound of the leaded butts like the kiss of billiard balls. "There's always stuff—there's always a way to regain the pawn—but if you want a nice simple defense, then you can do it this way no matter what white plays. Make sure you get this move in. There's even no rush to castle. You have no weaknesses."

He was beginning to sound more like himself, and he looked down at the position as though it was the work of a painter he admired and understood. I asked him to play again, but we made it through only five or six moves before it was clear that I was not enough of a force to distract him from the predicament of Kalmykia. He went back into lecture mode.

When there came a knock at the door, it seemed almost an imposition and it was a moment before we looked at one another and realized there was a stranger at our door in a remote corner of Russia.

It was a delegation in the hallway. A heavy Kalmyk man in a suit carrying a high-powered walkie-talkie, and a young pretty Kalmyk woman who I recognized right away as the translator who had walked between Chuck Norris and Ilyumzhinov at the Chess City construction site. The woman introduced herself as Bambusha. She spoke English. It had been Bambusha whom Glenn had spoken to on the phone, and the man, Sanal Kugultinov, was a personal adviser to the president.

"I spoke with Bair and asked him why he did not appear," Sanal said. "We are here to introduce ourselves. And to talk to you regarding the goals of your visit."

Bambusha looked about the clutter of Glenn's room and asked whether this was the proper setting for a meeting. Sanal said that he did not have much time as in an hour or so he was going to the airport. President Ilyumzhinov was scheduled to return to the republic at 10:00. The president was coming! It was an event in Kalmykia, and even Sanal and Bambusha seemed anxious.

"You would like to interview the president?" Sanal said.

Yes, I said, and I went on to explain our interest in Kalmykia. Sanal nodded as a call came in over his walkie-talkie. As a group, we began to move toward the hallway.

"I am the FIDE projects manager," Bambusha said. "We handle ratings and the magazine, *FIDE Forum*. I work in the FIDE office, which is situated in Chess City. Have you visited Chess City?"

Bambusha was sweet and beautiful with a round face and high, arching eyebrows and her hair neatly slicked back on her head and a pair of sunglasses perched at the peak of her brow, though dark had long since fallen. Her lips were decorated with a precise splotch of red. She was a lucky Kalmyk with perfect teeth and dimples.

"The FIDE office is in one of the cottages," she said. "You are, of course, welcome to come and ask us questions."

"Excellent," I said.

Sanal eventually went to the airport, and Bambusha offered to take us to Chess City to await the president's arrival. Our interview might take place that evening. We took a cab and visited the FIDE office first, a cottage that from the outside appeared to have never been lived in. It had the comfort of prefab architecture, the shallow pleasure of sheetrock walls. Underneath, the Chess City cottages were the same cement blocks as everything else, but the smell of the plaster exterior was to Americans like the smell of home cooking.

Here we met Altana, a woman every bit as beautiful as Bambusha, and Casto Abundo, a chubby Filipino who was in charge of FIDE's Elista branch. I had read about Abundo in a book about chess politics; he was a player who had given up playing to pursue a career in the game's administrative network. Abundo had heavy bags under his eyes. He welcomed us, then hurried off while Bambusha and Altana showed us around. There was little furniture in the FIDE cottage, and the walls were bare. I spotted a copy of Jeremy Gaige's *Chess Personalia* on a shelf, a famous text among historians, and Altana found Glenn's FIDE rating in their database. Neither Altana nor Bambusha actually played chess, but they handled the FIDE ratings of thousands of players from all over the world. They were amused by the many letters that came to them with the greeting "Dear Sirs."

The four of us walked to Chess Palace, a hundred meters from the FIDE cottage. The Congress on Traditional Medicine was over now, and the building was deserted. Glenn's mood had changed since the turn of events, and he was giddy now, anxious to entertain the women. He jumped onto the giant chessboard on the ground floor of Chess Palace, made himself erect on a center square, and announced, "Living chess!"

We had coffee on the second floor. Bambusha and Altana were distant cousins. They were both twenty-three and had spent time in the United States, Bambusha a year in Wisconsin, Altana a month in Atlanta. Bambusha revealed that she loved regional American accents, and before long Glenn was doing a medley of bad impersonations, caricatures of cartoon characters and movie figures, sometimes stepping away for a moment to practice and then lunging at Bambusha with a bad impression of Shaft or Foghorn Leghorn. Bambusha swooned and told us how people in America, intimidated by her name, had decided to call her Mitsubishi instead.

I smiled at Altana every chance I could. Bambusha was like a Kalmyk yuppie or dot-com phenom, professional and made up and equipped with a beeper and a cell phone, but Altana was more like a Kalmyk hippie, with long, straight hair and little makeup and a band of freckles across her eyes like the mask of a raccoon. The three feet between the two women was a continuum of the range of possible loveliness. I found myself fighting against the fear that they were another dupe. They were so kind. They seemed too overjoyed at the campy vision of America that Glenn was acting out beside me now with imitations of a number of characters from *Forrest Gump*, that text of idiot adventure and accidental success.

Bambusha called Galzanov to ask what they should do with us, and it was decided we would move to Chess City that evening after all. Bambusha and Altana would accompany us back to Hotel Elista to collect our belongings, we would have a brief meeting with Galzanov, and then we would return to a cottage already chosen for us. We stood up to go. Bambusha put on her coat and looked over the rail into the gut of Chess Palace.

"Oh, the president is here!"

We walked to the rail. Down below Kirsan moved into Chess Palace behind a handful of handlers. As in his pictures, Ilyumzhinov was thin and short, and his suits, I noticed, fit him loosely, jacket shoulders drooping past the bend of his actual shoulders. He had his hands in his pockets. I liked that, actually. He was showing off the building, his pride, to a group of five men who had arrived with him. Our foursome circled down the spiraling stairs to watch the great man be great up close.

"He looks so tired," Bambusha said.

He didn't look tired to me. But the precise sculpture of his hair called attention to a pocked aspect in his complexion. He looked worn. Kirsan had three prominent facial moles. He rarely smiled, I saw, because his teeth were bad. Now he was over by the model of Chess City, gesturing up at the pictures on the walls for his guests, those of himself with Chuck Norris. Sanal had arrived as well, and he approached to speak with Bambusha for a moment. Our interview would be delayed. The president himself spotted us as Bambusha translated, and he edged up a short of flight of stairs to where we were standing. Up close, Kirsan had the air of a celebrity with a lost sense of himself. The whole of Chess Palace focused on our landing as Ilyumzhinov shook hands with Glenn, then with me. For a moment he seemed as confused and distracted by the hubbub as we were. He seemed to glow, as with the knowledge that he might be assassinated at any moment. Every instant was primarily new. "I will be meeting with you after tomorrow," he said, in English, though it sounded more like a prophecy than a plan. He looked up into Chess Palace as though its architecture was new even to him, then nodded and moved on as if we were a pleasing but forgettable exhibit in a museum open for him alone.

We headed back to Hotel Elista for our bags. Upstairs, the flags of my paranoia went up again, and as Glenn and I packed I asked him what he thought the chances were that Bambusha and Altana would be gone when we returned downstairs.

"They'll be there," he said, confidence all he had left.

They were there, smiling and perfect. We needed two taxis now with our bags, two Volgas that waited for us outside the House of Government. Galzanov, still working up in his dark office, offered no apology for Bair, whose failure to appear was a mystery to him as well, he said. He took credit for both the president's arrival and our move to Chess City. He finished with the hope that Bambusha and Altana were adequate compensation for the loss of Bair. Our foursome smiled.

An hour later, in a warm Chess City cottage, still wet from my first hot shower in I wasn't sure how long, I sat in our kitchen, typing on my laptop late into the night. Glenn had gone to bed. Just out our window was a billboard commemorating the Olympiad. Lit from below, the poster depicted a massive hand descending on a chessboard, plucking a pawn from its home and shifting it to d4. The hand appeared disembodied in the electricless Russian night, and my eyes kept wandering to the huge luminous fingers playing chess in the dark. I felt guilty. My Russian paranoia had been persistent, and earlier, when Bambusha had suggested that she ride with our bags in one taxi, and Altana ride with us in another, I had flinched. Our taxi made it to Chess City first and Altana ran into the palace to collect our key so that for a moment, Glenn and I stood on a street in Chess City in the middle of the night, not knowing where any of our belongings were. It seemed almost an appropriate joke to plant us there. But then the lights of Bambusha's taxi appeared, and Altana came running out of the palace, like damsels coming to the rescue of knights in distress, and now all was well except that while I remembered that moment, savored its shame in the warmth of a Chess City kitchen, the lights flickered once—the city was autonomous, but not independent—and then went out, and even the godly chess-playing hand vanished into black.

I READ THE BULK OF *THE PRESIDENT'S CROWN OF THORNS* during our first two days in Chess City. It and the international journalists' version of the same story were tellings of a history still elusive.

The plot of the autobiography was framed by a pentangle of revelations. The president knew epiphany. The book opened with the first: The young Ilyumzhinov climbed a telephone pole on a neighborhood dare and, slipping, found himself suspended upside-down. His inverted vision of the world applied not only to what he could see then and there, but to the cultural state of Russia. It was political awakening.

His second revelation came just after high school—insignificance, this time. "Staring into the infinite abyss of the black, velvety night sky I suddenly felt consumed by love," the president wrote, "and I am just the merest speck of dust in this boundless, living world." The thought humbled him; and as his friends rushed off to college, Kirsan chose the more austere path of a job at an industrial plant.

Revelation number three was the comfort of predestination and arrived when he and several friends became lost driving the steppe. Two black dots appeared on the horizon. They made for what turned out to be two shepherds playing chess. "The two herdsmen," Kirsan wrote, "were holding sway and disposing of the destinies of their little chess soldiers in the infinitely complex world of the board's black-and-white checks. Is this not the way that destiny casts its shadow over us in the world?"

Number four came long after he'd gone to school and made his fortune. On a trip to France, he wandered into Notre Dame and looked up at the crucified Christ. Kirsan was a Buddhist, but he believed the stories of Buddha, Christ, and Muhammad were chapters torn from a single great book. He was in Paris on business, but the majesty of the cathedral carried him away from things earthly. It was the Big Picture revelation. Looking at Christ, he felt an acute yearning for the life he had lived prior to his reincarnation. Organ music streamed down, and his soul cried.

Kirsan reflected on all he'd done to that point and ideas for reform began to come to him. He considered running for the presidency. He knew that his popularity would not last if he ran, and because the decision was difficult, he flew to Bulgaria to consult with the famous clairvoyant, Vanga.

"Jesus, you are so young!" Vanga said. "I see flowers. Go to your people."

Kirsan then asked the Dalai Lama for blessings just as Ayuki Khan had done three hundred years before. A photo of their meeting decorated a street in Elista.

His last revelation came just after he took office, during the '93 coup attempt. Until hostilities began, Kirsan had managed to remain outside political coalitions in Moscow. Now he tried to bring about a peaceful solution to the crisis by staying in the White House for three days. When tanks opened fire, Kirsan led a delegation to remove women and children from the building. The revelation came as snipers' bullets streamed over his head. He cut his hand on a shard of glass, and his hot blood fell to the floor where it mixed with the cold blood of a dead other. The revelation was brotherhood, a bond formed with the casualties of every Russian atrocity ever.

The last chapter of *The President's Crown of Thorns* was entirely devoted to his assumption of the presidency of FIDE. As Kirsan imagined the future of chess, himself, and Kalmykia, it was indeed as though they were all one. Life itself was a game of chess, cerebral and pristine; and sometimes, at the end of a long workday, he looked to the heavens where there was lyricism and the potential for new revelation:

> . . . *I go up to the window of my office. In the thickened pre-dawn blackness of the sky I can see the sparkling, shimmering and twinkling stars. . . .*
> *The two halves of the cosmic chessboard have already been joined on the plains of the Milky Way. The chessmen have taken their places. I start a new game with fate and make my first move. May success attend me!*

IF THE KALMYKS' PROBLEM WAS THAT THEY WERE WANDERERS who had been forced to stay in one place, then our problem was that we were sedentary folk who had been kept on the move. I had hoped Glenn's shower and our new fixed home in Chess City would improve his mood, but the accommodations had simply kept him breathing. He did not stir from his fetal bundle when I opened his door in the morning and asked if he wanted to explore Chess City.

A walk through Chess City in the morning would become my routine. Without any conference underway, the city was a ghost town, though every morning several men appeared to sweep the streets with twig brooms. It did not seem to bother them that the city's landscaping had been slaughtered by steppe weeds and that their efforts did little to improve the appearance of the street. It was Kalmykia, after all, where weeds had come to stand for landscaping, and what should they know of boxwood or ice plant or juniper? I walked just across the street to Chess Palace, and looked at the model of Phase I on the ground floor. The small model cottages at the rear outskirts of the city were unfinished. But this was accurate: the structures they represented outside were cluttered brick affairs never completed. I walked through the palace, and began to notice the shortcuts that had been taken in its construction, the hints of its decline. The plastic floors had begun to curl with age, and amoebas of grime reenacted the birth of multicellular life in dark corners. A few windows had shattered, and others showed the scrape of wind and the bleeding excrement of birds.

Back outside, I discovered that Chess City had its strays, several cats and a little yellow dog, an odd breed with a plump dachshund's body. The little dog had a strategy like everything else trying to survive the steppe. Hers was to jiggle along beside anyone who appeared, and upon being given any attention whatsoever roll on her back and expose her belly. I named her Steppe Dog. Steppe Dog was dirty with three different colors of mud, but she chugged along happily and was chubby enough to suggest that her begging strategy was good enough to eke out a living here. I made a note to stuff a fruit bar into my bag for her.

Steppe Dog seemed to recognize that I was a good investment, and she followed me as I took a tour of the streets. Out in the parking lot near the gate, I saw several men dressed in camouflage climbing into a truck. This was the Chess City army. Really, they were more like a militia or a police force, but their fatigues and their truck were decidedly military, and sometimes I saw them tooling through the streets as though it were a combat zone. I walked around the edge of the city, casually scanning for Yudina's pond. Just north of the fence was a large depression in the earth, a few squared-off acres. It might have been a man-made lake once. I crimped my fingers into the chain link and looked into the hole. Overhead, the morning cloud cover lay still as a layer of moss on the pond I imagined, and the rhythm of two ropes banging against a flagpole seemed the inspiration for traditional Kalmyk music, played on two-stringed instruments. I sat on a bench near the Mickey Mouse pawn and listened. Steppe Dog panted at my feet.

I had spent the earlier part of the morning reading the president's autobiography. Chess City was beginning to fall apart just two years after it had been constructed, and so was argument enough against many of Kirsan's claims; but there were other irregularities in the book as well that made it an unreliable account. The night before Galzanov had asked that I submit interview questions for the president. I didn't intend to confront Kirsan on the irregularities, and began to compose a few softballs for him as I rose and walked toward the rear of town. I discovered a break in the fence that Chess City employees used as a shortcut in walking from Elista. I feared what the Chess City army would do if I left the city myself, and continued on inside the fence, passing the row of unfinished brick cottages, life-size this time but long since infested with plants and drifts of sand that threatened to pry them apart. Ilyumzhinov. In the preface to *The Defense,* Vladimir Nabokov's chess novel, Nabokov said that he chose the name Luzhin for his fictional grandmaster because "it rhymes with 'illusion' if pronounced thickly enough to deepen the 'u' into 'oo'." The 'y' in the president's name made this shift compulsory, and the English near-homonym was clear: illuminate. The president had a crown of thorns, and he had let there be light. There were as many saviors in Kalmykia as there were revelations, and I realized that the glowing hand out my window the night before had most certainly been Kirsan's.

I came to the road that was supposed to lead into the next phase of Chess City, the asphalt ending at a hopeful mound of dirt. Heading back to our cottage, I got my first look at the front of Chess Palace from a remove. What had been difficult to discern of it up close was obvious at a distance. It was a *kibitka:* the glass front of the palace was a giant modernized version of those round, dunce-capped tents. But what the ancient nomads had known about the steppe was lost on the modern Kalmyk architects who had constructed their vision on ground never meant for permanent structures. The nomads had been nomads for more reasons than one, and the buildings of Chess City already showed cracks and wear, as though from earthquakes. Indeed, I had to watch for sudden holes in the sidewalk where the land had receded beneath it. Walking back to our cottage, I noticed that there were manhole covers in the streets, but no sewer openings.

Bair was a no-show again that morning. We had seen him for the last time. Back in the cottage, I scribbled notes. The night before, the cottage had seemed warm and comfortable, but now it seemed too warm and was filled with flies. The house, like the city itself, had been put together on a shoestring budget and in the nick of time. The drapes were thin, the floor was plastic, the couches hard. The Kalmyk suburban vision was less an idealized America, than a real one. They had shot for Disneyland, but instead achieved a squalor only slightly more perfect than their own.

I was hungry. In a country known for hospitality, Glenn and I had not had a proper meal in two days. I was almost grateful for Glenn's sardines, and I thought of him now. It was typical chess player antics—and in the spirit of Fischer—to talk big and travel half the world only to gripe about conditions. Strictly speaking, I was frustrated with him not because he had failed to act like a chess player, but because he had. I made a new resolution to care for him. I checked in on him again, still scrunched on his bed, and told him that I was going out to look for food. He said he wasn't hungry.

"Glenn, you haven't eaten since Thursday."

"It's okay, Hallman."

He was back on emotional autopilot, and I left him there like a man leaving a wounded comrade on top of a mountain. Back out in Chess City, I looked down a few of the identical streets. Earlier, I had seen Abundo watering a plant outside his private cottage. I knocked, and he listened carefully to our troubles and allowed me to phone Bambusha and Altana. They promised to arrive at Chess City at 1:00. At 12:30, the doorbell rang and I thrilled: Our lovely Kalmyk champions were early.

But it wasn't them. It was Sasha, the Chess Champion of Kalmykia, and his father.

"Oh boy," I said.

Sasha's father wore a suit and a droopy Russian mustache. Somehow they had heard we were here. They came inside and we sat in the kitchen, and I set about trying to explain that Altana and Bambusha would be arriving shortly. Not much of this got through, and Sasha and his father exchanged a glance that said I had missed some profoundly simple point. Sasha's father took a moment to compose a short English sentence.

"You no want play?"

Drunk and paranoid, scared and hungry, submerged in chess politics, and finally cordoned off in the failed utopia of Chess City, I had simply forgotten that anyone might want to play chess just for the fun of it. I smiled and nodded and walked back to Glenn's room.

"Glenn."

"Yeah, Hallman."

"The Champion of Kalmykia is here."

Their match took place in Chess Palace. Sasha's entire family had accompanied him, brother, sister, and mother, all of them dressed as though for a formal function. We climbed to the second floor and moved one of the chess tables near the palace's slanted windows for light. The family gathered around, and admired our Chronos clock.

We taught Sasha how to use it and set it to the time control they would play, five minutes each. It was Sasha's mother who had been the chess player in the family prior to Sasha, and she took the chair closest to the table. The family was confused as Glenn took a few moments to draw out a grid that they would use as a scoresheet for a twenty-five game match. It was Glenn's practice to keep careful score even in informal matches, and usually he insisted that both players sign the sheet when the match was over. When Glenn was finished, he reached across the board to shake Sasha's hand, and they began.

Glenn had the better of it on time through the first four or five games. At the end of each, he wrote in the "1" and the "0" in the proper squares and he sometimes stared at the sheet for a moment before beginning the new game. When Altana arrived, tall and smiling, I excused myself to go to lunch with her. We would meet Bambusha downtown.

"Bring me back something safe," Glenn said.

Altana took me to a restaurant called Elista, a tucked away room down a back street. Like Kirsan, Altana had an interest in astrology, and when she asked me when I was born we discovered we had the same birthday, exactly a decade apart.

"You are the same age as Christ when he was—"

"Yes, I know," I said, and it was the third time in Kalmykia, after Galzanov and Bair, that I had been told it was high time for my crucifixion.

Altana longed to return to the United States to live. She had plans for a visit in just a few weeks, ostensibly to accompany her grandmother, but she hoped it would be permanent. It wasn't something that people in Kalmykia felt free to talk about, she said. She also admitted that she had no particular affinity for chess, that she found many of the people involved in the game funny, and that what she enjoyed about her job at FIDE was a sense of process. Bambusha met us after we had finished lunch, and I was passed off from one Kalmyk to another.

Bambusha and I walked about Elista, talking. She was married to a Korean man who worked for Ilyumzhinov's tax scheme company. Like Altana, Bambusha harbored no secret love for chess, but she was comfortable in Kalmykia and longed for children.

We stopped by the House of Government to check in with Galzanov, but before we could climb into the building's anemic elevator a guard stopped us. The president was about to arrive. We sat on a bench until Kirsan's car appeared and he rushed into the building alone. The elevator was an exposed cage, and we watched the president go up and the concrete slab that was his counterweight go down.

Galzanov sat in his office, smoking and playing chess with someone I didn't recognize. He confirmed that the interview would probably happen the following night, and he had taken the liberty of scheduling a trip for us to one of Kalmykia's outlying districts for Monday. We left him to his game.

As we came back into Chess City, we passed the depression I had stared into that morning.

"I read that there was a pond near Chess City," I said. "Was this it?"

"No," Bambusha said. She indicated the opposite side of Chess City, ahead and below us. "The pond was somewhere over there, I think. They drained it. The land was unstable. They used dirt from here to make it stable. Why do you ask?"

"I went for a walk this morning. I just wondered."

She glanced at me, smiling. "You are a journalist."

Back at the palace, the match was in its final game. The score was 12½-11½, and Glenn needed a win to even the outcome. The family had surrounded the players with chairs by then, and Sasha's mother had long since taken over the scorekeeping duties. Glenn lost the last game, but the mood afterward was friendly. We chatted for a moment as Abundo, over at the small café, held a beer bottle in one hand and a microphone in another and butchered Sinatra. Between songs, I went to speak with him.

"Bambusha is married," he advised me, "but Altana is a free spirit."

I'd brought Glenn a chicken dinner. He ate in the cottage. Chess and food improved his mood. "Sasha is good," he kept saying. "I mean, good!" He had kept the scoresheet and examined it as he ate. He indicated a string of four wins he had managed in the middle of the match. "Look at this, Hallman. I was hittin' him! His parents were worried! Bringin' the whole family to root for him. I thought that was it, but the kid can fight." He chewed for a moment. "Tomorrow, we interview the president, and then we can get out of here. Back to Moscow. Back to Boris, maybe."

I gave my interview questions to Galzanov in the morning. Bambusha had arrived at our door at 10:00 and informed us that she and Altana would be our permanent translators from then on, under Bair's terms. This would not be explained until we met with Galzanov, who revealed that Bair had not yet surfaced. He was considered missing. Galzanov said this as dryly as he might have recited crop statistics to a district newspaper. He told us to return to his office in the afternoon to await a call from the president.

The idea of using clocks to limit a game of chess first came about in the middle of the nineteenth century. Initially, they were hourglasses: After a move, you laid your glass on its side to stop it. Clocks gave birth to "time trouble," the phrase coined for the intense stress that came about when your sand ran low. Kalmykia seemed faster with the president in the country. It was as though everyone was afraid of failing to emulate Kirsan's frenetic work ethnic. The republic, I thought, was like a desert tucked inside one of those early chess hourglasses, between moves, dry and motionless. When the president appeared the glass was suddenly turned upright, and the whirlpool began. As we now drove closer to our interview and the president's swarm of duties, everything seemed to accelerate. Kalmykia with Kirsan in country felt exactly like time trouble, the sand sifting away beneath your feet and the president a presence even when it was only the fear that he might appear around a corner and see that you weren't doing anything.

There was still a significant wait from Galzanov's office that evening. Galzanov, Badminov, and Glenn played chess in the dead time, and Bambusha worked on translating my questions. Kirsan had only one translator that he trusted completely, and Chuck Norris's visit was the only other time Bambusha had worked for him. Everyone seemed intimidated, which diffused the tension between us as adversaries. The meeting was a common effort. "Don't scare interview, don't scare interview," Galzanov told me, as we looked over a chess problem together. "Don't *worry*," I corrected him, and he smiled his gap-toothed smile.

We got word that the interview would not happen for at least an hour, and Galzanov suggested we go for dinner. Galzanov was corrupted by power, I thought, but I was coming to realize that I had more in common with him than I did with Glenn. I had long since decided that Galzanov was the hidden author behind the as-told-to tone of *The President's Crown of Thorns.*

"What is your IQ?" Galzanov asked me at dinner, suddenly. It was loud enough to interrupt the other conversations, and Bambusha's expression, translating his words into the silence that followed, showed she thought the question rude. Galzanov leaned back with a young man's bravado, his ability to be at ease in a moment that was awkward for others a measure of his power. I told him that I had never been formally tested, and turned to Glenn to ask if he knew what his IQ was.

"I believe in passed pawns," Glenn said.

He also believed in a happier tone to the dinner, and when karaoke began, first with Abundo singing alone, and then doing a duet with Bambusha, Glenn disappeared into the room where they took requests and scheduled the Beatles' "Yesterday." When his turn came, he motioned that Galzanov and I should join him at the head of the restaurant. Galzanov looked at me, grinning, but wouldn't go unless I did. We mirrored each other's hesitation, then rose at once for what Glenn would later tell me was a repeat performance—the three of us had sung the same song on a night that now seemed so far away, and in the friendly interlude of this newer moment our three faces assumed orbit about the interrogation device of the microphone, and we bellowed sentiment until we received a call that the president was now ready for us.

Outside the president's office, in the gloomy hallway near the elevator, the delegation that would meet with Kirsan after us already waited their turn. With just a glimpse of their ceremonial garb, elaborate hats and billowy tunics, I had not enough time to formulate even a guess as to what continent they were from.

Ilyumzhinov's office had essentially the same blueprint as Galzanov's, though it was larger—a significant outer office, and off to the left a pair of closely set doors, two doors just centimeters apart as though to exponentialize their sense of threshold, that led into Kirsan's office proper. We waited in the outer room a moment. A number of people sat about this room, presidential consultants and members of the Kalmyk military dressed in what looked like band uniforms, all of them bored and haughty but happy to linger in the president's sphere of power. One of the uniformed men barked at Galzanov for being late. The president, it seemed, had been forced to wait for us.

The people in the outer office seemed to exist for no other reason than to make the president seem important. Their mood suggested Kalmykia was engaged in a war that had just turned for the worse, their faces sour but composed as the republic crumbled around them. I tried to log some of the room's details, but it was a small community of paralyzing stress and all I could take in was that tension—a cabinet trying to keep the republic going, trying to stay in power. There was no chess playing here as there was in Galzanov's office, and the room was wholly unlike the building in which it sat. It was posh and comfortable, the vast gap between rich and poor in Kalmykia drawn along the line between this room and the outer hallway. Here was the special intimidation of furniture: the bookcases of reddish wood, the overstuffed leather chairs Glenn and I found ourselves in, the ornate carpets and banker's lamps and indirect light all indicators of success and legitimacy. Two of the heavies sat behind matching desks like weary bookends. They had been there for a long time, on a schedule far different from ours. It was already late, and after us there would come the delegation in the hallway, and perhaps several others before their night was finished.

We were ushered into the president's room. Before I realized it, we had become quite a large party, Glenn, myself, Bambusha, Abundo, Badminov, Galzanov, and now Sanal joining our group. Kirsan approached us. He shook my hand and moved on to greet the others. A large Buddhist tapestry hung directly behind the president's main desk, flanked by the Russian and Kalmyk flags limp on upright poles. The bookcase that filled the back wall overflowed with books and knicknacks, and the desk was strewn with electronic gadgets and what appeared to be diplomatic gifts, a softball-sized sphere of some precious stone, a crystal mace. The president had as many elephants, wood and stone creatures standing all about, as he did Buddhas, but there were Christian icons as well, a row of framed pictures of Virgins and Baby Jesuses wearing their telltale shrouds and backlit in that Christian way. A portrait of Genghis Khan hung on one wall, and on another the president of Mongolia.

I took the seat just off to Ilyumzhinov's right, and Glenn sat beside me. The long table filled in. I watched Kirsan hold his double-dimpled tie to his chest as he eased into his chair. Under his jacket, his shirt was badly wrinkled, and I could make out the striped outline of his undershirt. I noticed his fingers, pale and bone thin and steady as though from exhaustion. I turned on my tape recorder and across from me Abundo produced a pad to take notes. Galzanov would take notes as well somewhere down the line. The room became quiet.

It began quite normally. My first question was simple, based on the obvious premise that chess had been introduced to Kalmykia to give the Kalmyks an added sense of identity. The president had once described his people as having been asleep for seventy years, I said, and I asked whether he had hoped to wake them up with the game. It turned out that Bambusha's work in translating my questions was unnecessary, as the president listened in English, but responded in Russian. I wasn't sure he always understood, and he often used the questions as platforms to spring into standardized stump speeches on the game.

"*Da,*" he said. "From ancient times, Kalmyks have played chess. Our nation has been familiar with chess for many years. My grandfather taught me how to play the old Kalmyk chess. As you have said, the game is sleeping in our nation, and it is necessary to wake it up. Up to now, we have had no grandmasters among our people. I became champion of our republic when I was fourteen years old, among our adults. And I was just a candidate master. The Kalmyk people liked to play chess before, but it wasn't as popular then as it is now. Back in 1993, when I became president of Kalmykia, I signed a decree that gave governmental support to the development of chess. Can we get them a copy of the decree?" He spoke down the table, toward Galzanov, who nodded. "Part of this program focused on the teaching of chess to young children. Second, it introduced the idea of holding tournaments among organizations, regions, plants, and factories. Chess is waking up now. We see very good results of chess development in Kalmykia. One hundred percent of Kalmyk children know how to play. As well, there have already been ten Russian championships held here. In 1996, we hosted a world championship match, and in 1998 we built Chess City for the 33rd Chess Olympiad."

The president paused, then lifted a hand to indicate the length of the table in front of us. "But right now we are just at the beginning of a very long road. We have made only the first step. The way is very long, like the end of this long table. I am certain that in the future we will produce more grandmasters and perhaps by 2020 or 2025"—here he banged the table two or three times, lightly but emphatically—"a Kalmyk chess player will become world champion. Two factors are important here. The first is that the future chess champion is going to be born here. The second is that a Kalmyk is the president of FIDE. FIDE and Kalmykia will get a boost from each other, and this will create an explosion of interest for both."

I noticed that I tended to cover my lips while I listened to the president. On the table just to my left sat a book, and on top of it was placed a medal of some kind, a colorful ribbon and heavy iron star meant for the delegation following us, perhaps. In just a few minutes, Kirsan had spanned the entire history of his chess decree. He seemed reasonable if not entirely levelheaded. He wasn't Kurtz or the Wizard of Oz, I decided, he was more like Goldfinger, a not entirely unsympathetic supervillain with a kooky plan to dominate the chess world. As he spoke of the future Kalmyk world champion, I thought of the chubby-faced Sanan, a talented boy whose significant intellect would be molded to the president's designs.

"Would you like me to speak a little shorter?" Ilyumzhinov said.

"No, no, that's okay," I said. "There're only a few questions. It's not a long—program."

I next asked for his thoughts on whether the nature of chess was closer to art or science.

"*Da,* chess," he said, "a sport, a science, or a culture? This is the debate. For me, chess is a philosophy of life. It's more than an art, or a sport, or a science. But there is a practical side to your question. Our goal has been to become an Olympic sport. Why? Because by becoming an Olympic sport the financing of national federations will double, and this will help with the popularization and development of chess in the world. As president of FIDE, then, I am very happy to announce that the International Olympic Committee has unanimously accepted chess as an Olympic sport, and FIDE as an international sport federation. But again, this is a very small step on the road to making chess the philosophy of people around the world, the philosophy of life and religion."

I tensed when I heard him use the Russian word for religion, and shifted anxiously when the translation arrived from Bambusha. The president went on.

"Because right now half a billion people in the world play chess. My aim is to make a billion people play chess. There are Muslims, Christians, Buddhists—I think the twenty-first century will be the century of the Internet. Humankind is making very large steps in its development. And there will be meetings. Humankind will meet other civilizations in the future. Not Earth civilizations. From other stars in our universe. A person in the twenty-first century will differ in many ways from a person in the twentieth century. And chess is a sport of the Internet. You cannot hold football championships on the Internet. Or Boxing. Or Karate. You can play chess on the Internet. Millions of people in America, millions of people in Europe, they can all be on-line at the same time, and they can all play chess at the same time. This is not possible in football. Maybe chess, then, can become a religion."

I glanced around the room to see how others were reacting to the president's words. The quick bleed from that which seemed logical and reasonable to that which was mystical and bizarre was an oddity the others appeared to have become accustomed to. It was as though the president had broken wind, and we all planned to ignore the noise and the stink. Power, I thought, was the ability to say anything that came into your head and have others nod at the wisdom. When Kirsan became impassioned in his speeches, his eyes darted as though his imagined audience was a cloud of gnats figure eighting before him; and when he made an expansive point, he smiled broadly like a salesman, like an evangelist. Just behind him was a large television, angled somewhat but turned enough toward me so that from where I sat his head was superimposed in the frame, as if he was appearing in it rather than before it. And even though I was close enough to him to make out the sinewy cables inside his fingers, to carefully measure with my eyes his delicate frame, and to catch his pleasant scent as his talking hands created currents in the room, it was, yet, as though he was still very far away from us, transmitting himself here from a vision of the future apparently difficult to describe.

I skipped down to my question about chess and religion. In it I quoted from the scene in his autobiography in which he has his third revelation on coming upon two shepherds playing chess in the steppe. Galzanov had seen the question and was ready with the Russian version of the book, and there was a scramble to locate the quote.

Kirsan read the passage to himself, then chuckled and told a joke about Brezhnev, his laugh at his own punchline breathy and inconsistent, an animal fending off pretenders to its meal.

"What was the question again?" he asked Bambusha.

She told him I had asked for a general reaction to the relationship between chess and religion.

"Ah. The author is right here," he joked, referring to his own book. "The last phrase he mentions, I agree with it, of course. I will cite another classic writer. Shakespeare. Shakespeare, *da?* The world is a theater, and people are actors in it. So the world is a chessboard. And we are like pieces. Sometimes we make our own moves independently. Sometimes we get played, we get moved. Sometimes those who move us, they get moved by others. And there is an eternity there, where here in Kalmykia it is said that the eternity of a soul is equal to the eternity of the universe."

I next asked whether chess's evolution could ever be truly controlled by an organization like FIDE. His response picked up from where he left off.

"Hm. The development of chess is closely connected to the development of civilization. Everything that happens is in one way or another connected to chess. In the 1970s, there were two worlds fighting against each other. The world of the capitalists, and the world of the Soviets. Two political systems were in conflict—which one is better? And then we have a situation on the chessboard with the representative of the capitalist world, Fischer, on one side, and Boris Spassky on the other side. These two worlds fought each other. Fischer beat Spassky; the capitalist system beat the Soviet system. It was like a fight on the stage of the Cold War, in the background of the Cold War. And in fifteen years, Gorbachev came to reign, and the Communist system failed. So chess was faster—it foresaw this event. Chess is a mirror reflection of our life. Then, during *perestroika*—this unclear situation mirrored our unclear situation in chess, the split of world champions. In 1995, when I became president of FIDE, I gave a press conference in Manilla and talked about our chess *perestroika*. But when I was first posted for FIDE, my motto was to move chess away from politics. Chess is politicized. But I would like chess to be larger than politics, to be like a religion. This is my position. Do you have many more questions?"

"Two more," I said.

The last two questions were about the business of chess, the political rift in the game that Ilyumzhinov had already referred to, and a backlash that had surfaced in response to one of his most recent proposals, the commercialization of the game. There was already some restlessness in the room, the fidgety signals that we were overstaying our welcome, but I posed them anyway.

"Our aim right now is to commercialize chess," the president said. "The main thing is to make chess make money for sustaining itself. That is why we are taking some revolutionary steps in winning the title of the world championship. That's why I changed the system of playing for the title. I made it more democratic. When Fischer, Karpov, and Kasparov used to play for this title, they would wait and play with the opponent they wanted. This is not democratic. Right now, the top one hundred players representing many countries of the world have the right to fight for the title, and each one has the chance to become world champion, just as in any democracy any citizen has the right to become president. In monarchies, this is not possible. Kasparov, and other champions, they created monarchies for themselves."

Despite all his talk of democracy, Kirsan did not sound like a man who was planning on holding free elections anytime soon. There was a moment of silence as I jotted down a note.

"*Spasibo*," Kirsan said.

"Just one more," I said.

"Yeah, please."

My final question was about opposition to his proposals—was there anything about chess or its players that explained why the game resisted becoming a business?

"There is always opposition. In my family there is opposition. I tell my son he has to go to sleep at 10:00 and he says no, I am going to watch television. There are two kinds of people: One person has one opinion; another has a different one. They have a right to choose. We're not going to skip the problem of the commercialization of FIDE. Chess is a game for chess players, for chess amateurs. This is one side. The second side is to provide decent conditions for chess players to play this game. That means that we have to find financing. And that means that I have to make the system work *for* the chess player. These two parts have one thing in common, and when there is harmony between them, then chess will become a religion."

CHAPTER 14

Infinite Variety

I am told that in the abstract world of mathematics, the methods of one man will reveal his individuality to fellow mathematicians. . . . It is the same in chess.

—Desmond MacCarthy, "Chess," 1935

Strange as though it may sound, I have found that the inclination of the different nations for chess shows that the chess mind is more closely related to the artistic rather than to the mathematical mind.

—Lajos Steiner, "The Chess Mind," 1937

PRINCETON UNIVERSITY SITS ADJACENT TO THE TOWN OF Princeton, New Jersey, the two shaping a peaceful symbiosis out of stone architecture and lush landscape, a brain split down the middle by the corpus collosum of Nassau Street. There is ivy everywhere in Princeton, and precious trees, and walking through town it's not unreasonable to scan for placards naming the shrubs. The city and school both have that feel of simulated travel, but it's not fake: The stone buildings are truly stone, and behind the beveled glass are the storied classrooms and book-filled offices of superscholars and laureates.

Glenn and I parked on Nassau. We tried for inconspicuousness, but just being in town without a syllabus felt like trespassing. We walked through a wrought-iron gate onto campus, and Glenn said, "No ID check or nothin'! Anybody could walk in here!" Because excellence in chess included precise defensive play, Glenn noticed lapses in security in real life out of habit. It was like a rook moving onto an open file. But he was basically right. Schools like Princeton could survive without walls and only a paltry security force because its intimidating academic history lent it an aura of invulnerability. It was just that sense of academic betterness that I had hoped to challenge by bringing Glenn to play chess at Princeton's famous Math Department.

I'd read about the Princeton Math Department in a biography of one of its aging faculty, Nobel Prize–winner John Forbes Nash. Nash was one of the fathers of game theory. Einstein was the most famous of the emereti, so Relativity was associated wih Princeton; but game theory—which has been used to help fight wars, predict economies, or simply gain insight into the foibles of human group thought—called Princeton its outright birthplace. Perhaps because of this, Princeton math students still play various games at Friday "afternoon teas" at Fine Hall. Games played at the teas include chess, go, kriegspiel, bridge, backgammon, and wholly new games invented by Nash or other members of the math select.

Chess has tried to nurture a relationship between itself and academia, but as a subject the game simply will not take its place alongside philosophy and anthropology. Harvard has a chess chair occupied by GM Boris Gulko, but most academics regard the game, at best, as a bothersome younger sibling. Long before Glenn and I were confronted with the cantankerous relationship between chess and the academy at Kalmykia's Institute for Humanities Research, I'd thought to tweak the academic sensibility by crashing the Princeton tea. At first it seemed like a devilish but impossible way to rock the boat. Then I realized it wasn't impossible at all, that basically no one at universities ever stops anyone to ask them what they are doing there. The idea was simple: Go to the tea, set up a board, and see what happened. Glenn, who sounded at times like a cocky chess mercenary, seemed energized for a confrontation. "I will crush them all," he said, nodding.

Our plan was to arrive at Fine Hall half an hour before the tea. We had some time to kill, so we wandered through the campus and sat for a time in a small botanical garden behind a spired faculty club. The grass was plush carpet, and a fountain gargled holy water. Not far off, a couple of maintenance men were setting up a tent for an event to be held later in the day. It was true that Glenn thought of himself as a chess player first, and black second, but I watched him scanning the endless white faces of the students, and now he noticed that even Princeton's gardeners were white.

"I haven't seen one black groundskeeper," he said. "Not *one!*"

I was silent, and he turned the problem over in his mind.

"I ain't leaving this place 'til I see a brother pullin' some weeds," he said.

Fine Hall was a modern building, a bland industrial structure plopped down in the middle of a campus whose emphasis was as much on atmosphere as accolades. Like Einstein and his apocryphal sets of identical clothes, mathematicians rejected fashion even in architecture. The building's lobby and stairs were that of an upscale parking garage. I'd already done one reconnaissance mission to the building, and I hurried along, excited. Glenn followed calmly.

We reached the third floor, official home of the Math Department. We walked down a hallway lined with bulletin boards marked with a plaid pattern of news clippings; notifications of Nobel wins and Fields Prize honors hung alongside job postings and class-cancellation notices. The corridor was a math Mecca, but to anyone unversed in the psychodrama of academic mathematics it was an ordinary hallway, probably too narrow, with a grubby tile floor and unhealthy lighting.

The tea room was relatively nice, a standard university conference room with a square of couches around a coffee table here, several long wooden slab tables there, a blackboard or two (these coated with the language of high math, sets of sloppily drawn symbols, and the occasional "=") hung on the walls between huge, framed photos of past faculty and graduating classes. These photos were as much the reason we had come as any other: If they were an honest record, then it appeared that Princeton's Math Department was void in both black faculty members and black students.* The rows of endless white faces were like the photos of major league baseball teams before integration: There was a nameless absence hard to pinpoint, invisible men lurking at the borders. Even though the Math Department's empirical relationship with the Bomb and the Cold War made its admissions practices tough to challenge, some little part of me hoped

---

*Later, then-Chairman Peter Sarnak told me that Princeton had employed two African-American systems professors at the time of our visit. Still, Sarnak acknowledged, both women and minorities were dramatically underrepresented in the math world.

Glenn's race would poke a hole in Princeton's illustrious facade. I secretly hoped that we would be thrown out, for a scene that would indict academia and rescue chess.

There were just a few people gathered in the room when we entered, reading newspapers and sipping from plastic cups. It was early yet for the tea, and no one looked at us. Glenn and I took a table in the center of the room and set up our board and clock quickly on the theory that it would be tougher to expel us once we were entrenched in the ritual of a game. We played, but I hardly paid attention. I sneaked glances about us. Off in one corner of the room stood a pair of ribbon statues. These were upright glass monoliths. Inside, some kind of mechanism caused a huge soap bubble to form, which clung to the glass walls as it grew and eventually broke into smaller soap bubbles, and these in turn broke into still smaller bubbles, etc. Presumably, it demonstrated a mathematical point of some kind, and I wondered if the relationship between bubbles and math was anything like the relationship between chess and math. Glenn and I actually disagreed on a chess/math connection. Even though Glenn had once gone to college with the intention of studying mathematics, he preferred thinking of chess as an art. "There's no numbers," he said, "it's just chess." But for me the ribbon statues were all about chess and academia: If bubbles popping inside a museum case said something useful to men who plotted doom with equations, then so should the game.

Glenn paid less attention to our contest than I did, but still crushed me. His moves, usually exceedingly quick, fluid swoops from the board to the clock, were now slow-motion versions of that same arc. He didn't want to scare anyone off. Math people were filtering into the room now, and I looked up at each of them between moves, trying to get their attention. Young, poorly dressed men glanced at us as they entered, failed to recognize us, and double taked before moving off to the back of the room where a woman was distributing doughnuts and tea. The room began to fill.

Finally, a portly kid executed a parabolic approach on our game. He stealthed his way in, polite.

"Hi," I said, and told him my name as I offered my hand.

He took it, smiling. "Charles."

"Wanna play?" I said, and stood up motioning to Glenn.

"No, no," Charles said. "I'm not very good."

I flashed back to my days in pool halls, talking people into trick games. "Play," I said. "Come on! What can it hurt?"

Glenn was already winding the clock. "Sit down," he said to Charles.

Charles smiled goofily, then shrugged and hurried into the chair.

By Glenn's standard of chess, Charles was not terrible. The first game went quickly, Glenn flushing the boy's king to the center of the board and forcing mate. They played again, and another kid walked over, a lanky Indian student. Glenn's manner at the chessboard betrayed his expertise—if ever he was as awkward as a mathematician in life, that awkwardness vanished over the board—but the two students watched only the opposing collections of pieces, seeing whatever it was mathematicians saw when they looked at a chessboard, patterns, groups of moves, quantities, the stylized thinking of mathematics translating to chess in some incomprehensible way. From a game theory point of view, chess is a finite, zero-sum, two-person game with perfect information. Its fatal flaw is that it frequently ends in a draw. That chess lent itself so easily to descriptions of academic mathematics had led me to conclude that the two were related. There was historical precedent for the thought: The creation of chess was often linked to the origin of the decimal system, and early Muslim texts showed a chessboard being used as a tool for calculation, like an abacus or early adding machine. In medieval literature, a number of poets had alluded to the doubling of the chessboard as a way to reference the infinite. More recently, chess player/mathematician IM Ed Formanek had compared the political infrastructures of chess and math, suggesting that chess was the more honest of the two because tournaments eliminated math's hollow braggadocio. More frequently, though, chess players invoked quantity in the game's defense. Of just the Sicilian Defense, Walter Korn once wrote: "Age cannot wither nor custom stale its infinite variety." It was a lyric variation on what Garry Kasparov preferred to state with numbers: "The number of possible moves in the average chess game is, according to the specialists, a superastronomic figure—10^{120}. To compare: the number of atoms in the universe is 'only' 10^{80}."

Which meant, basically, that while the total number of possible chess games was finite, the number was so large that it was useless to try to comprehend it. Mathematics, it seemed to me, enjoyed the same style of thinking: infinite within the finite, or, if you preferred it, the other way around. Both math and chess aspired to transcend primitive trial and error. They seemed to exist on the same plane of intuitiveness, a hope of finding pattern amid chaos, the aesthetic potential of thoughts drawn to order invisible until just now. And on top of the rest, both chess and math seemed to take a psychological toll on their practitioners. Russian mathematician Andrei N. Kolmogorov's suggestion that one's emotional development halted at the moment mathematical talent set in sounded like a diagnosis of many chess players who started playing at an early age. One didn't even need to leave Princeton to find damning evidence of the awful triangle of chess, math, and insanity: Nash, the father of game theory, was schizophrenic, and had fathered, besides his work, a schizophrenic child with a master rating at chess.

Glenn and Charles continued their game, the click of the clock loud in the industrial acoustics of the room. The Indian kid glanced at me.

"Are you guys math people?" he asked.

I ignored the question, and scanned the crowd. "So who plays? We're looking for a game."

"Sarnak plays," the kid said. "He's the head of the department." He looked around the room. "He was here a minute ago. If you sit here long enough, he'll find you."

He was right. Glenn's gunslinger ethic of chess applied even here, and before long Peter Sarnak appeared, a casually dressed middle-aged man. He passed through what had become by then a small crowd of math students, having been told that some serious chess was happening. As though he'd been called out, the head of Princeton's Math Department was ready to set himself before the black-and-white baize.

He introduced himself by first name, and Glenn and I eventually learned that he was South African. As a chess player, Sarnak had once been Junior Champion of South Africa, and then Champion of Rhodesia. His chess-playing days had ended years before, but the math was easy: Sarnak had played chess in South Africa during the height of apartheid, and in Rhodesia during the country's decade and a half of white rule. Sitting across from Glenn a quarter century later, Sarnak was simply a pleasant and gracious man, but still his nationality raised the question of race. Chess's race record was as suspect as Princeton's. Alekhine's ambiguous association with Nazi Germany threw chess a curve as he was world champion during WWII, and Bobby Fischer's open anti-Semitism reflects poorly on the game today. Chess projected a vision of itself as a color-blind game, yet there was dirt under the rug—Emmanuel Lasker's original *Lasker's Chess Primer* began with "Everyone should know chess, because the mentality and individuality of the white race has found expression in this game in its modern form." On the other hand, and to South Africa's credit, Donald Woods reported that only a single Afrikaner objected when he organized a nonracial chess club in South Africa during apartheid. "You have to understand," Woods said, "that the perception of whites under apartheid could only be dispelled by the evidence of their eyes and ears that here was a black man who could compete as an intellectual equal. . . . And in the field of sport, chess has this unique role as an intellectual pursuit."

As a mathematician, Sarnak was most famous for his work on proving the Riemann hypothesis, which has been called the most important open problem in pure mathematics. Sarnak's work had not resulted in a proof, and he wore his humility in the form of a sweet smile and fetching wrinkles. He was a kind man and appeared evolved well beyond the fray that had absorbed Lasker, Alekhine, and Fischer. It wasn't clear that he even noticed Glenn was black. The two men simply set the clocks and began.

They played calmly through the opening. Glenn would later say that just the first six or seven moves revealed Sarnak as an accomplished player. I backed away from the crowd that began to form about them, bodies crunching together. When a bridge foursome began to form, I volunteered for South so I'd have an excuse for being in the room. The foursome was made up of myself and three young odd men surely brilliant in their field but unversed even in simple greetings. The games of the afternoon teas, I thought, were as much an exercise in math as they were an attempt to break primordial ice.

On the other side of the room, I heard Sarnak grunt a bit of frustration after a mistake. I suited my cards and looked over. Glenn was silent, staring at the pieces. Around the board the students pinched their chins and let the processors of their brains run madly. Sarnak exhaled deeply, then gathered the pieces together to resign.

Then I saw Nash. Long retired and often thought dead, Nash maintained a relationship with reality in old age by continuing a relationship with the Math Department. He wandered the halls of

Fine, came to the teas, and scribbled math puzzles and math challenges on the blackboards. He was over by the buffet line now, a thin man with poor posture. He looked neither crazed nor quite right and, cup in hand, he surveyed the doughnuts. My attention veered between him, the bridge game, and the chess match: My partner bid four hearts as Glenn and Sarnak calmly discussed the final position of their previous endgame.

"Your two hearts promised more," my partner told me as I laid down my dummy hand. He was a tough twenty year old. He was unusual among the math students in that he was dressed well, yet he was bitter in the manner of the one sane man in the sanitarium. The closest of any of them to something like normal, the boy's math angst took the form of scorn for anyone whose intellect was not skewed in the same fashion as his own.

I shrugged and apologized. My partner frowned and began calling for cards, and I stopped paying attention. Glenn and Sarnak had begun another game, the first moves quick, and then trailing off into concentration. Nash had left the buffet line by then and moved about the room in an elliptical orbit, following a path that might have been determined by thirty years of routine. He hesitated when he saw the chess match, took a bite of a jelly-filled. He wandered over.

Nash, because of his oddness, had been dubbed "the Phantom of Fine Hall," and the way the students ignored him now gave credence to the thought of him as a ghost. He didn't attract the wake of students that Sarnak drew behind him, nor did he command the attention one would expect of a Nobel winner. It was as though only I could see him. Even just reading about Nash, his particular combination of brilliance and madness had reminded me of Fischer. Fischer's play was as legendary and unique as Nash's math talent, but Fischer's mental lopsidedness took the form of paranoia and that bizarre anti-Semitisim. I was worried. I'd hoped the Princeton chess match would produce a scene, but now I feared how Nash would react to Glenn. The whole potent moment could explode—a ribbon statue falling down.

I dealt and bid the next hand of bridge. My partner was an aggressive player, and refusing to incorporate into his calculations the fact that I was neither talented nor paying attention, he bid us up to another unlikely contract.

"Your three clubs was, uh, just about the *dumbest* possible thing you could have said," he said, on seeing my hand.

"Hey!" I snapped at him. "Don't sugarcoat it!"

His face filled with fear until he got the joke of it, then he rolled his eyes and climbed back into his conceited armor. I looked back at the chess match. Nash stood directly behind Glenn now, the only difference between their focused faces the slow movement of Nash's jaw as he worked his doughnut. The old prodigy, like Sarnak, gave no indication of noticing that Glenn was black at all. In fact, he gave no indication of noticing Glenn was even *there*. Steinitz, as much a father of chess as Nash was of game theory, had often been quoted as saying that he thought of his opponents as abstractions. Nash appeared to have gone farther down that same lonely road; and though he and Glenn were closer to each other than either of them were to the chessboard, their only communication was its language-less transmission of ideas.

Nash watched the position until Glenn calmly pushed a pawn and fingered the button of his clock. Nash took another jelly-filled mouthful and wandered away. In all the time I'd watched him, he had made eye contact with no one.

The match was over by the time I returned to the chessboard. Glenn and Sarnak had played three games, Glenn with the plus re-sult, two wins and a draw. Sarnak had just resigned the last game when I arrived, and he had to correct several of his students when they offered escapes from Glenn's final mating net. Glenn and Sarnak shook hands, and then Sarnak asked us who we were, what we were doing there. Glenn had achieved a status in the odd forum, and I waited for him to speak for us. He nodded coyly and said, "We heard there were chess players here." Sarnak didn't press further, and for all my off-color hopes and plans, the two opponents began to strike up a friendship. Their races were unimportant, the gravity of their histories irrelevant, the battleground of the chessboard neatly turned to a field of peace and union. I was struck by the irony that a game of combat could bring together two men who would otherwise never have met, one who studied constantly but struggled to pay his child support, the other paid handsomely to calculate problems of obscure practical value. It challenged the very notion that chess was a game of war, and for me it was the lesson of the encounter. If chess couldn't become a recognized tool of learning, if it would never become its own academic subject, then perhaps this was why it had managed to survive anyway, and why, at least in Russia, one could still achieve a Ph.D. in the game.

For Glenn and Sarnak it was incidental. They were simply engrossed in conversation, struggling over problems, preparing to exchange game histories over E-mail, becoming pals in a world that, without chess, would never have allowed them to meet.

It didn't stop there. Soon Glenn was nearly lecturing to the crowd of brilliant misfits, these kids whose brains ran at hyperdrive but who might, if you simply asked their name, feel their heart race. Glenn was at home here, a visiting lecturer, and these kids actually followed the questions he posed to them. They listened, sat down, and started scribbling until Glenn told them no writing, visualize.

Sarnak, who had wandered off briefly, returned to check Glenn's progress on a problem that Sarnak had recently devoted seven hours to solving. Glenn, who had looked only at a list of coordinates, not actually seen the pieces on the board, said simply, "I think it's queenside castle and mate in two."

"Oh, no, no, no," Sarnak said. "It's much more difficult than that."

They set up the pieces on the board and we all studied the position. Twelve faces fixed as though to witness the result of a months' long experiment.

"Queenside castle," Glenn said again, almost whispering. "There's no defense."

Sarnak's eyes fluttered over the board. "I, uh...something's wrong here...the pieces, they..." He was moving the pieces now, looking for the correct position, and he realized at last that the black king should be one file over. He laughed and blamed the error on the colleague who had E-mailed him the problem in the first place. Glenn admitted it was much more difficult now.

There was a moment of silence as those gathered around the board began a new assessment of the problem, and in the lull I asked Sarnak to comment on the relationship between chess and math, the old debate. The academic dismissal of the game was tough for him both because he had once been a player and because he'd just admitted to spending seven hours on the problem standing before us. Still, he said, he tended to think there was something artificial about the game. At the same time he acknowledged that those who were interested in chess were often interested in math as well. This produced a frenzy of discord, students and faculty both weighing in on the issue. Some said chess was more like art, others like economics or politics, and one faculty member, John Conway, discoverer of surreal numbers and inventor of the game Life, said fie to the very idea of chess because its rules were imposed and represented no natural order. Soon the debate was out of hand. One student argued with Sarnak so vehemently that it was natural to wonder whether his financial aid would be intact the following semester. Three separate skirmishes broke out. Glenn and I simply listened and shared a grin at having instigated the melee, and I wondered if all the theories that emerged from Princeton came from these kinds of discussions, ideas bounced and prodded like chess players discussing a game, concepts played against emotion and ego, until these quirky characters would have to either give it up or duke it out.

They decided to give it up, and the tea began to dismantle itself. Sarnak had a parting gift ready for us: a pair of photocopies of news clippings of his chess exploits from the distant past. A chess player's games are like his work, his equations, intellectual property invested with flaws and brilliance. "I've never done *this* before," he admitted, and later I would serve as Glenn's Cyrano in responding to the games that, Glenn said, were evidence of chess promise unfulfilled. Without additional matches, the friendship between chess player and mathematician soon fizzled, but I called Sarnak for an interview some time later and revealed why we'd been there. In our talk we discovered at least two more ways in which mathematics resembled chess. First, Sarnak agreed that his work on the Riemann hypothesis had been inspired as much by an aesthetic drive as a scientific one, which placed the impulse for math beside chess in the vanishing point where art and science converged. And second, a number of mathematicians believed that computers posed the same threat to mathematics that they posed to the game. For mathematicians, chess players were canaries choking on the air of the future.

"That was cool!" Glenn said, back in Princeton as we exited Fine. The evening was fresh and lively, and we headed back toward Nassau where our meter was three hours overdue. For Glenn, Princeton had been like a homecoming—he was a specialist in a problem every academic mathematician had a private interest in. The trip was validation, both of his skills and of the power of the game as a tool of friendship. We lingered a moment near a fountain, reluctant to leave Princeton's fine space, and Glenn counted off the victories on his fingers: "They didn't harass us. They didn't kick us out. They didn't arrest us." Each was a measure of the game's success, of its gutsy defiance of rules that kept like people apart. Glenn thought a moment longer, and added, "They could have offered us some tea."

CHAPTER 15

Developing Your Pieces: ♕

At nine I fell in love with the black queen.
Now democracy rules in my army.

—Boris Spassky, 1969

She is not merely the soft excitement of war
who bids her king go forth with her blessing;
no, she is the active, undaunted,
indefatigable leader of an army, herself a host!

—William Hone, The Year Book of 1832

THE QUEEN BEGAN AS THE WEAKEST OF ALL THE PIECES, stronger than a pawn only in that it could move backward. Originally thought of as a male counselor to the king, the queen was born as *mantri* in Sanskrit, became *farzin* in Persian, and was adopted as *ferz* or *firzan* in Arabia, which it would remain for the first half-millennium of its existence. The Muslims valued the *firzan* as an offensive weapon, and *ta'biyat* were designed to create lanes for it. The move of the *firzan* was the same as the original *mantri*: a single square along any diagonal.

The placement of the *firzan* beside the king helped in the gender transition the piece underwent a few generations after its arrival in Europe. Language helped as well: *firzan* was adopted as *fierge* in French, which sounded like *vierge,* meaning virgin or maiden. But the simple position of the *firzan* alongside what was immediately identified by the Europeans as the king was enough to make the gender shift inevitable. In Latin, the queen moved from the feminized *fercia* to simply *domina,* and in German and Swedish the piece became *dame,* lady.

In one morality, the queen was described as a soul that was white through confession or black through sin. In another, she was charity. Just as Arabia's understanding of the *firzan* as a counselor inspired them to use the piece as a weapon, so did Europe's queen metaphor instruct them to keep the piece back to protect the king. In addition to playing physically slower, one less weapon marching forward on the attack retarded European chess. Slower meant more tedious, and when the Christians began tinkering with moves to accelerate the game, the queen was an early target. The moralities had begun this experimentation long before, their popular chess metaphors overestimating the value of the queen to such an extent that the word *fierge* came to have a meaning completely outside of chess, that force without which it was difficult to win in war. The promotion of the queen reflects an interplay of influence between players themselves and nonchess-playing intellectuals who saw the game as rhetoric. But even from a realist's point of view, the queen's influence was not depicted on the board, and altering the move was a natural step.

Like all significant developments in chess, the modern queen move cannot be traced to an individual person or country, though Murray suggests Italy as the most likely candidate. The queen move first changed to that of the original *aufin,* the early bishop, but this proved insufficient, and the subsequent change to the modern move appears to have come about quite suddenly. Along with the bishop's parallel ascension, this signaled the birth of modern chess. Suddenly, the game on the board was faster in terms of how quickly the forces were in conflict and how swiftly a mistake could be exploited.

The queen had become a superpiece, combining the powers of the rook and the bishop into a single entity. The new game spread through Europe within the single generation spanning the turn of the sixteenth century. New names of the game specified not only the queen, but characterized the influence of the piece as well: France's *eschés de la dame enragée* and Italy's *scacci alla rabiosa* were two ways of calling the game "mad chess," a name later misinterpreted as evidence that the game drove its players insane. The power of the queen also inspired a new chess origin myth: The game had been invented during the reign of the mythical queen Semiramis, founder of Babylon.

The modern queen is generally considered stronger than any

other piece by nearly a factor of two. All else being equal, the queen is the equivalent of three minor pieces. Because it's the most powerful piece on the board, sacrificing one's queen is the most flamboyant and rare of all practical maneuvers, and chess history's "immortals"—classic games reprinted and replayed for instruction—are often queen sacks. A clever queen sacrifice against even a marginal opponent can travel the globe in the pages of chess magazines. As with the Knight's Tour, the modern queen spawned a puzzle: place eight queens on a single board so that no one queen threatens another. The puzzle caught the attention of mathematicians, who first solved the question of eight queens on an 8×8 board (twelve fundamental solutions, with many mirror images), and then expanded it to try to find a solution for n queens on an n^2 board.

Scacchi al antica or *axedrez del viejo*, "old chess," survived for a generation or two before being completely displaced. Chess had evolved to a new, viable state. The game continued to hammer out its fine points as it caught on and became the world's most widespread amusement. In the late eighteenth century, the Russians gave the queen the power of the knight as well, but Philidor, among others, bashed the idea so that it lasted but half a century.

Ironically, the queen move, meant to speed the game up, ultimately slowed it down. The conflict that now arose between forces early in the game also allowed players to target weak spots in their opponent's opening array from the first move. When Glenn told me that soon after seeing a chessboard for the first time, he noticed f7 was weak, it meant that even without playing he sensed the power of long-range pieces. Trick openings and traps—maneuvers designed to obtain a quick overwhelming advantage—gave rise to "opening knowledge," a vocabulary of known positions and the pitfalls or tricks they contain. Now the game was as much a study as an amusement. The first player who seemed to grasp all the possibilities of the modern game, Morphy, was criticized at first for treating the pastime too professionally. Preparation was like cheating. But the criticism had no effect, and by 1920, when schools of chess thought merged, a vast repertoire of openings was critical. Analysis of popular openings could run twenty-five moves deep. The game became as much a test of creativity as the ability to study and retain vast quantities of theory. Some regard this as further evidence of the genius of the game, but others find it a labor outside the spirit of play. The last generation has seen rumblings of frustration with a game that in the eyes of many has become dependent on rote memorization. The move of the queen made chess dynamic, but also may have set it on a path with no outlet.

CHAPTER 16

The Road to Lagan

To a Kalmuk Girl

My sweet Kalmuk, farewell! In mood
Content worldly affairs to flout,
My commendable habitude
Had nearly led me in pursuit
Of you, to tread a nomad route.
Your eyes are narrow, I admit,
Your brow is broad, and flat your nose;
To simper French your tongue unfit;
Clad not in silk your dainty toes.
No English lady you, at tea
To slice your bread in patterns trim
To quote Saint-Mars in ecstasy,
Or Shakespeare hold in scant esteem,
Or, void of any thought at all,
Affect profoundest reverie,
Or take to singing "Ma dov'é",
Or dance the gallop at a ball.

What need? For fully half an hour,
A saddle for my horse awaiting,
My mind and heart were contemplating
Your glance and your wild beauty's power.
My friends, what difference can you find:
It's just the same—on elegant
Divan to lie with vacant mind,
Or idle in a nomad tent.

—Alexander Pushkin, *Lyric Poems: 1826–1836*

KALMYKIA SO FAR WAS A LESSON IN SUDDEN FAME. WE
had been *nouveau riche* from the moment we stepped out
onto the weedy tarmac. For a while Glenn continued to answer every

"Hello!" we encountered on the street, and once he shook hands with two young men in black leather jackets on a street corner only to have Bambusha laugh and tell us they were Mafia. Children appeared in alleyways asking for chess games, people gave us their chess research or simply their poetry, and we each signed a thousand autographs. But the many calls for our attention had begun to seem bothersome, and even Glenn came to understand that all fame really meant was that some people would decide to dislike you for really no reason at all.

Altana sat beside me in the back of a cramped Volga scuttling down a thin highway splitting Kalmykia's semidesert steppe. We were headed to Lagan region. The land coaxed along like a fickle underlayer of cirrus. The landscape's desolation was profound, its beauty Martian, the chalky dirt solid on the ground but rising as dust as though evaporating. Too much time in such a place, I thought, could trigger an incurable agoraphobia. The steppe was not featureless, but what features there were served as reminders of the barrenness: a leafless oak home to thirty crows' nests like ornaments on a dying Christmas tree, the occasional shallow lake a bleary absence that mirrored the sky.

"Are you white bone or black bone?" I asked Altana. These were the ancient labels Kalmyks had used to distinguish between commoners and people of privilege.

She rolled her eyes and said that people didn't care about such things any more. She said her name meant gold in the Kalmyk language, however, and there was a rumor of a prince in her distant family. I looked up at our driver, Sergei, and took stock of the upside of fame: I had a car and driver, I was sitting next to a princess named Gold, and today I was being chauffeured to the farthest reaches of Kalmykia, where Galzanov had made preparations for my visit. And yesterday I had met Kirsan.

Glenn had decided not to come along. At the very instant Ilyumzhinov had made his final claim to turning chess into a religion the night before, Glenn had brought the interview to a conclusion by reading the line as resolution and attempting to initiate applause among the rest of us. He sat up and clapped five or six times, but it was out of place and didn't catch on. Kirsan, who looked as though he might have gone on talking for some time, seized it as an opportunity to shuffle us out the door.

Out in the hallway, a number of people congratulated me on the interview. It had gone smoothly, they felt. When someone asked if I had gotten the answers I wanted, I said that my questions weren't meant for specific answers. But it was a lie. In announcing that he wanted to make chess into a religion, Kirsan had said exactly the thing I had hoped he'd say, the thing I had suspected from the very first moment I'd begun reading about Kalmykia. And he'd made the claim with such confidence that I began to wonder whether it was as absurd as I thought it was.

I didn't have much time to think about it then, and just as I had ducked out of the hunting trip earlier in the week Glenn ducked out of the trip to Lagan when we returned to our cottage. He said good night, and he was still in bed when I left in the morning.

A third of the way to Lagan, Altana produced two apples from her purse and offered me one. We ate them and threw the cores out the window. Altana charmed me by pronouncing "laughing" as "loffing," and by saying, "Right you are," whenever she meant true or yes. The land began to checkerboard as we moved farther from Elista, alternating light-colored squares undulating toward the horizon. At certain spots in the semidesert, the horizon was quite close all around, half a kilometer off, as though the whole world was that small disk, an island in a sea of sky. At such moments Kalmykia felt like purgatory. Kirsan had written that his republic was the meeting point of certain infinities: nothingness, eternity. In meeting him I sensed another: weariness. He seemed to have long since accepted that international journalists would never comprehend the enormity of the task he had undertaken, the dismantling of the lingering Soviet regime and the baking of an economy from scratch in a land without natural resources. Kirsan had not seemed like a murderer to me. Murder was not too gross a tactic a for a chess player—players were often chilly and distant—but something about Ilyumzhinov made him seem frail and vulnerable, and it was hard to imagine him working through the logic of a killing so close to home, just at the moment when Kalmykia had finally drawn international attention. By contrast, the members of his staff seemed equipped with less of their boss's intelligence, and it was easy to imagine them snapping under the pressure of a relentless reporter. As with Ayuki Khan's villainy, the murder of Larisa Yudina was best understood as a chess exchange—why not simply remove her from the board?

Our Volga chugged along. We zoomed by an onion farm, low buildings set back a piece. The farmers sold their crop at the side of the road in torso-sized bags, the onions stacked so tightly that they stood upright and from a distance were indistinguishable from their crouching vendors. A line of telephone poles shadowed us for a time before shooting over a ridge, and we passed a number of small mock graves at the shoulder, markers of highway deaths, each with a miniature fence marking out a personal sanctified graveyard.

I had read a good bit about Kalmykia's ecological predicament. The North Caspian steppe was generally vulnerable due to lack of moisture and the fact that it had once been seabed. Beneath even the regions of remaining quality dirt there was a thick layer of saline soil. A gorge ninety kilometers south of Elista had challenged the theory that the climate of southern Russia had not changed in the last five thousand years—radiocarbon analysis of three distinct layers of strata suggested the climate had undergone a severe and sudden change sometime around the year 1040, in roughly the same epoch chess had moved north into Russia. The Caspian Sea normally went through periods of expansion and contraction, and when it receded the salty underlayer was revealed. Wind and the overgrazing of sheep destabilized the soil. The desert began moving westward, and experts had estimated that a meter-thick layer of saline could have appeared in less than one hundred years. Now Kalmykia's desert region was expanding by four hundred square kilometers per year. Ancient Kalmyks had worn shoes designed to go easy on the fragile grass, but the deserts of Central Asia had followed them as surely as bad weather.

I wanted to ask Altana what she thought of what was happening in the republic and tried to think of a way to ease into it.

"I am wondering about Bair," I said. "Do you have any guesses as to why he may have disappeared just when the president arrived?"

She tilted her head. "How can I guess if I do not know?"

"Well, it wouldn't be a guess if you knew."

"Right you are," she said.

"I think maybe he was KGB," I said.

"There is no KGB anymore."

"You know what I mean."

"Maybe someone told him to disappear," she said. "Maybe the president does not like him."

"What do you think about Ilyumzhinov?" I asked.

She smiled and looked away. She stared out the window, then turned to address the cavity between the front and backseats of the Volga. "It is difficult for me to say. I cannot say I like him or do not like him. I am not interested in policy. I know that his policy for young children is a good one. During the Olympiad, many people, many young people worked." She squinted over a thought. "I know it sounds stupid, but I don't have anything more to say."

"Last night Kirsan told me that he wanted to make chess into a religion."

"The president said that?"

"Yes."

Her eyes wandered. "Let me overthink it."

Lagan was a town of sixteen thousand, known as "Little Japan" because it was the easternmost point in Kalmykia. The Lagan government building was not equipped with indoor bathrooms, and the first thing I did after Sergei swooped us through the dusty streets was ask after the facilities. It was a concrete hut in an alley. The other day at lunch, Bambusha had spontaneously offered support for my theory of commodes. A good deal could be discerned of a culture from its toilets, she said. Now, as I leaned over another sloppy square hole I felt a waft of shit and piss rise up, the outhouse's ventilation system flowing backward and the bad air passing over my face.

In the Lagan government building we met Elena, who would escort us on a tour of the city. She was a matronly middle-aged Russian in a black leather vest and spiked heels. Apart from trees, Lagan was entirely without vegetation. And there was no traffic. The streets were unpaved, and it would have been the Wild West if a kid on a motorcycle hadn't sped past us, kicking up an arc of dirt that simply turned to dust and kept rising. Elena took us first to a small Buddhist gazebo that had been visited by the Dalai Lama. We walked three circles inside and left precious rubles as offerings.

Next, Elena took us to the Lagan museum, where a local historian gave us a tour through the history of the region; and from there we went to Lagan's Buddhist temple, a large cement-block structure on the outskirts of town. A short Tibetan monk met us out front with the youngsters who were his protégés, and he cuddled my hand in both of his and draped a white scarf around my neck. The youngest of the three monks-in-training wore a T-shirt that was part of the marketing campaign behind *Titanic, the Motion Picture Soundtrack*. The boy was a frolicking advertisement. Fortunately, there was Altana. Inside the temple, I watched her approach a wall of idols. She put her hands together and bowed her head. She was beautiful, and her faith, I decided, was the most genuine thing I had encountered in Kalmykia.

We were offered Kalmyk tea and crackers. We sat in a back room of the monastery, where it was dim and quiet, and suddenly there was nowhere that I was about to be rushed off to, and I noticed the serenity of the monastery as surely as if I had arrived here from a hectic metropolis.

"It's so peaceful," I said.

"What do you want?" Altana said. "It's a Buddhist temple."

Our monk opened a box of special chocolates. I asked him how he had come to be assigned to Kalmykia and Lagan, and he admitted that it hadn't been his first choice. He wasn't sure how long His Holiness intended to keep him here.

"Is it true," I asked, "that all forms of religion are welcome in the monastery?"

"Yes," the monk said.

"Last night President Ilyumzhinov told me that he wants to make chess into a religion. Do you think chess can become a religion?"

The monk looked confused for a moment. "I don't make decisions," he said.

On the ride home, Sergei interrupted from the front seat to point out first a steppe eagle hunting over the road and then a steppe viper absorbing late-day warmth from the asphalt. I asked Altana what she knew about the Pushkin poem, "To a Kalmuk Girl." A statue of Pushkin stood in Elista, but the poem and its story, engraved in the base, were all in Russian. Altana knew the story and told it to me in the back of the Volga as the steppe began to darken.

In a series of lyric poems, Pushkin had described a tour he had taken through southern Russia early in the nineteenth century. One leg of his journey had brought him to some Kalmyk *kibitkas*. He tied his horse and entered one of them, finding a Kalmyk family. He noted even then that the faces of the Kalmyks showed the influence of their time in Russia. Their savage features were disappearing. He spied a quite handsome Kalmyk girl, sewing and smoking, with crimson lips and pearly teeth. He sat near her. "What is your name?"

Pushkin asked. "***," the girl said. "How old are you?" "Ten and eight." "What are you sewing?" "Pantas." "For whom?" "Myself." "Kiss me," Pushkin said. "No way," the girl said. "It's a shame!"

They shared tobacco, and Pushkin ate breakfast with the family. He suffered through the trial of Kalmyk tea, and for his courage he believed he deserved a reward, which he then tried to extract from the girl. She bonked him on the head with a Kalmyk musical instrument. Pushkin tired of Kalmyk hospitality and left. The poem was a letter to the girl that he imagined would never reach her.

Altana finished her version of the story, and then we both smiled and looked out into the black steppe. It would be foolish to care for her, I thought. Both she and Bambusha could be plants from Galzanov, like Bair. Still, I thought of chess history and how often, before the modern era, romance cropped up in descriptions of the game: An ancient Arabian text described a chess-playing slave girl who was purchased for ten thousand dinars by a chess-playing caliph—the girl beat him three times, and he granted her a wish. The French poem *"Les Eschez amoureux"* ("The Chess Lovers") begins with a chess game between the author and a skilled lady in the Garden of Pleasure, and when the lady wins, her opponent is so pleased that he imagines neither Philometer nor Ulysses could beat her; and even one of the creation myths of the game, the eighteenth-century poem *Caïssa*, portrayed it as a kind of aphrodisiac—the god Mars, whose love for a particular nymph was not returned, asked the god of sport to invent for him a game that would win her heart.

Altana and I were quiet for ten kilometers. I asked her what her plans were if she managed to return to the United States. What would she do? She didn't know, but she was thrilled at the prospect. I told her to expect the transition from Russia to the United States to be difficult. She was a debutante in Kalmykia, but in America she could barely expect to be middle class on her own.

"It's like chess," I said. "You have to make a plan."

"Kalmyks are not good at making plans," she said.

"Maybe that's why you haven't produced any grandmasters," I teased her.

But Altana didn't care about chess, and for a while we both sat there convinced that the other's grass was greener. Like Bambusha, Altana had blind love for things American. After the interview with Kirsan, I was leaning more and more toward the use of chess as a religion. I went on a short rant about American pop culture—I didn't want to see Nike shoes on kids' feet in Nigeria, I did not want children in Borneo wearing Michael Jordan baseball hats, and I did not want monks-in-training in the Lagan region of Kalmykia, Russia, wearing T-shirts from movie soundtracks. "That's what I like about chess," I told Altana, defending my interest in the game to someone who worked in Chess City. "It's at least fourteen hundred years old. How old's rock and roll? Fifty years? So what. Chess has a history. Ilyumzhinov is right about this much."

Altana was a lovely listener. When I stopped, she looked away to overthink what I had said. At last she turned back to me. "Thank you for taking me with you. You have opened my mind to many things. I see now that I have not been thinking with my open mind."

Back in Chess City, Glenn, we learned, had just lost to Sasha again, 10½–9½. He had spent most of the morning killing flies in our cottage, he said. Sasha had arrived unannounced in the afternoon, and their daily matches would become Glenn's routine. Now he had a date with a girl he had met at the Chess City sundries store. He gave me the key to our cottage, and hurried off before I could tell him anything at all about the road to Lagan.

I WOKE THE NEXT MORNING TO TRUMPETS AND TROMBONES. A small band in faded uniforms had set up on the steps of Chess Palace to signal the start of an agricultural fair. I prepared for the day, resolving to attempt another search for Yudina's pond.

First I toured the fair. Scattered about Chess Palace were exhibition booths and jars of pickled everything—grapes, watermelon, basil leaves. There were stacks of lettuce like cannonshot, giant spools of bound wheat stalks, long squash that curled like fishhooks, peppers the size of fists, great green pumpkins, and coconuts that were not coconuts but some kind of vegetable that one would have to be starving not to mistake for rock. The carrots were fat, the eggplant was small, and whole-roasted baby pigs had been left in their fetal squeeze as they cooked. Mounds of decorative bread bulged like the fat *babushkas* who arranged them, and three chickens monitored the proceedings from within a small cage. Inside the bounty it was hard to believe that much of Kalmykia was reverting to desert.

Back out in Chess City it wasn't much of a stretch. Steppe Dog followed me to the edge of town; I looked around for the Chess City army, then ducked under the bent chain link where the city's residents had shaped their shortcut. From there, a dirt path led down to the open steppe behind the city, where Bambusha had indicated the pond had been. I descended as a group of crows cawed overhead, a message repeated over and over. The land was otherwise still and somehow frightening now that I was alone in it. On an earlier walk, I had seen a man standing in the field where I now paused. He had slowly sunk down into the shrubs, and he did not reemerge. The world suddenly struck me as a quite eschatological place, and I no longer wondered why the Oirats had become Buddhists, even if the reason had been ostensibly political. As the crows continued their argument, I bent down to examine the weeds that were the greedy culprits of Kalmykia. Most were of a small, pale green variety with leaves both small and large so they could multitask. Another brand was a creeping moss attached to the land itself, webs sucked down against the hard dirt.

I stood again and looked off to where a herd of cows spotted a far hill. A grasshopper popped up and bounced off one of my knuckles. Directly in front of me—and directly behind Chess City—stood a dense wall of reeds that made a perfect obstacle. It was a huge field of reeds, a couple hectares in size. I turned off toward a stand of trees on the theory that where there were trees there ought to be water. The international journalists' description of where Yudina's body had been found varied, but maintained a consistent theme: "...in a pond in Elista," "...in a river," "...in a pond near the Chess City site," "...a pond on the outskirts of Elista," "...by the 'Chess Pond' close to the Olympic Village." I looked back up to Chess City to triangulate on Bambusha's directions.

After Yudina was killed, her work was continued by her husband, Gennady Yudin, who continued to publish *Soviet Kalmykia Today*. He crusaded to publicize the murder, and the crime received far more attention than most assassinations in Russia. Closer to the date of the crime, however, Yudina found another supporter in the form of Bachar Kouatly, a French-born grandmaster and chess politician. But it was politics. Kouatly had run against Ilyumzhinov for the FIDE presidency and lost. He claimed irregularities, then represented Monaco at the 69th FIDE Congress, which was held in conjunction with the 33rd Chess Olympiad in Elista.

Yudina had died five months before the congress convened in a room only a short ways from where her body was found. What Kouatly said in his speech to the congress was not published in the official record, but the responses were. Kouatly was attacked repeatedly for making the murder an issue. A FIDE vice president said Kouatly's speech was evidence of the difficult conditions under which Ilyumzhinov had been forced to work. Others accused Kouatly of being like a chess player who refused to resign a lost game. In the end the delegates stuck to a familiar line of argument—no accusation against the president had ever been proven—and when the president was reelected, he vowed fairness and hard work. "No criticism or attack," Kirsan said, "can prevent me from serving the interests of my people of the Republic of Kalmykia, chess and chess players."

The stand of trees was a dump. I walked past piles of refuse that lay where they had spilled from the backs of trucks, and beyond I looked into the distance for a gully that might have held water. But there was nothing, and I abandoned the search.

On the way back to Chess City, I saw a Kalmyk man climbing a hill and reading a book. It was ritual somehow. He climbed, stopped, read a little, and repeated it. A dog sat above him on the hill, watching with effortless faith that the rite was necessary. The sun rose behind them, hiking up the horizon's padding of clouds, and I watched the man read and walk, read and walk, until he stepped out of sight, headed for nothing I could see.

BACK IN THE COTTAGE, GLENN LOBBIED FOR OUR DEPARTURE from Kalmykia. With food and warm water, we were better off than we'd been at Hotel Elista, but he was far from satisfied. We had the information we needed, he said. But we didn't have the information we needed. We had heard from Ilyumzhinov, and it sounded good: Perhaps he *was* the benign dictator the Kalmyks seemed to need. But we'd only heard what he wanted us to hear. Whether chess could be the thing he claimed was still a mystery. It was as dubious as my theory.

Glenn's real problem was that he was almost out of money by then. He had never figured how to translate rubles to dollars, and he had not realized that perhaps the only expensive thing we had found in Kalmykia was the laundry services. He was having his shirts done every day, and with more than a week to go it had just about drained him.

"There're no chess players here," he said. "Let's go back to St. Petersberg."

"No way," I said. "We're staying."

"Hallman. Actin' like a tyrant."

"If you're out of money, use your credit card."

"That's for emergencies."

"Running out of money *is* an emergency," I said. "And there are chess players here. There's Sasha."

"Sasha's a kid," Glenn said.

"Sasha beats you."

Bambusha could sense the tension between us as we ate lunch prior to the two interviews we were going to conduct that day. After the Institute for Humanities Research the week before, I had asked Galzanov if we could meet with Vaskin, the Kalmyk chess expert, and Basaev, the problemist.

To break the mood of the lunch, I told Bambusha about the road to Lagan. The land of Kalmykia, I said, was desolate but beautiful.

"Our desert is spreading all over," she said.

I WANTED TO TALK WITH VASKIN BECAUSE OF SOMETHING I'D read in Murray. In 1913, Murray had disagreed with other chess historians, who claimed that all the older forms of chess had vanished by then. Ninety years later, Vaskin was a still-lingering connection to that past, and even though the Kalmyk game showed distinct Western influence, it was quite different.

Vaskin still wore his beret and a long tie. His home was filled with wood trimming and comfortable furnishings, and we sat on chairs covered with sheets. Bambusha had to scream into Vaskin's ear. His wife gave us water. Vaskin started talking.

A rich Kalmyk had brought an ivory chess set from Djangharia to Kalmykia 150 years ago. He donated the set to a Kalmyk temple constructed in 1860, and it came into the possession of a monk who became Vaskin's woodworking teacher. The ivory set was the first chess set Vaskin ever saw. When the temple was destroyed by Communists, the board and the pieces were lost. Sixty years later, Vaskin reproduced the set in honor of both his teacher's one hundredth birthday and the five hundredth anniversary of the *Djanghar* epic. He brought out the board and pieces for Glenn and me to see. It was his most prized possession.

The board was a four-legged tray a couple of decimeters high. It was made of African rosewood, and the black-and-white squares were buffalo horn and elephant tusk, respectively. It had taken him a year and a half to complete. The chessmen were chiseled from Swiss beech, and came in the squatty shapes of a number of animals.

"This is the idea here," Vaskin said, "they reflect the life of the nomads. The rook is a bull. The bishop is a camel. The pawn is a boy."

"You could sell this to a museum," Glenn said.

A delegation from Germany had offered him twenty thousand dollars for the set, Vaskin said. He had refused. Glenn was astonished, and wanted to know why he hadn't simply pocketed the money and made another one.

Vaskin laughed. "I only make unique things. I never repeat."

"Would you like to play a game?" Glenn said.

"Of course!"

Vaskin again went step by step through all the peculiarities of Kalmyk chess. He made the first move. Glenn twice had to lean in close to distinguish camels from horses. He won the game with a clever use of the Kalmyk rule of promotion, and when Vaskin realized he had lost, he cackled and said that Glenn had done very well in his first time playing Kalmyk chess.

"It was a pleasure to play you," Glenn said. "I never played that way before. This is a very nice set, but next time take the twenty thousand and make another one."

Vaskin laughed again. I reminded him that at the institute he had mentioned his mother's chess prayer. He nodded and spoke the prayer in Kalmyk, a quick consecration like grace before a meal:

> Oh, God, thousand Buddha,
> I worship and pray to chess.
> Sanctify my play, bless my Knight's move
> and protect the Saint Khan.
> Bless my victory.
> Oh, God, thousand Buddha.

He nodded at the memory of it. I asked him the same question about chess and religion that I had asked of the monk in Lagan.

Vaskin was too old for political fear and disagreed plainly. "Chess is an intellectual game," he said. "It cannot be a religion; it's a culture. A national chess game is a national chess culture, but it cannot become a religion. Chess was created by an Indian or an Arab, and they made this game for competition. They wanted it to be an intellectual game. I have been Buddhist since I was three. And never have I seen chess in Buddhist books."

I wanted to argue with him. One of chess's creation stories said that the game had been invented by Buddhist monks as an alternative to violence, *buddhi* had once been a name of chess, and the spread of chess, in fact, closely followed the spread of Buddhism. And hadn't he just recited a Buddhist chess prayer? But Vaskin was on a lucid roll and would not be interrupted.

"Chess is a competition of mind. I am sure that this idea of the president's will not end well." He mimed a spit at the floor and accented his words with raps of his cane. "It will just not work! Here's why I think this. Because a long time ago when Kalmyk people started playing chess, men and women were equal in the game. There wasn't a single family where the members didn't play. Everybody played—it was widespread among the Kalmyks. But chess is different from Buddhism. In chess you play in order to capture the pieces of your enemy. You capture them, you surround them, you kill them. And religion does not foresee this. It is forbidden in any world religion. Chess has nothing to do with religion!"

"A LONG TIME AGO," BASAEV SAID, "IT WAS TRADITION AMONG Kalmyk people to bet the family animals while playing chess. One day a Kalmyk peasant lost a camel and a horse to his friend. They continued playing, and when the game had become decisive, they were faced with this position."

We met Basaev in Galzanov's office. Galzanov and Glenn played blitz in a corner as Bambusha translated Basaev's story. Basaev called himself a folklorist. Chess problems were his hobby. The story he was telling mixed the two: a short folk tale that accompanied the chess problem he now pushed across the table to me. I looked over the jumbled profiles scattered across a diagram four centimeters square*:

*White to move, mate-in-four.

"The peasant who had already lost his animals, he now has white. The other has black. We clearly cannot covet white. Black has clear advantage. The Kalmyk playing white only has his last sheep to bet. The position is very bad. He is embarrassed, and he is almost ready to resign."

The world of chess problemists is another sub-culture. Apart from solving two- and three-movers with Glenn, I had actively avoided chess problems because I recognized how well-suited I was to their weird psychology. I had once spent three hours futilely trying to generate a position that could only be resolved by the underpromotion of a pawn to a bishop. It was an abyss I could have easily fallen into. Chess problems are precreated positions that work like puzzles. They look something like a game frozen at a critical moment, and the task for the solver is to find the one and only solution that satisfies the problem's restriction—mate-in-two, mate-in-five, or whatever. Chess problems go as far back as the Arabian game, when they were used primarily as a tool for instruction. Problems would simulate predicaments that were likely to arise in games and illustrated the rules of good play, or exceptions to those rules. When chess arrived in Europe, both the game itself and chess problems thrived, but the sophistication of European problemists was sorely lacking. Early problemists were simply gamblers. They were out to win a quick stake, and it did not matter if their compositions were likely or even possible in actual chess. Hundreds of years would pass, and chess would change completely before Europeans caught up to the skill of Arabian com-

*(1.Rh8+ Kxh8 2.Be5+ Kg8 3.Rh8+ Kxh8 4.f7++) Double rook sacrifice on h8. Final move is discovered mate by the bishop.

posers from eight centuries before. It once again became important that chess problems be *possible,* however unlikely. The middle of the nineteenth century saw the emergence of themes in chess problems, and later there would be a number of clearly identifiable schools of chess-problem thought. Special tournaments for problems eventually emerged, as did international titles for accomplished composers. Problemists invented new pieces for unique problems—nightrider, orphan, equihopper, reflecting bishop. Hans Ree once called problemists the "conscience" of chess. "You get the impression that [they] have risen above everyday reality even farther than ordinary chess players," he wrote. In the tenth century, as-Suli described a "very old" study in the Islamic game that he considered unsolvable. He was right for a millennium, until 1986, when the first-known solution to the problem was published by GM Yuri Averbakh, who called it "a creation of genius."

Before chess problems became an art, however, they had often been accompanied by a tale or story that hinted at the solution. I wasn't able to solve Baseav's problem in the instant he allowed me to look at it, and he continued the narrative that went with it.

"Close by this peasant who was almost lost, his young daughter-in-law was standing. She was watching the game, but she did not reveal to the guest that she knew how to play. And he didn't notice that she knew what they were doing. The daughter-in-law understood the situation. But instead of interrupting the game, she stood and walked in the direction of the door. When she was close to the exit, she said, 'How dirty it is right now in the steppe. The boys will get lost in the steppe, and they will not be able to get their horses out of the dirt.'" Baseav now made the moves on the board, solving his puzzle as he spoke the coded words of the daughter-in-law to her father, references to the Kalmyk pieces and the puzzle's solution. "'It is necessary to break the wagon. We have to put the boys on the camel, and they will be saved.' Her father-in-law, he immediately understood even though his opponent did not, and he made the moves and won the game. Have you heard anything like this story before?"*

"I think I've heard that story," Glenn said. Galzanov was taking a phone call, and Glenn had wandered over to see what we were up to. I was surprised that he was interested because he tended to care for problems only when they were of instructive value. "I think I've seen this position, too."

Basaev nodded. It wasn't uncommon for a chess position to travel the world. Galzanov hung up, and Glenn returned to their match.

Basaev and I spoke for a time, but as at the institute, we had little common ground in the history of the game. He believed that the queen and bishop had evolved independently among the Oirats, acquiring moves identical to those that developed in Europe. To argue with him would have been to suggest evolution to one whose faith was grounded in creationism. Still, he showed me his collection of personal compositions, a flimsy packet of stapled-together paper. He had pasted a diagram to each page, and the solutions were scribbled out in his tiny Cyrillic. Sometimes, individual squares of the board and pieces were pasted over the diagrams, and many of the pages had been stained with juice or coffee. The puzzle on the cover had won Basaev an award when he was nineteen years old. Now he was a shifty, somewhat paranoid-looking, middle-aged man with hollow eyes, forever pursed lips, and a tendency to speak in short, contradictory remarks.

"Do you think chess problems are a higher form of art than normal chess?" I asked him.

"Yes," he said. "You make problems to show beauty. The men who make problems, it is like fighting against one's own mind. You have to think for both opponents. In chess, one opponent thinks for himself. A composer must think for both. The most important thing—and the most difficult—is that there must be only one way out, only one salvation. We can say that problemists, they are the poets of chess."

I WOKE EARLY THE FOLLOWING MORNING TO TYPE NOTES. I heard Glenn moving about earlier than usual, and when he appeared in the kitchen he handed me a piece of paper and went into the bathroom. He'd written:

Yo Hallman,

Our comparative use of logic is like examining a simple straight line and an exponential function of infinite magnitude. It is very clear to me that my use of logic far exceeds your daily usage.

GDU

I walked out onto our terrace. Across the way, I saw Abundo outside his cottage, tending to chores, alone on his street like a man left behind after a plague. Just below me, the mayor of Chess City— a chubby Kalmyk in dark sunglasses who kept a beauty who worked the Chess Palace souvenir stand as his mistress—was giving a tour to three other men. The mayor gestured up in my direction and spoke to the others, and I recognized the moment as the first in which Glenn and I had truly become residents of Chess City, noteworthy features. Down a bit, Steppe Dog barked viciously at a man who had probably kicked her once, each vicious yelp causing her to recoil slightly.

I thought, *Who's the straight line, who's the exponential function, and which one is more logical?*

Back in the kitchen I packed another treat for Steppe Dog, but she was gone by the time I got outside. I walked to the FIDE office to meet Bambusha. Their crew had arrived for the working day. Abundo had been complaining for several days about their Internet connection, and now they were without a connection completely. Abundo was furious because FIDE's annual rating list would be late.

"The whole world is waiting for this list!" he ranted. "They will blame me! We have it right here. The guy takes his money, he goes. When we try to send, it asks for the password! We don't know the password! We cannot work in Elista. Ah, this is the benefit of Germany, of being destroyed in the war. You must rebuild. You get better things."

I didn't have the heart to tell him that most of Elista had been leveled during the war, pretty much like everywhere else.

"So," Galzanov said, when we finally made it to the House of Government, "when are you leaving?" He smiled, but it was a diplomatic way of telling us that our business was concluded.

"A week from tomorrow," I said.

It was too long, but not so long that he could simply be rude about it.

"Well! What else can we do for you?"

I told him that I would call the instant an idea came to me.

"No problems," he said.

Just outside, in Lenin Square, there was an event honoring the Kalmyk militia. It was half-fair/half-parade. A line of tables manned by militiamen displayed their latest gadgets, and after a while everyone stepped back so that a bunch of militiamen could goose step on by. We found Sasha and his family in the crowd. They were anxious for another match. Glenn was ready, too. We agreed to meet at Chess Palace a short time later.

Back in Chess City, Glenn took a nap and Altana replaced Bambusha as our translator. Together, we conducted a short interview with the mayor of Chess City. He told us the plan for Chess City had originally been six hundred hectares, but currently only eleven were complete. Phase I had been built with the president's money, but now funds for other phases were coming from the republic and the process had slowed. But work was continuing on Chess City III, a small development adjacent to one of the microdistricts. He gave us directions.

The Utnasunovs arrived during the interview. Glenn and Sasha had formed a routine by then. Glenn drew the scorecard, and Sasha arranged the pieces. They set our Chronos clock, and both of them touched a corner of it as though to reorient their minds to its location. Then they shook hands and shared a sly smile at some secret of the game I would never know. And then the flurry began.

Sasha kept his head low to the board as he played, as though he had not yet outgrown a child's-eye view of its field. He cracked his knuckles when it was not his turn, his knees churned beneath him, and his lips often betrayed what he thought of his position. Glenn won the first two games, drew the third, and won the fourth. The Utnasunovs looked concerned. Although Sasha had won each of the matches so far, they had all been close. It looked as though Glenn had finally figured the boy out. The fifth game brought an extended moment of thought, an interval in which all of us watching became hypnotized by a tactic looming on the board. It was Glenn's move. He pressed his fingers to his forehead. He thought for more than a minute. Both he and Sasha held a pawn of the other's in their hands, spinning the pieces, making the little men do cartwheels like tiny acrobats, and when Glenn finally moved, it signaled a long furious exchange of pieces, slams on the board like a carpenter planting a nail in difficult wood, the sound carrying through the forlorn palace, until at the end of it I was left with one of Glenn's knights facing me directly. The game continued, but I lost its thread. Instead, I looked perhaps for the first time into the expression of the knight, the turn of its idol's mouth. The crevices of its jowls and the crook of its cheeks gave it a smile. The knight was the only piece that looked remotely alive.

Sasha made a final move, and didn't bother with the clock.

"Whoa!" Glenn said.

"Qb5!" Sasha said. "Checkmate!"

Glenn smiled, and began to gather the pieces together. He grabbed the knight that stood before me, and held it up. "No, no, no! Ng4!" he said, referring to a move from a game or two before. "Greatest move ever played!"

"Qb5! Checkmate!" Sasha said.

"No! Ng4! Shocking!"

"Qb5!"

"Ng4!"

The exchange would become the refrain of their friendship, the only real sentences they could share.

We heard a rumor that Galzanov was at Elista's six-table casino. I was curious to see Galzanov in a familiar environment. Altana and I left Chess Palace before the match was over and we bumped into Galzanov just coming out of the casino's attached restaurant in the company of a heavy-set man named Yvgeny who was in charge of all television in Kalmykia. Yvgeny was a rich, jolly Kalmyk. He offered to take us all for beer and crayfish.

"It is not a good idea to refuse this offer," Altana whispered.

A picture of Ilyumzhinov dangled from Yvgeny's rearview mirror. We drove to a bar, a large open room filled with booths. Yvgeny was affable, and waved his hand at wasted rubles or beer. A genocide of crayfish arrived at our table. We snapped them in half and sucked their heads.

The dance floor was empty, but the music blasted. Altana requested a song and asked me to dance. I begged off on an injury, then regretted it when she turned to Galzanov for politeness. He accepted at once. Yvgeny was potted by then, sinking into an aristocrat's depression because he was powerful but fat. The two of us fidgeted and watched them saunter toward the floor.

Altana's request began. It was a modern song, a then-worldwide smash, some rock artist's musical interpretation of a desert, a haunting and sad melody that lulled and repeated, I thought, like a Westerner's mistaken impression of the Kalmyk steppe. Like Duke Ellington's "Caravan" or Ravel's "Bolero," it was a borrowed ditty, a hybridized ethnicity, a map redrawn after colonization. Altana began to move her shoulders and hips in a fluid expression of approval for the song, suggestive enough so that even the music's revisionism seemed appropriate. It was just she and Galzanov on the floor, and Galzanov watched more than he danced himself, waving to and fro like a scarecrow in wind. Altana turned and her hair fanned behind her, her hands in fists and her eyes closed as she imagined the world of the song, translating it to movement. It was the distance between us, I thought. She saw hope in the song where I could see only irony.

For the rest of the night there was an inordinate amount of interest in my love life. Hundreds of years before, Kalmykia had been one of those cultures that fostered bonds with foreign powers by marrying off their princesses. It had basically worked for them. Galzanov suggested that if I truly wanted to understand the lives of Kalmyk people I should marry a Kalmyk woman. "Women," Yvgeny agreed, "are Kalmykia's *only* natural resource." Altana translated their words, smiled at their awkwardness, and looked into her lap during the lulls.

I rode back to Chess City by myself. Glenn was still awake. He'd won today's match, 13–7.

He was joyous again, and even had good words for Elista as he walked off to take a shower. "Man! This is the only city in the world where I can walk around without worrying about getting arrested for something. Woman gets robbed in an alley? I can just walk on by. Don't have to worry about nothin'!"

"IF YOU ARE NOT AFRAID OF DYING," ALTANA SAID, "THEN YOU will die calmly."

She spoke the words in the back of a taxi the next day as we rode about looking for Chess City III, concluding a conversation she herself had begun about death and reincarnation. A good philosophy for a Kalmyk, I told her.

Chess City III was back behind the monument to the Kalmyk deportation, a half-dozen squat, narrow homes going up in a row. It was midweek, but only two men were working in the development. Altana and I walked through the cramped rooms, the unfinished floors coated with sawdust and failed nails.

"Should we buy?" I said.

She smiled. "Let's keep looking."

Next, we walked through a microdistrict, a community square that felt abandoned and Soviet. The playgrounds for the children were all overgrown and all that could rust had rusted long ago. There were many car trailers parked about, but only one car, and laundry hanging everywhere showed the direction of the wind. We headed through a small market. I stopped to watch a *babushka* hack apart a headless pig. Further on, a man sold his personal catch of sickly fish in three wooden crates. Animals lounged as people milled and shopped between them, cats in the shade, dogs in the sun.

Earlier, Altana and I had passed a glistening white dome, a new structure that was supposed to be some kind of market. It had never been completed. Another building, brick and modeled after a castle, was supposed to be a supermarket, but the money had run out. Walking away from the microdistricts, we passed a huge pipe running alongside the road, half a meter in diameter, propped up on stilts, and branching off at street corners. I asked Altana what it was, but all she could say for sure was that it was another incomplete project.

"We get used to such things," she said. "It's ugly. They begin something, work for years, and then stop. It's okay. We stop looking at it."

I was afraid to ask if she thought chess in the republic would suffer the same fate.

"I like the word 'microdistrict,'" I admitted.

"Microdistrict," Altana repeated. "I like the word 'subdivision.'"

We returned to Chess City where Glenn had lost again to Sasha, 14½-13½. But Glenn was not displeased: He had done the calculations, and the total points of all their matches combined, 120 games, was dead even.

Galzanov arrived with two pieces of news. The republic would host a blitz tournament in our honor on Saturday. As well, right now, there was a community tribute happening for a Kalmyk boxer who had won a silver medal in Sydney. The president was there.

We arrived after it began. The theater was packed, and we stood back against a wall. The Kalmyk boxer was a quiet, shy man from one of the lower weight classes. His coach joked that they had preferred winning the silver medal because Kalmyks valued silver over gold anyway. Ilyumzhinov spoke briefly, offering pride and congratulations, and then there were a number of performers: an opera singer–accordionist duet, a singer who starred on a Kalmyk children's program, another singer accompanied by another accordionist. This last song was rousing, fast and jingly, and the mood of celebration seeped into the crowd, where it was apparently too much for some. Their only recourse was to leap up and begin dancing on their seats. Altana leaned close and said the song was perhaps the most popular Kalmyk song ever. The singer dipped into the crowd to drag the boxer to his feet to dance. Then the singer went for Kirsan, who smiled in his crisp suit and lifted one hand above his head to begin a strut to the music. The audience fell into hoots and rapture. The building shook under the feet of the joyous. It was nationalism as much as it was revival; and even though the accordion seemed entirely over-represented in the Kalmyk musical tradition, I decided that there was no real reason to conclude, as Kirsan had, that the Kalmyks lacked in culture. Even Altana was caught up in the happy moment of the republic.

"The president is dancing!" she said.

CHAPTER 17

The Narrow Way

Even at the best tournaments the players are a ragtag group, sweaty, gloomy, badly dressed, gulping down fast food, defeated in some fundamental way.

—Fred Waitzkin, Searching for Bobby Fischer, *1988*

Chess is a narrow way. I leave all pleasure behind. It is a time without pleasure, yes. You may not really follow this, ja. People normally go for fun, for pleasure, but chess players, through this very narrow way, try to get to God.

—Jan Timman, *1993*

"To win, I'll have to beat nine GMs," Glenn said, moving up the aisle of the dollar store. "Possibly eight. Eight might do it."

Before Kalmykia, before Baagi came east for the World Open and the bullet match I had organized, Glenn insisted that our tour of the chess world would be incomplete without attending the New York Open, one of the most prestigious open chess tournaments in the world. Glenn was thinking large as his previous results against grandmasters amounted to just a handful of points, but his enthusiasm was infectious, and I followed the line of his imagination just as I followed him up the glossy aisle.

"If I can start 4–0," he said, nodding, "I can have a good tournament."

We were at the dollar store to gather food for the week. Chess history was so littered with men starving for their craft that it was quite natural to count chess players as among the original hunger artists. As Glenn led us past the cut-rate food tins, merchandise scrapped by the larger supermarket chains, I considered what he had in common with chess's most tragic stories: lonely, obsessed, compulsive. But at least he wouldn't starve.

"So do you think I can do it? Do you think I can beat nine GMs?"

Chess players involved in matches often employ seconds, the word stolen from dueling ceremonies. On the surface, chess seconds serve as something like trainers or sparring partners, but on a deeper level they are the player's muse. I had decided that for the New York Open I would fill that role for Glenn. But I didn't think he could beat nine grandmasters.

"I think you're aiming beyond the finish line," I said.

He registered mock surprise and began loading tins of Maine sardines into a basket.

"I think you should try to make good moves," I tried.

"Hm."

He loaded us up with goods more appropriate to a camping trip—tangerine wedges, ravioli, cold beans, crackers, bottled juice, a jar of ginseng capsules. Then he looked at me.

"You don't think I can win, do you?"

On the bus to New York, Glenn took the wide backseat and stretched out to rest before his 6:00 game. The aging Greyhound shock absorbers still terrified me, but they rocked Glenn to sleep before we cleared the city. Out on the highway, I thumbed through a book called *Draw!* that Glenn had given me to close what he considered a gap in my chess understanding. Draws were what kept chess from being perfect mathematically, and to the casual fan a tie was like a broken promise, I thought. Glenn disagreed. *Draw!* was made up entirely of drawn games. Chess books are generally filled with thrilling victories.

Draws have long been a problem for chess. Early tournament rules called for drawn games to be replayed, but this quickly proved problematic as repeated draws put tournaments well behind schedule. The draw solution, devised in 1867, was to score half a victory for each player.

The standard elimination rules used in most professional sporting tournaments was abandoned by the chess world 150 years ago on the logic that they did not produce true champions. All-play-all systems were better, but couldn't accommodate large numbers of participants. The modern point-system and Swiss-style tournament reconciled the two. Each game was played for a point. Tournaments lasted a proscribed number of games, with winners playing winners, and losers playing losers. No one was eliminated. After several games, the formula became more complicated: In three rounds you might score 3 points for three wins, or 1½ points for a win, a loss, and a draw. (Or 1½ for three draws.) In each round, you were paired against a player with a like number of points, and whoever had the most points when all the games were complete won the tournament.

The main problem of the draw solution is that a draw winds up being closer to a win than a loss. A draw advances, a loss does not. Strategically, it becomes more important not to lose than to win. This favors careful play and colorless games. Even in the '20s and '30s chess players feared that the game was headed for *remistod*, death by draw.

But the author of *Draw!*, W. Heidenfeld, defended drawn games. He argued that the denial of a victor or a vanquished elevated the game above the gladiatorial. The games in *Draw!* were often thrilling, with flawless play from both sides of the board. "Who can doubt," Heidenfeld wrote, "that draws that are both well-fought and free from major error . . . constitute the highest form of chess?" But I couldn't get past their betrayal. No one had won.

"So do you understand draws now?" Glenn said, near New York, his eyes still closed behind me.

"I think so," I said.

He doubted it, but said nothing. The bus began a hissing breaking maneuver as we swung toward the Lincoln Tunnel. The passengers in the bus shifted all at once like eggs in a carton.

"The New York Open," Glenn said. "My chance to be famous."

THE MAIN TOURNAMENT ROOM WAS THE GRAND BALLROOM OF the New Yorker Hotel, owned by Reverend Moon, the Korean mass-marriage specialist. The New Yorker had taken the marriage of chess and hotel convention space a step further. As Mitchell had warned us, the New Yorker was now the home of the Manhattan Chess Club, in a pair of suites on the fifteenth floor.

Glenn and I settled in and arrived downstairs twenty minutes before the first round. The Grand Ballroom was deserted but set as though for a banquet, long conference tables arrayed cafeteria-style, boards and pieces already in place. As we arrived a team of tournament directors fanned through the room to distribute and wind clocks. The ballroom was loosely ornate. The carpet attempted a hybrid of fashion and fire codes, and a grand piano had been rolled off into a corner as punishment for irrelevance. A complex of chandeliers shed off the kind of diffuse incandescence that might equip a high-volume morgue.

Players began to filter in. I recognized Arthur Bisguier, the current Grand Old Man of U.S. chess, already seated at his board and waiting for his opponent. He seemed happy just sitting there. In neat cinematic contrast, eleven-year-old Hikaru Nakamura wobbled by just as I was watching—some months before he had set the record for a USCF master ranking: ten years, seventy-nine days. Pudgy and uncoordinated, Nakamura seemed to remain upright only because of the added weight. In an attempt to start the week with an interesting match, he had been paired on Board 1 against Vladimir Epishin, the tournament's highest rated player.

The tables filled with men, the room with chatter. Glenn headed off to his board, and I wandered the aisles of preconflict camaraderie. Chess players are prone to classism—grandmasters mix with grandmasters, masters with masters, etc., and though the tournament room was public and I could stand beside anyone I wanted to, it was easy to remain invisible; in fact, it was the players' idea that I do so. Leaning against a pillar, I witnessed the week's first controversy: A young, strikingly beautiful Dominican woman explained to a tournament director (TD) that she was entered in the tournament but didn't have a pairing. "You're in the open section?" the TD asked her. She scowled at him. The next time I saw her, she had been given an opponent and was frozen over her game in a position common to chess players everywhere: hands pressed into either side of her head as though attempting to juice an oversized orange.

Two minutes before 6:00, I realized that I had failed in one of the most basic functions of the chess second. I had not left my player with any encouraging words. I hurried quickly to Glenn's game, where he was chatting with those near him. His opponent had yet to arrive. "Hey, go get 'im, okay?" I said, but Glenn responded only distractedly, like a politician blindly accepting praise.

For the opening speech, I hurried upstairs to a balcony that over-looked the tournament floor. I saw why Glenn had been distracted—the players around him were all grandmasters, identified by placards. GM John Fedorowicz, GM Christian Bauer, GM Alexander Ivanov. Glenn's opponent, GM Igor Nataf, one of the strongest players of France, arrived at the last minute. Nataf had recently won an annual best game award from a prominent chess journal. Glenn smiled sheepishly and half rose in his chair to shake the young man's hand. The grandmasters chatted and laughed to ease the tension. Glenn was barely able to contain his excitement among that choice crowd. Watching it all at a distance, I was suddenly overcome with dread. Glenn would lose to Nataf. Not because he was scared of grandmas-ters, but rather because he wasn't. IM Josh Waitzkin once said, "Dur-ing the game, you want to kill your opponent—it's ridiculous." Glenn didn't want to kill anyone, he wanted to befriend them.

The opening speech was delivered by Carol Jarecki, a long-time chess supporter whose son had been a prodigy. She approached a microphone to the left of the stage where the top three boards were set and made a modest introduction. She cut to what she called the most important bit of information that the players would need: where the toilets were. This proved to be a complex set of directions involving multiple flights of stairs, and throughout the week, during play, I would see chess players rushing through the lobby of the hotel, the clocks of their games and their bladders ticking.

Jarecki dropped her notes to her side. "That's it, I guess," she said. "You may start your clocks."

The players complied, and the off-timed sputter of one hundred chess clocks enaged at once came like the report of distant musket-shot at the outset of a famous battle.

THE FIRST GRANDMASTER TITLES WERE CONFERRED BY CZAR Nicholas II at the conclusion of a tournament held in St. Petersberg in 1914. Or so goes the revisionism. The exact circumstances of the tale curiously resemble a knight's promotion ceremony: gallant war-riors honored for valor by the king. The problem is, the grandmaster title was in use as early as the 1830s, and Czar Nicholas II was in the Crimea in 1914, communicating with his capital only by post and courier.

The term *grandmaster* helped draw distinctions between very talented players. By the nineteenth century, "master" was no longer sufficient—even among the best, there was a broad range of ability. The separate "grand" category was born. History was repeating itself, but no one seemed to notice: Islamic players a few dozen generations before had recognized five classes of chess talent. The highest, *'aliyat,* translated as "grandee" before grandmaster even appeared.

Modern chess history would repeat Islamic chess history almost perfectly. Currently, there are the four formal classes of significant ability, but a recent proliferation of grandmasters has brought the GM title to saturation. An informal fifth title has come into vogue, cutesy and infantilized: "super-GM." A super-GM is a player superior to most grandmasters and may vie for the world championship. If history repeats itself, the title will be made formal and retroactively attributed to a politician who never heard of it.

GM Nataf was tall and dark, a thick tuft of hair visible at his throat. When Glenn started his clock, Nataf reacted not at all, pausing for what seemed like several minutes to acquaint himself with the silence that abruptly fell across the room. He filled out his scorecard, double-checked the spelling of Glenn's name, and settled in with his hands quietly at his sides. He looked about, either at the players near him or into some invisible dimension.

Nataf finally made his first move, e4. Glenn took more than a minute to respond to the most common first move in the history of the game, and then they began a leisurely trade.

I reclined in my seat and glanced about at the ninety-nine other dramas also unfolding. The ballroom had become about as silent as a room full of the zealous and anxious can become, the purity occasionally interrupted by a variety of nervous behaviors: shufflings, a rhythm of coughing as bacteria was passed about like pollen among flowers, the whisper, the chuckle, once in a while the hiss-pop of a soda can, all the agonized evidence of two hundred minds grinding away on a fourteen-hundred-year-old puzzle. I was struck by the fact that players in tournament games were frequently not at their boards—once the games had moved sufficiently into their openings, many players made their move, hit their clock, and left. This was what Glenn had tried to describe to me so long ago. The opponent, who might also have left, then returned, moved, and left again, so that in some games it was entirely rare for the players to sit face-to-face. It was as though every move was a period of intensity, like holding your breath underwater, and afterward the player would swim to the surface to recover.

I came down from the balcony to mill with the crowd and examine the faces I would come to know through the week. Players and observers moved about like customers at a yard sale, a slow steady gait punctuated by brief hesitations, pauses filled with analysis. I made for the head of the room to see how the little Nakamura was doing against Epishin. There were three rows of seats before the waist-high stage, and behind each of the games stood a demonstration board like the one Glenn used for his blindfold exhibitions. The audience would prove thin through the week; men keeping score or making experimental moves on small magnetic sets; men in postal or janitor's uniforms, or in suits; men nibbling on treats or listening to headsets; men with their heads tilted slightly back as though contemplating something suspect. The players on the dais often, even when it was their move, simply looked back into the crowd. It wasn't quite preening, but they were aware of being watched, regarding the gallery the way gorillas regard visitors at the zoo.

Epishin, even with his rating of 2667, was the kind of man I felt an instinctive pity for: he was a step beyond plump, his hair was disheveled, his clothes were old and unwashed, and his heavy glasses slid down his nose like wax on a candle. Throughout the week, between moves, he paced between the boards, shuffling forward as though working through some important presentation he was soon to give. The little Nakamura was already on the receiving end of a sweating lesson, and the boy seemed preoccupied with the audience, with the tournament, with everything but his opponent's pieces bearing down on his king. I felt sorry for him as well.

As would happen in each round, I found three or four boards that were interesting either for the player match-up or for what I could discern of the position. I amassed a cast of characters to follow: Anna Khan, a young, sexy, sleepy-eyed Latvian as well-known in the chess world for her play as her presence; Julen Arizmendi, a handsome young international master who somehow seemed to have acquired chess talent without the usual sacrifice of health and hygiene; GM Igor Khenkin, a man who looked to be teetering on the edge of an exhaustion-inspired insanity; Immanuel Guthi, a tall, bearded, and smelly Israeli whom Glenn and I knew from our casino—he was a regular—where he was known simply as "Moses" for the likeness; GM Alexander Ivanov, who, like Epishin, went for little walks between his moves, holding his hands in a lotus-style pinch and closing his eyes as though to recall a fragrance; GM Alexander Galkin, a friendly looking Russian who could have passed for a young literature professor in tweed and jeans; and Timoleon Polit, a thin, nervous, little old 1390 guy who would be on the lowest board all week, and who looked like the kind of man Jack Lemmon would play, the washed-up business stooge attempting to use chess to fulfill a criteria for having led an eventful life. All these faces I committed to memory.

Eventually, I came back to Glenn's game. I had to look at the clock to determine whose move it was because neither man appeared to be thinking about the game. Glenn's eyes were trained on Fedorowicz's position next door, and Nataf was frozen, either communing with his angel or accepting a data transmission from a satellite. Of the game I could make out little: Glenn had begun what was perhaps a premature queenside attack, one of his pawns lurched forward to a square threatening but vulnerable. Nataf had castled, but his knights looked cramped. After ten minutes, I left the two men just as I had found them.

The tournament was an hour old. Out near the directors' desks, I eavesdropped on a debate over Bu Xiangzhi, the tall, bad-toothed fourteen year old who had just become the youngest grandmaster in the history of the game. Lines of argument formed over whether the boy had deserved the title. Some were impressed by his achievements, but others alluded to a well-known phenomenon in chess—the organization of tournaments for the sole purpose of creating grandmasters. The debaters didn't know it yet, but back in the ballroom Bu was minutes away from dropping a piece to a much weaker player.

The tournament spilled into some of the hotel's common areas. I headed into a hallway where the standings would be posted for the week, bulletin boards that attracted great crowds before each round. Between these boards, on the floor against the walls, stood the work of painter Jovan Prokopljevic, a literal chess artist. Prokopljevic traveled from tournament to tournament to sell prints of his chess paintings, modest, cartoonish works with chess themes and images of gnomish chess players, whose large noses and rotund bodies made them look a little like Prokopljevic himself. Prokopljevic sat behind a table and watched people watch his work. His business was quiet now, and he would wait the entire day to make a few sales as the games began to finish.

I bought a cup of coffee in the lobby and watched players weave through the hotel guests, minds on their games. On the way out of the tournament area they were composed and relaxed, but on the way back they were rushed, breaking into power walks. I was surprised to spot Nataf, calm and steady, having a laugh with the bearded man who was his own second. They went on in French; and though they might have been talking about anything, I immediately concluded that they were having some fun over Glenn's position. The role of the second in real duels, I knew, was pretty simple—make sure the guns are loaded right—but four-hundred years ago, in France no less, seconds were honor bound to take part in the hostilities. I had no problem with this. A hatred for the bearded man, my counterpart, welled inside me; and I fertilized it with quiet scathing criticism of his dress and manner. I hurried back to the tournament, almost at a jog, to see what had brought their happy mood.

In 1921, shortly after Lasker lost the world championship to Capablanca, Lasker gave a description of his opponent's style that proved an accurate description of how chess would come to be played in the coming decades. Capablanca's strength was to "by almost imperceptible degrees increase a trifling, scarcely more than theoretical, advantage until it became real and eventually decisive." When I returned to Glenn's game, I found him in the middle stage of this degeneration. He had lost a pawn. The very pawn that had attacked prematurely had become the theoretical advantage Nataf had set about exploiting, and with the pawn now in his pocket all he had to do was convert that real advantage to a decisive one. Glenn had managed to wedge a bishop near Nataf's king, but by itself it was little more than a nuisance. I could see nothing in the position that compensated for the pawn, but Glenn was steady over the board, massaging his chin in thought.

I flushed. I hadn't thought Glenn would win, but now that the loss was imminent, it surprised me. I wandered through the tournament, distracted by the emotion but checking up on the games I had followed. Guthi sneered a prophet's recognition at me as I caught his scent and watched him work the nerves of an excitable eighteen year old; Anna Khan had the vise on old man Polit; Bisguier had used his half-century's worth of tactical knowledge to win in seventeen moves; and the little Nakamura's tenuous position looked not so tenuous anymore, even if the boy himself sat the stage like a nervous kid riding a parade float.

Back at Glenn's game, the race had begun. Nataf had returned to the board, and he used his bishops to chase down Glenn's king. With each move the advantage became more real, more insulting, and twenty minutes later another of Glenn's pawns was hung out to dry.

He offered his hand across the board. My body seized.

A number of games were finishing up: Players signed one another's scorecards and turned in the moves to the directors' desk. Slightly dazed, I moved through a louder and busier room. I stopped in place when I saw the final result of Epishin-Nakamura: ½–½. The kid had managed the draw. Suddenly, I knew exactly why a draw was closer to a win, and I fretted that Glenn had not managed even the semivictory. I looked around until I found the little Nakamura edging his way between tables, expressionless, as though it had been nothing at all to be eleven years old and draw one of the best chess players in the world.

Glenn tapped my arm from behind, and indicated that I should follow him. I felt at once ill-prepared as his second—I had no consoling words for him. But it didn't seem to matter to Glenn, who appeared to be in a pretty good mood despite the loss. He led us into the common room outside the tournament hall, where Nataf waited for us. We would do a postmortem of the game. It turned out that Glenn had known Nataf from the ICC—they had played and chatted across the Atlantic—and so even though the game had been routine, they would discuss it before retiring.

Glenn introduced Nataf by title—Grandmaster Nataf—and we found a board on which to reconstruct the game. Nataf was the senior player present and set about giving what amounted to a workshop session. The game boiled down to Glenn's fifth move, b5.

"This is not good move," Nataf said. "Black is behind in development. Needs to castle. Premature."

Glenn admitted that he had had luck with b5 against strong players on the ICC.

"You had me worried," Nataf said, "after h5. Do you know what I was afraid of?"

Glenn studied the position for a moment, but didn't want to look as though he needed to think about it. "Bc5?"

"h4!" Nataf said, and made Glenn's move himself so that a threat for Glenn's pieces appeared quite suddenly. "Now black can play. These pieces—you see?—can maneuver. But still, after b5, I have advantage."

"Yo," Glenn said later, as we headed to our room. "Grandmasters are good!"

I was surprised at how he was taking the loss, and I was a little sore that he hadn't played safer. "Why did you play a speed move in a tournament game?" I said.

"It worked before."

"In five minutes. Not in six hours."

Glenn shrugged. We were quiet until we reached the room and got ready for bed.

"I got outplayed," Glenn said. "But you know what? I didn't play scared. And tomorrow I have white."

SATURDAY MORNING GLENN SHOWERED AND DRESSED AND prepared what would prove to be his preround meal, a concoction designed to boost his play. First, he unscrewed three ginseng capsules and sprinkled the magic powder over a tin of sardines. The little fishes' spinal chords were clearly visible as he munched them down. Next, he worked open a can of tangerine wedges, stabbed each crescent with a fork, and swallowed them whole. Finally, he drank a glass of sugar-water juice, gulping the sweet potion as though its hit would help him prevail.

Saturday would be his best day in the tournament.

Just before the second round, the crowd around the pairing board stood three bodies deep. The players were still fresh, but sleepy. Glenn's opponent for the round was a sixtyish 1900 man from the Dominican Republic. He appeared to be the leader or coach of a group of young Dominicans, including the young woman I had seen. Against Glenn, the man played quickly, allowing a slow drizzle of pawns to eventually soak him. Glenn ended it with a tactic on the man's pinned king, and the attack was so decisive there was no need to discuss it afterward. Glenn smiled and shook my hand, and we left the ballroom where, three hours later, many games of the second round would still be in doubt.

Out near the pairings board we spotted Guthi. He sat off in a corner, sprawled across a chair beneath a tall window. Guthi was dressed in the same rumpled, ill-fitting suit he had worn the day before, the same suit, in fact, that Glenn and I had seen him wear almost every day at the casino.

Glenn walked over to say hello. Guthi had won the night before, but he had been paired on stage against the 2622 Khenkin that morning, and he had been put away easily. Guthi smiled, and spoke whimsically, "These guys—too good!"

We left him in the corner that would serve as his squat for the week. Across the street at a fast-food joint Glenn admitted that he had given money to Guthi in Atlantic City on a number of occasions for food or bus fare. Glenn didn't particularly approve of Guthi, but he had helped him on occasion.

At the fast-food counter, Glenn bought a special two-for-one chicken sandwich and hot apple turnover deal. He had the meals bagged separately, ate one, then excused himself to run outside with the other. When he came back the sandwich and pie were gone.

"He looked hungry," Glenn said.

We took the subway to Washington Square Park to kill the hours before round three. It was May, the day was perfect, and in the park the drug trade flourished alongside the chess business. Sweet Pea was there, haunched up on his newspapers, but Russian Paul was not to be found. There were ten or twelve games in progress, some gamblers, some looking to charge the usual rates. Glenn played several games with the current cock of the roost, a wiry black man named Harry. Glenn won the first game and in the second he ran his clock down to :34 before beginning a hyper assault. He promoted one queen at :09, another at :03, and gave mate with 0.4 on his clock. Several observers shook their heads, and a man carrying a book of Pablo Neruda poems gave a low whistle.

"Double the bet," Harry said, angry. "This one for five."

Glenn smiled faintly and reset the clock. "I'm up four, right?"

"Yeah. Five dollars. Come on!"

They played the game, and Glenn won more handily. Harry wanted to double again—he was on the line—but Glenn quit him, taking five dollars and calling it even. Harry was furious, but all he could do was spit his anger at us in quick half sentences, continuing his sermon even as we left earshot.

Back at the hotel, the tournament was beginning to take shape. As players accumulated points, they moved up in the boards, playing closer to the stage. The pairings went up at 5:00. Glenn was to play Ronald Simpson, a handsome man about forty.

Simpson's manner at the board was slightly nervous. His eyes cruised between the pieces as he jammed his fingers into his mouth, chewing their tips. His rating was significantly higher than Glenn's, but for the duration of the game he looked like a man awaiting test results in a hospital corridor. This was in part due to Glenn's play. Their game began hypermodern, both players exerting abstract influence on the critical center squares, and after the first eight or ten moves there was a prolonged period of probing and jabbing, as though neither man was sure if they wanted the contest to be a tactical pyrotechnic display or a sublime ballet of positional proofs. On Glenn's twentieth move, he played on the board what to that point had been a looming threat—he sacked a pawn to open Simpson's kingside. This exposed Glenn's own king, and though it was not clear whether the sacrifice was sound, the move decided once and for all that the game would be tense and upsetting, at least in chess terms, and that if Simpson went on chewing his fingers as a function of Glenn's threats he would need sutures when all was said and done.

Several moves later, Glenn's sack had proved useful and sound. His queen had advanced up to the h-file. Each of his remaining pieces had quick and potentially lethal access to white's king. Simpson's intensity betrayed his nerves; his knights jogged on his back rank. Glenn rose from the game and climbed up to the balcony to see me. He smiled, and whispered, "Now, I'm in his grill! He's gotta play e3."

e3 was on the board before he got back. Simspon had been forced to block his own active rook. Two moves later Glenn had a rook-queen battery on the h-file, and the game seemed well in hand.

I took a break to wander. I came downstairs and dwelled on the tournament's range of peoples and fashions. Strangely, the more disheveled a player was, the more he was to be feared. There was a similar rule in place for children, who because they tended to improve quickly between events often had ratings that did not reflect their strength. The age range in the room was as wide as the style of dress— from Glenn's neat suits to Guthi's wrinkled antifashion to GM Maurice Ashley's Negro-league Pittsburgh Crawford T-shirt to Anna Khan's easy allure, the sexy twist of her thin frame as she leaned forward to enter the depth of a position. Many players' clothes were out of style, either temporally or geographically, and sideburns were in, sometimes accidentally. Most of the grandmasters were Russian, many with beard shadows that seemed to darken with the strain of their thinking. The coughing in the room had become more frequent now, a low-grade virus catching and spreading, a chess epidemic. A sense of anxiety was building as well, in the way of people trapped together and beginning to starve. There was a natural tendency to look about and speculate on who was expendable and of possible nutritious value.

I just missed crashing into Epishin as he came around a corner, the nerdy powerhouse hurrying back to the stranglehold he had on some hapless IM. I dodged him, then listened in for a moment on the conversation of the strapping Arizmendi, who while his clock was ticking flirted with a woman named Mercedes, another Dominican. She smiled and twisted a predictable finger through her hair, and Arizmendi joked with her in a common tongue. The two would become the tournament's lovers, the week like a tryst. I gave them their privacy, moving on to those lower boards where players with few or no points pushed their wood, older men like Polit addressing in retirement a passion that the tournament would prove they should have addressed long ago.

I headed back to Simpson-Umstead.

In chess, brilliancy has a very particular meaning. A one-sided contest executed with style and panache is inferior to a game in which the dexterity of the defense matches the lust of the attack. Simpson began a brilliant defense. He returned a pawn to keep a critical file half closed, then forced the queens off. The men traded a pair of rooks, a swap that gave Glenn a passed pawn that would gestate for seventeen moves before figuring huge in the ending. But well prior to that, around move thirty, Simpson came up with a resource the effectiveness of which he could not have been aware, a weapon that, had he played the man rather than the board, he might have used with more frequency and greater consequence. He sneezed. Perhaps battling the tournament flu, Simpson's body convulsed violently on itself. Glenn reacted just as suddenly, rearing back in his chair as though from a devastating combination. He was stunned and thrown. Simpson might not have noticed—he wiped the residue of the sneeze onto the thigh of his jeans and went on chewing his gum—but Glenn hesitated for almost half a minute, allowing the air to clear, before righting himself and toggling back into concentration mode.

The players used the next four or five moves to attempt exploitation of the refitted pawn structures. Then Glenn found a tactic, using a bishop to snap off a protected pawn. If Simpson took it, he would lose his remaining rook. He was forced to bring his king into the fray, committing it to the defense of a pawn that would eventually fall anyway. But the move gave him play, and fully half of his remaining moves would be with a single knight that weaved through Glenn's territory threatening a series of forks. For the next short interval, both players found the only moves that would preserve the game's complicated balance. A few weeks later, Glenn would put a computer to work on the game, and in several hours it would verify the exactness of moves the players intuited in minutes.

Glenn finally grabbed Simpson's exhausted knight on c5, an exchange that gave him another passed pawn alongside his first from thirteen moves before. Connected passed pawns: Valued sometimes as high as a rook and more powerful further up the board, connected passed pawns advance like a bolo leap-frogging through the air. The race on the board—Simpson's king slicing across to harass Glenn's knight, and Glenn's pawns sneaking forward to defend it—had already been run in the player's minds but was no less exciting in the creep of its realization. The three stages of a chess game have been compared to the beginning, middle, and end of a story; but narrative prose, I thought, would not quite do justice to the fine torture of watching such a brilliant equilibrium sustained. Climax and denouement were delayed, the brain suspended in a vortex of stress. There were moments watching when I would rather have been torn apart by the gravity that drives a black hole than be forced to continue tottering at that event's horizon. Glenn pushed a pawn with check. Simpson inched closer to the knight, now protected. I felt pulled toward the end of the game in the same way a musical scale draws toward resolution. Glenn gave check with his bishop in a surprise move awful and wonderful. Simpson took it, and then, very suddenly, the two men spoke a few scripted words, smiled and shook hands, and I realized what I had just seen, and I was exhilarated and spent, though no one around me would have guessed that I had any stake in the matter at all.

It was a draw.*

The end of a good chess game is more like a birth than a death—it's a beginning. Once completed, games become public fact and property that are scrutinized, appreciated, distributed, retold. They may achieve a fame of their own, wriggle into databases both figurative and literal, and eventually constitute lore. Glenn and Simpson paused not at all at the end of their contest. They and a few others hurried off to the Skittles Room to analyze what they had wrought. The game had attracted some attention, and the session that followed in the adjoining chamber was like a celebration after a complex plan has come to fruition. The two men played through the moves again, smiling and laughing now at the maneuvers they had considered or feared. Observers offered alternatives almost always explained away by the players.

Among the watchers was Emory Tate, a flamboyant member of the black chess sub-subculture. Glenn admired Tate. He had shown me one of Tate's games in *Chess Life* a year back, and we had spoken to him briefly the day before. Neither tall nor wide, Tate was nevertheless a kind of super-aggressive man, dominant in his element, with wide, wild eyes and a manner that suggested amphetamine enhancement. Tate had a tendency to think quickly and translate his thoughts into words at once. His whole being seemed derived from speed chess.

Tate had watched the analysis of Simpson-Umstead from a distance. When he finally suggested a line, he did it in grandiose fashion, stepping no nearer the board but assuming the floor.

"Takes! Retakes, takes, takes! Bg7, rook up, pawn takes, and black's cooked!"

The watchers were stunned at the outburst, but no one looked at Tate. They all watched the board, eyes attempting to follow whatever line he had described.

Anticipating criticism, Tate went on: "If Kg3, push! Takes, takes, takes, takes! Rh3! And same thing. Thank you for the game. Analysis

*See appendix for game.

courtesy of Emory Tate, five-time U.S. Armed Forces champion! Good night!"

He was four or five moves ahead of the position on the board. Simpson was about to call Tate on some section of the analysis, but Tate would not go down easily.

"Don't talk about it! Analyze!" He pointed at the board, meaning they should execute the moves he described. "Play chess! Play chess!"

The game wasn't over, according to Tate. A game of chess was never over.

Tate's moves turned out to be just as inconclusive as the text of the game. The delicate balance was preserved, and Tate's suggestion was really more of a test, pressure applied to its purity. Tate simply waited until his own moves revealed no lopsided advantage to grant it his approval.

"A game like that," he said. "It's studylike."

The proclamation allowed the group to disband. There were a number of speed games in the room by then; but there was another round in the morning, and Glenn wanted to sleep. We stopped to relax at a bar a block away. I pulled out my peg set so I could ask a few questions, and we played through not the decisive victory of the morning but the inconclusive draw of the evening.

At the end of it, each of my questions answered with a simple gesture—an overlooked capture, a revealed check—Glenn finally came down from the high.

"Tate said it was studylike," he said, wondrously. "That's a great compliment."

SUNDAY WAS A DISASTER FOR GLENN. IN ROUND FOUR, HE WAS paired against a 2300 Spaniard, and achieved what looked like a good position. Then, perhaps overconfident from the day before, he sank his queen deep into his opponent's territory, going after an undeveloped rook. The Spaniard threatened to trap the queen, and in the scuffle Glenn overlooked a move that gave check and attacked one of his pieces at the same time. He resigned at once. The thrill of the day before was gone in an instant. That night he was back in the rear of the room again, matched up against a jumpy 1900 high-school junior. It was the first game to which Glenn arrived late—the clocks began ticking at 6:00, regardless of whether either player was present—and he made his first move after he had lost thirteen minutes. It didn't matter, though. The blunder of the morning had killed his spirit, and he played a dull draw.

"How could I miss the queen check?" Glenn said later, in our room.

It was the third or fourth time he had asked the question, and there still wasn't an answer. He had been too aggressive, I thought, but he had come to his senses in the second game. He had opted for the safe half-point. At least we had that.

I attempted to remain impartial as a second should, but it was difficult. I was also a disappointed fan. "You're playing like these guys are no good," I told him. "Too much ICC."

"Hm," Glenn said.

"Hey. How can I be your second when you won't listen?"

He paused. "You're not my second."

"Sure I am," I said. "A batting coach doesn't need to be a great hitter. He just needs to know how to bat."

"What color is f6?"

"White."

"Man," Glenn said, "You had a fifty-fifty chance."

By morning he had recovered a little. We caught the subway downtown and stopped at a used bookstore where Glenn found a treasure: a text with an entire chapter devoted to a move he liked, 6. Bg5 in the Samisch Variation of the King's Indian Defense (KID). Back at the hotel, for half an hour before round six, he described the move to me—it was a little-known but strong maneuver he had picked up from an early tournament opponent. Complicated move names are best understood in reverse: The King's Indian Defense (KID) went as far back as the nineteenth century, but hadn't become popular until the '20s. Played from black, the KID basically amounts to a fianchettoed bishop on the kingside, which granted white a central pawn structure that black proceeded to attack. The Samisch Variation refers to Friedrich Samisch, a German bookbinder. Samisch's greatest success was a match victory over the hypermodernist Réti, so it's not a surprise that the Samisch Variation, 5. f3, is considered one of the best replies to the hypermodern KID. The next move, 6. Bg5, has remained somewhat unexplored: It is unnamed and questionable, and Glenn preferred it, I thought, for its vague romanticism.

I left Glenn to his shower and sardines and went upstairs before the next round. I wanted to check out the new digs of the Manhattan Chess Club. The most recent move of the club was suggestive of a transformation in the game itself. Just as chess was going high-tech, the old clubs, with their classical soundtracks and colonies of dust mites, were being forced to retreat to suites with Internet capacity.

As soon as I stepped off the elevator I could hear the click of pieces, the crackle of a hushed conflict. The club was laid out like a doctor's office, a corridor alongside three rooms crammed with tables. The photos on the walls were those of the old location, but they seemed out of place in the new context. It was weirdly *clean*. But the players who sat in the front room didn't notice anything amiss as they sat around a board and talked about e3s and g6s, and Benonis, and Scotch games, laughing at odd moments.

In the back room a children's tournament was underway, eight or nine silent children making moves and punching clocks. Some of them sat as still and grim as memorials to children lost. I glanced at my watch: 6:05. The larger tournament had begun again.

The week had hit its peak. The grandmasters had broken away from the pack: Bu Xiangzhi had recovered from his shaky start and was making a run to prove his name; Khenkin had won four straight; Ivanov was steadily moving up, though in his lotus trance he might have been oblivious to even his own score. I stopped to watch Galkin, the Russian literature prof—at four points he was doing quite well. It wasn't just Galkin's clothes that made him seem human: He was the only player I saw all week who was expressive as he played. He squinted at the pieces, moved his lips, scrunched his nose as he debated his own ideas. His manner made chess seem possible.

Players were up and moving about more now, I noticed. If the previous Friday time away from the board had been used as a tool to maintain composure, it was now an extra weapon. Wastes of time delivered messages of intimidation. You knew a player was nervous when he appeared in a rush just after his opponent moved—he was watching from somewhere, but wanted to appear casual. Players attempted to confuse one another with off-the-board tactics, the psyche game overlapping with chess's tendency to draw out the hungry animus. This feeling was transmitted to the crowd of observers, which had grown substantially by then. I became a member of this group, and as a group we shuffled from board to board, searching not, as one might expect, for decisive moments of subtle drama. Rather, we descended on games where the outcome had been decided, where the pieces were coming off quickly, where at least one frustrated player was digging deep for the courage to resign. Our quest was for blood. It was the same instinct that preferred the execution to the trial, and the faces in our circle, gathered around a struggling master, were like the silent gawkers who watch a stoning and who would participate if they could.

Glenn's game had good news and bad news. The bad news was that his opponent was thirteen years old. Traian Tasu was a gawky, shy, 1659 boy in a funny baseball hat. I got the idea that he was Romanian somehow. Tasu was bad news because, having already scored victories over two players rated higher than 2000, he seemed to be one of those dramatically improved children. Just a year younger than Bu Xiangzhi, there was really no telling how strong he might be. The good news was that I recognized the position on the board when I arrived: Glenn had just played 6. Bg5 in the Samisch Variation of the KID. The boy hadn't really fallen for a prepared line, but at least Glenn was playing something he was familiar with.

I walked out to the pairings board to see how Tasu was doing. He had two victories against strong players and two draws. Back at the game, the sacrifice that Glenn was about to play on the board was not nearly as surprising as the fact that GM Nick de Firmian was watching the game. De Firmian was quite famous, an ex-U.S. Champion whose ragged blond hair and lingering youthfulness gave him the air of a surfer guru. Like Xiangzhi, de Firmian had stumbled in the first round, but he had played quite strongly since. Glenn was in the room's back row for round six, and it was surprising to see de Firmian strayed so far from his board. The grandmasters tended to avoid the lower boards as though their lesser chess could rub off. At first, I guessed Tasu was a student—de Firmian had been living in Europe, I'd read—but de Firmian's intense study of the position suggested it was Glenn's sacrifice that had caught his attention. De Firmian studied the board as deeply as the players. Deeper. He tried to walk away not once, but twice, each time pulled back by something striking in the position, something so vexing he couldn't yank himself away even as his own game continued across the room. Before the New York Open, I had been under the impression that sacrifices in tournament chess were relatively common. Chess magazines published many sacrificial games, and players who sack frequently are almost always popular. But in reality, sacrifices without immediate compensation are rare, and in four days at the tournament, four days in which I had observed hundreds of games, I had seen only four. Three of them were Glenn's.

De Firmian scurried back to his game just before Glenn played the sack. Tasu recaptured, and Glenn went on to lay siege to the boy's broken position. Later computer analysis would show that Glenn had already passed up a winning move, but a sacrificial attack is like watching a tightrope artist—it's more dramatic when they slip. Tasu could fight back. Stuffed into his corner, he found a way to skewer Glenn's rooks with a bishop, and when Glenn pushed a pawn rather than retake, the boy thought for thirteen minutes before returning Glenn's sacrifice. Two moves later Tasu was on the offensive. He played methodically, harvesting material, launching his own high-wire act. Much later, the computer would offer smarmy, prepro-grammed criticism after various moves through this stage of the game: **Black** [Tasu] **can already relax; Black keeps a firm grip; White** [Glenn] **chokes on his own greed; Even a better move would not have saved the game; No good, but what else?** Before his twenty-third move, Tasu thought for twenty-two minutes and then pushed his king forward, a bit of sly bravery that allowed an end-around by his rooks. Glenn replied at once, got up, and we hud-dled in a corner.

"That's bogus!" he said. "No 1600 player in the world thinks for twenty-two minutes. The kid can play."

Tasu tightened his headlock, forcing a series of trades that left Glenn down three pawns and the exchange. Tasu moved his queen for the first time on his thirtieth move, and Glenn was left wriggling, slowly suffocating. **Doesn't get the cat off the tree,** the computer would say when he moved a knight. **Doesn't get the bull off the ice,** when he moved it again. Tasu was excited now. His queen had hibernated for most of the game, he had fended off Glenn's attack using only a fraction of its influence, and now it was released. Glenn played a quiet king move, suspicious as he had not been in check. Tasu ignored it and continued building influence like drawing back the string of a bow. Glenn then moved his queen, and I saw that he had lined up all his remaining pieces along the same file as Tasu's king, and I realized that this was no accident, and that Tasu was too excited to notice it. I had just enough time to calculate each of the trap's lines, to recognize that there was just one move that would let it all work, before Tasu grabbed his queen and shuffled it to f4, the only loser. Glenn hesitated for politeness and moved his knight again.

The final blow, the computer would say.*

Suddenly, Tasu was thirteen again. After his eyes computed the equation of his demise, he looked back at me, mouth pried wide. De Firmian was nowhere to be found. Tasu absently shook Glenn's hand, and then his parents were on him. They had held a more distant vigil than my own, and their simultaneous ministrations were incomprehensible, even to their son.

Glenn and I fought giggles as we left the ballroom. The happy greed of a point! One point and advancement! A swindle in chess is far from the finest form of win, but the point was the same. Back in our room, Glenn and I toasted victory with special cookies we had purchased from the dollar store, squares of shortbread with profiles of chessmen printed into them.

"Did you see it coming?" Glenn said. "I thought he just might fall for it."

I was too giddy to respond.

"You know," Glenn went on, "there's gonna be one person in this hotel who can't sleep tonight! One!"

And we laughed out loud at the misfortune of a thirteen year old with promise.

IN ROUND SEVEN WE GOT WHAT WE DESERVED. GLENN'S OPPO-nent was a thin young man named Kriventsov who looked as though he was recovering from chemotherapy. But Kriventsov was not un-happy looking—he had the sickly glee of remission—and his rating was 200 points higher than Glenn's. I first approached their game when Kriventsov was away from the board. Glenn and I had gone to Washington Square Park again that day, the entire afternoon filled with the guilty rush of the previous night's victory. But Kriventsov was the weakling sheriff who would bring us to justice.

Now I glanced to my left and saw Kriventsov just beside me, both sets of fingers to his lips as though watching pain in one he loved.

*See appendix for game.

When Glenn moved a piece, Kriventsov strode forward and played a devastating move to end things—the unlikely retreat of a knight that revealed an unstoppable attack. Glenn resigned, and his joyousness of the day turned to a despondency he nurtured all night long.

Back in our room, he refused to play through the game to answer my questions. I set up a board and pieces on my mattress and made the moves myself, reading from the yellow score-sheet duplicate. I didn't know why, but I had the idea that if I could show him an improvement it would cheer him up.

"Does this save it?" I said, and played a bit of home-cooked nonsense.

Glenn was splayed across his bed as though tossed there by a bomb. He glanced up for just an instant, exhaled, and said, "f3." There was no way to commute the knight's sentence, and so I resigned myself, to Glenn's sadness and the gloom of the rest of the evening.

Before round eight Guthi sneaked into the ballroom and twiddled on the grand piano for a while. Despite his clothes and stench he could play. Snippets of melody, a minute of *Moonlight Sonata*. The connection between chess and music is deep and well-known, but the tournament directors told him to knock it off anyway. Round eight began. The tournament was grinding down. Six or seven grandmasters still had a shot at the win, but everyone else was playing for their rating. A number of players had given up completely—the directors had to dredge up an opponent for old man Polit. Everyone was visibly tired now, and the virus that had run its course earlier in the week had simply evolved and spread again. Anna Khan's sleepy eyes were bruised holes, and Professor Galkin studied his game with a frown as though over the grammar errors of students. De Firmian, with a shot at first place, looked like a man emerging from a car wreck, flushed and shocked. Only Ivanov and Epishin looked the same as they had all week, their sustained focus the product of a kind of used-up punchiness.

I saw only a few moments of Glenn's eighth game. It was a short draw against a young 1900 man named Fernandez, who had made chess his life by working for the ICC's New York office. The game was drawn with all sixteen pawns on the board.

Outside the ballroom, Glenn revealed why the game had gone so quickly.

"Hallman, I'm leaving. I'll be back tomorrow."

"You're leaving?"

"I'm going to Atlantic City. I'll be back for the last round."

He nodded. He was going to see a girlfriend, another doomed romance. I felt as though he had played a tactic on me, a combination I hadn't seen coming.

"You're just upset because you're losing," I said. "It's like running away."

"No, it's not," he said. "I'll see you tomorrow."

I WENT TO SEE A MOVIE THE NEXT DAY, A HOLLYWOOD spectacle of gladiatorial Rome whose production costs probably exceeded the amount of all the prize money awarded in every chess tournament ever held. The film inflicted an improbable story line onto the body of known historical fact in the same way chess distorted its history. I forgot about chess for two hours and stepped back into the light of the New York afternoon. Through the week, I realized, I had bought stock in chess's combat metaphor: The players were valiant warriors even if, to all external appearances, they were goofy and haunted. The spell was broken now. The metaphor was gross, and the fact that chess players themselves were often its source made them seem more wily than dangerous.

I went to Washington Square Park to play for a while. I used my *ta'biya* opening against a young black man who quickly became convinced that I was a master and then I played it against a grizzled, raisin-skinned old man who queen sacked on me, shrugged, and said he just saw it. I sat under a nearby tree and read a book that suggested the word "gospel" was related to the German word ending for game, *-spiel*. Thirty yards away, in the chess arena, an argument erupted over a money match that was technically not gambling. There was hollering and a threat of violence, and for a minute it seemed I would witness another contest between gladiators that day.

Glenn arrived for the final round just minutes before it began. His final opponent was a Canadian named Jean Herbert. Their game focused on a pawn Herbert moved into Glenn's territory. I thought of the chess language for pawns—pawn storms, pawn shields, pawn thrusts—but now they all seemed like childish exaggerations. Herbert had simply moved a pawn onto Glenn's side of the board. It wasn't a man sneaking behind enemy lines, it wasn't a planted bomb ticking away, it was just an idea that Glenn's ideas weren't good enough. Something of a balance was reached, but then Herbert used the slight advantage of having been more the proactive of the two men. This idea was perfect if protracted, and after a dozen moves Glenn rose from his seat and approached me.

"I'm going to resign in a few more moves. Get our bags. We can catch the 8:20."

The game was full of tactics; the position was intricate. Yet now I agreed that it was dull and unimportant, so far removed from tournament victory. It was habit and formality. I realized that Glenn had returned to New York only because I wanted him to, and even this seemed a poor decision.

The bus was crowded. We had to sit in the same double seat, thighs and shoulders pressed. We were quiet until we made the turnpike, and then Glenn reached to shake my hand.

"There was only one good thing about this tournament," he said. "I didn't play scared."

I didn't respond. I was angry. Like all fans, but not at all like a second, I was perfectly unforgiving. But at the same time I knew that his result was a function of his refusal to play a kind of chess that was bad for the game. Glenn was a creative player. I knew he was right—I knew that courage was more admirable than a trophy or a title—but I couldn't shake the competitiveness, the ego stake I had invested for the duration of the week. And all the way home I despised him for indulging in failed brilliance when he might have saved me the heartache and played for a draw.

CHAPTER 18

Developing Your Pieces: ♔

He moves on slow, with reverence profound
His faithful troops encompass him around,
And oft, to break some instant fatal scheme,
Rush to their fate, their sov'rign to redeem.

—Marcus Hieronymous, Scacchia Ludus, *1513*

And their glory is departed, they are annihilated
When they see how their lord is slain.
Yet does the battle begin over again,
And the killed ones once more stand up.

—Abraham b. Ezra, *1283*

To the moralists, the king was our lord jesus christ, as surely surrounded by rooks and knights as the King of Kings was surrounded by angels. Among chess players, everyone west of India agreed that the leader of the chessmen was a battlefield king—*shah, raja, khan*—but in Korea, China, and Japan, the king became a general and remained so. As chess had arrived in Europe around the time Christianity was replacing the Roman Empire as the unifying force in Western Europe, the king became associated with kings who wore crosses in their crowns to identify themselves as spiritual leaders: carved chess kings, which had always been equipped with some evidence of royalty—a sceptre or orb—went on to be shaped with a crucifix on their heads.

The king moves one square in any direction. As its capture is the goal of the game for each player, the importance of the king is obvious, but the strength of the piece as a weapon is more difficult to calculate. Efforts have been made to estimate the value of the king in the same way the other pieces have values, but it's tricky—while the power of the other pieces may increase or decrease according to the position, the king's fluctuation in strength is more a function of the stage of the game. The king is weak at the outset; but in an endgame with only a few pieces on the board, the king's value may exceed that of a bishop or a knight. King power is another opportunity for unlikely beauty in chess, and the king's unique combination of strength and vulnerability demonstrates the childish limitation of chess software: at least one program had to be told that the king had a value of 1,000 so it would not waste time calculating a king exchange.

The most reasonable theory of the origin of chess suggests that the game emerged from a kind of protochess, a board and men that were used in the conduct of a ceremony in the astrological spirit of the *I Ching*. The ritual used dice; a primitive dice chess would emerge and linger for five hundred years. The authors of *The Oxford Companion to Chess* took a somewhat whimsical view of the theory: "Then someone was sacrilegious enough to convert this process to a game, perhaps eliminating the dice. The person who secularized the religious ceremony has, perhaps, the best claim to be the 'inventor' of chess."

All chess historians have agreed that the point of the invention was the elimination of chance—a shift from faith in the justness of fate to faith in man's own intellect. The creation of a game based entirely on man's skill influenced the rules of the game itself in terms of the king. It now became "illegal" to move one's king into harm's way—it was against the laws to blunder so badly that the game would be lost for simple oversight. A rule for the reverse emerged as well: when attacking an opponent's king, a player was required to point out the attack by announcing "check." To give check ensured first that the opponent was aware of imminent danger, second that the eventual checkmate, a check that could not be blocked or dodged, would not be sullied by an opponent's error. Fate would receive neither credit nor blame in chess.

Announcing check has long since vanished from the laws of the game—a subarticle specifies that to announce check is not obligatory. Still, the announced check is a facet of the game that has caught the public imagination, and even those with little or no knowledge of the game know what a check is, and what it suggests. To give check is to announce your position as potent and significant, to cast influence and force others to acknowledge your threat.

In the Islamic game, the king was never allowed to move more than one square, and in East Asian games the generals are limited to a small grid of squares called the Nine Castle. In Europe, players were quick to note that the king was more easily protected in a corner of the board than in the center. The king's initial weakness was the bit of antirealism that led to the maneuver now known as castling. Surely the king should be as strong as a knight, and as early as the thirteenth century, the king was granted an initial leap, moving once like a knight. But when rooks came to be carved as towers, a metaphor presented itself—the king would retreat to his castle and seat of power. In castling, the king and rook perform a simultaenous flop of position, the only time in chess two pieces move at once. The verb "to castle" appeared around 1650, and the move was popular almost everywhere by the end of the century. In the modern game, to prevent an opponent from castling is advantageous, and early castling is one of the first lessons for students.

Because a king may attack all the squares immediately around it, two kings alone on a board cannot give check to each other. They repel one another like magnets. Endgames in which two kings shuffle about and try to escort a pawn to promotion revealed to chess players a phenomenon known as *zugzwang*, a German-derived word (*zug*: move; *zwang*: constraint, obligation) that meant the creation of a position on the board in which whoever moved next necessarily lost. To create *zugzwang* in a simplified ending, players were forced to understand repellent kings. The principle behind repellent kings is called "opposition." When artist Marcel Duchamp, also a chess player, wanted to write a book about an obscure chess phenomenon, he chose opposition and wrote *Opposition and Sister Squares Are Reconciled*, a compilation of problems that were possible but "so rare as to be nearly Utopian." According to the *Oxford*, king opposition was calculated by the measurement of the "distance between the centres of two laterally adjoining squares." It was an effort to determine in advance whether white or black was going to be able to create *zugzwang*. But the math of it all was tricky—everything either "partly depend[ed]" or was "loosely" understood—and king opposition is still not completely solved. It is evidence of the complexity of chess that even its most simple pieces, alone on a board, creates a function yet to be resolved after a millennium of effort.

CHAPTER 19

Nothing New Under the Sun

God moves the player, he, in turn, the piece.
But what god beyond God begins the round
Of dust and time and dreams and agonies?

—*Jorge Luis Borges, "Chess," 1960*

Explain, O supereminent in virtue, the game on
the eight times eight board. Tell me, O
my master, how the Chaturaji may be played.

—*Raghunandana,* Tithitattva, *late fifteenth century*

GLENN'S VICTORY OVER SASHA WAS THE HIGH POINT OF
his time in Chess City. He had crashed badly since then, and we
hadn't spoken for a few days. He didn't even write me a note. By
then he was completely out of money. Cash was even more important
than hot water, and he slipped back into his profound depression.
He began losing badly to Sasha, 20-10, 22½-15½. He went to sleep at
7:00 in the evening and often didn't wake for fifteen hours. For the
most part he stayed in the cottage, locked in his room, until Sasha
arrived, and then stumbled to the palace.

Bambusha helped arrange our flight back to Moscow. We made
the reservations five days in advance. Outside the travel agency was
a billboard with a shot of Kirsan with the Djangharchi. I had been
trying to figure out the Djangharchi for a while. He was the Kalmyk
singer who was the official holder of the famous Kalmyk epic *Djanghar,* a bald, middle-aged man who looked like a monk. But he was
neither a political nor a rigidly spiritual figure. The Djangharchi was
a performer, but he sang only one song that was a kind of history.

The Djangharchi was a historian, and Vaskin had told us that there were chess references in the *Djanghar*.

Bambusha and I went to see Galzanov to arrange a meeting.

The Djangharchi lived in Chess City with us, it turned out. His house was one of the largest in the subdivision, a multilevel prefab at the front of town. It was clean and spacious, sparingly furnished. The Djangharchi's wife let Bambusha, Glenn, and me inside, and led us to a living room with a long sofa. We sat to wait. Across from us, the Djangharchi's bench stood against a blank wall. It was made of heavy wood, and a cylindrical pillow was set carefully at either end. After a time, the Djangharchi appeared in his traditional baggy robes, the triple-spiked symbol of his clan prominent on his chest. He wore a pair of pointed boots like an elf. He carried a small guitar with him, a sophisticated ukulele. The Djangharchi spoke for a time before beginning a personal performance for us, employing sentences carefully measured, never hurrying his words, all the while twiddling on his instrument, plucking it for the sheer joy it seemed to give him. One of its strings sounded like a banjo, the other like a violin played pizzicato.

The Djangharchi's house was the center of the *Djanghar*, he said, a meeting place for those who felt called to sing the Kalmyk epic. The Kalmyks had come from a region thick in epics. Scientists had counted forty epics from the land of the Kalmyks' predecessors. The *Djanghar* was just one. Twenty-seven songs of the *Djanghar* had survived—originally it was much longer—but even so, to sing what remained from beginning to end would take more than a month. Some people believed that singing it had the power to change weather, to change many things.

The Djangharchi cleared his throat before he began. He had a heavy smoker's cough. We were about to learn why. He strummed his instrument, gripping its frets and wiping the fleshy strips of his fingers across the two strings, making both the beat and the chords he would follow, and after a brief semimelodic introduction he looked off to the right, down at the floor, at the singular spot he would study all the while he sang. Then he began the throaty vibrations that constituted the epic, that were his singing, a singing wholly different from the Kalmyk music at the tribute for the Olympic boxer. It was closer, I thought, to a monk's deep throat chant, but this was much more difficult because it was quicker and made up of many words, and there was a melody that went with them that climbed and descended and repeated. Like Altana's song, it seemed to want to capture the spirit of the steppe, but it succeeded where that popular other had failed, its grumbling turns and repeats like a low-altitude glide over the broad unpredictable sameness of the steppe. It was beautiful and painful to listen to the Djangharchi. The music was tribal and contemplative. But, as well, I couldn't listen without wondering what kind of damage he was doing to his vocal chords. Glenn stared on, and looked as though he might leap up to offer emergency medical attention. Both of us were confused but rapt, and completely unprepared for the weird magic that the Djangharchi had in store for us.

The Djangharchi rocked back and forth on his bench slightly as he played. His expression throughout was calm transcendence. He came to a point in the epic in which his voice was silent for a time, banging the same notes again and again as though gearing toward something, and then he took a long breath and hit a single deep throat note. The note remained steady a moment. Then it began an incredible change. It shifted first to a deep hum, then achieved a kind of choral resonance and seemed to be made up of many notes at once. Already it was entirely inhuman, a mechanical whirring, a perfect speedy engine. Then it began to fade even though the Djangharchi seemed to be doing fine without oxygen, but as the chord approached silence it began to morph again, and was replaced—no, *joined*—by another noise, a new and entirely different sound that could only be described as having come directly from the Djangharchi's soul. It was like a whistling. Or it was like the sound of a moist finger rubbed along the rim of a crystal glass, electric and fantastic. Somehow, it came from within the Djangharchi, a sometimes-trilling, sometimes-dissonant hissing pitch that I decided at once was the necessary escape of energy that occurred when the natural scratched against the supernatural. It was the whoop of another world's wind, the mating call of a wizardly imp trapped within the birdcage of the Djangharchi's ribs. He conjured the specter a number of times over the next immeasurable while, but could not control it, I realized, once he had rasped his voice to its frequency. He was only its conduit, and its unearthly play, its climb along scales, vibrating and sticking, seemed to have inspired the random melodies of the epic itself. It was indeed evidence of a better place. And when the Djangharchi fell silent, ending the song on a simple drunk's grunt, the silence in the room was heavy with disappointment for its absence.

We clapped lightly and the Djangharchi nodded and tinkered with his tuning pegs. The part of the *Djanghar* that he'd sung, he said, was a story about a very prosperous land—the land of the Kalmyks' ancestors. It was an ancient civilization. The ruler of the state was called Djanghar, a king who loved the whole world and who considered the whole world to be his.

The Djangharchi coughed heavily and fell silent. I wanted to ask him about the sound. I wanted to ask him what set of muscles he was exercising to make it. His face had remained impassive so that it was impossible to tell, but I just wanted to know what *region* of the body he was flexing. Instead, I asked about the title he held, and how he had come to obtain it.

The title, he said, was not passed down from father to son, but there had been such cases. The Djangharchi was a psychological state, a gift from God. The Djangharchi's real name was Tsagan Khaalg. He was educated as a civil engineer. One night, he had dreamt of himself singing, and that was the beginning for him.

"The song I just sang for you," the Djangharchi said, "was the same as the one I sang in the dream."

I mentioned Vaskin. "He told us there was chess in the *Djanghar*," I said.

"Yes," the Djangharchi said.

One section of the epic told the story of feuding brothers in the middle of the seventeenth century. A war brewed between rival clans. One afternoon the armies of the two brothers appeared across a field from one another. According to custom, the conflict would begin with a fight between two men in the middle of the field. A son of each brother was chosen for the contest. The cousins approached. The armies looked on, tense and quiet. When the men were just about to fight, they embraced instead. One produced a set of chessmen, the other a board, and they began to play. The battle was avoided.

The Djangharchi's wife had prepared tea and treats in the kitchen. A modern stereo system sat near the table, and as we sat down the Djangharchi laid a shiny CD into a gliding tray. The recording was the Djangharchi. He cranked it up and his voice boomed through the house louder than he ever could have sung. On the CD, he was accompanied by synthesizers and guitars, modern pulses and beeps. He was working with a French composer, he explained, on a remix that would make the Kalmyk style of singing more popular with young people. This would get them interested, he said. Then they would return to the epic.

When he turned the music down again, I asked him if he thought it was strange to be the keeper of such an old tradition yet live in Chess City in such a new home. He shrugged and said that the Kalmyk tradition conceived of time differently, that the difference between past and present wasn't so marked in their thinking.

Glenn had been quiet for the entire evening. That afternoon, he had refused an invitation from the Utnasunovs to attend a football game so that he could remain in Chess City and woo a Russian girl named Ludmilla. Ludmilla was half Glenn's age. They had walked about the palace taking pictures with a disposable camera. Before we visited the Djangharchi, Glenn and I had argued over the choice, and this explained his silence. But now he saw an opportunity to weigh in.

"In the West," he said, "we have a saying. 'There's nothing new under the sun.'"

The Djangharchi liked it. "It is a very wise saying," he agreed.

We stayed for a while longer, then excused ourselves. Once we were out in the street, Glenn and I had the opportunity to continue our argument, but we didn't. Instead, I asked him how he would describe the amazing sound that had come from within the Djangharchi.

"I don't know, man."

"It was like whistling," I said. I meant to tease him. The chess players of Russia had bested him, and now we had found a better whistler as well.

"That wasn't whistling," he said.

"Then what was it?"

"I don't know. Wasn't whistling." He hit a few notes for comparison. "*That's* whistling."

At the cottage we turned on the Kalmyk news. There were five consecutive stories about Ilyumzhinov. In one, he offered ten thousand dollars to the first person who could write a play about chess. We watched without comment, and then suddenly we heard the Djangharchi again. His sound filled the room, his ghostly song, and for a moment the only explanation was that he had walked down from his house and was serenading us from the street. Then we figured it. It was still the news. The Djangharchi was their theme music, and he was taking them to commercial.

Two log cabin–sized prayer facilities stood near Chess City for convenience. One was a miniature Buddhist temple with a giant meditation spool always spinning in the middle of its four-meter-square room, the other was a generic Christian church that was locked tight for our entire stay. The latter amounted to another break in the fence around the city, and several days before Galzanov's blitz tournament I approached the church, tried the door for show, then attempted another search for Yudina's pond.

I went south of the city this time, on the other side of the huge field of reeds, following a dirt road that led down into what looked like an abandoned neighborhood. Just out in the steppe, a shepherd was taking his flock out for the day, the bell of the lead cow jangling slowly through the morning. A swarm of little birds whizzed by me like a ball of wind.

The front of the neighborhood was guarded by a rusted wrought-iron gate. I passed through into a deserted town that stood on the same hill as Chess City. Its buildings and homes stood old and crumbling, with warped porches and ancient drapes waving through broken windows. I passed a building that looked as though it had been struck by a bomb, half intact, the rest reduced to rubble. Crows barked. Then I saw laundry hung out to dry, a wardrobe stiff in steppe wind, and I realized the place was not abandoned. A woman walked by carrying a large sack. She ignored me. Nevertheless, I was suddenly aware of everything foreign about me—my satchel, my jacket, my face. It had been a community once. The remains of benches and picnic tables. A gazebo. Now it was reverting to nature faster than its neighbor, and even the trees seemed frustrated. There was no way out, I discovered, no way through to Yudina's pond. I hiked back to Chess City on my same route.

"Where do you go on your walks, please, if you don't mind my asking?" Bambusha said.

She had picked me up so that we could try to find Muzraeva, the smirking woman from the Institute for Humanities Research. I wanted to confront Muzraeva with the president's proclamation of making chess into a religion, but as well I hoped she would talk to me about Yudina. I told Bambusha that I was just wandering, that the steppe reminded me a little bit of the hills I had explored as a boy. Her question may have come more from Galzanov than from curiosity. They knew where Yudina had been found. They knew what I was looking for. As we were both nonplayers caught up in the chess world, Bambusha and I had become friends. I truly had an affection for her, but it was impossible to know the extent to which she had been called upon to report on us. The power of paranoia was its ambiguity. The challenge of Russia was to manage love and affection even as the apparatus of the state tried to undermine it.

At the Institute for Humanities Research, we wandered around looking for Muzraeva. We knocked on a door at a computer center, and a young Asian man answered. Bambusha began in Russian, but he interrupted.

"*Ya ne gavarit' po ruskiy,*" he said, and I recognized his accent just as if I was looking in a mirror. He was Korean-American, one of a group of missionaries in Elista. He knew Muzraeva and directed us down to her office, but she was not in. We returned to the young man, and I asked him if he would join us for a cup of coffee.

His name was Rick. He was from California. He had been in Elista for only a few months, and didn't really know that you shouldn't talk to journalists.

"It's very poor here," Rick said. "We're trying to help people. You know, there was this murder here. A reporter. I forget her name."

He looked to Bambusha for help, but though the name, two years later, was poised on the lips of Russians thousands of kilometers away, she claimed she couldn't recall it.

"Yudina," I said. "Larisa Yudina."

"Oh, yes," Bambusha said. "I remember now."

It was the first moment when I had admitted to anyone that I knew about the murder. I was grateful Bambusha had played dumb—it meant we could continue as friends even as it revealed the boundaries of our friendship.

"Do people talk about it still?" I asked Rick.

"Oh, yes," he said. "A lot."

"Do people think Ilyumzhinov did it?"

"Well," he said. "Yes."

We chatted for a while longer, drank our coffee, and walked back to the institute. Muzraeva was still out, and Bambusha and I hopped in a cab to return to Chess City.

"If you want to have a better society," Bambusha said in the car, moved by her mood and the passing concrete neighborhoods, "you need to do for others what you would do for yourself. Look. The gardens of Russians are cleaner than those of Kalmyk people. They are more accurate. It is strange for me to say this because I am Kalmyk, but it is true. We need more accuracy. Things will not get better without changing these things. We do not have them. It is sad."

MIDWEEK, ALTANA ACCOMPANIED US ON ANOTHER DAY TRIP ARranged by Galzanov, to a region called Ketchenery. Ketchenery was like everywhere else in Kalmykia: farming, dust, blight. We took a van. I sat in the front seat, facing the rear, and Glenn and Altana sat side by side in the back, facing forward. They bounced in tandem on the rough road. Glenn fell asleep, and Altana stared out the window at the struggling farms, the voided ground where even the slight rise of hills had names and each tree had a significant history. Altana was sad looking out at her land, sometimes gnawing at the inside of her lip, but she insisted her sniffles were only allergies. When we had met she had said she wanted to return to the United States forever. But now she said she might not return at all. It was Glenn and I who had changed her, I thought. She recognized our celebrity as fake, and meeting us, I imagined, dispelled the magic of America. We were too convenient, too free. We had come to Russia to seek its absurdity, but the most absurd thing we had found was us. I stared at Altana, beautiful for the moisture in her eyes, and I came to the same conclusion as Pushkin: One can overstay Kalmyk hospitality.

"I THINK I WILL BE GIVING YOU HALF YOUR BOOK," MUZRAEVA said, smirking.

Bambusha and I caught up with her two days before the blitz tournament. I had repeated the president's words for her and she had spoken for a time, seeming at first to defend the chess decree. A few pages of my notebook had filled with her comments, sometimes in her own English, sometimes through Bambusha. Her smirk was beginning to annoy me.

"I don't think so," I said.

The uselessness of simile was apparent in Kalmykia. You couldn't say that the little flags that hung outside Buddhist temples were like those that hung at used car lots because in Kalmykia they weren't. You couldn't compare the wriggling shoulders of traditional Kalmyk dancers to those of strippers spinning their pasties because there were no strippers in Kalmykia. And you couldn't say that every telephone in Kalmykia—like the one that sat on Muzraeva's ugly desk—was like a child's toy because that was all they had. Metaphors didn't work. But it was just this plastic gadget, flimsy and made as though for tiny hands, that started to ring; and Muzraeva answered it before we continued.

"I think it's not just words that he wants to elevate chess," she had said so far. "It's not unreasonable." She described a concept in Buddhist texts called *chakravartin* that stressed the importance of religion in a leader's rule. The development of religion was linked to the prosperity of a king's reign: If it went well, then the country would be prosperous. There were many references to *chakravartin* in Tibetan, Mongol, and Oirat texts, and when you translated those texts they sounded very modern. "Maybe Kirsan is aware of some of these texts. Maybe he is hoping to make the republic prosperous through chess and this process."

When she hung up, her lecture turned a corner. She smirked again—she still had me pegged as a government flunkie. "The idea of making Kalmykia prosperous through religion is right," she said, "but to choose chess for this purpose—I am not sure chess can work in this way. I am not a counselor to the president, but I would advise that he concentrate on the religions that already exist. I am judging this by seeing the situation from the *inside*. You see?"

She meant that I was outside, and so could not see. I had hoped for a moment alone with Muzraeva, a moment in which the name Yudina would serve as a password into the world of Kalmyk dissidents. But I realized now that Muzraeva wouldn't have spoken to me even if I'd said the name, even if Bambusha wasn't there, even if she was a dissident herself. She wouldn't talk to me because there was no way for her to know whose side I was really on.

. . .

CHESS CITY WAS TRULY INDEPENDENT, IT SEEMED, AT LEAST IN the sense that our welcome thinned there more quickly there than it did in Kalmykia proper: They needed our cottage for attendees to the next Chess City conference. Bambusha offered the use of a two-bedroom apartment above the FIDE office, and we stopped by to clear it with Abundo. Abundo was still having problems with the Internet connection, and now he was planted before a monitor, writing a letter to settle things. "Dear Kirsan," I read over his shoulder.

"This'll light a fire under their ass," Abundo said.

Glenn was just then losing to Sasha over in Chess Palace. When the match was finished, we packed our belongings and carried our bags through the streets of Chess City. Glenn claimed that he had played with Sasha for the last time. He couldn't win, so there was no point to it. Upstairs at the FIDE office, he chose a bedroom and shut the door.

I waited half an hour, then went to see him. He had retrieved a chess book from downstairs, and he was studying the Botvinnik Variation of the Semi-Slav. It was an opening he had played with Sasha.

"Seems I've been too aggressive with my h-pawn," he said. "Guys in the *Informant* have been playing 13. g3. I've been playing Qd2. I think I need to reinvent all my openings."

Before Russia, I had liked watching Glenn win. I savored his thrilling sacrifices. But now I had learned the pleasure of watching him lose as well. Glenn was my friend, and I loved him as I would love a painter or a cellist, but I could hate him, too, for what he'd given up to be even that good at the game. I had come to enjoy seeing him punished. I liked seeing his ego destroyed—this was chess as well. Glenn's failed games were still works of art; they were simply failed works of art. To watch him was to watch the process of the game. For twenty years he had linked his identity to his improvement as a chess player, but coming to Chess City proved he was no longer improving. Kalmykia itself had the same lie of progress, I was beginning to think. Glenn was not concerned that his coworkers found him an oddity, and Ilyumzhinov did not care that the world's reaction to Chess City was condescension.

I prodded Glenn to keep playing with Sasha. "Maybe it's time to make your matches about more than just ego," I said.

"Nah. It just doesn't make sense for me to play with him any-more."

"Maybe now you should think of yourself less as Sasha's oppo-nent than his trainer. Or second. Or friend. Sasha knows you're not at your best here. But he also knows that even if he messes up just a little bit, you'll be all over him. Plus, he likes you. Didn't you tell me that Sasha doesn't play king pawn openings? Maybe what you can do is just force him to play king pawn against your Sicilian."

"I'm not an expert on king pawn defenses."

I paused. "I think you realize that you're never going to be a grandmaster."

"Maybe," Glenn said.

"But that doesn't mean you can't make an important contribu-tion to the game. If you teach Sasha even a few things, if you even keep the pressure on him, then you're doing good work. For him, for chess."

He didn't buy it. He wanted to go to sleep. I sat beside him for a time. Glenn was as temporary as Chess City, I thought. He had no novelties or openings to his name, no games that were replayed by other players around the world. He would exist for a time in the memories of Sasha and Sanan, the hopes of Kalmykia, as evidence of the worldliness of their undertaking, but when they were gone he would be gone, too. Most chess players' lives were just as fleeting.

GALZANOV'S BLITZ TOURNAMENT WAS HELD IN CHESS PALACE in a large room on the second floor. Sixty Elistans arrived for the event that had been put together on just a few days' notice. Glenn wore his finest suit, and many of the other players, including the children, wore suits as well. The chubby-faced Sanan ran by me in a perfect dollhouse three-piece. The Kalmyks banged out practice games while the tour-nament directors set up their computer. Several people asked Glenn to play before the tournament began, but he refused.

A girl began following us. She was small and shy, plain but pretty. She stared at Glenn, and her glance held even as her body and head tried to turn away. Finally she could stand it no longer and walked up to Glenn and said, "What is your name?" Her name was Oksana, and she was a chess player. She looked about thirteen, but she was eighteen, she said.

Glenn did well through the first six rounds, winning five and drawing one. Oksana followed him everywhere. After round six, a rumor that the president had entered the palace moved through the room like a charge, and we all tensed as though for a smack of thunder. Ilyumzhinov's force field preceded him, a berth of power that stretched out five meters in front of him, clearing away bodies. He was there to address the Kalmyk chess players, but for a time he simply held an upright court from the room's threshold, flanked by bodyguards and shaking the hands of those who approached him. "We should pay our respects," Altana said, and though I wanted to stay in the rear of the room and watch, I agreed to approach and shake the president's hand. But there were rules to it. People gathered in front of him, and when Kirsan looked at them they approached and were received. But he did not look at me. I waited my turn and prepared my line for him, but he passed over us. Altana seemed to read it as failure.

Kirsan moved to one side of the room and arranged a chess table as a makeshift podium. Glenn sat down near Oksana, and Altana and I squeezed close together so she could whisper translations. Il-yumzhinov gave a pep talk. With the five-year anniversary of his FIDE presidency just around the corner, he said, he wanted to take this opportunity to report to Kalmyk chess players on what he had accomplished so far. The most important change he had made was the abolishment of the world championship system. "Chess is not a democratic kind of sport," he said. Also, the president said, he had promised to build Chess City, and here we were sitting in it. Two weeks ago chess had been a demonstration sport in the Sydney Olympics, and the only question that remained was whether chess would be a winter sport or a summer sport. Regarding his plans for the future, there was an effort underway to shorten the length of tournament games. Six hours was too long. A decision had been made to reduce the game to two hours. "You are the first to hear of this," Kirsan said. "Chess will become a more democratic game."

Altana flinched beside me whenever the president seemed to directly contradict himself. Sometimes there were long pauses when she did not translate his words at all, and I wondered how much she was editing as we went along.

The president went on. He had just returned from a meeting with Bobby Fischer in the Philippines. He announced that he had offered to host a tournament of Fischer's recently invented chess variant, a game called Fischer Random. The president detailed Fischer Random. It was the same as chess, he said, but a computer was used to randomly scramble each player's back row of men. Kirsan was optimistic about Fischer Random. There would no longer be chess theory. "I lost four times in this new game," Kirsan said. "Fischer is a god of chess. He has agreed to play here, but no journalists will be invited. We spent a whole evening together, and I felt as though I had spent an evening with a god. One hundred thousand centuries may pass, but people will still talk about Bobby Fischer. The history of Chess City will be linked to this system."

Kirsan took questions for a while, and then an older man rose from the audience to challenge the president to a game of blitz. Kirsan rarely played anymore, we had been told, but now he agreed and a huge crowd formed. The man had been an opponent of the president's when Kirsan was just a boy. I couldn't get close to the game, but Glenn pushed his way in and peered past the lump of gathered men. They played a Caro-Kann, and the room was quiet but for the click of the clock until the president produced a clever tactic, and his opponent resigned. Everyone cheered, and it was over.

"It was a decent game," Glenn said afterward, "but Qh6 would have won faster."

Galzanov had been lurking about, and he and I and Altana sat down for coffee after the president left. "Did you get the game?" he asked, excitedly. He wanted to know if Glenn had seen enough of the president's game to reconstruct it for publication. He was strangely enthused, and I wondered if the game, like Kirsan's autobiography, had been composed for us. I told him I didn't know.

"No problems. So what do you think of the president's idea for Fischer Random?"

I thought it was ridiculous. Kirsan had first said he wanted to make chess into a religion, and now he had said Fischer was a god. I had liked the idea of chess as a religion when it was a way to grant the Kalmyks an identity. Our interview had gone well, but his speech now made him seem like a cultist, the high priest of an order that would worship Fischer. Fischer *was* a god of chess, but he was Old Testament, cranky and vengeful, with different plans for the chosen people. It was hard even to believe in him now. Kirsan had bragged of millions for tournaments while the Kalmyks starved. He had promised them airports and submarines and subdivisions when they didn't even have toilets. He had teased them with visions of the twenty-first century when he could barely deliver the twentieth. But I didn't say this to Galzanov. Instead, I told him that the plan worried me because if the history of chess proved anything, it was that no one man could alter its path. It had evolved of its own accord, and no single intelligence could determine the course it would take.

Galzanov nodded and smoked. Then he offered to arrange a trip to another region. The president was planning an inspection of Chernozemelsky the following day, and we could ride along in the convoy.

"We leave at 5:30 in the morning," he said. "The president does not sleep much."

I went back to the tournament. Glenn had lost four games in a row. He was shocked and sad and couldn't explain it. But Oksana still followed him, quite loyal, and he won his last five games to finish in tenth place.

I asked Oksana to join us for dinner. The restaurant was empty as always. I took Glenn to the bathroom when we arrived. When I had first started writing about Glenn, he had revealed that he was a regular at a number of massage parlors in Atlantic City. He had offered to take me with him once. "You can write about that, I don't care," he said. Now, in the bathroom, I reminded him that Oksana was eighteen years old, but might be lying about that. I expected another spat.

"I know," he said. "Don't worry."

Oksana found it incredibly difficult to look away from Glenn's face. She told us that she had had a dream about meeting an African-American man. She was shy, but her shyness made her competent in the use of translators. The rest of us bumbled through conversations with awkward introductions—*Tell him . . . Ask whether . . . Say this . . .* But Oksana simply spoke her words, sat quietly as Altana repeated them, and went on. She had begun playing chess in the sixth grade, shortly after the president's chess decree. Her father had died when she was twelve, her mother when she was fourteen. She lived in an orphanage. She had learned the game by studying chess problems from a book, and once she played in a chess tournament and won a pair of gold earrings. Now she played at the Elista Chess Club. When she joined, they had asked her a question: "What would you do if you had a million dollars?" She would buy a color television, she told them.

We hadn't been told of the existence of the Elista Chess Club until that day, when its manager stood during Kirsan's Q&A. The manager had complained that there was no money for the Elista Chess Club and that it was becoming run down. "I know, I know," Ilyumzhinov had responded. "I am ashamed. Write a letter. Everything will be all right."

Glenn asked whether Oksana had noticed anything during the tournament about how he moved chessmen. He wanted her to comment on his style and flair. "About how I pick up the pieces," he said.

"Oh, yes," Oksana said. "I noticed everything. Things I will practice at home."

Glenn grinned. It was a question he often asked of beginners who watched him, but this was the first time he had received the reply that he had searched for. He untied his chess tie from around his neck, a splotchy black-and-white pattern littered with recognizable bishops and knights, and presented it to Oksana as a gift. She was overwhelmed, and pulled a ring off her finger, a round ying-yang emblem, to return the gesture. It barely fit Glenn's pinkie. He wore it for the rest of our time in Russia.

That night, back in our apartment, Glenn said, "I've been thinking about the president's game. I was wrong about Qh6. Ilyumzhinov's move is better. He looks Asian, but he plays like a Russian. Good posture, good breathing. There's no gambit play; he's not risky. He's very aware of king safety. He picks a simple opening, plays it mechanically, and when the time comes he gets creative. He waits until there's a weakness, then he pauses and calculates. When he's seen all there is to see, he goes in for the kill."

SERGEI PULLED UP IN FRONT OF THE FIDE OFFICE PROMPTLY at 5:30. It was still dark. The office was empty, and I had to wake Glenn so he could lock the door behind me. As he stood in the doorway, I nodded past him at the glow of FIDE's computers, running through the night.

"Here's your chance to be a grandmaster," I told him.

He looked back and his lips cracked. It was the first time he had smiled at me in a week.

In Chernozemelsky, we caught up with the president's motorcade just as Kirsan was climbing out of his Rolls to dedicate a spa. We followed from the spa to a new gymnasium, then to a local hospital. Even the idea of hospitals in Kalmykia seemed stuck in time—before helping sick people become well, their first funtion seemed be to keep them away from healthy people. Bambusha and I followed along in Ilyumzhinov's comet's tail of photographers and reporters. We all watched him walk about, gesturing at things, moving through the entire place without ever touching anything except, once, a lace curtain that served as a door. I strayed off down a hallway to take some notes, but ran into Kirsan coming back around full circle. He looked at me and could not ignore me this time. He approached and shook my hand, his handshake soft like Glenn's, supple and without pretension. He moved on to sign a wall mural in the hospital lobby, those behind him speeding up and slowing down like the trail of a long robe.

The motorcade stopped again at a park. The park had everything that a park was supposed to have—benches and pathways and a gazebo—but there was no grass and no plants, only a few scraggly trees taking their time to die. Chernozemelsky was one of the regions most profoundly struck by desertification. Here, you could witness the process: On the outskirts of town, small dunes were beginning to appear, smooth knee-high strips of beachy sand like the backs of fabulous creatures surfacing briefly in the sea of dirt.

I climbed back in the car with Galzanov. Outside, stray dogs weaved at the feet of the president. Just across the street, a woman emerged from a small hut that was her home. She was dressed in desert rags, and carried a wide bucket of dirty water toward her outhouse. Galzanov saw me watching the juxtaposition of Kirsan's guided tour with the oblivious woman going about the chores of her survival.

"We hid nothing from you," he said. "You see? You see everything in Kalmykia."

I nodded. It was a lie, but not a complete lie.

Our motorcade slinked to a school. A band heralded the president, and girls rushed forward with Kalmyk tea. Everyone gathered in a theater so the president could distribute prizes to local herdsmen. A parade of schoolchildren followed the ceremony, singers and dancers. When it was over, Galzanov suggested that we return to Elista. Kirsan was headed to another region. The motorcade went one way, our Volga went the other, and I never saw the president again.

ALTANA HAD NEWS. SHE WAS LEAVING TOMORROW FOR MOSCOW to work out the details of her visa. She had decided to go to the United States after all, but her clearance had hit a snag. She hissed at the bureaucracy of it, but was certain the matter could be taken care of in person. She would leave in the morning, and conveivably she might never return to Kalmykia again.

As with Bambusha, I would never be certain who Altana was exactly, but I had long since decided I didn't care. She was a plant from Galzanov whether she knew it or not. Early the next day, I asked to speak with her alone, and we talked at a restaurant. She was leaving in a few hours; we were leaving in two days.

I told her I was worried that we had spoiled the idea of America for her. She was lovely and wise, I said, and the United States would provide her with many opportunities if she went there. She still didn't have a plan, and I told her that I hoped we could see each other if she came. She said she hoped so, too.

I looked at her. She could have been Galzanov's spy, or she could have been a beautiful, naive young woman confronting the world as an adult for the first time. She looked back at me quizzically. I told her that I simply wanted to pay her that compliment. She was wise and lovely, and in the United States she would find a welcome home. She looked into her lap and said she was not sure what to say.

Outside, we were headed in separate directions. She raised her arm to a taxi and climbed inside.

"Good-bye," she said.

In Chess City, Sasha arrived for a match with Glenn, but true to his word Glenn refused to play. Instead, the three of us sat around a table and Glenn tried to give Sasha instruction on how to handle grandmasters at the FIDE World Championship tournament he would be attending in Delhi. Sasha was confused but listened carefully, and when Glenn put problems on a chessboard the boy solved them so effortlessly that even Glenn was surprised. Soon there was nothing left but the awkward knowledge that Glenn had nothing more to teach Sasha. Late in the afternoon, the three of us went to the Elista Chess Club. The club was in a small house on a residential street, its outhouse a smelly wooden shack the size of a telephone booth—though Kalmykia had no telephone booths. Inside the chess club, there were a few rooms with pipes running around the walls for heat. The top board—where the best players played blitz—was simply the board nearest an open window that got light, and kibitzers stood outside to watch the games from over the sill.

Glenn played. I interviewed the club's manager.

I hoped he would talk about Ilyumzhinov's rebuff at the tournament. It had been an insult. But he said no, he had simply asked Kirsan for help, and the president had pledged help. The only promise on which Kirsan had truly delivered, I thought, was hope, and the Kalmyks wouldn't relinquish it easily.

I wandered back out to where the games were going on. Vaskin was there in his beret. He kibitzed and drank a Coke. Just as with the old chess clubs in the United States, no one seemed to care that the house looked as though it might fall down at anv moment. It was our last day of chess in Kalmykia. Glenn and Sasha did not play a match, but instead the top board became a kind of mountaintop for king-of-the-hill—whoever won played whoever was waiting.

Glenn held the board for a few games. He licked his lips in concentration and banged our Chronos. One of his opponents was a young man who beat him on time with a cheap trick meant as a joke. In a quick endgame he called "Check!" loudly when he had not in fact given check, and Glenn ran out of time looking for the phantom threat.

"Yo!" Glenn said, "You can't do that! Somebody tell this guy he can't do that!"

The words were translated, and the young man smiled and agreed. They played again, and this time the young man made a sudden move and announced, "Chuck . . . *Norris!*"

Even Glenn laughed, and before long Kalmyk players throughout the room were calling "Chuck Norris! Chuck Norris!" as the afternoon turned to evening.

CHAPTER 20

Salt in the Coffee

John Huss, when in prison, deplored having played at chess "whereby he had lost time and run the risk of being subject to violent passions."

—Brian Chapman, "The Game of Kings," 1936

. . . he spoke of the fact that all around them was a bright, free world, that chess was a cold amusement that dries up and corrupts the brain, and that the passionate chess player is just as ridiculous as the madman inventing a perpetuum mobile *or counting pebbles on a deserted ocean floor.*

—Vladimir Nabokov, The Defense, 1929

I STARTED DREAMING ABOUT CHESS. CHESS DREAMS, Glenn had told me, were common among strong players and dedicated students. They tended to offer solutions, the subconscious weighing in with weird insights like gifts from the soul. But my chess dreams were not like this. In my dreams the pieces moved just as illogically as they did when I was awake. I was void of inspiration, primitive. I didn't have chess dreams; I had chess nightmares.

I was coming to dislike the game, I realized. It wasn't because I had little aptitude for it. Rather, in learning its history, I had come to realize that a game with the potential to reconcile art and science instead frequently served as a fulcrum for ugliness. The failure of chess to popularize itself was one of the few things all chess players seemed to agree on. "Chess should be on a higher level than any other sport," GM Yasser Seirawan said. "The fact that it's on such a low scale is a collective failure." As long as chess has existed, great thinkers have found it distasteful. "I hate and avoid it, because it is not play enough," said Montaigne. "The struggle for power and the competitive spirit expressed in the form of an ingenious game [has] always been repugnant to me," said Einstein.* The list of actual players who have abandoned the game or come to dislike it while continuing in the profession is long and full of talent.

I researched the usefulness of chess to remind myself that the game had an upside. The usefulness of the game was assumed but had never been proven. The assumption was that chess made you smarter. A more refined understanding of the game led to the more refined traits it was supposed to imbue. "A chess mind is logical and imaginative," said one chess writer, in 1937. "If people, from their schooldays on, could be trained to be logical and imaginative, it surely would help to increase the intellectual standard of our race." In the Middle Ages, skill at chess and tables was a significant part of the curriculum for noble children. Ben Franklin signed his name to a document that claimed that "by playing chess, then we may learn" foresight, circumspection, caution, and perseverance in the search of resources. Others claimed that "fathers of families should hail [chess] as a powerful auxiliary in training their children in the pleasures of domestic life," and that "chess [was] a playground on which the intellect may acquire useful habits of lasting benefit." More specifically, a California experiment claimed that 55 percent of students showed significant academic improvement after only a "brief smattering of chess instruction," and a Pennsylvania study showed test scores skyrocketing 17.3 percent for children in chess classes. *The Oxford Companion to Chess* took a more cynical view, admitting that "where chess has been a compulsory subject at school there is no conclusive evidence [of development] in a higher degree than would have followed if a different but academically relevant subject had been taught." The authors listed benefits for prepubescent students, but ended with the abrupt warning that "the ability of chess to engage interest and encourage concentration can lead to obsession."

Ironic, then, that chess has also been used as a tool for rehabilitation. The game has been tried as a prop to assist in the recovery of adolescent alcoholics ("... it seems to be helping them stay sober"),

---

*Others include Melville: "...an oblique, tedious, barren game hardly worth that poor candle burnt out in playing it"; and Wells: "You have, let us say, a promising politician, a rising artist, that you wish to destroy. Dagger or bomb are archaic, clumsy and unreliable—but teach him, inoculate him with chess!"

and to smooth the readjustment of discharged psychiatric patients ("Finding the right moves—in life and over the board").

I thought of the uses Glenn had culled from the game. He was a loner who had come to prefer loneliness. He was a careful thinker, but even after a great deal of careful thought he frequently blundered—in life. Chess seemed to have given him little beyond the ability to confront failure with poise.

The chess world has long claimed that the game works like a drug, but the simile is always delivered with a coy grin, as though to suggest chess players are hip after all. The chess drug is alternately akin to aspirin, Valium, peyote, ginseng, and some kind of destructive psychedelic.

I tried to think of a way to put the usefulness of chess to the test. But my impulse was different this time. Through most of my tour of the game I had defended it. Now I would attack.

An idea came at once. I called Glenn and told him that I had another chess adventure for us.

"What would really be cool," he said, "is if we went to a prison."

Another benefit Glenn had gleaned from the game: anticipation. I told him my idea of having him perform a simultaneous exhibition for a group of inmates, but he was playing on the ICC while we were talking.

"Look at this guy," he said, speaking to his computer and me at once. "Tryin' to harass my men! Listen, Hallman, if you want to know about prison chess, you should talk to this guy, an inmate. He's in Virginia." He returned to his game a moment. "Whoa! Weak check? And you call yourself an IM!" Then he returned. "I think his name is Bloodgood."

"BACK IN THE 1830s," BRUCE AMBS SAID, "THE TOWN OF Jackson had a choice. It could become the capital of Michigan, it could be home to the University of Michigan, or it could be the site of Michigan's first big prison. Well, we chose the prison."

Obtaining permission to enter a prison to play chess wasn't difficult. I got a list of prison chess clubs from the USCF, then called recreation directors all around the country with a pitch. I fibbed, suggesting that studies had found reduced recidivism rates among inmates who took up the game. The lie resonated with what many recreation directors had come to suspect about chess anyway, and almost every prison I contacted was interested in having us come. The first to obtain approval from their warden was Parnall Correctional Facility in Jackson, Michigan.

We came into Jackson early to meet with Ambs. He was a former president of the Jackson Historical Society, an older man who had found an impassioned second calling in dispute resolution programs. Dispute resolution, he said, was a kind of mediation aimed at resolving difficult matters.

He spelled out the town's history for us. Jackson had existed for less than a decade when it won the right to build Michigan's first penal facility, and the town's fiscal health was still linked to the prison, its prosperity waxing and waning along with the prison's policy of rehabilitation. The facility had moved north of town in 1934, a single-wall home to almost six thousand prisoners, at the time the largest prison population in the world. Overpopulation became a problem in the '80s, and as the city of Jackson reeled from the loss of its motor-parts industry a corresponding riot broke out in the prison. A 1994 court order split the prison into four separate facilities, of which Parnall was one. The area north of Jackson, once dominated by that one wall, was now an unlikely suburb, the whole thing growing in an odd, slow sprawl. But the town's future was bright again and, as always, linked to the concept of progressive incarceration.

Glenn had spent most of the meeting hiding behind a chess book, studying openings. But when it began to wind down, he produced a challenge for Ambs.

"One more question. What's your opinion of chess as an aid in prison rehabilitation?"

Ambs's passion for dispute resolution flared at the thought of its natural association with chess. Every game was a dispute. "Oh, I think it's fine," he said. "Chess is an activity that people can enjoy. It gives them a chance for some competition. It gives them a skill they can practice. It's a positive kind of experience."

Glenn nodded in agreement. Ambs had basically described what the Soviets had tried seventy years before, and what Ilyumzhinov had tried just recently. But I doubted them. How could a game that lent itself so easily to bad dreams and visions of combat do anything to teach patience, morality, or forgiveness?

. . .

I drove all night from New Jersey to meet Bloodgood.

James River Correctional Center sat in the middle of rich, rolling farm country west of Richmond. The region was in a slow transition from the era when houses had names—Chanticleer, Maranatha—to a more modern time when whole neighborhoods had names—Old Oaks, Hunters Woods, Kimberwicke. It was amid these tiny incorporations that the Virginia Department of Corrections had sectioned off several thousand vivid acres for the second prison I would visit for chess. James River was like a plantation. Near the fenced housing units for inmates stood the manicured homes of wardens and higher-ups. I saw a sign that read POWHATAN CORRECTIONAL CENTER: 1.9 MILES. This was my goal, and the whole stretch of it was inside the James River complex.

I drove over the James River itself and then across a set of railroad tracks, both of them beelining through the compound. I passed motor shops, storage huts, something labeled the MEAT PLANT. I finally came to Powhatan, a huge concrete structure surrounded by a double billing of electric fence. I parked and sat for a moment to collect my Bloodgood material.

Claude F. Bloodgood III was a chess player doing a life sentence for murdering his mother. He had the usual story: He had confessed to the crime, then taken it back. Like asking to take back a move in chess that left his freedom *en prise*. Since then—three decades ago—he had consistently proclaimed his innocence. But no one really listened anymore. Bloodgood was famous for having once used chess to help him escape, but he denied this as well.

After Glenn gave me the name, I sent out a batch of E-mail to get information about Bloodgood, but I didn't actually find him until I stumbled across one of his books, a thin volume detailing a hustler's opening line. Bloodgood had published several chess books from prison in the '90s.

Bloodgood had been sentenced to death in 1970 after a two-day trial. He flirted with execution dates until 1972, when the Supreme Court ruled the death penalty unconstitutional. He had been an average tournament player in Virginia prior to the murder, but after incarceration his postal game took over. Correspondence chess is categorically different from over-the-board play. You have three days to deliberate a move. The result is departure from chess theory at the outset. With seventy-two hours, the potential for detailed analysis during play is greater. Postal players are pioneers into uncharted chess territory. At one point, Bloodgood conducted twelve hundred postal games simultaneously.

He attracted the attention of the chess world in 1996 when his over-the-board rating suddenly shot up over 2600. This was a better reflection of the flaws in chess rating systems than it was a measure of his talent, but still his name slipped onto top ten lists in the United States, which qualified him for an invitation to the U.S. Championships. This raised the ugly specter of the last time Bloodgood had made headlines, in 1974, when he escaped from prison while on furlough to help organize a chess event. In the early '70s, the Virginia Department of Corrections had entertained a progressive policy of prisoner activity like Jackson, Michigan's, and Bloodgood had made them pay for it. He and another chess player inmate overpowered a corrections official. They escaped, and Bloodgood lasted a month before he was recaptured.

It was my recent distaste for chess that had drawn me to the story of the escape. Like a scientist bent with bias, I was looking for data that would conform to a cynical hypothesis. Not only had the game proved useless for Bloodgood, he had turned the tables and used the game itself. Bloodgood was chess's dark side.

I gathered my tape recorder and notebook and made for the gate that led to the Powhatan Medical Unit. Bloodgood had lung cancer. More than a year before he had been told he had less than a year to live. In chess terms, it was as though the flag of his life clock had fallen, but God had yet to notice.

I approached the double gate. The fences to either side were wired. I was buzzed through, and once inside I noticed all the guards' holsters were empty: No weapons where the prisoners had access to them. I entered a small foyer in the building, checked in at a box office–style window. While I waited, several batches of prisoners filed in wearing cuffs and leg irons. They barely looked at me.

I was taken to a small, cold, cinder-block room just a few yards inside the building. Three metal benches ran along the outside of the room, and I stupidly tried to move one of them. There was an observation window, and two knobless doors. I looked up at the fluorescent lights and a smoke detector, then down at an electric plug long since cemented over. The prison air tasted bad and was filled with noise: a rhythm of security buzzers and heavy gates slamming on springs. There were voices from far and near, and occasionally someone humming, taking advantage of the building's acoustics. I double-checked my tape recorder and waited for Bloodgood. The cold of the bench moved through my slacks. I heard someone start to sing and joined them, softly, my own poor voice bouncing sweet off the horrid walls.

GLENN AND I SCOUTED THE JACKSON PRISON SUBDIVISION AN hour before we were scheduled to appear. It was a huge, five-sided structure, like a child's drawing of a house. Since the court-ordered breakup, additional structures had popped up all over. What really drew our attention was the razor-ribbon wire hung on everything. The number of coils and the number of fences changed with the security level of each facility. We passed the old prison graveyard, caught in a kind of institutional limbo: twenty old tombstones tilted like bad teeth, standing just outside the giant wall of the old prison and just inside the razor wire of a newer one.

We parked in Parnall's crowded lot. For some time prior to the trip Glenn had been warning me about men in prison—he feared that I would say or do something that would get us in trouble. Now he made a wry crack about returning to jail. All morning he had been acting like a man who had once done a healthy stint way upstate. He wore a snarl like a mug shot. It was all bad memories of those five days he'd spent in county with crazy men and paper pieces.

We entered a waiting/reception area like a small bus terminal. Kathy Merkey appeared to greet us after ten minutes. I had done most of the organization of the event through Merkey, Parnall's recreation director. She was a friendly blonde woman with clever, intensely light eyes. She seemed to have to make a sustained effort to remain calm, but probably I was transferring my own anxiety to her. Lines on the floor of the reception area told us where to stand while waiting for the prison portal to open. The heavy glass door moved aside hydraulically, and Merkey led us in. In an instant, it seemed, we were outside again, walking along a concrete path lined with pretty flowers. This was the yard. Because Jackson Prison had been broken into separate installations, each sharing a portion of the old wall, all the new facilities had a kind of unfinished appearance, an oddly put-together quality. The yard was long and diagonal and immaculate. There was no litter, no decay, and extra light reflecting off the razor wire gave the air a light, magical feel.

As we walked toward the gym, Merkey gave us some details on the prison. It was considered a Level 1 facility, which meant minimum security. But this didn't mean that its inmates were guilty of only minor felonies. "We've got murderers here," Merkey said confidently. "We've got assault. We've got sex offenders." Most of the prisoners had been moved here to serve out the final portions of long sentences. "We think of it as moving down in the system."

Close to the gym, a dozen picnic tables sat beneath half as many shade trees. We came upon a man at the nearest table, a chess set arrayed before him.

Glenn's eyebrows jumped, and he said to Merkey, "Can I give him a position?"

"Sure," Merkey said, though she didn't really know what it meant.

The man's name was Lee. He was black, Glenn's age, and at first sight he looked so unlike someone you might find in a prison that it was easy, even in the first moments of being there, to forget that this wasn't a nice park in the middle of Manhattan. Lee had on a white shirt and orange shorts. Prisoners either wore this getup, or a pair of blue pants with an orange stripe down the side like a Civil War uniform. Lee had heard we were coming and greeted us as though we were long lost cousins, strangers but blood. Glenn set up a problem before him, a little queen-and-rooks two mover that he liked because its first move was what he described as a "quiet" move—it neither gave check nor directly descended on the king that was to be mated. Lee looked at the position and started to move the pieces to solve it.

"Well, if I go here, then that looks good! Oh, no. 'Cause he can just go here. What about if I go here?"

"Just takes," Glenn said, and indicated the capture that spoiled Lee's solution. "It has to be two moves. You move, he moves, mate."

"Okay, okay." Lee was sinking into the position now. He wasn't a particularly good chess player, but a policy of becoming enthusiastic over things that were supposed to be good for him seemed to have served him well here. "Okay, I'm onto it now. Yeah, I see what you're doing. I'll get it, don't you worry."

"Two moves," Glenn reminded him, and we headed off toward the gym.

Card games were underway on the other picnic tables. Everyone looked up at us as we passed. Ninety percent of the prison population was black, including the guards. As we neared the prison's free-weight area, one huge inmate approached with two free-weight disks in his hands, like danishes. Just a thought would turn the weights into weapons, but Merkey remained calm. It turned out the man just wanted to point out that the weights had been chipped. Merkey nodded and said she'd take care of it.

Just then, Lee began hollering. "I got it! I got it!"

We looked back, and Lee made cartoonish pointing motions at the board.

"I got it! Yes, I got it!"

"Think he got it?" I asked Glenn.

"No," Glenn said.

Merkey smiled, and we headed into the gym.

The gym was impressive. There were six retractable basketball hoops, several sets of plastic retractable bleachers, and the floor was covered with a hard carpet to dampen sound. The front wall was glass as a security measure—the inside could be monitored from outside and vice versa—but it made for a pleasing architectural accident: a fully enclosed gymnasium with natural light. The only feature that revealed the gym as a prison facility was its exposed bathroom. Set back in a large nook, a cut-away alcove, the bathroom was like a movie set of a bathroom. It was strange to see urinals from far away. The stalls for the toilets were chopped low, as though for dwarfs. Later, I watched one inmate enter a stall, and when he squatted down I could still see his bald scalp, like the head of a black pawn.

They had a row of tables ready for us, lined up before the bleachers. On the plane, Glenn had expressed fear about the pieces that would be used in the simul. These fears turned out to be warranted: The eight or ten sets already in place were undersized boards with black-and-red squares, and the pieces were tiny, plastic and hollow, the pawns molded to fit inside one another like stackable chairs. Glenn was concerned about this. Chess was about spatial intelligence, he explained, and in a simul, where he would move from one board to the next, spending just a few seconds at each, it took discipline to reorient again and again. When this reorientation included disparate visual cues of smaller squares or different pieces, the change of gears was that much more difficult. Glenn called the little sets "El Cheapos."

A guard was assigned to us, a short man whose attitude more than his physique proved him capable in his position. We walked over to the boards, where two prisoners were already waiting for us. One had a cardboard chessboard under his arm like a framed canvas, the other wore a wool hat in the middle of July. Both were black, perhaps a few years older than Glenn. The first was called Chicago, a nickname, the other Sueing.

Merkey nudged my arm. "I think these two think they are about the best here," she whispered.

It was just then that Lee caught up to us again. "I got it, I got it now," he was still saying, quieter now in the sanctuary of the gym. We cleared off one of the boards and Glenn set up the position again.

"I go here!" Lee said.

A number of inmates gathered around to see if the chess master had been bested so easily. Glenn slid a rook over one square and the solution was ruined.

"Oh," Lee said, touching his lip. "Oh." Immediately, several inmates began studying the position together, trying out moves and correcting one another. Glenn left them to begin a game with Chicago.

"Why don't you play them both?" I suggested, gesturing to Sueing.

"Okay," Glenn said.

"Play us both?" Sueing said. "Shoot!"

I edged others into the game until Glenn was playing an informal five-board simul while at the same time consulting on the puzzle. "Listen. The first move. It's a *quiet* move," Glenn said, and it was clear that he hoped the context would bring them to an understanding of what a quiet move was.

"That means it's not a check," one inmate said.

"Right!"

Glenn returned to his other games. The inmates were generally a docile bunch. It was impossible to tell if their manners were genuine or put on for a system that rewarded good behavior; but even if it was fake, I thought, it was probably pretty good practice for the real world, where feigned courtesy tended to win out over the real thing anyway. The thought was a variation on what I had lately come to think of chess. The surface of the game was pure and good, but underneath was a rotten core where politics, bickering, and paranoia went unchecked. One of Glenn's opponents was a man in dreadlocks like Medusa's snakes. He sat poised over his board with a double-palm visor to his forehead to block extraneous data. As I watched him, he suddenly looked about like a wolf from its meal, and I feared he would catch my glance. But he did not, and when he returned to his game I wondered if what he was learning, if what chess would give to him, was simply a more sophisticated understanding of deviousness than the one that had landed him here. Chess might make you smart, but it didn't make you good.

Glenn had finished off a few of the players already, but the seats were filling in quickly.

"He made me look like a baby tryin' to crawl!" one inmate announced. "Couldn't even stand up!"

Two other men compared the quality of their losses.

"He say I know how to play!"

"Yeah, right."

"He said I needed to find good people to play. I told him I couldn't find none in here, and I named you first!"

I checked on Chicago's game. If Chicago and Sueing thought they were better than the others, they were right. Both men's games were still going. Chicago's board and set were remarkable. The cardboard board was drawn in—the dark squares black ink, the light squares still the original brown. He had marked the coordinates so he could replay games from *Chess Life*. Chicago's pieces were tournament size, but they looked to have spent several hours in an oven. The crenelation of the rooks were worn down completely, their tops smooth. The crucifixes on the kings and the crowns of the queens had been shaved down so that they were identical in height. It wasn't until I noticed that the clefts of the bishops had been filled in with something, like nail holes plugged with sawdust, that I realized all the sharp surfaces of the pieces had been removed.

"Chicago has a pretty good position," I told Merkey. He was a pawn up heading into the endgame.

"Really?" she said.

A prisoner named Chapman finally solved Glenn's queen-and-rooks puzzle, after simply staring at it for quite a while. Lee never did figure it out, and he headed back to the yard, disappointed. Glenn gave Chapman another mate to solve, this one a difficult position based on underpromotion that emphasized the player's need to consider all possibilities at all times. This was Glenn's contribution to the idea of chess as rehab—to help generate an instinct to stop and think, to weigh all options.

Chicago's position crumbled suddenly. The slight material lead he had managed collapsed before a mysterious positional concern, and mate reared on the horizon. He resigned with a smile of missed opportunity.

A prison journalist arrived and asked me for an interview. His name was Baynes. He was an older black man with bleary eyes and a long face; and like a clever newspaper reporter he had found that by exhibiting a kind of mild confusion, a not entirely feigned dumbness, he got the kind of interviews he wanted. After all the games were complete, Glenn began a lecture to the gathered prisoners. As much as I would have liked to listen, Baynes insisted on a moment's time and pulled me aside.

We sat on chairs near the exposed bathroom. He had a notebook and pen ready. So did I. We were going to interview one another.

"Now, let me think," Baynes said. "Let me think of what kind of information I need here. So. What is it exactly that you're doing here?"

It was a good enough question to dodge. I had already asked myself whether in fabricating a link between chess and rehabilitation so that I could conduct an experiment, I was taking advantage of the prisoners' captivity and boredom. But I sidestepped the question, giving Baynes a little information about myself and Glenn, all the while watching Glenn address the inmates gathered around him. He gesticulated broadly, but the prisoners watched only his eyes.

"So," Baynes said, pointing his pen off at Glenn, "he's like a—a chess master, huh?"

"Yes."

"And you, too?"

"No, I don't play, really."

Baynes eyed me as though suspecting a con. "So what are you then?"

"I'm kind of an organizer."

"I see."

There was a pause. We both scribbled down what the other had just said. I saw Glenn wrapping up his speech, and told Baynes to come back that evening for the simul.

"Oh, I'll do that, I'll do that," he said. "I hope I can get a few words with the master, too."

Glenn had moved from teaching the inmates chess to telling them about his career as a card dealer, sneaking in his basic philosophies of life. "I've seen guys betting twenty-five thousand or fifty-thousand dollars a hand," he told them, and they were fixed at the thought of so much money. "More than what most people have in the nation. But it's like Big Macs, you know, or any nice burger. They're good! But really, how many can you eat in one day?"

He grinned and paused. Glenn saved his most charming smiles for when he felt he had made an illustrative point.

"Hey," I said in the lull, "why don't you play Chicago again? I think he deserves another shot."

Chicago was at the back of the small crowd.

"No," Glenn said, "let's do a blindfold. But wait!" He looked back at Chicago. "Can you name me one chess book by Nimzowitsch?"

"*My System.*"

"Can you name me another?"

"Uh, what's it called? *Chess ... Praxis?*" Chicago was unsure how to pronounce the words he had found in the pages of *Chess Life.*

Chapman chimed in with the knowledge that *The Arabian Knights* was based on chess. Glenn complimented him on his knowledge. He went on to make suggestions as to what the inmates could do when they got out of prison—how they might further their chess careers with study and the assistance of computers. He was halfway into a detailed explanation of how to pirate expensive chess software when he realized that this was probably not the best information to give to men who had been put away for worse. He let the thought dribble away into nonsense before any of them caught the thread of it.

"How do you, like, get really good at chess?" one inmate asked. "How do you remember it all, and get it all down, and put it all together?"

The others fell quiet. The question was not so much about chess as it was about using the game to adopt a regimen of study and practice. It could apply to chess; it could apply to anything.

"Well, I'm good at chess," Glenn said. "I'm very good. But there are guys much better than me. Guys who make me look terrible. If I wanted to get *really* good, I'd have to study all the time. Work all the time. Maybe quit my job."

He was right, and his answer gelled with my disenchantment with the game. The worldwide structure of tournament play, the entire existence of FIDE and Ilyumzhinov and other chess organizations, it was all designed for one thing—to create a patriarchal pseudogovernment whose only purpose was to perpetuate itself. Chess was like an aircraft carrier forever at sea, at war with the world and always on the brink of mutiny. Even its first world champion had suggested the world might be better off without it. It was virtually impossible for a player of Glenn's caliber to feel as though he had accomplished anything. As a black man, Glenn had achieved what only a few dozen black men had done before him, ever, and though chess was his identity wholesale he was forced to think of it as a glorified hobby. The prisoners wanted it to be something else. They wanted it to be the tool that the chess world occasionally claimed it was. But there was no infrastructure for that. The odd program appeared now and again; but left by itself, chess amounted to chaos—the chaos of our dealers' lounge, the chaos of Washington Square Park. On the level of the amateur, chess offered benefits, but as you got closer to professional chess the game began to revert. Men left their wives for the game. They quit their jobs for the game. They stopped washing, their eyes went bad, they became paranoid, depressed, anxious. The inmate, whether he knew it or not, had asked Glenn how to use chess to learn how to live life without committing felonies. But all Glenn could do was put him on the path that the chess world had adopted, a path to produce champions.

Glenn nodded a few times, filling in the gap of what he did not know how to say.

Sueing volunteered to play the blindfold, and I sat down to move Glenn's pieces. Before the afternoon was over, rumors of the blindfold would reach all corners of Parnall. Glenn immediately established an advantage.

"Man," Sueing said, "he's doin' the same thing to me again!"

Nineteen or twenty moves in, Sueing moved a knight to d6. It was free.

"Nd6," I called over my shoulder.

"Nd6?" Glenn said. "Gimme that knight!"

There was laughter and applause, and Sueing smiled and re-signed. Then yard was over, and the inmates began to scatter. Glenn shook a few hands and told them all to develop their pieces. In thirty seconds, the gym was deserted.

Merkey wandered off to call the warden to see if we would be allowed to eat lunch with the prisoners. While she was gone, Glenn and I complimented our guard on the gym, its clean floors, and pleasant space.

"It's a fucking disgrace, if you ask me," the guard said. "One point three mil on a gym for a bunch of convicts. My kid's high school can't even have a basketball game."

Merkey returned with the word from the warden. No. But she had the idea that if we went to meet him he might change his mind.

"It's hard to remember that it's a prison," I told her, as we made the reverse trek across the yard.

"Really." She reminded us that we were being shown just a small portion of the facility. "Don't worry. Now we're headed to the other side."

BLOODGOOD WAS COMPLETELY BALD, AND APPEARED, AT FIRST, to be an old man regressed to childish bliss though he might have simply been happy to be out from wherever he'd just been. A guard pushed Bloodgood's wheelchair through the door, then sat down on one of the benches and opened a newspaper. Bloodgood smiled. His pleasure was unfettered by an oxygen-feed apparatus that shot tubes up his nose and hooked over his ears. Bloodgood's chest tumor was inoperable for a number of reasons, he said. His doctors had given him its dimensions without the usual allusions to fruit—one inch wide, two inches tall. Maybe a kiwi.

I asked Bloodgood the obligatory first question of chess inter-views—how did he start playing—and received the standard answer—he was taught by his father. Before I knew it, he launched into the question of how he had wound up on the U.S. top-ten player list. This involved an explanation of the rating process, and his dazed serenity vanished as the talk turned to the game.

"If you're unrated," Bloodgood began, "and you play someone, and you win from 'em, you get their rating plus 400 points, as a provisional rating. If you lose to 'em, you get their rating *minus* 400 points. This is not reasonable." Many players in the real world agreed with Bloodgood, but the flaw of it was more problematic in prison because in prison high-rated players more frequently wound up playing unrated players. "Then the USCF has the bonus points," Bloodgood went on, "where if you do so much better than the percentage you are *expected* to, you get bonus points in the ratings. This doesn't work. It reached a point in here where we had players rated over 2400, and players up around 2600. And I didn't play that well, and nobody else did, and I was much better than anyone. The thing simply started to snowball. I sent the USCF information on it. But they never did anything! And the bottom line was, gee, I was manipulating the hell out of 'em. Everyone was catching flak, so we all said the hell with it. That's what happens when nobody gives a dang."

I didn't give a dang either, actually. The ratings scandal was tame, unlikely to turn up the dirt on the game I was looking for. Even if Bloodgood had inflated the ratings intentionally, it was just weird vandalism, the misdemeanor of Bloodgood plugging his name into *Chess Life* where it didn't belong.

At first I had been uncomfortable in Bloodgood's presence, spooked at being so close to a murderer, but now I was getting used to it. I decided to switch gears and ask him about the darker corners of his history. The time limit on our interview didn't allow for smooth transitions.

"What are you in prison for?"

"I was convicted of the murder of Margaret Bloodgood, who was my father's second wife," he said, fielding it like a lawyer. "I pled not guilty to it, and I offered to take polygraphs, sodium pentathol, hypnosis. But truth is not necessarily what people want in a courtroom. It's a piece of theater, it's politics. The trial in front of the jury was two days. The testimony of Michael Quarick was that he watched me beat, strangle, and smother her in the foyer. Quarick got a six-month suspended sentence. His testimony was bought."

Like a grandmaster going through the variations of a well-known opening, Bloodgood could rattle off the complex variations of his life, the lines he had explored in intimate depth. I could follow it only vaguely.

"I was defended by Barry Willis, who I tried to fire daily," he went on. "It came down to it that half the men on Virginia's death row had been his clients. He was appointed. He went over and sat at the prosecutor's table during the trial because I would have killed the son of a bitch. Court-appointed attorneys are a gyp."

I needed to get the conversation back to chess. Bloodgood was more animated when he weaved the weird facts of his life, but he didn't sound quite as honest as when he talked about the game. I decided to head for the heart of what interested me.

"Do you think chess is useful in any way?" I said.

He frowned, not because I was changing the subject, but because the answer was obvious. "At the penitentiary, we had over a hundred players who were USCF members. Of them, fifty-nine were paroled. Twenty years later, eight were returned. Now that's a pretty good recidivism rate for a state that has got a seventy-some percent rate otherwise."

Bloodgood had conducted the experiment I had lied about. I quickly threw him another question to hide my surprise. "Is chess different from poker or backgammon?"

"I think chess does something that . . . it gives people constructive use of their time. If it does anything, it gets them away from their associations. It's more respectable. It's not the guys down at the corner who are talking about breaking into a place. You can find chess clubs anywhere. Poker does not cross social lines. In chess you see doctors, lawyers, playing with workers. It crosses lines. See. This is the thing. Chess crosses more social lines than any other game."

Bloodgood was ruining my theory completely. Without knowing it, he was adding plausible and lucid argument to a debate he didn't know was being conducted. I had to shift the action to the other side of the board, where there was still his 1974 escape to talk about. I decided to move back in history first, commit him to some facts. Bloodgood's birthdate had been a matter of conjecture, chess historians, newspapers, and government agencies failing to agree on how old he was exactly.

"When were you born?"

"July 14, 1924."

"Bastille Day."

Bloodgood nodded. "Bastille Day. That's fitting. You know, you're the first person to register what that was. It's a blank for most people. Today, I don't play 2300 chess because I'm getting old. To compare what I'm doing now is not a reasonable way of evaluating my chess. Today, I can only handle a couple hundred postal games. But I still hold a 2000 rating."

"How do you afford postage?" I interrupted. It was a question I'd been wanting to ask since I first heard of him.

"I'm a disabled veteran. Money is not a problem."

"Did you serve in a war?"

"Several of 'em. Didn't have a scratch in Korea. Came back and was assigned to a roller-skating rink in Quantico, Virginia."

"Were you in WWII?"

Bloodgood paused and looked at my eyes. A creepiness came over him, and he glanced at the guard to see if he was paying attention. "I was, but not for the United States. My father was German."

The cold of the bench ached into my bones.

"I was born Klaus Bluttgutt in La Paz, Mexico," Bloodgood said.

THE ADMINISTRATIVE OFFICES IN JACKSON WERE THE KIND OF cramped fluorescent space that people who worked in offices in the real world compared to a prison in and of itself. Rooms like cells, stale air, few windows, specific times for eating, a furlough at the end of the day.

We were introduced around. Apart from Glenn, the only other man in a suit was the warden. He was a wide, solid black man whose authority made him seem fatherly, and he stood perfectly erect at all times. Merkey told us that he was unusual among wardens in that he would walk the yard by himself.

The warden asked a few questions about our background. He asked me to describe the contents of my satchel. Then, apparently satisfied, he said, "Allow me to invite you to visit our dining hall for lunch."

This drew snickers from the prison personnel for its hat trick of euphemisms: invite, dining hall, lunch.

We were taken to the cafeteria shortly before the general population arrived. One hundred years before the Jackson Prison cafeteria had been called a commissary; now, it was called a chow hall. The chow hall was a large space with cement floors and high ceilings, something like a multipurpose shed. The seating was not the cramped conference tables that I associated with prison claustrophobia—rather, there were dozens of metal square tables with spindly seats attached. The room would have looked futuristic thirty years before, and perhaps still did to inmates who had been incarcerated all that time. As though to complete such a vision, the first dozen tables at the front of the chow hall were filled with what appeared to be teams of futuristic doctors, men decked out in fantastic surgical attire.

It was the chow hall kitchen team covered in plastic to prevent epidemics. They had eaten first and now waited for the crowds of prisoners. The kitchen staff watched as we approached the head of the room, first one shower cap turning toward us, then another, then a cascade of rustling plastic and intense stares. The prisoners who had beards wore U-shaped protection sheaths for these as well. Merkey was right: this was the other side, and the attention we received here was wholly different from the low-level celebrity of the yard. Here it was something the prisoners themselves might have identified with—indictment, a walk to a gallows. I sensed that even Merkey was apprehensive now, like a dog in the presence of other dogs. Glenn's suit and my notebook were unlikely features in the room, making it unpredictable, explosive. She steered us into the chow line, where Glenn and I gathered trays, plastic forks and spoons.

"No knives?" I asked Merkey, trying to make a joke of it.

"No knives," she agreed.

The food was cooked but mysterious. Mashed potatoes, something that looked like fried egg but tasted like pizza, and hockey pucks of meat like the leftover scrapings of a botched autopsy. The food was the worst punishment I had seen at the prison. But it was this same food the inmates had converted to the hard chests and thighs on so many of them, the musculature that measured their tedium.

Once our trays were loaded—even the chow hall staff thought of the food as a joke, and piled our plates high—Glenn led us into the heart of the prisoners already seated. One table was clear among them. Nodding at everyone who made eye contact with him, Glenn wound up explaining who he was before he sat.

"I'm a chess player," he said.

"A what?"

"Chess. You know! Chess!"

I sat down and looked at my meal. A dozen other faces looked at my meal as well. I tried to figure out how to cut away bite-sized portions of my meat pucks without a knife. It was too difficult, and finally I just picked one of them up and gnawed away a chunk. Later, I saw a man neatly sawing his own puck with the handle of his spoon.

"Yo, Chief!" a prisoner called out. He was a white kid, twenty-five, covered with tattoos and acne. He was seated with several other white men who did not look at me and who seemed to think it was a bad idea to try to talk to us. Still, the kid, hair wrapped in plastic, tipped his head back and offered a piece of advice.

"The po-lease sits over there!"

He indicated the other side of the cafeteria, where a few guards were seated. Merkey was among them, not having followed us, and none of them were eating the prison food. Glenn was still explaining who he was, behind me.

"We're not police," I said.

"You don't work for the state?"

"No."

He smiled and looked for support among his friends. "Who are you, then?"

"He's a chess player," I said, gesturing back at Glenn, "and I'm a writer."

"A chess player?"

"Yes." I told him about the simultaneous exhibition that Glenn would perform at 6:30.

He nodded, concentrating to hear me in the clamor of the room. The population of the prison had begun to file in by then, and we were both speaking loudly enough so that twenty or thirty of the closest prisoners could easily eavesdrop on our conversation.

"I used to gamble at chess over the wall," the kid said. "But it's different there. Not nice like here. They don't like me here. I got a bad attitude."

I nodded to indicate that it was okay with me if he had a bad attitude.

Merkey came over to check on us. She walked with a guard's meaningful swagger, a teacher checking up on the new kids. Glenn waved at a few more prisoners.

"Everything okay?" Merkey said.

Sure, sure, we told her, and she nodded and headed back to her lunch. Glenn sat and began a kind of triage on his meal, picking through its parts as though attempting to decide the best way to put it all back together. I had managed to gobble down one of my pucks by then, and I was about to set to work on my pizza doughnut.

The kid across the way was determined to spill his guts. He checked the room for guards and nodded at us again.

"So you're a writer?"

"Yeah."

"You want a story? I'll give you a story. I'll tell you a story about the po-lease. Some of the shit they do. Some of the shit they pull."

He glanced around again. The two dozen inmates who could hear him did not react.

"What's your name?" Glenn said.

"Mark," the kid said. It was a shock to hear someone's first name.

"You want to sit down?" Glenn gestured to one of our table's extra seats. Mark bounded to it.

"Yeah, I'll tell you some stories," he went on. "They make you work in here. Even if you're a cripple. Seventeen cents an hour." As though on cue, a prisoner with some kind of degenerative disorder limped up an aisle carrying a box for the kitchen staff. To Mark it was proof of his claim. "See?"

"Hm," Glenn said.

"So you're not getting paid or nothing? To be here? You just came of your own recognizance?"

"Yes."

"I like that. Lot of people forget about us. We're the scum of the earth. It's nice people thinking about us. You know, I tried to sign up for that chess thing, I remember now. But I work until 7:00. They said there was a conflict. They don't like me."

I told him that we would probably be there well after 7:00, and that he could join us at the gym then. Mark nodded, and then beat it when Merkey came back to check on us again. The chow hall had filled. There were more prisoners than there were seats, and it was a rotation—prisoners appeared and ate and were replaced. Eating was chore, not ritual. Glenn and I were left alone for fifteen minutes to pester our food.

"Man," Glenn said, "I'm tired. Hallman gettin' me up at the crack of dawn. I need to sit down. I need to rest."

"We're resting now," I said.

Glenn looked at me and gave a little shrug, an inconspicuous gesture to the room, the men, the food, the awkward seats, and the noise like a beehive echoing on itself.

"This is not rest," he said.

I WAS CONVICTED OF THE MURDER OF MARGARET BLOODGOOD, Bloodgood had said, *who was my father's second wife.* The words repeated in my ears even as Bloodgood prattled off the rest of his romantic meander. The trick nearly fooled me. In newspaper accounts of his trial, it was always clear: Bloodgood had murdered his mother. Beat reporters pommeled to death the quirky Oedipal-style twist to the story: Margaret, dumped along a road, was found with a bloody pillow under her head. Thirty years later, Bloodgood described her as his father's second wife, just a tiny emphasis on second to suggest she wasn't his biological parent. It was misdirection, a lie to cover the squares of other lies, and just that one tactic shed light on everything about him.

There were a million possible ways to recombine the facts that orbited Bloodgood, but his own version and the most likely version struck me as most interesting. The former went like this:

Bloodgood was born July 14, 1924, in La Paz, Mexico. He was a Mexican citizen. His father, an agent for the Abwehr, the German high-command service for sabotage, took him to Germany at an early age and taught him to play chess. He was a prodigy, and played with the world-class likes of Euwe and Bogoljubow, as well as Rommel and Himmler. At the same time, Bloodgood attended boot camp at Kiel, learning to be an agent of the Abwehr himself, which included skills such as rapid safecracking. Bloodgood and his father found themselves back in the United States during WWII, in Norfolk, Virginia. His father worked as a land operator, Bloodgood as a courier between Germany and the United States. The young Klaus hopped off and on U-boats that deftly avoided submarine nets in the Chesapeake Bay. Bloodgood was lucky enough to wind up in the States after the war, and he and his father attempted to blend in, transliterating their names, the younger shaving a dozen years off his age to obscure his difficult past. Bloodgood Senior kept Abwehr money that had wound up in a Swiss bank account, and arguments over the Nazi treasure led to disruption in the family and the eventual dispute with

Margaret. In 1954, Bloodgood joined the marines and served in Korea. When he returned, an accident crushed both his feet and he was sent to Camp Pendleton in San Diego to recover. While hospitalized, he chanced to meet Humphrey Bogart, who had stopped by to cheer the troops. Bogart spotted Bloodgood playing chess, and Bogie, a player himself, initiated a chess friendship. Bloodgood would go on to run with the likes of Gary Cooper, James Cagney, and David Niven, all of whom had become enthusiasts when chess became Hollywood vogue for a time. Bloodgood even married Kathryn Grayson, star of *Kiss Me Kate,* in a Tijuana ceremony that was quickly annulled. Attempts at playwriting and acting were also quickly annulled, and Bloodgood returned to Virginia in the late '50s to continue playing chess: From 1957–61, he won the Virginia Open twice and the Norfolk Open four times. It was then that Bloodgood began to turn to crime, attempting to defraud banks and putting his Abwehr training to good use in breaking into post offices to crack their safes. "The average length of time I was in a post office was twelve minutes," he bragged. A B&E wrap landed him in a Delaware jail in 1962, widening the gash between himself and his father. When the elder died in 1968, he bequeathed his son only one hundred dollars, and Margaret blamed Bloodgood for her husband's death. She accused her son (or stepson) of forgery, and in a trial over an endorsed check Bloodgood boldly announced to the courtroom that he would kill his mother (or stepmother). Nine days after he was released on the forgery stint, Bloodgood and another man, Michael Quarick, broke into his mother's house, and Quarick killed Margaret. Knowing the crime would be pinned on him, Bloodgood fled. A crazy road trip ended with Bloodgood handing himself over to authorities to protect a girl he was with. 1,988 blank postal money orders were found in the car. In the ensuing murder trial, Bloodgood pulled the same judge who had presided over his forgery trial. The judge refused to recuse himself. No one believed that Quarick had killed Margaret, and Bloodgood was convicted and sentenced to death. He started out as No. 8 on Virginia's death row, moved up, but was saved by the Supreme Court. Then he started a chess club. Bloodgood and Lewis Capleaner, who was in jail for stabbing a woman seventeen times, arranged events with high cash prizes even by nonprison standards. Both men were then victimized by George Winslow, the prison supervisor of the chess club. In 1973, Winslow somehow lost all the money the chess club had raised for a tournament. In a panic he arranged for furloughs for Bloodgood and Capleaner, ostensibly to organize the tournament, but really so that the two could rob a casino and get the money back for him. Bloodgood and Capleaner, of course, refused to participate, but Winslow was crazed. They had no choice but to tie him up and escape with their girlfriends. Once again, Bloodgood went on a long road trip, staying at motels and not doing much of anything, eventually being called upon to do the right thing when it became apparent that the girl he was with would be implicated in the robberies he was committing. He allowed himself to be captured. Winslow, in part of a VDOC cover-up, quit his prison job and joined the army before Bloodgood was returned to Virginia. Of the escape trial, Bloodgood said, "I was found guilty of overpowering a man who wasn't there to testify that it happened." After that, Bloodgood was punished by prison officials for implicating one of their own: He was sent to a special ward for three years. He didn't play chess again until 1992, when other prisoners pressured him to start up a club once more. But that only led to the ratings fiasco, followed in turn by his chest tumor, and last year's prediction that he would be dead before this year.

This was Bloodgood's version, and I understood now why I was just the next in a line of journalists anxious to interview him. Bloodgood had already done an interview with the British paper *The Guardian*, and another writer from Paris's *Le Monde* was scheduled for the week after me. What Bloodgood did, I realized, was manipulate the enthusiasm of writers by leading them into inviting water. He was part lawyer, part chess player: Learn your opponent, generate doubt.

The more likely version of Bloodgood's life was shorter and less interesting: he was born somewhere in the United States in the late '30s. He'd grown up in Norfolk, near a beach where a railroad tanker had washed up years before; locals took it for a submarine. He learned to play chess at a young age, and engaged in postal chess matches even before going to prison; in 1959, he was investigated by the FBI for a game he conducted with a Soviet player. Although Bloodgood had told me that chess helped keep people away from the associations, it didn't seem to have had this effect on him. He went to jail in '62 for B&E, again for forgery in '68. He was released in 1970, and was free for a week before looking for vengeance against his mother. More than one psychologist during the trial testified that Bloodgood was a sociopath, and Bloodgood himself told the prosecutor, under oath, that he was "a very convincing liar." He was convicted, skirted the death penalty. Then he caught wind of a U.S.-Mexican prisoner exchange program that offered him a shot at freedom if he could demonstrate Mexican citizenship. He concocted the story of Mexican birth, and added a dozen years to his life with the risky ironic flourish of a French independence day birthday. But no one noticed. A fictional German heritage, which drew on the railroad wreck of his youth for inspiration, explained why Bloodgood had lied about himself. One simply couldn't fess up to being a German spy. But the new year of birth, 1924, did not jibe: His mother was fifty-eight when she died, making her twelve years old in 1924. No problem, she just became his father's second wife. But Bloodgood had never bothered to explain how it was that his father had been only fourteen at the year of his son's birth. Still, the Simon Wiesenthal Center conducted an investigation. But Bloodgood's Nazi party number was too low for one who was supposed to have joined in the '40s. In 1974, Bloodgood's chess club offered him a second chance to escape, and this time it worked. But, as with a postal chess player who plans well in private but is not as sharp over-the-board, Bloodgood's escape was better planned than executed: He was recaptured when authorities tracked his use of a credit card. Prison officials did not appreciate Bloodgood's attempt to pin the escape on them—a *Wall Street Journal* reporter was lulled by the story's romance, and Winslow was temporarily detained—and not only did they punish Bloodgood, the incident changed the entire direction of Virginia corrections.

In the end, which of the Bloodgood stories were fact didn't really matter, and Bloodgood knew it. "I've spent thirty-some years in prison," he told me in summation. "Whether I'm guilty is immaterial."

When he finished his story, he eased into a coughing fit that confirmed at least one of his claims—he was very sick. As the attack came, he produced a roll of toilet paper from a side compartment on his wheelchair and quickly made a mop of tissue to clean himself.

Our interview was almost over. It seemed he wasn't going to give me what I wanted. "Why do you keep playing chess?" I asked him, a final effort.

Bloodgood's face slackened. It was the first moment when he did not have to keep up a pretense. His eyes were sad and intelligent.

"To keep from going completely buttfuck," he said.

As we ended our talk, Bloodgood suggested that we play a couple of games by mail—it was something he generally did with journalists. I agreed, and we exited into the hallway together, his guard pushing him from behind. "I gotta pee," Bloodgood said, and the guard assured him it would be taken care of. I reached to shake Bloodgood's hand. "Take care, Claude," I told him, and I meant it. Whether Bloodgood was evil, whether his use of chess to escape prison proved the uselessness of the game, was as immaterial as his guilt. Bloodgood himself, significant only for his clever web of lies, remembered only for the holes he had punched in the USCF rating system, was also immaterial. There was no reason to hate him. Bloodgood's stories were like one of his postal games: infinitely more imaginative than his real life and created to give him something of hope, something to keep him from going completely buttfuck. This was a use of chess itself. Bloodgood had tried to swindle the world, but the maneuver had gone horribly wrong. He had been sentenced to death, to a lost position, but even this had been snatched away from him. For thirty years, he had been forced to shuffle the pieces of his life, to calculate traps in hope of further play, but each of these had proved fruitless; and he had continued to lose material until there was almost nothing left of him. Now Bloodgood ran his king around the board, dodging threats and begging for attention. His history was a score sheet full of gorgeous tactics; and he desperately longed for someone to analyze it with him, a writer who would come to the conclusion that he had lived, at least in his own mind. But the thing was, you couldn't be sure that Bloodgood's scoresheet was accurate—his life, already in postmortem, was full of lies and erase marks. Looking back at the game, its beauty was marred by the knowledge that, as a game, it might never have been played.

GLENN SAT IN MERKEY'S OFFICE ON THE FAR SIDE OF THE GYM, gathering himself like a concert pianist. The walls of Merkey's office were thick glass, so I could see him from where I stood over near the inmates. Most of the players were already seated, and the sets of various sizes—from Chicago's melted wax to the tiny El Cheapos—

stood in their opening arrays along the row of conference tables. Twenty boards. The inmates sat along the side with the black pieces. When the time came, Glenn would walk up and down the opposite row.

Merkey asked me to go over the procedure for the simul one more time. Simuls are often quiet, formal affairs. They can last for many hours, depending on how many players participate. I told Merkey that it was okay if our simul wasn't quite as structured as a formal exhibition.

"Oh, but we like structure," she said. Merkey had already explained that every day in the prison was pretty much like every other day in the prison, and that slight variations in routine raised the ire of inmates long before it bothered anyone else. She spoke of structure as though it was part of the prison's philosophy of rehabilitation. I wondered about the logic: Structure was supposed to be good for the prisoners, but many of them seemed simply mollified by it. Chess players, I thought, could be equally dulled and resistant to change.

Merkey introduced me, and I stood. "A simultaneous exhibition works like this," I said. "Glenn will play white in every game. He will walk up the row making his first move on each board. You don't move until he returns to your board." The prisoners nodded. I might have been giving them instructions on how to enter and exit their cells. The inmates were like a group of savvy undergraduates who had learned that convincing their instructor they were paying attention would net them a better grade. "That's very important—do not move until he returns to your board. This will make things kind of slow in the beginning—you will want to move quickly, but don't. When you get further on in your game, you will want to think some more. If Glenn comes to your game, and you're not ready to move, you can pass."

I turned the floor back to Merkey, and she nodded. "Okay, we're going to bring him out."

Glenn appeared to muffled applause. The prisoners weren't quite sure what the etiquette should be, but they were trying. In addition to the twenty players ready to begin their games, a dozen observers were scattered across the stands. I saw Baynes off in one corner, notebook at the ready, hidden in plain view. Glenn gave a short speech and pointed out a few of the players he had played earlier in the afternoon.

It was silent as the simul began. Glenn hurried his first trip down the line, making his initial move on each board. Not all of Glenn's first moves were the same. Against the players he did not recognize he played a simple king pawn opening, while against those he recognized and in whom he perhaps saw a little talent, he played queen pawn. Against just two players, he played Nf3, a hypermodern, to perhaps throw them off their plans from the beginning.

Just a short time into the simul, I climbed into the bleachers to observe the scene from a distance. An inmate who was just there to watch nudged my arm and said, "This is the most peace and quiet I ever got in prison in my life. Thanks." It was true, the room was remaining calm. Glenn cruised the row again and again, pausing just a second or two at most boards, fifteen or twenty at a few of them. Of all the games, only Chicago had come prepared to keep score: he'd arrived with his scoresheet ready with Glenn's name written across the top and forty handwritten innings already scribbled in, waiting for the moves. Another man had brought a manual for a hand-held computer game because it had a chart of openings in the back. No one from the audience had yet risen to look at the games. A kind of formality seemed to be the only privacy available to an inmate, and they were reluctant to step on one another's intellectual turf. The scene might have been sacred, Glenn like a priest walking the line and blessing a gang of twisted altar boys. When he reached the end of the row, he turned and immediately rushed to the front, moving back to the first game where he would start again, without breaks.

I came down to walk the row myself. The first in line was Lee. When I approached his board, he smiled broadly—he was quite optimistic about his position even though he appeared to have the worst of it.

"If I was to win, or even come close to winnin', I'd feel so good!" he said.

Just then, Glenn appeared and quickly made his move like a wave washing over a beach picnic. He was two or three boards down the line before Lee and the man next to him were able to assess the damage to Lee's position.

"Who's close to winnin', loser?" said Lee's neighbor.

Peeking over Chicago's shoulder, I saw that pronunciation of obscure chess words was not his only problem—his notation was a baffling mix of algebraic and descriptive, like a line of music written in multiple clefs, pawn moves in the former, piece moves in the latter. But his game was far more interesting than those near him. The pieces of both players had exploded toward one another on the board, and the forces had collided without the usual exchanges and simplifications. They were mounded together in a sumo press.

When Glenn came to Chicago's game, he paused much longer than at the others, placing a large palm to either side of the board and looming directly over the position as though over a sacrament. Chicago did not look at Glenn at such moments. After Glenn appeared once more, the two men sharing the trance of the game for another quick interval, Chicago looked up at me. I noticed that he did not mark his pawn move on his scoresheet, that in fact he had not marked the score for several innings.

"Why aren't you marking it down?" I said. "It's a good game."

Chicago's steely chess player vanished, and he broke into a grin. "I was gonna. But it got, like, too intense!"

I complimented him and continued. I passed two games in which Glenn had already won a piece, and came to the game of an older white man whose crime was difficult to imagine—it was difficult to imagine him jaywalking. He was smallish, with tousled white hair and impeccable manners. He played on one of the red-and-black boards with the El Cheapo pieces, but his attack against Glenn's king was complicated and vicious. The heft of triple-weighted pieces in speed chess sometimes helped give a sense of potency to an attack, but the little criminal's advance on Glenn's kingside was significant even as it was represented by thin thimbles that could be moved with a breath. Glenn was using both his rooks, his queen and a knight to defend against a two rook-queen-bishop attack, and a little black pawn marching up the h-file threatened to amount to the difference. One board over a young man was engaged in a slow positional contest. I asked him what he thought of his chances, and he said he liked them even though the game was dull. "Black be on defense anyway," he said. "I'm tryin' to get me an open, but he ain't give me none yet." Two boards down from him, a large man was lecturing on the hopelessness of his position. "He's playin' me for a chump!" he said, his voice carrying over the room and the bleachers. "He ain't moved but one pawn, this motherfucker." He pointed to the one man of Glenn's that he had managed to capture so far. With knight, bishop, and queen, Glenn had infiltrated the man's kingside in a kind of guerrilla maneuver. "Wait! I see it now! He's coming here," he said, gesturing broadly to a square that, if occupied, would cripple him. Glenn arrived in the next wave, not even really stopping completely as he came to this board, and made the move the man had anticipated. Then he was gone. "I knew it! Damn! Motherfucker!" And just down from him, another two or three quick victories away, Sueing sat at the end of the row, still in his wool hat, having captured one of Glenn's rooks for a bishop. As compensation, Glenn had one of his own bishops protected on a long central diagonal that ended at Sueing's king. Flanked by his remaining bishop and his queen, the three made a slanted swath of attack down the board. The position seemed to be of some interest to Glenn, and even as he pivoted on his heels to turn away his eyes lingered on the pieces.

Mark appeared in the gym, at last released from work. He sauntered in alone. I barely recognized him without his plastic chow hall gear. He walked up beside me and we surveyed the simul together, discussing his chances of getting a board. A few players had resigned already only to be replaced by others, and I had been organizing a list of those wanting to squeeze in. I told Mark I was not sure there would be time. He nodded at the hopelessness of his lot—another bit of injustice—and changed the subject.

"So you're a writer, huh?"

"Yes."

"I'm a writer, too."

"Oh, yeah?"

He nodded like a scribe keen to the ugly ways of the publishing industry. "I got two novels written. I'm lookin' for an editor, whatever. They're sci-fi/fantasy. I like that shit. 'Cept in my books the bad guys always win. So far, anyway."

I came to understand that I was standing beside perhaps the most dangerous man in the prison. Of all those whose muscles bulged, of all those who towered over me like kings over pawns, none scared me so much as this one small man who was unafraid to put what little freedom he had managed to collect on the line just to satisfy a personal vision of right and wrong. Mark found the world unjust and used this as an excuse to behave unjustly. The bad guys won. It was like a chess endgame: sword and pen vs. pen. The pen had a lost game.

Mark headed up to the bleachers and sat with two other white prisoners. I walked over to where Baynes was sitting, and he tried to hit me up for contacts as well. He thumbed through a copy of his newspaper, showed me the stories and poetry he had written, and then adopted a fatherly tone. "Now, I'd like you to write to me," he said. I told him I would, and I made him promise to send me a copy of his chess story when it appeared.

My trek up the line had opened the floodgates to observers, and now inmates were peeking over the shoulders of their peers, attempting to assess who had winning chances. Several guards were among them, their uniforms interspersed with the uniforms of the inmates like pieces of wholly different games mixed together. Mark caught my eye from the stands, nodded his head at an officer craned over a board, and spoke just loudly enough so I could understand. "How come none a these po-lease playing?" Part of what frightened me about Mark was his ability to tap into that which, I had to admit, I found interesting. Glenn had offered to play a number of the guards, but they had refused. Merkey came up beside me then with the news that we would not be able to begin any more games. It was coming up on 8:00, and she was calling it. Just as we agreed to this, a man resigned and began to gather his pieces together. I tapped Merkey and gestured to Mark. Mark looked up, but Merkey froze him with ice from her eyes, a skill of hers, and Mark sank back down in his seat, hiding to continue his long wait.

"About how much longer do you think he's got?" Merkey said.

She meant Glenn, the sentence of his simul. I told her I wasn't sure, probably not much—most of the remaining games were already decided. Merkey and I were put into the position of chess organizers forced to make a difficult call. When Glenn ended his next round of moves, I pulled him aside and asked him to speed up a bit. "Okay," he said, and marched away. At the same time, Merkey made an announcement to the inmates, asking them to resign lost positions.

Glenn did not speed up at all. From then on, I gave him minute by minute updates. He may have been the first chess player in history to encounter time trouble while conducting a simul. Eight-thirty came and went. Most of the observers had cleared out by then, and before long only six games remained. Glenn had yet to lose or draw a contest. I asked Merkey what our status was and she pointed outside, into the yard, where we could still see a few figures moving in the failing light. "When you don't see anyone out there," she said, "we absolutely have to leave."

Two more players resigned, and Glenn took his time at his games. Sueing, Chicago, the older white man, and one other player remained, each as calm as Glenn in their moves, steady as grandmasters. Those most anxious at the hour were myself, Merkey, and the guard who had told us the gym was a disgrace for its pricetag. But now his tune had changed a bit. He was rooting for Chicago, standing behind him and pulling for him, and when Merkey and I wandered over to look at the position, he said, "Merkey, we've got to let him finish this one! He's so close!" It was true. Chicago had flushed Glenn's king from its castled hideaway and was making it dance behind a screen of pins and attacks. Chicago still did not look at Glenn when he appeared. Chess sometimes became a medium of communication, I thought, a secular technology of communion. Eye contact became irrelevant, hopelessly tangential. My distaste for the game and my search for its usefulness had made me forget this. And it was this that was perhaps the finest use of chess, a use that tended to go overlooked because descriptions of the game were always lacking. But it was precisely a kind of covenant that chess players sought; and when they found it, a mood surrounded the game that was hypnotic even to those who could not quite fathom its depth or meaning. It was at such moments that chess became literally holy, a religion. And if I had come to doubt the game for how it had been abused in the world—for the fact that it was used to compare rather than share—it was this moment, this game, in which chess showed its resilience, its ability to withstand and survive and to be used for the purest of reasons, that brought me back to its appreciation. Like an idea of God, chess would not fully succumb to the petty influence of organized veneration. Its purity would occasionally resurface, like statues crying or bleeding in odd corners of the world, a school, a monastery, a throne room, a prison. Its grand metaphor was something beyond politics and certainly beyond war or simple melee, but it was also beyond that which language was yet able to describe, and it was malleable, immune, and immortal. The game had come from man, but it was alive now and, like a computer, beyond him—and it cared not how men tried to use it.

It was past 8:45. There was no one in the yard. Mark was gone,

Lee was gone, Baynes was gone, only the four players remained. Among the survivors was the furtive excitement of breaking the rules, a sensation compounded by the context of the prison.

"Okay," Merkey said. "Here's what we're going to do. I'm going to ask Glenn to pick one game to complete. We don't have time for the others."

Glenn demonstrated wins in three of the games that remained. His central bishop in Sueing's game would prove decisive, the older white man's queen was to be trapped in a move or two, and the third was a long-projected win in which Glenn's king would sneak around to pick off a critical pawn. He decided on Chicago's game to complete, and the two men shuffled through the final few moves quickly, all of us gathered around. The mood of the moment was totally unlike the climactic ending of a sporting event or a story. Rather, it was an observance or a tribute, a structured ritual that must be completed and whose function was to bond us into an absurd moment of humanity.

"Okay, I resign this one," Glenn said, as though pronouncing death over one who had lived long. There was collective relief, and a sense that things had ended affably. There was quiet handshaking and farewells, and the prisoners rushed off to be accounted for. We did not see where they went, or even in which direction they headed. Chicago's win was the true conclusion to the event, and everything after was anticlimax as we were ushered out of the prison. Merkey took us back through the security lock, where gas masks and oxygen hung on the walls. It was the end of her day as well, and she escorted us to our rental.

We got out onto the highway, and I watched the remnants of Michigan's northern dusk fade in the rearview mirror. Glenn watched the cars going the other way.

"Way to go, Hallman," he said, "you didn't say anything to get us killed."

I nodded and suggested that he jot down the game with Chicago in my notebook while it was fresh. It would be nice to have it.

"I don't need to write it down," he said. He tapped the side of his head, and gave a solemn rapper's nod. "It's here."

I had received this answer from him before and knew it to be true, to an extent. Immediately after a game, Glenn could recall each and every move of even the most complicated contests. After several days he would remember positions but perhaps not how he had arrived at them. And after a few weeks, he would recall not even this, though he would remember some feature of the position, some idea, something the game had demonstrated. But most of all he would remember whether he had fought well, whether his opponent had fought well, whether it had been good chess. And even though I asked him, each time, to write down his games, to enter himself into the world of recorded data and chess civilization, he would only agree and then abruptly forget, his formidable memory either selective or above such base concerns, so that I was reminded that the many games published throughout the world, those in books and magazines, the million on my computer database and millions more locked into the Internet—these were but a fraction of the chess games that had been played, a hint of the billions that had been lost, the billions that proved that chess, like ice sculpture or cave painting or architecture, was an art of dreamlike impermanence.

CHAPTER 21

Reentrance

Considered merely as a chapter in the social history of mankind, chess is equally worthy of admiration.

—Nathaniel Bland

I have always a slight feeling of pity for the man who has no knowledge of chess, just as I would pity the man who has remained ignorant of love.

—Dr. Siegbert Tarrasch

I WENT FOR ONE LAST WALK ON THE MORNING OF OUR final day in Kalmykia. The Christian minichurch was locked as always, so I walked out past the lone member of the Chess City army sitting a lazy sentinel at the gate and headed up the road to the small Buddhist temple. The giant spool turned inside, persistent as a clockwork, and a man in a corner chanted verse from a small book. I watched the mantras printed on the prayer drum, spinning.

Om, Ma HH, Ne Me, XYHR

At the head of the room sat vases of flowers, candles long since burnt down, photos of famous lamas, peacock feathers, and a statue of the Buddha wrapped in a linen shawl. I left two rubles on a table.

I had one last chance to find Yudina's pond. From the temple I took the pipe-lined road that Altana and I had walked on together, and at the end of it I cut off into the steppe.

Sometimes jets flew low over the republic. Now, in the October chill, vapor trails striped the sky, thick layers of ordered mist only five hundred meters up. They would remain for hours. I swerved out and around Chess City. Bambusha had warned me of bandits this far out, but there didn't seem to be anyone around at all and I descended into my first steppe gully, one of the crevices that from the sky looked like wounds in the earth. At the bottom it was reeds as water gathered there, and I squished through a fetid puddle. Up on the other side, three little dogs became angry with me for approaching an abandoned construction site, a large unfinished house. It would have been a grand property, an estate, and was probably the effort of one who had banked and lost on the success of chess in the republic. I continued into the steppe, making another thousand meters and cutting under rows of power-line towers and telephone poles. Then suddenly I saw them, off to my right, the hulking cows, motionless and munching on weeds near a stand of trees. Most were actually bulls with portentous horns, and now they were between me and Chess City. I was beyond them. I watched their shepherd weave between the quiet living beef.

I moved on carefully. Down in the flat between Chess City and the far hills, it was all marsh. I passed over a makeshift bridge made of the flat sections of a car's metal body. Another two hundred meters and I was back within sight of Chess Palace, and from a distance it appeared to be what it had been billed as, a fulfilled promise, the president's dream come true. If it was sinking, I couldn't see it from here, and even the unfinished cottages appeared inviting and modern. It was a Potemkin village, but it was perhaps too easy to call it just that. Farther on I came to the huge field of reeds. They were as solid up close as they were from a distance, but as I walked by I glanced something in among them, a pale splash of unexpected brown. I stopped and pried back the sharp stalks. Then I walked into them, like walking into a wall of corn.

It was just a few steps in and down before it opened up again, onto ground that at first sight looked to be made of porous bones, brown and soft and moldy. They weren't really bones, of course, and now I figured that the reeds had been the clue all along. This was Yudina's pond. The reeds grew where the shoreline had been. The dry bed of it was the dirt that Bambusha had said was used to fill the pond in, the fabric of sandbags decaying so that it looked like mummified skin stretched across rotting bone. I walked out onto the sacks. There was junk here, random garbage, tires, and what looked like a bedpan, and the reeds made a wall all around. Weeds had sprouted up near the middle of the pond. Even the plants in Kalmykia knew that the center was important. I could see nothing of the world outside the pond except the tip of Chess Palace a good ways off. It was this that made me wonder under what circumstances Yudina's body had been found. I had come across this place only by accident. If it was a given that a corpse was difficult to transport, then it was reasonable to conclude that after Yudina had climbed into that car in the middle of the night, she had been driven to Chess City and killed here. It was only Yudina's death that kept the story of chess and Kalmykia from being simple comedy. She was an ambiguous martyr. Her murderers had dumped her in this pond, but somewhere where they knew that she would be found. The exact site was a message. Looking around the creepy floor of the pond, like a parched African desert, the only place in Kalmykia where there had been an attempt made to drain the land rather than irrigate it, a hiding place so perfect that something's being found here seemed to necessitate intent, the meaning of the murder, committed by whoever, was perfectly clear: Don't mess with chess.

I panicked when I realized that I had lost the spot where I entered the pond. I took my best guess and pushed back through the reeds. I climbed back to Chess City. I passed the Djangharchi's house, windows covered with a metallic-looking material for warmth or acoustics and a spiffy Volga parked in the driveway. In Chess Palace, there were boys and girls everywhere. A children's blitz tournament was to be held that day. A gang of boys surrounded me to ask the English questions they chanted in school, then swarmed the model of Chess City, Phase I. They peered into the little houses, finished and unfinished, and when one of them leaned too hard against the base, part of the model tipped down and in, like some ungodly quake let loose upon the city. The boys reared back and laughed, and the model righted itself. But it was like a prediction of the subdivision's demise, the end of chess in the republic, at fast forward, half of it sinking into the earth and the other half pitching up in the air like a ship in breech before the plummet to the ocean floor. But again the simile didn't work, I thought, because Kalmykia was already ocean floor, or had been, and just as its people had nowhere left to roam, there was no farther depth to which its fragile land could sink.

• • •

WE ARRANGED A BANQUET ON OUR LAST EVENING IN KALMYKIA for the staff of the FIDE office and the Utnasunovs. The Utnasunovs took us to their home before we all headed to Elista for dinner. Their microdistrict apartment was small and cramped, three teenagers in one room. Sasha's father gave Glenn a gift: a small chess trophy, a knight on a wooden base. "Ng4!" read the inscription. We gave Sasha our Chronos.

At the restaurant Glenn surprised everyone just as we were sitting down to dinner. "I'm sorry, I have to go," he announced to the crowd that was gathered to see him off. "I, uh, have a date. Sorry."

The Utnasunovs looked to me for an explanation, but I didn't have one. Glenn started to leave, then waved me out into the hallway.

"These people are here for you," I told him.

"I have to go. Listen, I'm going to take a hundred dollars. I'll pay you back from my first paycheck when we get home."

He nodded and tried to shake my hand, but I wouldn't. I had never refused Glenn a loan, and this was the first time he was going to take money from me without asking. I thought of all the things I had been for Glenn in our adventures: organizer, friend, second, supporter, teacher, student, fan, benefactor, critic, biographer. But before all that, the very first thing I had been was his opponent. I felt opposed to him now. Glenn had the same problem with me that he had with women—we would never truly connect because I would never truly understand the game that was his litmus for meaning in life. My problem with him was the same as my problem with Kirsan— they were both using chess, but what might have been used as a device for enlightenment was instead a greedy, lesser form of spiri- tuality. Our relationship had begun with the premise that Glenn was obsessed with chess, but now I was obsessed with him, with what he might have become had chess been the thing I wanted it to be. But it wasn't, and he wasn't, and I knew it now.

I let him have the hundred dollars. But I took the rest of the money he was carrying in his belt.

"You can count it," he said. "It's all there."

"I will."

He left, and I returned to dinner. The guests asked me what had happened. I explained that where Glenn and I lived in the United States there was no one nearby who understood Glenn's chess talent.

This made him very lonely sometimes, and as a result he occasionally made poor decisions.

Glenn returned a short time later with Ludmilla. They sat down near the end of the table. The dinner continued happily with people laughing and singing karaoke. Galzanov arrived, but he wasn't there for us—he was already on to his next job, the next project that would keep the republic in the news. I watched him sit down at a table and light a cigarette as he waited for whoever would be joining him. The flame from his lighter shot up tall as a finger, and for a moment it jumped to the end of his cigarette and stayed there, a brief flare. At the other end of the restaurant, Glenn was bragging to Ludmilla and the others around him. He would be forty in a year, but he flexed his biceps for Ludmilla and told her to squeeze the muscle, and promised to make a tape of songs for her and send them along once he was home.

MOSCOW FELT MORE LIKE HOME THAN HOME, AND ERASED much of the tension between Glenn and me. We shared a room at the Intourist and bathed in the water we had feared. Glenn insisted we eat at the McDonald's on Tverskaya Street. The restaurant felt the same, but for Russians a Happy Meal cost half a day's pay. We were safe.

On the morning of our departure, I woke Glenn by accident as I dressed before our view of the city.

"Hallman," he said, groggy, "you're a shadow in the window."

In all my chess study, I had never tried to complete a Knight's Tour. It had been the artfulness of chess that had first drawn me to the game, and I had never understood the mathematical appeal of calculating a knight's leap across the board. But I could imagine it, and in the same way checkmate was anticlimax in the game, the position long imagined in the players' minds, so were the last few moves of a Knight's Tour formality, a ritual like filling in the final line of a maze. When Glenn and I returned to the United States, it was like the end of such a puzzle. It all went as we had planned, and when we landed again in Boston our tour was reentrant.

We rode in silence to the home where we would stay that night. We would drive to Atlantic City in the morning. We ate a quiet dinner, and our host asked Glenn what he had learned in Russia. "I learned that I have a lot more money than I thought I did," he said. Then he asked if he could borrow the computer in the next room. He played chess on the ICC until 6:00 A.M.

On the drive south, I asked Glenn if we could try to play a game of blindfold together. I thought I could handle it now.

"No way," he said. "You're driving."

I argued, but he refused to try unless I pulled over and let him drive. Finally, I agreed. He was right. After just two moves I could barely think of anything else and keep it straight. After four moves, I was in trouble, and after six I was guessing. Glenn made his replies at once, and took us south through the morning. We had to be back in Atlantic City by 3:00 to register with our casino. At move nine, I thought for ten minutes and forgot moves seven and eight completely. I gave it up.

Closer to Atlantic City, I asked Glenn what his plans for the future were. He said he would probably move in with one of the women he was dating here, then try to get custody of his daughter. I asked him how long he planned to stay in the casino business, to work as a dealer rather than for the thing he loved.

"I don't know," he said. We were nearing home, heading directly for the casino. "Probably awhile. But it's all right, I have an idea."

"For what?"

"A perpetual motion machine."

"Really?" I said. "What is it?"

"I can't tell you, man."

He refused to reveal what it was until I promised not to write about it. Then he laid it out, and to be honest I wasn't sure it wouldn't work. We checked in at the casino office, our last bit of business together, and then he walked me out to the boardwalk to say good-bye. I spoke the line I'd waited a month to deliver.

"Develop your pieces," I said.

"Hey!" He smiled, and then he waved and walked back through the tinted doors.

CHAPTER 22

Check-O-Rama

O thou whose cynic sneers express
The censure of our favourite chess,
Know that its skill is science' self,
Its play distraction from distress.
It soothes the anxious lover's care,
It weans the drunkard from excess;
It counsels warriors in their art,
When dangers threat, and perils press;
And yields us, when we need them most,
Companions in our loneliness.

—b. Mu'tazz, *K.* yawaqit al-mawaqit fi madh
  ash-shai' wadhammihi, *1038*

The spirit of the professional is no longer the true play-spirit; it is lacking in
spontaneity and carelessness. This affects the amateur too, who begins to
suffer from an inferiority complex.

—Johan Huizinga, Homo Ludens, *1950*

IF MY ADVENTURES WITH GLENN WERE A TOUR OF THE
chess world conducted over the course of a year-and-a-half, then
Baagi's first day on the East Coast, months before Glenn and I went
to Russia, was a tour completed in twenty-four hours.

Let me warn you, Baagi had typed to me on the ICC a day or so
before she and EK climbed on a plane, *I am no Miss of America!* Emerging from the gate at the terminal, Baagi was lively and expressive in
a way that made her quite pretty really. You could see chess had made
her famous in Mongolia. She was entirely comfortable with the formal greeting we went through in the terminal, the idea that we were

there to drive her. EK was tall and quiet beside her. He looked like a man who had spent years studying variations on kindness.

We were already in time trouble. The first leg of Baagi's tour would be the dealers' lounge. The best time to play the Baagi-Glenn match was just before the start of swing shift, when the dealers who were about to begin for the night mingled with the day shifters just getting off. We made the casino with a few minutes to spare. Glenn kicked the players off the boards when we arrived, and he and Baagi set up a better board and heavier pieces. Under the table's plastic sheet was an old *Chess Life* cover with a picture of a young Asian woman completing a free-standing statue from a full set of chessmen. The resemblance to Baagi was only slight, but it was enough to cause Lynell, one of the lounge players, a cursing, righteous, acne-scarred man of many words, to nudge her and ask her if she was the cover girl. Baagi was beginning to look a little uneasy, but she only smiled and said no.

"Three minute?" Glenn asked, when they were ready.

"No," Baagi said. "One."

He smiled, fixed the clock, and they began to play. Baagi was immediately fast. She was tired even then, but as soon as the game began she came to life. To the uninitiated, one-minute over-the-board looks sloppy, pieces falling to the floor or lying on their sides and rolling circles, often while they are still in play. Bullet has a character of an entirely different sort from any other spectacle in chess. It was not the lecture of a simul, nor was it was the séance of a blindfold—it was more like knife juggling. You couldn't possibly understand all the action, but there was thrill and weird fear to watching its execution.

A crowd gathered. People in the lounge who never played chess came by to watch. People who had listened to rumors of Glenn's exploits for years, who had seen his picture in local newspapers and posted on the walls, people who had been shuffled out of precious seats so that chess players could play twenty-minute games, they were all watching now, gap-mouthed, and a refrain began to run through the room. Who is this girl? Where's she from again? And though Glenn announced it several times, between games, Mongolia was not on the collective map of the place. The dealers' lounge was a cosmopolitan collection of cultures, but it wasn't just the cultures that melted, it was nationality, history, and geography. Here, Asia was one vast country, very far away, and Baagi was of a place and a gender that these people had never before associated with chess.

Glenn lost the first few games. All his predictions that there was no woman in the world faster than him were proved false. Baagi was faster. Even the crowd could sense it, and Queenie, a woman who had never watched chess before, rooted for Baagi exuberantly. "You go, girl! You beat that man! He needs it. All that talkin' all these years! You go, girl!" To that point the crowd had been in kind of a state of shock, trying to reconcile the solemn reputation of the game with a more primal instinct to root and cheer. Baagi herself was confused by all the shocking identical shirts. It was as though she had been transported to a world of overly affectionate ETs.

Baagi's style was different from Glenn's. Her captures were less like Glenn's snapping slams than they were dextrous, sleight-of-hand shiftings. Her men moved like skaters, not like combatants at all, and she picked up fractions of a second every time she hit the clock. When she made captures, the pieces seemed to atomize at her touch. To the crowd it didn't matter—their ignorance of the game granted them through to a purer form of its appreciation. They couldn't understand the specifics of bishops and rooks, but they could re-spond to the vague idea of it. They watched silently during the games, an odd selection of information—Glenn's frowns, Baagi's confidence, the hesitations, the speed—allowing them to tap into the fundamen-tal drama, and when either one of them quit, pushing the pieces forward, or when mate suddenly appeared on the board, it was a signal for cheering, for random raucousness.

"You ain't my teacher anymore!" Lynell announced to Glenn, af-ter a loss. There was a round of laughter. Lynell produced two folded sections of newspapers and fanned the players during the break, steal-ing the stage for a moment. Glenn asked someone to bring him a glass of water, and a wry young Asian girl brought him a cup of boiling water from the coffee machine.

Glenn was laughing even though he was losing, happy that every-one was watching, that they would understand his game a little better now. "Everyone, this is Baagi," he said, introducing her for the fourth or fifth time. "She's an international master from Mongolia."

Baagi produced several interesting mates—in-your-face rook mates with escape squares covered by pawns or distant bishops. There were no draws. Several times in endgames the tension heightened dramatically, and the crowd gasped audibly. Baagi played two-handed at such moments, both raised over the board like a pair of cobras on the hinges of her elbows, sometimes still clutching the last piece of Glenn's she had taken, the little man lynched in the crotch between two fingers.

"Who's that girl?" a new observer asked.

"She's the Queen Grand Master!" Lynell announced, and no one argued with him.

It was over at 8:00. The dealers could not delay their departure to the casino floor, and in the middle of the thirteenth game they filtered out.

Baagi had won, 9-4. Glenn vowed revenge, and they made a date to play again after the World Open.

Baagi needed to get on a computer by 9:00 for the next stop on her tour. It was a tournament in Mongolia. Not just any tourna-ment—a tournament that was *named* for her, for her chess accom-plishments. She would play in the live event from my apartment via the ICC. Baagi was under pressure from her brother to participate. He was running for Parliament, and hoped to parlay her result into votes.

The Internet hookup was clean, and we were just in time. Baagi began a game against a young Mongolian grandmaster. Mongolia was the exact flop of New Jersey, timewise—noon was midnight. We cheated. We played the moves on the board on my table. EK sat in the opponent's position, and as the digital clocks on my screen dis-played the time, Baagi and EK moved the pieces, analyzing four or five moves ahead. Sometimes Baagi took EK's suggestion, sometimes not. He never complained when she preferred something more ag-gressive; he simply accepted the new position. The young GM, eight thousand miles away in a straight line, proved tough, and Baagi's position began to deteriorate. EK finally looked at me and said, "We are going to lose this game."

They played a few more moves, and Baagi resigned. I was still unsure of what to say to chess players when they lost—I told her to shake it off.

We walked to the hotel nearby where I had arranged a room for them for the night. I left them there to shower and prepare for the next game, scheduled to begin at 1:30 A.M. Baagi had been awake for nineteen hours at that point, and there were already dark wedges under her eyes. Her next pairing was against a 1900 player. She told EK she could handle it alone, and he lay down on my futon. I fell asleep on my bed only to wake an hour later when I heard Baagi mutter, "Gosh!"

Baagi's skin showed green in the computer light. She was leaning forward, inches from the screen. Oh, it's nothing, she said, easy game. She had three pawns on the sixth rank, and was ready to either force mate or promote.

The final round was half an hour later. Baagi's last opponent played the first eight or ten moves and offered a draw. Baagi weighed the decision both in terms of her result and in terms of how it might affect her brother's hopes for the election. The sun came up just as it set on the other side of the world. She took the draw.

Two hours later I drove her to the World Open for the final stop on her tour. Like Glenn on the bus to New York, Baagi had no trouble sleeping in the backseat of my car on the way to Philadelphia. EK and I talked chess history; Baagi's snoring harmonized with the highway. She grunted herself awake when we arrived at the hotel, and we checked into their room to rest. Baagi took a bed, and EK produced a chess magazine and played through a few games from its dense pages, slowing down from the hectic day-and-a-half of travel and strange places. EK and Baagi were an ironic chess couple. Baagi's reckless life and giggly charm were an extension of her tactical style— it was why she could bounce out of bed and produce interesting combinations. EK, on the other hand, was a quiet, positional player, content with slight advantages; and his careful movements, slow thought, sweet demeanor, even his study before the tournament, these were all analogues of his quiet, powerful play. Baagi and EK saw their differences as a value—alone, they had weaknesses, but together they were a complete chess team, ready to meet whatever strategies the world chose to throw at them.

I walked down to the pairings room to look around before the tournament began. My reaction to the tournament this time around was much different from the previous year when Glenn had introduced me to chess. It was exciting. The Skittles Room was as packed as a discotheque, and the pairings room had a Grand Central Station feel to it, people bouncing about like lottery balls. The hallways churned with men carrying zippered cases that held their little sacks of weighted chessmen. The sense of anticipation was like a fog—for the children of the lower-rated sections, it was unbearable, and they ran off the mysterious energy, zipping between adults like bicyclists through gridlock. I felt butterflies in my stomach. It seemed silly when just a short time before it had all struck me as sad. In the pairings room, I looked to see who Baagi and EK would be playing: EK was paired down, a game that would prove easy, but Baagi had drawn GM Joel Benjamin. I knew Benjamin. At least, I felt I did. Reading through Glenn's collection of old chess magazines, I had watched Benjamin's entire life, his childhood and chess career, from the very first mentions of his play as a goofy Brooklyn kid with a charming smile, to his quick development following in the New York footsteps of Fischer. Benjamin was world-class. He had assisted the IBM team that programmed Deep Blue to beat Garry Kasparov, and he would go on to win that year's U.S. Championship. And since his days of T-shirts and goofy grins for *Chess Life,* he had grown into the serious, balding, spectacled man that I passed in the hallway when I left the pairings room. I recognized others as well: GM Gregory Serper, winner of the World Open the year before, looking dazed with a red razor swipe along his cheek; Fedorowicz from the New York Open, who looked as though he was about to enter a hockey game rather than a chess tournament; and Ivanov again, who had not yet sunk into his meditation for the week and who was looking somewhat cleaner than he had in New York.

Baagi and EK had slipped by me and they had seen the matchups for themselves. The final stop on Baagi's tour was the most depressing.

"Tough pairing," I said.

"Well, you know, you just play chess!" Baagi said.

The open section was predictably quiet, and the players filed in and began their games without fanfare. I wandered back out to the main hallway between playing rooms. The wide corridor I had once thought of as a tunnel had become a kind of chess market for the week, a chess mall to answer Chess City. The artist Prokopljevic was there, his prints spread all over the floor, and beside him a craftsman displayed handmade chessboards and jewelry boxes. A beautiful woman sat at a desk to promote a Web site called chessherbs.com, which offered herbal and nutritional supplements "designed specifically for the competitive chess player." There was a display for a piece of software called Bookup, and another display for a limited series print based on a glorified history of the Sicilian Dragon opening system. The hallway had a Main Street feel to it. People milled about or chatted away the hours while their friends or relatives played games in the distant quiet. An old woman sat knitting on a sofa. Several men inexplicably walked by in Superman shirts. Kids wore basketball tank tops marked with the names of chess teams, and a grown woman wore a baseball hat with "chess" printed where a logo should have gone.

I wandered into the Skittles Room where two players had broken into an impromptu duet of "Mona Lisa" using the metronome of their clock to time the melody. Just up from them several teenagers were playing bughouse—a four-man chess variant—calling out instruction to their partners, "I need a knight! Trade, trade! Now give me a pawn! Whatever!" At the next table, an old man lamented a trap he had fallen into and repeated a sad chant: "Prepared variation, prepared variation, prepared variation."

By the time I wandered back to the tournament room, EK had already finished off his opponent. He was sitting near Baagi's board, but betrayed nothing of what he thought of her position. Baagi and Benjamin sat across from each other carefully. Baagi was ahead half an hour on the clock, but neither of them had castled. The board was a complicated mess. I couldn't begin to work out its complexities, so when EK walked outside for a cup of water I followed.

"Her position is very good," he said. "She likes this kind of position. She said she thinks she will win ten moves ago."

We walked back into the tournament room, and I looked for excitement on Baagi's face. There was none. Baagi's normal, happy clamor disappeared over the board during tournament play. She looked perhaps ten years older, wore a poker player's grimace, and sometimes glanced at her opponent's eyes as though he was the source of all evil in the world. Baagi allowed her legs to spasm to release nervousness, and sometimes she wrote down her moves before she made them. Because she was a woman, many players stopped to see how she was doing. She seemed used to the attention, though, and did not notice when several grandmasters examined the position. Word, it seemed, had gotten around that Benjamin was having difficulty with this girl few of them knew. Fedorowicz stopped to look, and Serper gave it a long study from the next board. I was surprised when Ivanov took time to look at the game. Earlier, he had spent ten minutes with both hands over his eyes during his move. But as Baagi started to beat Benjamin, Ivanov had somehow come to know of it, and he politely leaned over someone's shoulder to look. Benjamin himself gave no sign that he was in trouble except in the time that he allowed to tick off his clock. He then needed to make fourteen moves in fifteen minutes. I cheered away his seconds. I tried to paralyze him with my eyes like the Soviet specialists. By then I had played at least ten thousand games in less time than he had left on his clock, but the thought of fourteen moves in fifteen minutes seemed like an impossible task. Baagi was calm and malicious. I watched her eyes cook Benjamin slowly. There was a quick series of moves the import of which I was unable to follow, and then Benjamin was stuck again, seven moves in three minutes. Inconceivable. The first sign of his defeat came as he passed a hand over his head, a slow massage of his scalp as his clock ticked past a minute. He let it wind to under ten seconds, and then he reached across the board and shook Baagi's hand lightly.*

The crowd that had gathered exhaled and dispersed. Outside the tournament room, Baagi smiled and shook my shoulder to transfer some of the energy burbling inside her. We stifled our grins as Benjamin walked by us. It was almost 10:00 then. Baagi had had three hours of sleep in two days. Her tour had stretched from the very dregs of chess to near its pinnacle. Her next game was tomorrow at noon. I said good night to her and EK in the Main Street hallway, deserted now, and then I watched them, the chess couple, walk off toward the elevators hip to hip, drawn together by victory and love.

FOR THE EXPERT SECTION, GLENN WAS AN ACCIDENTAL sandbagger.

Sandbaggers are tournament hustlers—players who allow their rating to drop below their true playing ability. Glenn had lost his master ranking a few months before, and now he was eligible for the expert section's ten-thousand-dollar first prize.

He didn't arrive until Sunday, planning to play in the three-day schedule. This made for a five-game initial day of play. I found him

*See appendix for game.

before his first game in the Skittles Room. He had lost his 2500 rating on the ICC a few weeks before, but what I saw now was more troubling: he was giving 5-2 time odds to a 1900 guy for a dollar a game. A number of people had gathered to watch, and between games Glenn looked up at them and smiled, enjoying the attention. I left before he saw me.

I went upstairs to visit Baagi and EK before their first Sunday game. Saturday had been successful for both of them, a win and a draw each, and they were both poised to post strong results for the week. Baagi's win against Benjamin had created some buzz, and there was already talk of publishing the game in *Chess Life*. Ten minutes before round four, EK was again studying at the table, and Baagi was drying her hair.

"Where's Glenn?" Baagi said.

"He's downstairs giving time odds for a buck a game."

"Oh, no."

We might have been talking about a friend who'd fallen off the wagon. At a tournament, only one kind of chess is truly appropriate.

I found Glenn again just after he had seen his pairing. "I pulled a Russian," he said. It was still two months before we were headed to Kalmykia, and he didn't know what it foreshadowed. "That means he's studied Bronstein, Tal, Petrosian. Russians study Russians."

"What's his rating?"

"Ratings don't matter in the expert section. You have to be strong to win. Anybody could be anything. He could be a sandbagger."

"That's basically true of you, isn't it?"

He shrugged. "Yeah."

The expert section was played in the hotel's main exhibition center. The number of boards here was accordingly greater, rows of white-sheathed tables stretching off to near vanishing points, the many bodies hunched over the pieces like crowds gathered in the wake of disaster. I looked at the board nearest me: "547." The exhibition center was home to the expert section along with the Under-2000 section, the Under-1800 section. There were more playing rooms upstairs. Tournament directors walked about with their fingers to their lips, but could really do little to stifle the hum of whispers.

It took me awhile to find Glenn once things began. I approached and stared meanly at his opponent, but his Russian was clearly more versed in the menacing glare. He was an older man, but age was as ambiguous an indicator of chess talent as youth: The old brilliance could flare at any moment.

Glenn was studying the next game over. He seemed to have reason for confidence—the Russian's king was precarious, and it appeared that after a series of exchanges Glenn would have the better endgame.

The Russian made a rook move, and Glenn thought for only a moment before launching the series of exchanges that would bring about his favorable resolution. They were halfway through the combination when Glenn reached out for a knight and stopped. I felt it in my chest. Pausing over the board was a peeve of Glenn's. "You know what I hate about chess in movies?" he had told me. "There's always this big moment at the end when the player reaches out to move his piece and stops. He hesitates like he's stupid. GMs don't stop, man." But this wasn't true, I'd found. GMs did hesitate. GMs stopped, and so did everyone else. For some players the act seemed a tool, a way of accessing intuitiveness—reach for the piece, see how hot it was, and if it *felt* wrong, draw back and calculate. But this didn't really apply to Glenn, and when he paused now, it wasn't because he realized that he was about to make a mistake, it was because he already had. He had blundered, and he was lost. He was suddenly sad. He was low on time, and the seconds began to accelerate away. And in the final minute, the player who I had come to know for his pride in his ability to move quickly, moved not at all until the last few seconds when he shuffled his king about the board until his time ran out.

The Russian rushed off to report his victory. Glenn gathered his pieces, and we headed down Main Street.

While most players at the tournament carried their pieces in special bags, Glenn carried his in a simple plastic grocery bag that hung from his fingertips. Now, near the pairings room, the bag broke, scattering his chessmen all across the floor. Glenn scrambled after them, gathering pawns and bishops and stuffing them back into a bag with a hole in the bottom. I did not help him. I stepped back and saw him not only as those on Main Street saw him, but also as a man spiraling toward nothingness, a waste of twenty years of effort and energy. He was broken. Glenn tied a knot in the bag's hole, dumped the pieces inside, and stood up again.

"2099," he said. "No way that dude's 2099."

"I thought ratings didn't matter."

"They don't. Man. *Sandbaggers*," he said.

He lost his next game as well, and quit the expert section with six rounds to play.

THE TOURNAMENT SOURED FOR BAAGI. FIRST, SHE SACKED A piece against GM Sergey Kudrin, a longtime U.S. chess personality with the eyebrows of a demon, and then sacked again the next game against a pouty 2400 high school senior, who seemed annoyed that she thought she could get away with it. She lost both games, but said that she had been brave. It was the same thing Glenn had said after the New York Open, and I wondered if I had been too hard on him.

Glenn and I returned that evening for a speed chess side event. As we waited in line to register, a man approached Glenn for an autograph—he was collecting the signatures of all the significant black players at the tournament.

"You're in the expert section. You lose two games and drop out. And still people are asking for your autograph," I teased him.

"True, true," Glenn said.

The speed event would be my first official tournament. I was already a little burned out on the atmosphere of competition but decided to play at least one game in the setting. When the pairings went up, I felt the pull of it, a kind of excited yank.

The tournament rooms were a mess by then. The white tablecloths were layered over with dust mice, clusters of hair, Styrofoam cups, beer bottles, clock boxes, and forgotten pawns. The tablecloths were wrinkled and marked with single-cell coffee stains, and the linen was beginning to yellow. Next to my board was a doodle that perhaps a twelve year old had inked out while waiting for his opponent to move. It was a clown's face with a dialogue bubble.

"FU!" the clown said.

My first opponent was an older man, the father of a talented youngster. Neither one of us was sure how to set his clock, and when we finally got our game going, I won his queen for two pieces, then blundered my own and resigned. At the front of the room Glenn had drawn his first game, against a friend.

"If we were GMs," he said, "it would be a grandmaster draw. It kind of backfired on me, though. I got Blatney coming up."

He meant Pavel Blatney, a 2608 player with an international reputation. That Blatney was playing in the side tournament at all demonstrated the financial straits of most professional chess players. Blatney was among the eight players who would finish tied for the lead at the end of the open section. He was a nondescript man who fit the profile of a serial killer—short, well-groomed, quiet, and very dangerous. His game with Glenn was highly complex, with few exchanges and a great deal of tension on the board. Both men wound up with several pieces in their opponent's territory, and if most chess games made good metaphors for conflicts with clearly defined battle lines, then this game was a good metaphor for a guerrilla conflict where there was no battle line, where the enemy was entrenched everywhere. Knights jumped from outpost to outpost; and amid the broad range of tactical options, the potentially violent trades and sacrifices, a quiet positional dominance shaped the fight. It would have been a weaker player's instinct to simplify the game. But Glenn wouldn't do it. Some vague notion of courage was more important to him than hanging on or even winning; and perhaps because Baagi had seconded the philosophy, I rooted for Glenn to add to Blatney's complexity. I just wanted to see the little man flinch. But Blatney was cold. And when he eventually forced a hole in Glenn's kingside, Glenn resigned with a thousand times the dignity he had displayed in the expert section. This was Glenn's role, I realized. He was neither a chess professional, nor a politician, nor a teacher, nor a promoter. Instead, he was the player who allowed grandmasters to be grand, and the game would really be nowhere without him and the droves of others like him. He had fought well.

I lost my next tournament game from a won position and dropped out.

BAAGI WOUND UP WITH AS MANY POINTS IN THE WORLD OPEN as Glenn had scored in the New York Open. EK went into the final day with a chance to share first place, but the impossible happened— he lost twice.

Among the tournament leaders, the final round created an unusual situation. At the beginning of the round, a number of players shared the lead at 6½ points. This meant there would be draws. Ehlvest-Benjamin and Serper-Fedorowicz were drawn even before the players sat down—they finished with 7. It was board three that gave the tournament its storybook ending. Ivanov, also at 6½, was paired down with the black pieces against GM Julian Hodgson, at 6. If Ivanov won, he would win the tournament outright; and if he drew, he would tie for first. For Hodgson, only a win would make a difference. The game played for a win came not because the players wanted it, but because the tournament ended in a quirk that allowed it. This was how chess players tended to talk about luck in chess, I had found. There was no luck over the board, but there was luck to the pairings; there was luck in one's health. In a game so far removed from chance, designed in fact to be without it, there was simply a readjustment of the threshold of what constituted it, so it was perhaps not a surprise that chess players tended to be odd and paranoid. Or that when pressure mounted, they began to act strangely, eccentricities surfacing. Which is precisely what happened when Hodgson-Ivanov was six hours old, when their endgame reached a feverish pitch of speed and anxiety, and there were two hundred people watching, and the whole week was on the line. Ivanov began to come apart. I saw in those final minutes what his trancelike state had been meant to contain, both at the New York Open and here, what his meditation controlled. When his time began to dwindle, his position to crumble, Ivanov began to rock forward and back in his chair like a lizard decrying its territory, doing little push-ups on the rim of the game, his face cruising through a series of contorted expressions and his head cocking back and forth like a puppy's. The audience began to shuffle forward as the game approached its climax, and for everyone it was an exercise in the restraint of primitiveness, a test of civility. There was a pull to return to that chess from which the tournament game had evolved. People wished to cheer, to root, to rush the board and study it inches from the game, and it was only the frailest of ethics that kept them in their seats. The boy who was recording the moves on the demonstration board lost the position as Ivanov and Hodgson began to move quickly, and soon the game that looked back out at us had little to do with the game between the players. The crowd did not care. Like the crowd that had watched Glenn and Baagi's match at the dealers' lounge, we were now tapped into a fundamental drama, into Ivanov's breakdown and whether he could manage the storm of it, whether a man could ride the stress of chess all the way to its end. The specific meaning of the contest was lost, until all that mattered was a vague notion of struggle and compromise. The game ended at some critical moment—it was another draw—and the clapping that filled the room was as much for the aesthetics of the game as it was for the joyousness of life, like the joy of passengers on an airliner whose pilot has managed a crash landing. And Ivanov, our captain, raised his hand and acknowledged the applause, worn and beaten, but smiling now, and normal again.

THE NEXT MORNING THERE WAS AN EXODUS OF CHESS PLAYERS from the hotel. By 11:00, all that was chess had been removed from Main Street. A new group was setting up for a new convention.

"It's Mensa," a man told me.

Back in Atlantic City, I escorted Baagi and EK down to the boardwalk, and Baagi produced one hundred dollars to play at the casinos. Despite her concise chess skills, Baagi couldn't get her mind around the logic of blackjack and made all kinds of impulsive decisions. Later, we went to my apartment to meet Glenn. We were all tired, but the week wasn't over yet, and Baagi introduced the reason we had gathered there.

"You ready to lose?" she asked Glenn.

"Me?" Glenn said. "No, are *you* ready to lose?"

They rose and began a smiling strut. They made for my table and chessboard. They set the clock for one minute, and when Glenn first engaged the device it was an inverted blastoff.

Away from an audience—away from either the audiences of the tournament, the Skittles Room, even the dealers' lounge—Baagi and Glenn's play was suddenly much different. The chess came with an addendum of talk, a chattery debate conducted in batches of repeated words, a kind of tribal chant of conjuring. It was almost possible to follow their game from the odd play-by-play, each move calling for some comment.

"Whoa! Where's that guy going?" Glenn started.

"I don't know!"

"Where's he going, Baagi? Is that the Grünfeld?"

"Could be!"

"You forcing me to move?"

"Just, just—*Gosh!*"

"You forcing me?"

"Just too much close!"

"You understand I need that guy, Baagi?"

"Sorry! Didn't mean to!"

"Drats. Where you going?"

"I don't know; you tell me."

"Where you going?"

"I don't know." Baagi put a strong move on the board and announced it. "Bam!"

"Whoa!" Glenn said.

"BAM!"

"Are you sure?"

"Positive. You chasing me now?"

"Not me, man."

"You chasing me all over the world? Gosh!"

"Look out, Baagi!"

"Gosh. Gosh! GOSH!"

"How come you're a rook down?"

"I don't know."

"How come you're a rook down?"

"Don't ask me."

"Mate-in-one!"

The talk sometimes degenerated to odd grunts, like children puppeting the efforts of miniatures. My windows were open, and as Glenn and Baagi raised their voices to match the tension of the game, I wondered if my neighbors would have been able to guess that it was chess happening in that apartment over the bleak street.

"Check-o-rama," Baagi said.

"You checking me?"

"CHECK-O-RAMA!"

"Drats!"

"Castle-o-rama!"

"Why you running?"

"Gotta run!"

"Where you going?"

"I don't know. Talk to me."

"Is that mine?"

"Talk!"

"Bam!"

"You think that scares me?"

"Bam again!"

"Ughhh!"

"Gaaahh!"

"UGHHH!!!"

"GAAAHH!!!"

They accelerated until the sound of the clock was like a playing card strapped to the spokes of a bicycle tire. It was as fast as I'd ever seen chess played. When Glenn finally won the game, they were both laughing. Baagi bounced onto my sofa giggling like a tickled child. It was a thousand-year-old mood of chess. We all laughed for several minutes before they settled down to begin again, to complete the match. Glenn finally won, 7–4. But by the end of it, I think I was the only one who was keeping score.

CHAPTER 23

The Upside-Down Urinal

*I myself have been travelling around the world for twenty years, and I have
never met a chess player who would agree to join me for a visit to an art
gallery.*

—*Anatoly Karpov*, Karpov on Karpov, *1991*

*A sport or activity where absolute expertise has no convenient slot in
society . . . can produce angst and neurosis.*

—*Alexander Cockburn*, Idle Passion: Chess and the Dance of Death, *1974*

GLENN AND I DID NOT SPEAK FOR A WHILE AFTER WE
settled back into our lives in Atlantic City. One day in the dealers'
lounge, I heard him respond to a young woman who asked if he had
enjoyed Russia.

"I survived Kalmykia," he said.

"CHESS HAS NO SOCIAL PURPOSE," MARCEL DUCHAMP HAD
said. "That, above all, is important."

Duchamp had been a painter and chess player. As an artist, he
was Warhol before Warhol. *The Bride Stripped Bare by Her Bachelors,
Even* or *The Large Glass,* Duchamp's major piece, has been called the
most prophetic work of art of the twentieth century. It was this and
the "readymades," common manufactured items promoted to art by
Duchamp's signature on them, that had made him famous. But he
was also known for having abandoned the art world in favor of a
chess career that lasted half a century.

Glenn and I had talked about Duchamp before we went to Russia. Just as with math, I'd suggested chess was similar to modern art. Its practitioners were colorful. It was difficult to appreciate. But Glenn wouldn't hear of it. When I approached him with the proof of Duchamp's chess paintings, he was simply annoyed that a patzer could become influential in the chess world just because he was famous for something else. I found fifty of Duchamp's games in my database, but waited until after Russia to invite Glenn to look at them. It was our first chess meeting since we'd come home.

There is debate over whether Duchamp's games show anything of his artist's inclination. Some have said he preferred a beautiful loss to a boring win. Others examined his games and decided he was talented but showed no more bravado than others of his generation. He threw Glenn for a loop. A game Duchamp had played against Frank Marshall in 1930 struck Glenn as having been played no earlier than 1980. Another game from 1928 struck him as modern as well. "Two players trying to find exotic novelties in a baroque-type opening," he said. A game against IM Hans Kmoch revealed the weaknesses in Duchamp's defensive game, while a 1924 game placed him in the company of modern 2600 players.

He was surprised when I revealed who it was.

It was then that I told Glenn I was leaving Atlantic City. He asked where I was going, then thought about it and said, "They have any chess players there?"

I had other news as well. The Philadelphia Museum of Art had a special room devoted to Duchamp. They had *The Large Glass,* the chess paintings, and *Etant Donnés,* the secret work that Duchamp had labored on for twenty years. Playing there would be our final chess adventure.

THINGS DID NOT IMPROVE IN KALMYKIA AFTER GLENN AND I left. Unemployment hovered at 23 percent and wages held at about half that of the rest of Russia. The BBC reported that the republic had not paid its power bill in two years, and inflation in Kalmykia continued to rise even as it finally began to go down in the rest of the country. Members of a group called People Against the Regime of Kirsan Ilyumzhinov claimed to have been assaulted by masked men, and Yabloko reported that its candidates had received death threats. A legal challenge to Kirsan's extension of his presidential term was shot down by the Kalmyk Supreme Court, and Moscow decided to allow Ilyumzhinov and other autonomous leaders to pursue third terms in their presidencies.

Kirsan himself kept busy. In between chess outings, he met with Saddam Hussein to foster ties between Iraq and Russia's autonomous republics, called for the international recognition of Tibet, and worked on a border dispute with a neighboring region. His vision of communication with extraterrestrials came closer to home: He recommended that Kalmykia become a launch site for the Russian space program. Kalmykia already had a cosmonaut training center, and the republic had been passed over for the first launch site only because its rich earth was sheep pasture. Now that the dirt was dead and the sheep were gone, why not?

Kirsan's dealings were met with a frown from the new Russian president, Vladimir Putin, who awarded Larisa Yudina the Order of Courage, though some felt it was just a tactic to change his KGB image.

In 2002, Kirsan bought another FIDE election by giving his challenger a vice-presidency, and he won that third term as president of Kalmykia. But while in 1995 he'd been the only candidate on the ballot, this time around he had eleven challengers, and only won after a runoff. "Elections are a celebration, elections are a revelation," he told a radio station. A *Moscow Times* editorialist promptly compared the Ilyumzhinov regime to The Taliban and General Manuel Noriega. Kirsan will be president of Kalmykia until 2009.

The Dalai Lama once again made arrangements to visit Kalmykia, but Telo Rinpoche doubted it would come off when I called him a few months after our interview. A warming trend between Russia and China would probably kill it, he said. Rinpoche had changed jobs since I last spoke with him. Now he was working at home, but wouldn't tell me what he was doing.

"I'm only on the first step," he said. "I'm not going to talk about it until I get to the third."

GLENN HAD A NUMBER OF THINGS IN COMMON WITH DUCHAMP. Both had preferred math in school. Both had learned chess along with their brothers. Both had had brief marriages with honeymoons interrupted by the game.

Chess was a recurrent theme in Duchamp's early paintings. *The Chess Game,* 1910, *Portrait of Chess Players,* 1911, and *The King and Queen Surrounded by Swift Nudes,* 1912, demonstrated not only his fixation with chess but also the evolution of his aesthetic. Even *The Large Glass* showed chess influence. In one panel of the work, a gathering of figures clearly recalled chessmen. In 1963, a photo of Duchamp playing chess with a naked woman in front of *The Large Glass* caused a scandal.

Duchamp became more interested in actually playing chess when *The Large Glass* was finished. His focus seemed to shift entirely. "The only thing which could interest me now," he said, "is a potion that would let me play chess *divinely.*" Duchamp's chess career started late, but he was once described as ranking among the top twenty-five players living in the United States. He designed his own set of chessmen and later his own pocket set. In a short film about Duchamp by Hans Richter, Richter asked, "Why chess, Mr. Duchamp?" Duchamp replied, "Why not, Mr. Richter? Do you think that life is so important and chess is not?"

Glenn wouldn't talk much about his marriage and honeymoon. He and his wife had traveled to Jamaica, but it had gone poorly. Duchamp had returned to chess seriously after his honeymoon, and artist Man Ray provided the uncorroborated story that one night Duchamp's wife glued her darling's pieces to his board. Duchamp had lasted six months from marriage to divorce, Glenn ten weeks.

By the time we headed to the Philadelphia Museum of Art, both of the women Glenn had been dating when we went to Russia were out of the picture. He had a new girlfriend now. He had moved to a new room, and a chess admirer had sold him his first car for one dollar. He offered rides to everyone he knew and cruised the streets, honking at women.

He drove us to Philadelphia. We walked through the museum slowly, taking the scenic route to the modern art wing. Glenn was skeptical as we strolled along. We passed part of a chapel facade, and he paused to look at the small card that identified it. It was from France, dated at 1533, but Glenn only looked at one word, "purchased."

"Everything you can hold can be bought," he said.

It was a sentiment he might have shared with Duchamp, who seemed to favor chess because it could never come to have the value of a painting. Chess was pure because it was worthless, useless.

Glenn was flabbergasted in the modern art wing. At the work of Howard Hodgkin, he said, "I could bang that out in twenty minutes. Emerald could!"

In the Duchamp room, we walked past the works before we sat down to play. Glenn didn't consider them much. *The Large Glass* was uninteresting because it was broken. It had shattered once during transport. *The Chess Game* was dull, and *The King and Queen Surrounded by Swift Nudes* was incomprehensible. He paused slightly longer at *Portrait of Chess Players*. A Duchamp biographer had once written that the real subject of *Chess Players* was "the process of thought," and that after this painting each new Duchamp work was a "step in unique direction."

"Could you bang that out in twenty minutes?" I asked.

"Maybe longer," Glenn said.

He scoffed at the readymades: a bicycle wheel fastened atop a common stool, a bottle rack, an overturned urinal whose basin vaguely recalled a seated Buddha. The twenty-year secret of Duchamp's *Etant Donnés* was in a room around a corner. It was this: An ancient arched wooden door set into the back wall. It appeared featureless until you got close and noticed eye holes. You peered like a voyeur into a meadowish scene in which a woman lay naked. Her head was out of sight, her legs were spread wide so that her shaved groin was exposed, and in her hand she held a small lantern. For the Duchamp biographer, the woman was "queen of the game, as powerful and dominant as the queen in chess."

Glenn looked at the door and shrugged. "It's a door." He edged closer, spotted the holes, and looked through. "Whoa!" Then he backed up and looked for other cracks or holes in the door to get an angle on the woman's face.

A security guard had been eyeing us for a while. We briefly debated whether we should simply set up our board and begin or ask permission. Glenn produced one of his business cards and approached the guard. He explained that we were chess players there to play chess in the room devoted to chess's greatest artist. The man was friendly enough but knew the matter was outside his jurisdiction and disappeared to call a curator. He returned shortly.

"Go ahead," he said.

· · ·

THE CHESS WORLD WAS IN FOR SOME BIG CHANGES IN THE months immediately after Glenn and I came home. GM Vladimir Kramnik beat Garry Kasparov in a match that was considered a title contest by just about everyone but FIDE. The sponsorship frightened some. The involvement of Brain Games Network, an Internet company, seemed to amount to the corporatization that the chess world had previously resisted. Brain Games eventually sold the title to a London-based group called Einstein. The next FIDE World Championship tournament was held in Delhi. Through the ICC Glenn and I checked up on Sasha Utnasunov's performance. He was paired in the first round against GM Alexander Chernin. Sasha traded three pieces for Chernin's queen, then lost in 147 moves. He was eliminated.

After the tournament, chess was still bottlenecked with world champions. Kasparov still had the highest rating in the world by a good margin, and arguments could be made for him, Kramnik, the FIDE champion, and of course Fischer, still lurking somewhere. Il-yumzhinov's proposal to accelerate tournament chess to two hours was met with rare, unified distress from Kramnik and the two previous world champions. They wrote an open letter to the chess world: "Drastically shortening the amount of time available during a game is an attack on both the players and on the artistic and scientific elements of the game. . . ."

As well, the effort to include chess in the Olympics fell apart, derailed in part because chess players did not want to undergo drug testing.

On another front, the chess world was out to correct the popular notion that Kasparov's loss to Deep Blue meant that computers had conquered the game. IBM had canceled the Deep Blue program, but Kasparov arranged to play a program called Deep Junior, and Kramnik played a program called Deep Fritz in a match billed as "The Brains in Bahrain." "I think that in the public eye the computer is already stronger than any chess player," Kramnik said. "I'm very eager to win and to prove that this is not the case." He took a 3-1 lead against Deep Fritz, then lost two in a row, committing in the first game what was arguably the worst blunder ever made by a sitting world champion, and trying a doomed sacrifice in the second. "I was seduced by beauty," Kramnik said. The match was drawn, and a month later, Kasparov played a similar match against Deep Junior. Another draw. Forty-five thousand newspapers covered the event.

In 2003 the world championship appears to be coming together again. Four players representing both the efforts of FIDE and Einstein will play matches to determine who will participate in a unification match scheduled for November. Bobby Fischer isn't invited. The last anyone heard of him was just after the 9/11 terrorist attacks. Fischer came out of hiding to give another rare interview just hours after the World Trade Center fell. For international journalists, Fischer was always good copy, and his words were published across the world. "Death to the U.S.," Fischer said. "They are the worst liars and bastards. This is a wonderful day."

GLENN PRODUCED HIS ORNATE CLOCK AND SETTLED IT TO ONE side of the bench. He set the needles to an hour each, and casually started my clock. I didn't move at first. I didn't move, in fact, for almost seven minutes. It seemed hopeless already. I had played hundreds of games with Glenn by then, and no first move I'd ever made had ever really turned out any better than any other. He knew my habits and weaknesses better than I did, and no matter what move I made, a line ending in a clear advantage for Glenn was already proscribed in his mind. I just sat there for a while. I thought of all the meanings that had been assigned to chess. The initial meaning had been war, of course, first battle, then protracted conflicts between opposed cities or societies. As the game had evolved to a more complicated set of rules inspired by aesthetics rather than realism, chess had come to represent intimacy, economics, politics, theories bleeding from rhetoric to outrageous science. GM Rueben Fine, a psychoanalyst, had argued that "a combination of homosexual and hostile elements are sublimated in chess." Literary critic and poet John Irwin had used the game to arrive at a theory of the analytic process: "Given the notion of chess as a kind of microcosmic world . . . one is reminded of Aristotle's summary in the *Metaphysics* of the Pythagorean belief that 'the original constituents' of 'Being' are a series of ten opposing pairs." And K. Cherevko in an article for the Russian magazine *Science and Religion*, headed more directly for the magical: "Thus, the quantitative complex is coincided: 64 chess squares on a chessboard and the same number of kodons [sic] in a DNA molecule . . . Maybe this coincidence is not accidental?" These were ideas that forced chess to be something it was not. I preferred the attempts to simply describe it, and Duchamp's *Portrait of Chess Players,* his process of thought, seemed as appropriate as any: The game approximated not just one's intelligence or emotions or wits, but all of these things, the interplay of them networking in our brains. Lines of force. But if this was chess, I thought, then what did it mean that I couldn't imagine a first move against Glenn that wouldn't lead, invariably, to defeat?

I moved at last, and Glenn responded politely. Art classes came through periodically as we played, instructors explaining to a dozen students at a time why Duchamp's *Nude Descending a Staircase. No. 2* was significant in the history of art. Regular museum patrons walked through the room as well, most of them as baffled by Duchamp's readymades as they were by our board.

I found a sacrifice to play against Glenn, the trade of a knight for two center pawns and a tempi. I thrilled as he considered the move for five minutes. I got up and walked around. When I returned he simply refused it, and the game turned positional. He forced the trade of rooks and queens, and bore down on me until it would have been an insult not to resign.

Out in the hallway, Glenn complained about the people who had walked by us. "I'm creating mate with two knights, a bishop, and a pawn, and these guys are looking at upside-down urinals."

We headed for the entrance.

"Nobody looked at the art I was making," Glenn went on, "Paying more attention to a silly toilet. Society is not ready for chess players. Amazingly enough, the opposite is true, too."

A FEW DAYS AFTER I RETURNED FROM VIRGINIA TO INTERVIEW Bloodgood, I received his first moves for our two correspondence games. Bloodgood's handwriting was small and neat, and he always signed off, "Best, Claude."

I'd seen the games that the journalists from *The Guardian* and *Le Monde* had conducted with Bloodgood. They had both played soft so Bloodgood could shine for their readership. I decided to use my computer and crush him. I didn't take all the computer's moves, but I stuck to its basic plan. After move six in both games—about two months later—Bloodgood scribbled a note below his notation: "Healthwise, I'm coughing more blood and have trouble keeping meals down." At move nine, Bloodgood took a month to respond and wrote that he had been sick and unable to focus. At move thirteen—two more months later—I won a pawn and the exchange in the second game. Bloodgood resigned: "I'm not sure what I had in mind for Game B, but I'm lost now." My computer seemed to think he was lost in Game A as well. I sent along my next move, a crusher. A week later, I got a letter in another man's hand:

Dear Sir:

Mr. Claude Bloodgood has requested me to inform you, he regrets that his health has forced him to end all games. He had hoped he could play a few personal games. He thanks you for your friendship and sportsmanship, which is what sets chessmen above the others. On behalf of Claude Bloodgood.

Sincerely,
Allan A. Burroughs

I attached a trailer to the rear of my car and left Atlantic City at the end of May, heading west. Several months later, Baagi and EK attached a trailer to the rear of their car and left Utah, heading east. Baagi had been offered scholarships from both the University of Texas and the University of Maryland. She opted for Balitmore, and they stayed with me for one night as they crossed the country. By then, Baagi had been in the United States long enough to qualify for the U.S. championships. She played the following January in Seattle. She placed third among women.

I had lived once before in the town I moved to. But I hadn't been a chess player then. Now I found that chess was popular there. I saw men playing in bars, on tables outside coffee shops, and in the pedestrian mall where I came to live there was a large chessboard set into the bricks. On Friday nights the games attracted crowds of thirty and more.

An old friend had a four year old by then. The boy had wheatish brown hair and deep blue irises threaded through with thick lines. He had a mild autism that caused stimming behaviors, hand flapping and a tendency to cock his head and cover his ears. He spoke in a private language of soft consonants and cut syllables. He seemed interested in ritual—when my friend and I drank coffee together, he was more interested in the coffee than in us. Auspiciously, the boy's initials were "G.M."

I had an idea for a final chess tour. Bring G.M. to my apartment, show him chess first on the big board outside, then on the ICC, and then on live sets on my coffee table. I didn't think he would learn to play, but Glenn had taught me that the first lesson in chess was not how the pieces moved, but a basic understanding of the game. I thought G.M. might make an association, might see that the game was trying to speak to him. I thought it could focus him, and reasoned that Baagi had been four years old when she learned to play.

The tour was too ambitious of course. The big board was of interest to G.M. only because it lay directly between a slide and a fountain, and he ran across it leaving wet footprints that described the path of a piece yet to be invented. Two grandmasters spitting out a speed game on the ICC captured G.M.'s attention for only a second. He did better with the live sets. I had three ready for him— a weighted speed set, a wooden set I'd bought in Russia, and a small stone set from Mexico. G.M. approached these carefully. He gathered a number of pieces in his hands, representatives from each, and bundled them against his stomach. I held a rook out to him.

"Rook," I said.

"Roo," G.M. said.

I grabbed a queen. "Queen."

"Kwee."

I tried one more. "King."

G.M. took it and turned it in his hand. "King," he said, and then he ran away.

From page 310.
Battsetseg Tsagaan (U.S. 2256)–Joel Benjamin (U.S. 2650)
2000 World Open, Round One
(Notes By NM Enkhbat Tegshuren)

1.e4 g6 2.d4 Bg7 3.Nc3 d6 4.Be3 a6 (4 . . . Nf6 would be a main line of the Pirc defense) 5.Qd2 Nd7 6.f3 b5 (Black is preparing to meet white's potential queenside castle) 7.h4 (with idea of h4-h5 and opening the h-file) 7 . . . Ngf6 8.Nh3 h6 (black controls g5, but must protect h6-pawn now at all times.) 9.Rd1 (White king is safe on center, so no hurry to castle.) 9 . . . Bb7 10.a4 c6 11.g4 e5 12.g5 hxg5 13.Nxg5 (another alternative is 13.hg5, but white preferred to activate the knight on h3) 13 . . . Qe7 14.axb5 cxb5 15.dxe5 dxe5 16.Bh3 Rd8 (16 . . . Rxh4 loses to 17.Bxd7+ and 18.Rxh4) 17.Qf2 (a multi-purpose move: protects h4-pawn, controls g1-a7 diagonal, and removes the white queen from potential discovered attack by rook) 17 . . . Rc8 18.0-0 (finally time for white to connect rooks)18 . . . b4 19.Na4 Bc6 20.Nc5 Bb5 21.Nxd7 Bxd7 (of course, if 21 . . . Bxf1 then 22.Nxf6+ wins) 22.Bxd7 Nxd7 23.Rd2 (overprotection; also d2-rook would be transfer to K-side via second rank) 23 . . . f6 24.Nh3 Rc7 (24 . . . g5 deserves attention) 25.Qg3 Kf7 26.f4 Rhc8 27.Rg2 Kg8 (this is an error; black is in time trouble. Better is 27 . . . Rxc2 28.Qxg6+ Kg8 with counterplay)

28.Rff2! (after this all white's pieces are actively placed; black has no counterplay) 28 . . . Nf8 (black has to protect g6-pawn) 29.fxe5 (white opens f-file for attacking black king) fxe5 30.Ng5 (knight returns to very active position close to black king) Qd7 31.Qf3 Rc6 32.h5 Rf6 33.Qe2 Rxf2 34.Rxf2 gxh5 35.Qxh5 Rd8 (with idea of Qd1+ and exchange queens; still, better is 35 . . . Rc6)36.Kg2 Rc8 (if 36 . . . Qd1 then 37.Rf8+! and with checkmate in next move) 37.Rf7! Qe8 (if

37 ... Qd8 then 38.Rxf8+ giving checkmate on next move or 37 ... Rxc2 38.Kg3
and black is helpless) 38.Bc5!

White threatens 39.Rxf8 followed by 40.Qh7 checkmate. If 38 ... Rxc5 then
39.Rxg7 Kxg7 40.Qxe8 and white wins the black queen, so black resigned. 1–0

From page 232.
Ronald Simpson (U.S. 2338)–Glenn Umstead (U.S. 2173)
2000 New York Open, Round Three
(Notes by WIM Battsetseg Tsagaan)

1.Nf3 g6 2.g3 Bg7 3.Bg2 c5 4.c4 e5 5.Nc3 Ne7 6.0-0 0-0 7.d3 Nbc6 8.Rb1 a6 9.a3
Rb8 10.b4 cxb4 11.axb4 b5 12.cxb5 axb5 13.Bg5 h6 14.Bxe7 Nxe7 15.d4 (white
weakens the c4 square, which can potentially be occupied by a black bishop
or knight) d6 16.Qd3 f5 17.Qd2 e4 18.Ne1 d5 (better is 18 ... Be6 with the bishop
eventually headed to c4 and the knight to d6 after d5) 19.Nc2 Be6 20.Rfc1 f4
21.gxf4 Nf5 22.Rb3 Qh4 (better is 22 ... Nd6 with an attack on the hanging f4
pawn after 23 ... Nc4) 23.Nd1 Nd6 (not bad, but this allows white to eventually
trade queens and relieve pressure—better, perhaps, is 23 ... Ra8 with the idea
of Ra2) 24.e3 Rf5 25.f3 Rh5 26.Bh1 g5 27.f5 Bxf5 28.Qf2 Rc8 29.Qxh4 Rxh4 30.Rc3
(after trading queens, white looks good with black's kingside rook misplaced
on h4) Rc4 31.Rxc4 dxc4 32.Nc3 exf3 33.Bxf3 Kf8 34.Ne1 Bh3 (prevents the trap-
ping of the black rook via 35. Ng2) 35.Bc6 Nf5 36.Nd1

36 ... Bxd4! (white bishop is hanging, and black knight threatens fork on e2. If 37 exd4 Nxd4 38. Bf3 g4.) 37.Kf2 Bb6 38.Nf3 Rg4 39.Ne5 Rf4+ 40.Ke2 Bg4+ 41.Ke1 Nxe3 42.Ng6+ Kg7 43.Nxf4 Nxd1 44.Ne6+ Kf6 45.Nc5 Bxc5 46.bxc5 Nb2 47.Kd2 b4 48.Bb5 c3+ 49.Kc2 Bd1+ 50.Rxd1 ½-½

Glenn Umstead (U.S. 2173)—Traian Tasu (U.S. 1659)
2000 New York Open, Round Six
(Notes by WIM Battsetseg Tsagaan)

From page 238.
1.d4 Nf6 2.c4 g6 3.Nc3 Bg7 4.e4 d6 5.f3 0-0 6.Bg5 Nbd7 7.Qd2 a6 8.0-0-0 c6 9.h4 b5 10.g4 bxc4 11.h5 gxh5 (better would be 11 ... e5) 12.e5 Ne8 13.f4 (white shows an adventuresome spirit as 13. Qh2 is clearly winning [13. Qh2 dxe5 14.dxe5 Bxe5 15. Qxh5 Nef6 16.Bxf6 and wins]) ... h6 14.Bxh6 Bxh6 15.g5 Bg7 16. Bxc4 (threatening mate on h7 after Qc2) Nb6 17.Rxh5 Bg4 18.Qh2 Bxh5 19.f5 Bxe5 20.dxe5 Nxc4 21.Qxh5 Ng7 22.Qh2 Nxf5 23.Nf3 Kg7 24.g6 Rh8 (black believes he cannot play fxg6, but actually the threat is an illusion and lines after 24 ... fxg6 are generally good for black) 25.Qf4 Nce3 26.Nd4 Rh4 (26 ... e6 also works for black and saves the piece, but lines are tricky) 27Nxf5+ Nxf5 28.Qxf5 fxg6 29.Rg1 Rh6 30.Qe6 Qf8 (black now with clear advantage) 31.Ne2 Qf7 32.Qd7 dxe5 33.Ng3 Rf8 34.Kb1 (good prophylactic move that avoids black's potential Qf4+) Rh2 (not an accurate move—black should be patient and play 34.Kh8) 35.Qg4 Qf4??

36.Nh5+ (black must take the knight, or lose his queen) 1–0

Of the many works on chess I consulted, several stood out and deserve additional recognition. These were H. J. R. Murray's comprehensive *A History of Chess,* Cathy Forbes's *Meet the Masters,* Hans Ree's *The Human Comedy of Chess,* Andy Soltis's *Karl Marx Plays Chess,* Hooper and Whyld's *Oxford Companion to Chess,* and both works of Edward Winter, listed below.

CHESS

Bell, R. C. *Board and Table Games from Many Civilizations.* New York: Dover, 1979.

Belyavsky, Alexander. *Uncompromising Chess.* London: Cadogan, 1998.

Bloodgood, Claude F. *Blackburne-Hartlaub Gambit.* Grand Prairie, Texas: Chess Digest, 1998.

Botvinnik, Mikhail. *One Hundred Selected Games.* New York: Dover, 1960.

Burgess, Graham. *Chess Highlights of the 20th Century.* London: Gambit, 1999.

Cockburn, Alexander. *Idle Passion: Chess and the Dance of Death.* New York: Simon & Schuster, 1974.

Darrach, Brad. *Bobby Fischer vs. The Rest of the World.* New York: Stein and Day, 1974.

Davidson, Henry A. *A Short History of Chess.* New York: David McKay, 1949.

Euwe, Max, and John Nunn. *The Development of Chess Style.* Seattle: Batsford/International Chess Enterprises, 1997.

Forbes, Cathy. *Meet the Masters.* Brighton: Tournament Chess, 1994.

Gollon, John. *Chess Variations Ancient, Regional, and Modern.* Vermont: Charles E. Tuttle, 1968.

Hanke, Timothy. "Finding Bobby Fischer." *American Chess Journal,* No.1 (1992).

Hannak, J. *Emanuel Lasker, The Life of a Chess Master.* New York: Dover, 1959.

Heidenfeld, W. *Draw!* London: George Allen & Unwin, 1982.

Hesse, Hermann. *The Glass Bead Game (Magister Ludi).* New York: Henry Holt, 1969.

Hooper, David, and Kenneth Whyld. *The Oxford Companion to Chess.* New York: Oxford University Press, 1996.

Hurst, Sarah. *Chess on the Web.* London: Batsford, 1999.

Kasparov, Garry, with Donald Trelford. *Unlimited Challenge.* New York: Grove Press, 1990.

Korn, Walter. *Modern Chess Opening.* 11th ed. New York: McKay-Pitman, 1972.

Kotov, A. and M. Yudovich. *The Soviet School of Chess.* New York: Dover, 1961.

Kotov, A. *Think Like a Grandmaster.* London: Batsford, 1971.

Mednis, Edmar. *King Power in Chess.* New York: David McKay, 1982.

Mitchell, Edwin Valentine, ed. *The Art of Chess Playing.* New York: Barrows Mussey, 1936.

Murray, H. J. R. *A History of Chess.* Cambridge: Oxford University Press, 1913.

Nabokov, Vladimir. *The Defense.* New York: Vintage 1964.

Pandolfini, Bruce. *Kasparov and Deep Blue*. New York: Fireside, 1997.

Pandolfini, Bruce. ed. *The Best of Chess Life and Review, vol. 1*. New York: Simon and Schuster, 1988.

Ray, Satyajit. *The Chess Players*. London: Faber & Faber, 1989.

Ree, Hans. *The Human Comedy of Chess: A Grandmaster's Chronicles*. Connecticut: Russell Enterprises, 1999.

Schonberg, Harold C. *Grandmasters of Chess*. New York: Lippincott, 1973.

Schultz, Don. *Chessdon*. Florida: Chessdon Publishing, 1999.

Soltis, Andrew. *Karl Marx Plays Chess and Other Reports on the World's Oldest Game*. New York: David McKay Company, 1991.

Tevis, Walter. *The Queen's Gambit*. New York: Random House, 1983.

Waitzkin, Fred. *Searching for Bobby Fischer*. New York: Penguin, 1988.

Waitzkin, Josh. *Josh Waitzkin's Attacking Chess*. New York: Fireside, 1995.

Winter, Edward. *Chess Explorations, A Pot-Pourri from the Journal*. Chess Notes (1996).

Winter, Edward. *Kings, Commoners and Knaves: Further Chess Explorations*. Connecticut: Russell Enterprises, 1999.

Zweig, Stefan. *The Royal Game and Other Stories*. New York: Holmes & Meier, 2000.

KALMYKIA

Bormanshinov, Arash. *The Lamas of the Kalmyk People: The Don Kalmyk Lamas*. Bloomington, Indiana: Indiana University, 1991.

De Qunicey, Thomas. *Revolt of the Tartars*. New York: American Book Company, 1895.

Ilyumzhinov, Kirsan. *The President's Crown of Thorns*. Moscow: Vagrius, 1998.

Khodarkovsky, Michael. *Where Two Worlds Met: The Russian State and the Kalmyk Nomads, 1600–1771*. New York: Cornell University Press, 1992.

Meyer, Karl E., and Sharon Blair Brysac. *Tournament of Shadows: The Great Game and the Race for Empire in Central Asia*. Washington D.C.: Counterpoint, 1999.

Nekrich, Aleksandr M. *The Punished Peoples: The Deportation and Tragic Fate of Soviet Minorities at the End of the Second World War*. New York: Norton, 1978.

MISCELLANEOUS

Huizinga, Johan. *Homo Ludens*. Boston, Beacon Press, 1950.

Ilf, Ilya, and Yevgenii Petrov. *The Twelve Chairs*. Illinois: Northwestern University Press, 1997.

Irwin, John T. *The Mystery to a Solution*. Baltimore: Johns Hopkins University Press, 1994.

Nasar, Sylvia. *A Beautiful Mind*. New York: Simon & Schuster, 1998.

Riasanovsky, Nicholas V. *A History of Russia*. 3rd ed. New York: Oxford University Press, 1977.

Sanuillet, Michel, and Elmer Peterson, eds. *The Writings of Marcel Duchamp*. New York: Oxford University Press, 1973.

Tompkins, Calvin. *Duchamp, A Biography*. New York: Henry Holt, 1996.